Blockchain Consensus

An Introduction to Classical, Blockchain, and Quantum Consensus Protocols

Imran Bashir

Apress®

Blockchain Consensus: An Introduction to Classical, Blockchain, and Quantum Consensus Protocols

Imran Bashir
London, UK

ISBN-13 (pbk): 978-1-4842-8178-9   ISBN-13 (electronic): 978-1-4842-8179-6
https://doi.org/10.1007/978-1-4842-8179-6

Managing Director, Apress Media LLC: Welmoed Spahr
Acquisitions Editor: Aditee Mirashi
Development Editor: Laura Berendson
Coordinating Editor: Aditee Mirashi

Cover designed by eStudioCalamar

Cover image designed by Freepik (www.freepik.com)

Distributed to the book trade worldwide by Springer Science+Business Media New York, 1 New York Plaza, Suite 4600, New York, NY 10004-1562, USA. Phone 1-800-SPRINGER, fax (201) 348-4505, e-mail orders-ny@springer-sbm.com, or visit www.springeronline.com. Apress Media, LLC is a California LLC and the sole member (owner) is Springer Science + Business Media Finance Inc (SSBM Finance Inc). SSBM Finance Inc is a **Delaware** corporation.

For information on translations, please e-mail booktranslations@springernature.com; for reprint, paperback, or audio rights, please e-mail bookpermissions@springernature.com.

Apress titles may be purchased in bulk for academic, corporate, or promotional use. eBook versions and licenses are also available for most titles. For more information, reference our Print and eBook Bulk Sales web page at http://www.apress.com/bulk-sales.

Any source code or other supplementary material referenced by the author in this book is available to readers on GitHub (github.com/apress). For more detailed information, please visit http://www.apress.com/source-code.

Printed on acid-free paper

This book is dedicated to my father, the most affectionate, selfless, and hard-working person I've ever known.

If you are stuck at a research problem, rigorously read all relevant literature, you will find the answer.

—*Scientist Bashir Ahmed Khan*

Table of Contents

About the Author

 **Imran Bashir** has an MSc in information security from Royal Holloway, University of London. He has a background in software development, solution architecture, infrastructure management, information security, and IT service management. His current focus is on the latest technologies such as the blockchain and quantum computing. He is a member of the Institute of Electrical and Electronics Engineers (IEEE) and the British Computer Society (BCS). His book on blockchain technology, *Mastering Blockchain*, is a widely accepted standard text on the subject. He has worked in various senior technical roles for different organizations worldwide. Currently, he is working as a researcher in London, UK.

About the Technical Reviewer

Prasanth Sahoo is a thought leader, an adjunct professor, a technical speaker, and a full-time practitioner in blockchain, DevOps, cloud, and Agile, working for PDI Software. He was awarded the "Blockchain and Cloud Expert of the Year Award 2019" from TCS Global Community for his knowledge share within academic services to the community. He is passionate about driving digital technology initiatives by handling various community initiatives through coaching, mentoring, and grooming techniques.

Acknowledgments

This book would not have been possible without help from many people. First, I would like to thank Aditee Mirashi from Apress for her time, patience, and dedication to this project.

Over the years, I have gone through many books, papers, online resources, and lectures from experts and academics in this field to learn about this subject. I want to thank all those researchers and engineers who have shared their knowledge. I also want to thank the reviewers whose suggestions have improved this book greatly.

I want to thank my wife and children for their support and bearing with me when I was busy writing during weekends, which I was supposed to spend with them.

Finally, I want to thank my father, my beacon of light. He sacrificed everything for me, guided me at every step in life, and empowered me to achieve the best in life. Thank you, Dad! He motivated me to write this book and suggested that I publish it in 2022. And my mother, whose unconditional love for me has no bounds. Thank you Ammi!

Introduction

This book is an introduction to distributed consensus and its use in the blockchain. It covers classical protocols, blockchain age protocols that emerged after Bitcoin, and quantum protocols. Many enthusiasts have come from different backgrounds into the blockchain world and may not have traditional distributed systems experience. This book fills that knowledge gap. It introduces classical protocols and foundations of distributed consensus so that a solid foundation is built to understand the research on blockchain consensus. Many other people have come from traditional distributed systems backgrounds, either developers or theorists. Still, they may lack the understanding of blockchain and relevant concepts such as Bitcoin and Ethereum. This book will fill that gap too.

Moreover, as quantum computing will impact almost everything in the future, I have also covered how quantum computing can help build quantum consensus algorithms. A clear advantage can be realized in the efficiency and security of consensus algorithms by using quantum computing. Therefore, an entire chapter is dedicated to quantum consensus.

This book is for everyone who wants to understand this fascinating world of blockchain consensus and distributed consensus in general. A basic understanding of computer science is all that's required to fully benefit from this book. This book can also serve as a study resource for a one-semester course on blockchain and distributed consensus.

The book starts with a basic introduction to what distributed consensus is and covers fundamental ideas such as causality, time, and various distributed system models. Then to build the foundation for understanding the security aspects of blockchain consensus, an introduction to cryptography is provided. Then a detailed introduction to distributed consensus is presented. Next, an introduction to the blockchain is given, which gives a solid understanding of what a blockchain is and how it is fundamentally a distributed system. We then discuss blockchain consensus, focusing on the first cryptocurrency blockchain, Bitcoin, and how it achieves its security and distributed consensus goals. Starting from Chapter 6 is an introduction to early protocols covering classical work like the Byzantine generals problem and its various solutions. After this, classical protocols such as Paxos, DLS, and PBFT are covered. Next, the blockchain protocols such as ETHASH, Tendermint, GRANDPA, BABE, HotStuff, and Casper are introduced. These protocols are the latest in the research on blockchain consensus mechanisms. Of course, we cannot cover everything due to the vastness of the subject. Still, this chapter dedicated to blockchain consensus introduces all those protocols which are state of the art and in use in mainstream blockchain platforms, such as Polkadot, Ethereum, and Cosmos.

The next chapter is another exciting topic, quantum consensus. With the advent of quantum computing, it has been realized that quantum computing can significantly enhance the classical distributed consensus results. Even results such as FLP impossibility might be possible to refute using quantum properties like superposition and entanglement.

Finally, the last chapter summarizes what we have learned in the book, introduces some exotic protocols, and suggests some research directions.

As this book focuses on the foundations of the blockchain and consensus, I believe that this book will serve as a great learning resource for all enthusiasts who want to learn about the blockchain and blockchain consensus. Furthermore, I hope that this book will serve technologists, researchers, students, developers, and indeed anyone who wants to know about this fascinating subject well for many years to come.

CHAPTER 1

Introduction

In this chapter, we explore the foundations of distributed computing. First, we will answer the questions about a distributed system, its fundamental abstractions, system models, and relevant ideas.

Distributed Systems

In the literature, there are many different definitions of distributed systems. Still, fundamentally they all address the fact that a distributed system is a collection of computers working together to solve a problem.

Some definitions from famous scholars in this field are as follows:

> *A distributed system is one in which the failure of a computer you didn't even know existed can render your own computer unusable.*
>
> —Leslie Lamport

https://lamport.azurewebsites.net/pubs/distributed-system.txt

> *A distributed system is a collection of autonomous computing elements that appears to its users as a single coherent system.*
>
> —Tanenbaum

www.distributed-systems.net/index.php/books/ds3/

Here is my own attempt!

© Imran Bashir 2022
I. Bashir, *Blockchain Consensus*, https://doi.org/10.1007/978-1-4842-8179-6_1

A distributed system is a collection of autonomous computers that collaborate with each other on a message-passing network to achieve a common goal.

Usually, this problem is not solvable by a single computer, or the distributed system is inherently distributed such as a social media application.

Some everyday examples of distributed systems are Google, Facebook, Twitter, Amazon, and the World Wide Web. Another class of recently emerged and popular distributed systems is blockchain or distributed ledgers, which we will cover in Chapter 4.

In this chapter, we lay the foundations and look at the distributed systems in general, their characteristics and properties, motivations, and system models that help reason about the properties of a distributed system.

While distributed systems can be quite complex and usually have to address many design aspects, including process design, messages (interaction between processes), performance, security, and event management, a core problem is consensus.

Consensus is a fundamental problem in distributed systems where despite some failures in the system, the processes within the distributed system always agree to the state of the system. We will do more of this in Chapter 3.

In the first chapter, we will lay the foundation of distributed systems and build an intuition about what they are and how they work. After this, we will cover cryptography, blockchain, and consensus, which will provide a solid foundation to then move on and read the rest of the chapters, covering more in-depth topics such as consensus protocols, design and implementation, and some latest research on quantum consensus.

But first, let's have a closer look at the distributed system foundations and discuss what characteristics a distributed system has.

Characteristics

What makes a system distributed? Here are some fundamental properties:

1. No global physical clocks

2. Autonomous processors/independent processors/
    indepedently failing

3. No global shared common memory

4. Heterogeneous

5. Coherent

6. Concurrency/concurrent operation

No global physical clock implies that the system is distributed in nature and asynchronous. The computers or nodes in a distributed system are independent with their own memory, processor, and operating system. These systems do not have a global shared clock as a source of time for the entire system, which makes the notion of time tricky in distributed systems, and we will shortly see how to overcome this limitation. The fact that there is no global shared memory implies that the only way processes can communicate with each other is by consuming messages sent over a network using channels or links.

All processes or computers or nodes in a distributed system are independent, with their own operating system, memory, and processor. There is no global shared memory in a distributed system, which implies that each processor has its own memory and its own view of its state and has limited local knowledge unless a message from other node(s) arrives and adds to the local knowledge of the node.

Distributed systems are usually heterogeneous with multiple different types of computers with different architecture and processors. Such a setup can include commodity computers, high-end servers, IoT devices, mobile devices, and virtually any device or "thing" that runs the distributed algorithm to solve a common problem (achieve a common goal) the distributed system has been designed for.

Distributed systems are also coherent. This feature abstracts away all minute details of the dispersed structure of a distributed system, and to an end user, it appears as a single cohesive system. This concept is known as distribution transparency.

Concurrency in a distributed system is concerned with the requirement that the distributed algorithm should run concurrently on all processors in the distributed system.

Figure 1-1 shows a generic model of a distributed system.

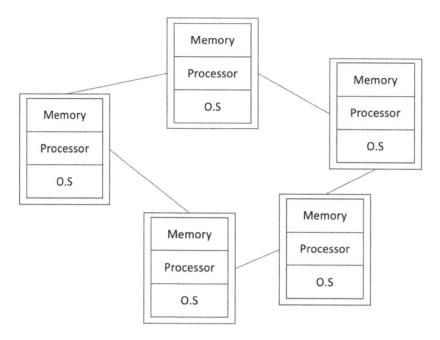

Figure 1-1. *A distributed system*

There are several reasons why we would want to build a distributed system. The most common reason is scalability. For example, imagine you have a single server serving 100 users a day; when the number of users grows, the usual method is to scale vertically by adding more powerful hardware, for example, faster CPU, more RAM, bigger hard disk, etc., but in some scenarios, you can only go so much vertically, and at some point, you have to scale horizontally by adding more computers and somehow distributing the load between them.

Why Build Distributed Systems

In the following, we introduce some motivations behind building distributed systems:

- Reliability

- Performance

- Resource sharing

- Inherently distributed

Let's have a look at each one of these reasons separately.

Reliability

Reliability is a key advantage of distributed systems. Imagine if you have a single computer. Then, when it fails, there is no choice but to reboot it or get a new one if it had developed a significant fault. However, there are multiple nodes in distributed systems in a system that allows a distributed system to tolerate faults up to a level. Thus, even if some computers fail in a distributed network, the distributed system keeps functioning. Reliability is one of the significant areas of study and research in distributed computing, and we will look at it in more detail in the context of fault tolerance shortly.

Reliability encompasses several aspects including availability, integrity, and fault tolerance:

- **Availability** simply means that when a request is made by a client, the distributed system should always be available.

- **Integrity** ensures that the state of the distributed system should always be in stable and consistent state.

- **Fault tolerance** enables a distributed system to function even in case of some failures.

Performance

In distributed systems, better performance can be achieved naturally. For example, in the case of a cluster of computers working together, better performance can be achieved by parallelizing the computation. Also, in a geographically dispersed distributed network, clients (users) accessing nodes can get data from the node which is closer to their geographic region, which results in quicker data access. For example, in the case of Internet file download, a mirror that is closer to your geographic region will provide much better download speed as compared to the one that might be in another continent.

Performance of a distributed system generally encompasses two facets, responsiveness and throughput.

Responsiveness

This property guarantees that the system is reasonably responsive, and users can get adequate response from the distributed system.

Throughput

Throughput of a distributed system is another measure by which the performance of the distributed system can be judged. Throughput basically captures the rate at which processing is done in the system; usually, it is measured in transactions per second. As we will see later in Chapter 5, high transaction per second rate is quite desirable in blockchain systems (distributed ledgers). Quite often, transactions per second or queries executed per second are measured for a distributed database as a measure of the performance of the system. Throughput is impacted by different aspects of the distributed system, for example, processing speeds, communication network quality, speed and reliability, and the algorithm. If your hardware is good, but the algorithm is designed poorly, then that can also impact the throughput, responsiveness, and the overall performance of the system.

Resource Sharing

Resources in a distributed system can be shared with other nodes/participants in the distributed system. Sometimes, there are expensive resources such as a supercomputer, a quantum computer, or some industrial grade printer which can be too expensive to be made available at each site; in that case, resources can be shared via communication links to other nodes remotely. Another scenario could be where data can be divided into multiple partitions (shards) to enable quick access.

Inherently Distributed

There are scenarios where there is no option but to build a distributed system because the problem can only be solved by a distributed system. For example, a messaging system is inherently distributed. Mobile network is inherently by nature distributed. In these and similar use cases, a distributed system is the only one that can solve the problem; therefore, the system has to be distributed by design.

With all these benefits of distributed systems, there are some challenges that need to be addressed when building distributed systems. The properties of distributed systems such as no access to a global clock, asynchrony, and partial failures make designing reliable distributed systems a difficult task. In the next section, we look at some of the primary challenges that should be addressed while building distributed systems.

Challenges

Distributed systems are hard to build. There are multiple challenges that need to be addressed while designing distributed systems. A collection of some common challenges is presented as follows.

Fault Tolerance

With more computers and at times 100s of thousands in a data center, for example, in the case of cloud computing, inevitably something somewhere would be failing. In other words, the probability of failing some part of the distributed system, be it a network cable, a processor, or some other hardware, increases with the number of computers. This aspect of distributed systems requires that even if some parts of the distributed system fail (usually a certain threshold), the distributed system as a whole must keep operating. To this end, there are various problems that are studied in distributed computing under the umbrella of fault tolerance. Fault-tolerant consensus is one such example where the efforts are made to build consensus algorithms that continue to run correctly as specified even in the presence of a threshold of faulty nodes or links in a distributed system. We will see more details about that in Chapter 3.

A relevant area of study is **failure detection** which is concerned with the development of algorithms that attempt to detect faults in a distributed system. This is especially an area of concern in asynchronous distributed systems where there is no upper bound on the message delivery times. The problem becomes even more tricky when there is no way to distinguish between a failed node and a node that is simply slower and a lost message on the link. Failure detection algorithms give a probabilistic indication about the failure of a process. This up or down status of the node then can be used to handle that fault.

Another area of study is **replication** which provides fault tolerance on the principle that if the same data is replicated across multiple nodes in a distributed system, then even if some nodes go down the data is still available, which helps to keep the system stable and continue to meet its specification (guarantees) and remain available to the end users. We will see more about replication in Chapter 3.

Security

Being a distributed system with multiple users using it, out of which some might be malicious, the security of distributed systems becomes a prime concern. This situation is even more critical in geographically dispersed distributed systems and open systems such as blockchains, for example, Bitcoin blockchain. To this, the fundamental science used for providing security in distributed systems is cryptography, which we will cover in detail in Chapter 2, and we will keep referring to it throughout the book, especially in relation to blockchain consensus. Here, we study topics such as cryptography and address challenges such as authentication, confidentiality, access control, nonrepudiation, and data integrity.

Heterogeneity

A distributed system is not necessarily composed of exactly the same hardware nodes. It is possible and is called homogenous distributed system, but usually the hardware and operating systems are different from each other. In this type of scenario, different operating systems and hardware can behave differently, leading to synchronization complexities. Some nodes might be slow, running a different operating system which could have bugs, some might run faster due to better hardware, and some could be resource constrained as mobile devices or IoT devices. With all these different types of nodes (processes, computers) in a distributed system, it becomes challenging to build a distributed algorithm that works correctly on all these different types of systems and continues to operate correctly despite the differences in the local operating environment of the nodes.

Distribution Transparency

One of the goals of a distributed system is to achieve transparency. It means that the distributed system, no matter how many individual computers and peripherals it is built of, it should appear as a single coherent system to the end user. For example, an ecommerce website may have many database servers, firewalls, web servers, load balancers, and many other elements in their distributed system, but all that should be abstracted away from the end user. The end user is not necessarily concerned about these backend "irrelevant" details but only that when they make a request, the system responds. In summary, the distributed system is coherent if it behaves in accordance with the expectation of the end user, despite its heterogeneous and dispersed structure. For example, think about IPFS, a distributed file system. Even though the files are spread and sharded across multiple computers in the IPFS network, to the end user all that detail is transparent, and the end user operates on it almost as if they are using a local file system. Similar observation can be made about other systems such as online email platforms and cloud storage services.

Timing and Synchronization

Synchronization is a vital operation of a distributed system to ensure a stable global state. As each process has its view of time depending on their internal physical clocks which can drift apart, the time synchronization becomes one of the fundamental issues to address in designing distributed systems. We will see some more details around this interesting problem and will explore some solutions in our section on **timing, orders, and clocks** in this chapter.

Global State

As the processes in a distributed system only have knowledge of their local states, it becomes quite a challenge to ascertain the global state of the system. There are several algorithms that can be used to do that, such as the Chandy-Lamport algorithm. We will briefly touch upon that shortly.

Concurrency

Concurrency means multiple processes running at the same time. There is also a distinction made between logical and physical concurrency. Logical concurrency refers to the situation when multiple programs are executed in an interleaving manner on a single processor. Physical concurrency is where program units from the same program execute at the same time on two or more processors.

Distributed systems are ubiquitous. They are in everyday use and have become part of our daily routine as a society. Be it the Internet, the World Wide Web, Bitcoin, Ethereum, Google, Facebook, or Twitter, distributed systems are now part of our daily lives. At the core of distributed systems, there are distributed algorithms which form the foundation of the processing being performed by the distributed system. Each process runs the same copy of the algorithm that intends to solve the problem for which the distributed system has been developed, hence the term distributed algorithm.

A process can be a computer, an IoT device, or a node in a data center. We abstract these devices and represent these as processes, whereas physically it can be any physical computer.

Now let's see some of the relevant technologies and terminologies.

Parallel vs. Distributed vs. Concurrency

The key difference between a parallel system and a distributed system is that parallel systems' primary focus is on high performance, whereas distributed systems are concerned with tolerating partial failures. Also, parallel processing systems have direct access to a shared memory, whereas in distributed systems all processors have their own local memory.

A comparison is shown in Table 1-1.

Table 1-1. *Parallel vs. distributed systems*

Resource/ Property	Parallel	Distributed
Memory	Shared memory, a common address space	Each processor has its own memory
Coupling	Tightly coupled	Loosely coupled
Synchronization	Through a global shared clock	Through synchronization algorithms
Goal	High performance	Scalability
Algorithms	Concurrent	Distributed
Messaging	No network, shared memory	Message-passing network

There are some overlapping ideas in the distributed computing, and sometimes it becomes a bit difficult for beginners to understand. In the next section, I will try to clarify some of the pertinent terminology and some ambiguities.

Centralized vs. Decentralized vs. Distributed

A centralized system is a typical distributed system where clients connect to a central server or a service provider. There is usually an administrator in control of the entire system. A typical example is the standard client-server architecture, where all clients send requests to a central server and receive responses. These systems are usually easier to develop and maintain. However, they are not fault tolerant (in the stricter sense of client-server where there is only one central server); if the central server fails, the clients cannot connect and make requests.

A decentralized system is where there is no central owner of the system. Instead, there can be multiple owners in different locations who oversee different parts of the system, or there is no controller as in blockchain systems.

A distributed system compared to a centralized and decentralized system can be thought of as a system where there may or may not be a central controller in the system; however, the resources and nodes are distributed.

Figure 1-2 shows a depiction of three types of systems.

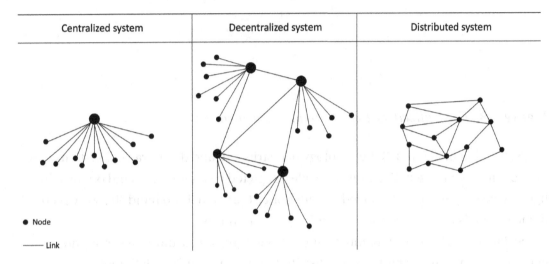

Figure 1-2. *Centralized vs. decentralized vs. distributed*

Figure 1-2 shows the traditional view of centralized, decentralized, and distributed systems. However, in recent years a slightly different picture started to emerge which highlights the notion of a system with a central controller and the one with no controller at all and where all users participate equally without any dependence on a trusted third party. These new types of distributed systems are blockchains, especially public blockchains, where there is no central controller, such as Bitcoin blockchain. We will cover more on blockchain in Chapter 4 and then throughout the book. However, let's now look at Figure 1-3, which depicts this type of architecture and highlights the differences from a control point of view.

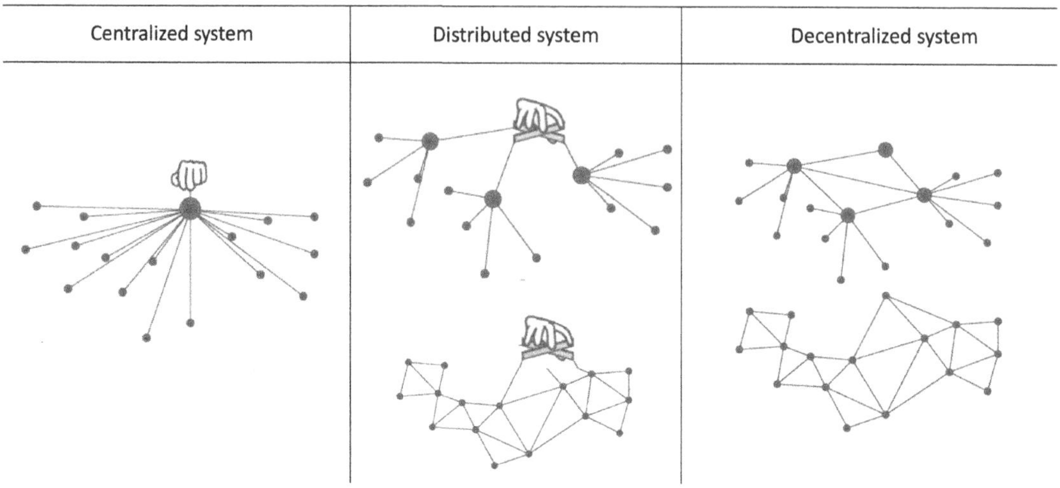

Centralized system	Distributed system	Decentralized system

Figure 1-3. *Centralized vs. distributed vs. decentralized*

Notice that in Figure 1-3 the topology of distributed and decentralized systems may be the same, but there is a central controller, depicted by a symbolic hand on top of the figure. However, in a decentralized system notice that there is no hand shown, which depicts there is no single central controller or an authority.

So far, we have focused mainly on the architecture of distributed systems and generally defined and explored what distributed systems are. Now let's look at the most important fundamental element of a distributed system, that is, the distributed algorithm that enables a distributed system to do what it is supposed to do. It is the algorithm that runs on each node in a distributed system to accomplish a common goal. For example, a common goal in a cryptocurrency blockchain is to disallow double-spending. The logic to handle that is part of the distributed algorithm that runs on each node of the cryptocurrency blockchain, and collectively and collaboratively, the blockchain (the distributed system) accomplishes this task (goal) to avoid double-spending. Don't worry if some of these terms don't make sense now; they will become clear in Chapter 4.

Distributed Algorithm

A distributed algorithm runs on multiple computers concurrently to accomplish something in a distributed system. In a distributed system, the same algorithm runs on all computers concurrently to achieve a common goal.

In contrast with a sequential algorithm where each operation in execution comes one after another, distributed algorithms are algorithms where the operations are performed concurrently. Concurrent algorithms and concurrency are quite common in computing, for example, multiple threads running simultaneously in a processor, multiple applications running in a computer, multicore processors in a computer, or multiple processes running concurrently in a distributed system.

We can define a distributed algorithm as an algorithm that runs concurrently on multiple machines.

There are several advantages of distributed algorithms, including but not limited to better performance where some computation can be parallelized to achieve higher performance as compared to sequential algorithms. In addition, distributed algorithms allow for fault tolerance; for example, if a certain threshold (which we will explain in Chapter 3) of nodes fails, the distributed algorithms continue to operate.

There are message-passing algorithms where processes communicate over the network by sending and receiving messages. Another type is shared memory distributed algorithms, where the algorithms communicate by reading and writing from shared memory.

Centralized algorithms execute sequentially, whereas distributed algorithms execute concurrently. Centralized algorithms are not usually characterized by failures, whereas distributed algorithms are designed to tolerate various types of failures. Sequential algorithms tend to be more intuitive as they are designed for sequential execution, whereas distributed algorithms can be challenging to understand. This is one of the reasons why the correctness proofs of centralized algorithms are comparatively easier to do and, in most cases, even apparent by observation. This is not the case in distributed algorithms, where correctness can be deceiving. A seemingly correct algorithm may not behave correctly in practice and could be subject to various failures and violations of properties. For this purpose, several formal specifications and verification techniques are used to ascertain the correctness of distributed algorithms. We will cover some of these methods in Chapter 9. Distributed algorithms tend to be more challenging to design, debug, and implement as compared to sequential algorithms. Moreover, from a complexity measure point of view, it's generally the measure of the number of instructions in a sequential centralized algorithm; however, the complexity of distributed algorithms is measured in the number of messages.

Elements of Distributed Computing/Pertinent Terms/ Concepts

A distributed system is composed of several elements. We are only interested in an abstracted view of the system instead of specific hardware or network details. The abstracted view allows designers to design and reason about the system under some assumptions by building a system model. More on that later but let's first look at the basic elements in a distributed system.

A distributed system can be presented as a graph where nodes or processes are depicted by vertices and communication links are depicted by edges. Some common topologies are shown in Figure 1-4.

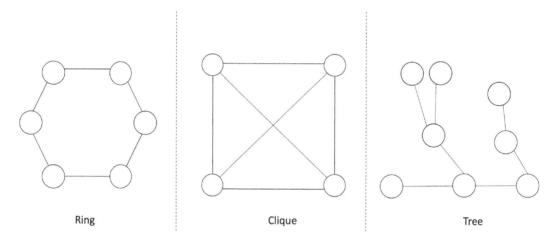

Figure 1-4. *Distributed system topologies depicted as graphs*

A distributed system is usually represented as a graph composed of nodes and vertices. Nodes represent processes in the network, whereas vertices represent communication links between the processes. These graphs also show the structural view or topology of the network and help to visualize the system.

A distributed system can have different topologies (structures) and can be presented as graphs. Common topologies include **ring** which depicts a topology where each node has two adjacent nodes. A **tree** structure is acyclic and connected. **Clique** is a fully connected graph where all processes are connected to each other directly.

Other elements

- Processes

- Events
- Executions
- Links
- State
- Global state
- Cuts

Let's look at them in detail now.

Processes

A process in a distributed system is a computer that executes the distributed algorithm. It is also called a node. It is an autonomous computer that can fail independently and can communicate with other nodes in the distributed network by sending and receiving messages.

Events

An event can be defined as some operation occurring in a process. There can occur three types of events in a process:

> **Internal events** occur when something happens locally in a process. In other words, a local computation performed by a process is an internal event.
>
> **Message send** events occur when a process (node) sends a message out to other nodes.
>
> **Message receive** events occur when a process (node) receives a message.

The diagram shown in Figure 1-5 presents this visually.

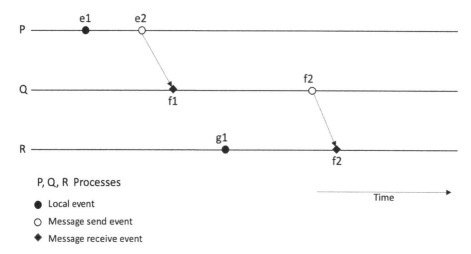

Figure 1-5. *Events and processes in a three-node distributed system*

State

The concept of state is critical in distributed systems. You will come across this term quite a lot in this book and other texts on distributed systems, especially in the context of distributed consensus. Events make up the local state of a node. In other words, a state is composed of events (results of events) in a node. Or we can say that the contents of the local memory, storage, and program as a result of events make up the process's state.

Global State

The collection of states in all processes and communication links in a distributed system is called a **global state**.

This is also known as configuration which can be defined as follows:

The configuration of a distributed system is composed of states of the processes and messages in transit.

Execution

An execution in a distributed system is a run or computation of the distributed algorithm by a process. There are two types of executions:

- Synchronous execution

- Asynchronous execution

Cuts

A cut can be defined as a line joining a single point in time on each process line in a space-time diagram. Cuts on a space-time diagram can serve as a way of visualizing the global state (at that cut) of a distributed computation. Also, it serves as a way to visualize what set of events occurred before and after the cut, that is, in the past or future. All events on the left of the cut are considered **past**, and all events on the right side of the cut are said to be **future**. There are consistent cuts and inconsistent cuts. If all received messages are sent within the elapsed time before the cut, that is, the past, it is called a consistent cut. In other words, a cut that obeys causality rules is a consistent cut. An inconsistent cut is where a message crosses the cut from the future (right side of the cut) to the past (left side of the cut).

If a cut crosses over a message from the past to the future, it is a graphical representation of messages in transit.

The diagram shown in Figure 1-6 illustrates this concept, where C_1 is an inconsistent cut and C_2 is a consistent cut.

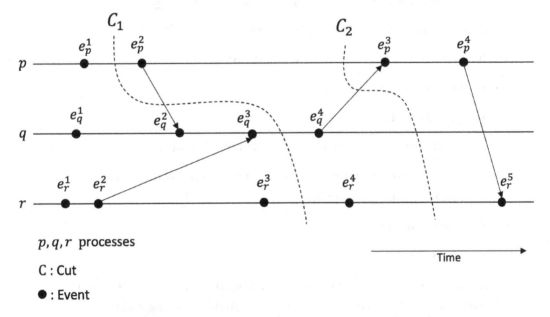

Figure 1-6. *A space-time diagram depicting cuts in a distributed system execution*

Algorithms such as the Chandy-Lamport snapshot algorithm are used to create a consistent cut of a distributed system.

Taking a snapshot of a distributed system is helpful in creating a global picture of the system. A snapshot or global snapshot captures the global state of the system containing the local state of each process and the individual state of each communication link in the system. Such snapshots are very useful for debugging, checkpointing, and monitoring purposes. A simple solution is to synchronize all clocks and create a snapshot at a specific time, but accurate clock synchronization is not possible, and we can use causality to achieve such an algorithm that gives us a global snapshot.

Assuming no failures, unidirectional FIFO channels, and existence of a communication path between any two processes in the system, the Chandy-Lamport algorithm works as follows:

- An initiator process initiating the snapshot algorithm does the following:

    - Records its own state

    - Sends a marker message (a control message) to all processes

    - Starts recording all incoming messages on its channels

- A process receiving the marker message does the following:

- If it is the first time it sees this message, then it

    - Records its own local state

    - Marks the channel as empty

    - Sends out a marker to all processes on its channels

    - Starts recording all incoming channels, except the one it had marked empty previously

- If not the first time

    - Stops recording

- A snapshot is considered complete, and algorithm terminates, when each process has received the marker on all its incoming channels.

- The initiator process is now able to build a complete snapshot containing the saved state of each process and all messages.

Note that any process can initiate the snapshot, the algorithm does not interfere with the normal operation of the distributed system, and each process records the state of incoming channels and its own.

Types of Distributed Systems

There are two types of distributed systems from the communication point of view. Shared memory systems are those where all nodes have direct access to the shared memory. On the other hand, message-passing systems are those where nodes communicate with each other via passing messages. In other words, nodes send and receive messages using communication links to communicate with each other.

Now let's discuss some software architecture models of distributed systems. Software architecture models describe the design and structure of the system. Software architecture answers questions such as what elements are involved and how they interact with each other. The central focus of the distributed system software architecture is processes, and all other elements are built around them.

Software Architecture Models

There are four main software architecture types which include the client-server model, multiple server model, proxy server model, and peer-to-peer model.

Client-Server

This model is a common way to have two processes work together. A process assumes the role of a client, and the other process assumes the role of a server. The server receives requests made by the client and responds with a reply. There can be multiple client processes but only a single server process. For example, a classic web client and web server (browser to a web server) design follows this type of architecture. Figure 1-7 depicts the so-called physical view of this type of architecture.

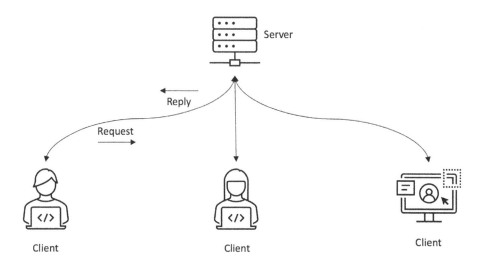

Figure 1-7. *Client-server architecture*

Multiserver

A multiserver architecture is where multiple servers work together. In one style of architecture, the server in the client-server model can itself become a client of another server. For example, if I have made a request from my web browser to a web server to find prices of different stocks, it is possible that the web server now makes a request to the backend database server or, via a web service, requests this pricing information from some other server. In this scenario, the web server itself has become a client. This type of architecture can be seen as a multiserver architecture.

Another quite common scenario is where multiple servers act together to provide a service to a client, for example, multiple database servers providing data to a web server. There are two usual methods to implement such collaborative architecture. The first is **data partitioning**, and another is **data replication**. Another closely related term to data partitioning is **data sharding**.

Data partition refers to an architecture where data is distributed among the nodes in a distributed system, and each node becomes responsible for its partition (section) of the data. Partitioning of data helps to achieve better performance, easier administration, load balancing, and better availability. For example, data for each department of a company can be divided into partitions and stored separately on different local servers. Another way of looking at it is that if we have a large table with one million rows, I might put half a million rows on one server and another half on another server. This scheme is called **data sharding** or **horizontal partitioning**, or **horizontal sharding** depending on how the sharding is performed.

We can visualize the concept of partitioning in Figure 1-8.

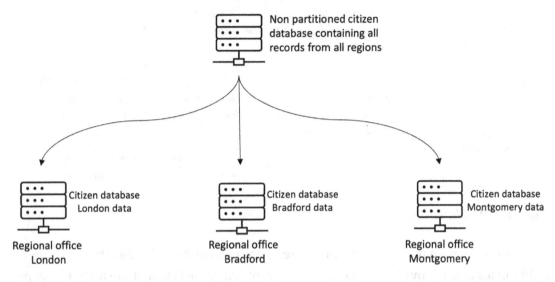

Figure 1-8. *Data partitioning*

Note that data partitioning shown in Figure 1-8 is where a large central database is partitioned into smaller datasets relevant to each region, and a regional server then manages the partition. However, in another type of partitioning, a large table can be partitioned into different tables, but it remains on the same physical server. It is called logical partitioning.

A shard is a horizontal partition of data where each shard (fragment) resides on a separate server. One immediate benefit of such an approach is load balancing to spread the load between servers. This concept is shown in Figure 1-9.

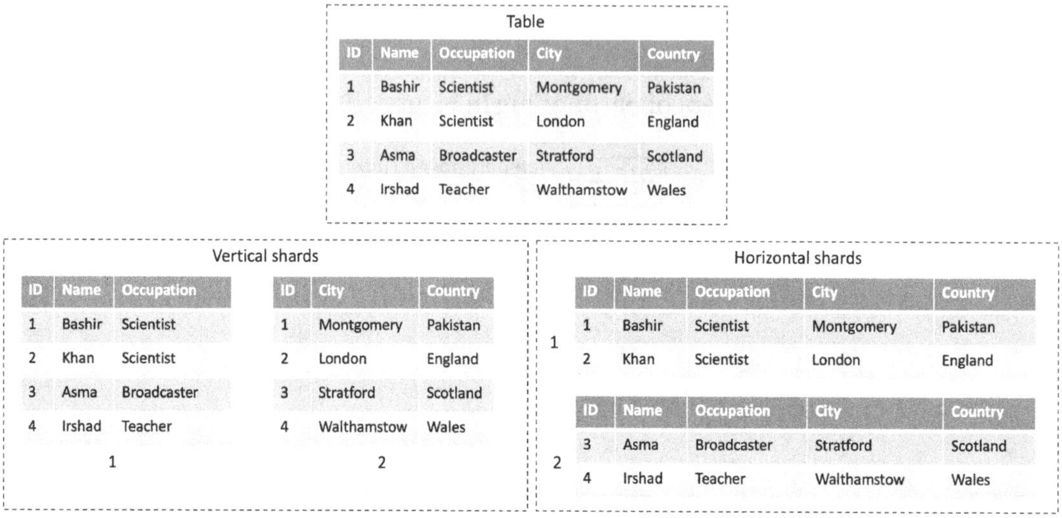

Table

ID	Name	Occupation	City	Country
1	Bashir	Scientist	Montgomery	Pakistan
2	Khan	Scientist	London	England
3	Asma	Broadcaster	Stratford	Scotland
4	Irshad	Teacher	Walthamstow	Wales

Vertical shards

ID	Name	Occupation
1	Bashir	Scientist
2	Khan	Scientist
3	Asma	Broadcaster
4	Irshad	Teacher

1

ID	City	Country
1	Montgomery	Pakistan
2	London	England
3	Stratford	Scotland
4	Walthamstow	Wales

2

Horizontal shards

1

ID	Name	Occupation	City	Country
1	Bashir	Scientist	Montgomery	Pakistan
2	Khan	Scientist	London	England

2

ID	Name	Occupation	City	Country
3	Asma	Broadcaster	Stratford	Scotland
4	Irshad	Teacher	Walthamstow	Wales

Figure 1-9. *Sharding*

Data replication refers to an architecture where each node in the distributed system holds an identical copy of the data. A typical simple example is that of the RAID 0 system; while they are not separate physical servers, the data is replicated across two disks, which makes it a data replication (commonly called mirroring) architecture. In another scenario, a database server might run a replication service to replicate data across multiple servers. This type of architecture allows for better performance, fault tolerance, and higher availability. A specific type of replication and fundamental concept in a distributed system is state machine replication used to build fault-tolerant distributed systems. We will cover more about this in Chapter 3.

Figure 1-10 shows multiserver architectures where a variation of the client-server model is shown. The server can act as a client to another server. This is another approach where multiple servers work together closely to provide a service.

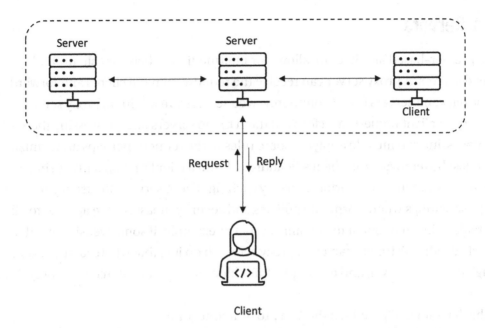

Figure 1-10. *Multiple servers acting together (client-server and multiple servers coordinating closely/closely coupled servers)*

Another diagram in Figure 1-11 shows the concept of data replication.

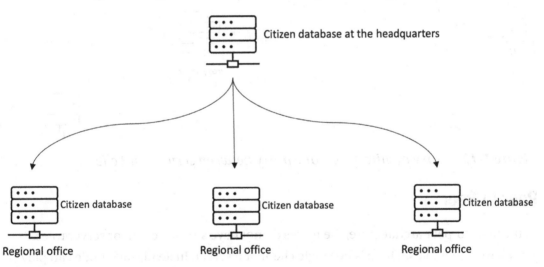

Figure 1-11. *Data replication*

In summary, replication refers to a practice where a copy of the same data is kept on multiple different nodes, whereas partitioning refers to a practice where data is split into smaller subsets, and these smaller subsets are then distributed across different nodes.

Proxy Servers

A proxy server–based architecture allows for intermediation between clients and backend servers. A proxy server can receive the request from the clients and forward it to the backend servers (most commonly, web servers). In addition, proxy servers can interpret client requests and forward them to the servers after processing them. This processing can include applying some rules to the request, perhaps anonymizing the request by removing the client's IP address. From a client's perspective, using proxy servers can improve performance by caching. These servers are usually used in enterprise settings where corporate policies and security measures are applied to all web traffic going in or out of the organization. For example, if some websites need to be blocked, administrators can use a proxy server to do just that where all requests go through the proxy server, and any requests for blocked sites are intercepted, logged, and ignored.

The diagram in Figure 1-12 shows a proxy architecture.

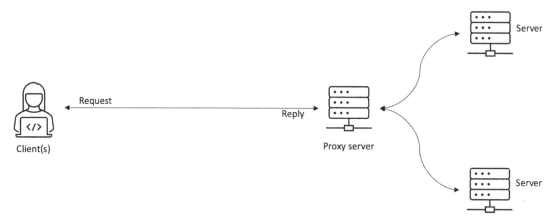

Figure 1-12. *Proxy architecture – one proxy between servers and clients*

Peer to Peer

In the peer-to-peer architecture, the nodes do not have specific client or server roles. They have equal roles. There is no single client or a server. Instead, each node can play either a client or a server role, depending on the situation. The fact that all nodes have an equal role resulted in the term "peer."

Peer-to-peer architecture is shown in the diagram in Figure 1-13.

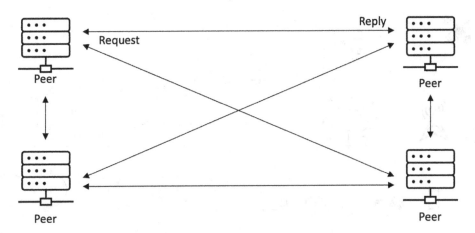

Figure 1-13. *Peer-to-peer architecture*

In some scenarios, it is also possible that not all nodes have equal roles; some may act as servers and clients to each other. Generally, however, all nodes have the same role in a peer-to-peer network.

Now that we have covered some architectural styles of distributed systems, let's focus on a more theoretical side of the distributed system, which focuses on the abstract view of the distributed systems. First, we explore the distributed system model.

Distributed System Model

A system model allows us to see a distributed system abstractly. It captures the assumptions about the behavior of the distributed system. It will enable us to define some properties we expect from our distributed system and then reason about them. All of this is at an abstract level without worrying about any technology or implementation details. For example, a communication link abstraction only captures the fact that a channel allows messages to be communicated/exchanged between processes without specifying what it is. From an implementation point of view, it could be a fiber optic cable or a wire.

We are not concerned with the specifics of the implementation of hardware technology in a distributed system model. For example, a process is a node that performs some events, and we do not concern ourselves with worrying about the exact hardware or computer type.

In this book, we are interested in the abstracted view of the system rather than physical infrastructure. Figure 1-14 demonstrates this concept.

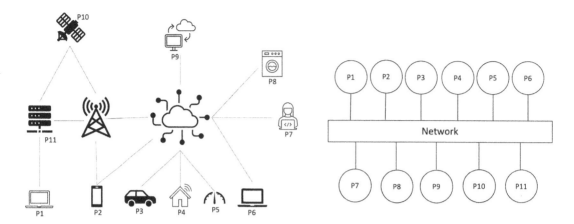

Figure 1-14. *Physical architecture (left) vs. abstract system model (right)*

Now let's see what the three fundamental abstractions in a distributed system are. Failures characterize all these abstractions. We capture our assumption about what fault might occur in our system. For example, processes or nodes can crash or act maliciously in a distributed system. A network can drop messages, or messages can be delayed. Message delays are captured using timing assumptions.

So, in summary, when a distributed system model is created, we make some assumptions about the behavior of the system. This process includes timing assumptions regarding processes and the network. We also make failure assumptions regarding the network and the processors, for example, how a process can fail and whether it can exhibit arbitrary failures, how an adversary can affect the processors or the network, and whether processes can crash or recover after a crash. Is it possible that the network links drop messages? In the next section, we discuss all these scenarios in detail.

Processes

A process or node is a fundamental element in a distributed system which runs the distributed algorithm to achieve that common goal for which the distributed system has been designed.

Now imagine what a process can do in a distributed system. First, let's think about a normal scenario. If a process is behaving according to the algorithm without any failures, then it is called a correct process or honest process. So, in our model we say that a node running correctly is one of the behaviors a node can exhibit. What else? Yes, of course, it can fail. If a node fails, we say it's faulty; if not, then it is nonfaulty or correct or honest.

There are different types of failures that can occur in a process, such as

- Crash-stop

- Omission

- Crash with recovery

- Eavesdropping

- Arbitrary

Crash-Stop Failure

Crash-stop faults are where a process crashes and never recovers. This model of faults or node behavior captures an irreparable hardware fault, for example, short circuit in a motherboard causing failure.

Omission Failure

Omission failures capture the fault scenarios where a processor fails to send a message or receive a message. Omission failures are divided into three categories: send omissions, receive omissions, and general omissions. Send omissions are where a processor doesn't send a message out which it was supposed to as per the distributed algorithm; receive omissions occur when a process does not receive an expected message. In practical terms, these omissions arise due to physical faults, memory issues, buffer overflows, malicious actions, and network congestions.

Crash with Recovery

A process exhibiting crash with recovery behavior can recover after a crash. It captures a scenario where a process crashes, loses its in-memory state, but recovers and resumes its operation later. This occurrence can be seen as an omission fault too, where now the node will not send or receive any messages because it has crashed. In practical terms, it can be a temporary intentional restart of a process or reboot after some operating system errors. Some examples include resumption of the normal operation after rebooting due to a blue screen in Windows or kernel panic in Linux.

When a process crashes, it may lose its internal state (called amnesia), making a recovery tricky. However, we can alleviate this problem by keeping stable storage (a log) which can help to resume operations from the last known good state. A node may also lose all its state after recovery and must resynchronize with the rest of the network. It may also happen that a node is down for a long time and has desynchronized with the rest of the network (other nodes) and has its old view of the state. In that case, the node must resynchronize with the network. This situation is especially true in blockchain networks such as Bitcoin or Ethereum, where a node might be off the network for quite some time. When it comes back online, it synchronizes again with the rest of the nodes to resume its full normal operation.

Eavesdropping

In this model, a distributed algorithm may leak confidential information, and an adversary can eavesdrop to learn some information from the processes. This model is especially true in untrusted and geographically dispersed environments such as a blockchain. The usual defense against these attacks is encryption which provides confidentiality by encrypting the messages.

Arbitrary (Byzantine)

A Byzantine process can exhibit any arbitrary behavior. It can deviate from the algorithm in any possible way. It can be malicious, and it can actively try to sabotage the distributed algorithm, selectively omit some messages, or covertly try to undermine the distributed algorithm. This type of fault is the most complex and challenging in a distributed algorithm or system. In practical terms, it could be a hacker coming up with novel ways to attack the system, a virus or worm on the network, or some other unprecedented attack. There is no restriction on the behavior of a Byzantine faulty node; it can do anything.

A relevant concept is that of the adversary model, where the adversary behavior is modelled. We will cover this later in the section "Adversary Model".

Now we look at another aspect of the distributed system model, network.

Network

In a distributed network, links (communication links) are responsible for passing messages, that is, take messages from nodes and send to others. Usually, the assumption is a bidirectional point-to-point connection between nodes.

A network partition is a scenario where the network link becomes unavailable for some finite time between two groups of nodes. In practice, this could be due to a data center not speaking to another or an incorrect/unintentional or even intentional/ malicious firewall rule prohibiting connections from one part of the network to another.

Link Failures

Links can experience crash failure where a correctly functioning link may stop carrying messages. Another type of link failure is omission failure, where a link carries some messages, and some don't. Finally, Byzantine failures or arbitrary failures can occur on links where the link can create rogue messages and modify messages and selectively deliver some messages, and some don't.

With this model, we can divide the communication links into different types depending on how they fail and deliver the messages.

Two types of events occur on links (channels), the **send event** where a message is put on the link and the **deliver event** where the link dispenses a message, and a process *delivers* it.

Fair-Loss Links

In this abstraction, we capture how messages on this link can be lost, duplicated, or reordered. The messages may be lost but eventually delivered if the sender and receiver process is correct and the sender keeps retransmitting. More formally, the three properties are as follows.

Fair-Loss

This property guarantees that the link with this property does not systematically drop every message, which implies that, eventually, delivery of a message to the destination node will be successful even if it takes several retransmissions.

Finite Duplication

This property ensures that the network does not perform more retransmissions than the sender does.

No Creation

This property ensures that the network does not corrupt messages or create messages out of thin air.

Stubborn Links

This abstraction captures the behavior of the link where the link delivers any message sent infinitely many times. The assumption about the processes in this abstraction is that both sender and receiver processes are correct. This type of link will stubbornly try to deliver the message without considering performance. The link will just keep trying regardless until the message is delivered.

Formally, there are two properties that stubborn links have.

Stubborn Delivery

This property means that if a message m is sent from a correct process p to a correct process q once, it will be delivered infinitely many times by process q, hence the term "stubborn"!

No Creation

This means that messages are not created out of the blue, and if a message is delivered by some process, then it must have been sent by a process. Formally, if a process q delivers a message m sent from process p, then the message m is indeed sent from process p to process q.

Perfect (Reliable) Links

This is the most common type of link. In this link, if a process has sent a message, then it will eventually be delivered.

In practice, TCP is a reliable link. There are three properties.

Reliable Delivery

If a message m is sent by a correct process p to a correct process q, then m is eventually delivered by q.

No Duplication

A correct process p does not deliver a message m more than once.

No Creation

This property ensures that messages are not created out of thin air, and if they are delivered, they must have been created and sent by a correct process before delivering.

Logged Perfect Links

This type of link delivers messages into the receiver's local message log or persistent storage. This is useful in scenarios where the receiver might crash, but we need the message to be safe. In this case, even if the receiver process crashes, the message is not lost because it persisted in the local storage.

Authenticated Perfect Links

This link guarantees that a message m sent from a process p to process q is indeed sent from process p.

Arbitrary Links

In this abstraction, the link can exhibit any behavior. Here, we consider an active adversary who has the power to control the messages. This link depicts scenarios where an attacker can do malicious actions, modify the messages, replay them, or spoof them. In short, on this link, any attack is possible.

In practical terms, this depicts a typical Internet connection where a hacker can eavesdrop, modify, spoof, or replay the messages. But, of course, this could also be due to Internet worms, traffic analyzers, and viruses.

Note   Here, we are talking about point-to-point links only; we will introduce broadcast later in Chapter 3.

Synchrony and Timing

In distributed systems, delays and speed assumptions capture the behavior of the network.

In practical terms, delays are almost inevitable in a distributed system, first because of inherent asynchrony, dispersion, and heterogeneity and specific causes such as message loss, slow processors, and congestion on the network. Due to network configuration changes, it may also happen that unexpected or new delays are introduced in the distributed system.

Synchrony assumption in a distributed system is concerned with network delays and processor delays incurred by slow network links or slow processor speeds.

In practical terms, processors can be slow because of memory exhaustion in the nodes. For example, java programs can pause execution altogether during the "stop the world" type of garbage collection. On the other hand, some high-end processors are inherently faster than low-end processors on resource-constrained devices. All these differences and situations can cause delays in a distributed system.

In the following, we discuss three models of synchrony that capture the timing assumption of distributed systems.

Synchronous

A synchronous distributed system has a known upper bound on the time it takes for a message to reach a node. This situation is ideal. However, in practice, messages can sometimes be delayed. Even in a perfect network, there are several factors, such as network link quality, network latency, message loss, processing speed, or capacity of the processors, which can adversely affect the delivery of the message.

In practice, synchronous systems exist, for example, a system on a chip (SoC), embedded systems, etc.

Asynchronous

Asynchronous distributed systems are on the other end of the spectrum. In this model, there is no timing assumption made regarding the timing. In other words, there is no upper bound on the time it takes to deliver a message. There can be arbitrarily long and unbounded delays in message delivery or processing in a node. The processes can run at different speeds.

Also, a process can arbitrarily pause or delay the execution or can process faster than other processes. You can probably imagine now that distributed algorithms designed for such a system can be very robust and resilient. However, many problems cannot be solved in an asynchronous distributed system. A whole class of results called "impossibility results" captures the unsolvable problems in distributed systems. We will look at impossibility results in more detail later in the chapter and then in Chapter 3.

As several types of problems cannot be solved in an asynchronous model and the synchronous model is too idealistic, we have to compromise. The compromise is called a partially synchronous network.

Partially Synchronous

A partially synchronous model captures the assumption that the network is primarily synchronous and well behaved, but it can sometimes behave asynchronously. For example, processing speeds can differ, or network delays can occur, but the system ultimately returns to a synchronous state to resume normal operation.

Another way to think about this is that the network usually is synchronous but can unpredictably, for a bounded amount of time, behave asynchronously, but there are long enough periods of synchrony where the system behaves correctly.

Another way to think about this is that the real systems are synchronous most of the time but can behave arbitrarily and unpredictably asynchronous at times. During the synchronous period, the system is able to make decisions and terminate.

In summary, we can quote Leonardo da Vinci:

Time stays long enough for anyone who will use it.

Figure 1-15 shows how a partially synchronous network behaves.

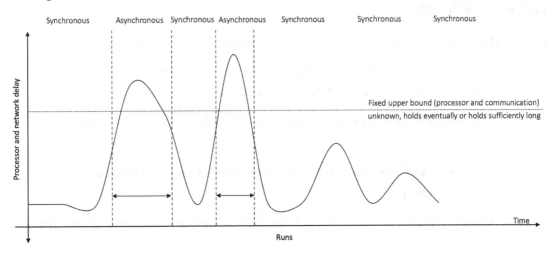

Figure 1-15. *Partially synchronous network*

Eventually Synchronous

In the eventually synchronous version of partial synchrony, the system can be initially asynchronous, but there is an unknown time called global stabilization time (GST), unknown to processors, after which the system eventually becomes synchronous. Also, it does not mean that the system will forever remain synchronous after GST. That is not possible practically, but the system is synchronous for a long enough period after GST to make a decision and terminate.

We can visualize the spectrum of synchrony models from asynchronous to synchronous in Figure 1-16.

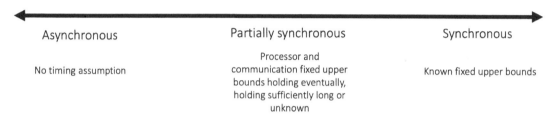

Figure 1-16. *Synchrony models in distributed systems*

Both message delivery delay and relative speed of the processes are taken into consideration in synchrony models.

Formal Definitions

Some formal definitions regarding the partial synchrony model are stated as follows:

- Delta Δ denotes a fixed upper bound on the time required for a message to reach from one processor to another.

- Phi Φ denotes a fixed upper bound on the relative speed of different processors.

- GST is the global stabilization time after which the system behaves synchronously.

With these preceding variables defined, we can define various models of synchrony as follows:

- Asynchronous systems are those where no fixed upper bounds Δ and Φ exist.

- Synchronous systems are those where fixed upper bounds Δ and Φ are known.

Partially synchronous systems can be defined in several ways:

- Where fixed upper bounds Δ and Φ exist, but they are not known.

- Where fixed upper bounds Δ and Φ are known but hold after some unknown time T. This is the eventually synchronous model. We can say that eventually synchronous model is where fixed upper bounds Δ and Φ are known but only hold after some time, known as GST.

- In another variation after GST Δ holds for long enough to allow the protocol to terminate.

We will use synchrony models more formally in Chapter 3 in the context of circumventing FLP and consensus protocols. For now, as a foundation the concepts introduced earlier are sufficient.

Figure 1-17 shows synchronous vs. asynchronous communication using a space-time diagram.

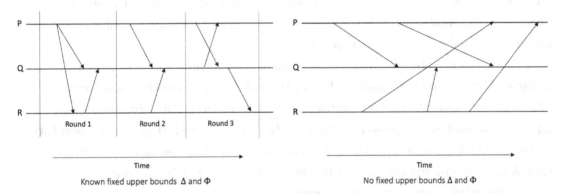

Figure 1-17. *Synchronous and asynchronous system*

Now that we have discussed the synchrony model, let's now turn our attention to the adversary model, which allows us to make assumptions about the effect of adversary on a distributed system. In this model, we model how an adversary can behave and what powers an adversary may have in order to adversely influence the distributed system.

Adversary Model

In addition to assumptions about synchrony and timing in a distributed system model, there is another model where assumptions about the power of the adversary and how it can adversely affect the distributed system are made. This is an important model which allows a distributed system designer to reason about different properties of the distributed system while facing the adversary. For example, a distributed algorithm is guaranteed to work correctly only if less than half of the nodes are controlled by a malicious adversary. Therefore, adversary models are usually modelled with a limit to what an adversary can do. But, if an adversary is assumed to be all-powerful who can do anything and control all nodes and communication links, then there is no guarantee that the system will ever work correctly.

Adversary models can be divided into different types depending on the distributed system and the influence they can have on the distributed system and adversely affect them.

In this model, it is assumed there is an external entity that has corrupted the processes and can control and coordinate faulty processes' actions. This entity is called an adversary. Note that there is a slight difference compared to the failure model here because, in the failure model, the nodes can fail for all sorts of reasons, but no external entity is assumed to take control of processes.

Adversaries can affect a distributed system in several ways. A system designer using an adversary model considers factors such as the **type of corruption**, **time of corruption**, and **extent of corruption** (how many processes simultaneously). In addition, **computational power** available to the adversary, **visibility**, and **adaptability** of the adversary are also considered. The adversary model also allows designers to specify to what limit the number of processes in a network can be corrupted.

We will briefly discuss these types here.

Threshold Adversary

A threshold adversary is a standard and widely used model in distributed systems. In this model, there is a limit imposed on the number of overall faulty processes in the system. In other words, there is a fixed upper bound f on the number of faulty processes in the network. This model is also called the global adversary model. Many different algorithms have been developed under this assumption. Almost all of the consensus protocols work under at least the threshold adversary model where it is assumed that an adversary can control up to f number of nodes in a network. For example, in the Paxos protocol discussed in Chapter 7, classical consensus algorithms achieve consensus under the assumption that an adversary can control less than half of the total number of nodes in the network.

Dynamic Adversary

Also called adaptive adversary, in this model the adversary can corrupt processes anytime during the execution of the protocol. Also, the faulty process then remains faulty until the execution ends.

Static Adversary

This type of adversary is able to perform its adversarial activities such as corrupting processes only before the protocol is executed.

Passive Adversary

This type of adversary does not actively try to sabotage the system; however, it can learn some information about the system while running the protocol. Thus, it can be called a semi-honest adversary.

An adversary can cause faults under two models: the crash failure model and the Byzantine failure model.

In the crash failure model, the adversary can stop a process from executing the protocol it has control over anytime during the execution.

In the Byzantine failure model, the adversary has complete control over the corrupted process and can control it to deviate arbitrarily from the protocol. Protocols that work under these assumptions and tolerate such faults are called crash fault–tolerant protocols (CFT) or Byzantine fault–tolerant protocols (BFT), respectively.

Time, Clocks, and Order

Time plays a critical role in distributed systems. Almost always, there is a need to measure time. For example, timestamps are required in log files in a distributed system to show when a particular event occurred. From a security point of view, audit timestamps are needed to indicate when a specific operation occurred, for example, when a specific user logged in to the system. In operating systems, timing is required for scheduling internal events. All these use cases and countless other computer and distributed systems operations require some notion of time.

The notion of time in distributed systems is tricky. Events shown in Figure 1-18 need to be ordered for a distributed system to be reasonably useful. Ordering of events in a distributed system is one of the fundamental and critical requirements. As there is no global shared clock in distributed systems, the ordering of events becomes a challenging problem. To this end, the main concern here is to accomplish the correct order of events in the system. We have this notion of time in our daily lives where we can say that something happened before something else. For example, if I sat an exam and the results came out a week later, we can say confidently that the exam must have occurred or happened before the results came out. We can visualize this relationship in the diagram in Figure 1-19.

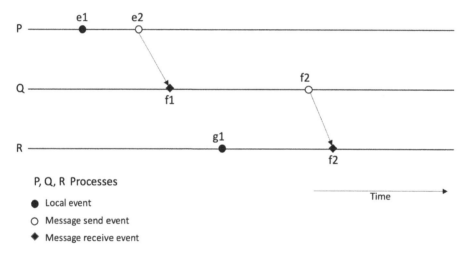

Figure 1-18. *Events and processes in a three-node distributed system*

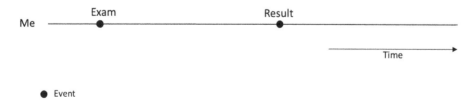

Figure 1-19. *Exam happened before the result – a happened-before relation*

Usually, we are familiar with the physical clock, that is, our typical day-to-day understanding and the notion of time where I can say something like I will meet you at 3 PM today, or the football match is at 11 AM tomorrow. This notion of time is what we are familiar with. Moreover, physical clocks can be used in distributed systems, and several algorithms are used to synchronize time across all nodes in a distributed system. These algorithms can synchronize clocks in a distributed system using message passing.

Let's first have a look at the physical clocks and see some algorithms that can be used for time synchronization based on internal physical clocks and external time source.

Physical Clocks

Physical clocks are in everyday use. Now prevalent digital clocks are based on quartz crystal, whereas traditional mechanical clocks are based on spring mechanisms or pendulums. Digital clocks, from wristwatches to clocks on a computer motherboard, make use of quartz crystals. In practice, an oscillator circuit regulated by a quartz crystal is used to generate an accurate frequency. When the electric field is applied to a quartz crystal, it bends and starts to resonate at a frequency depending upon its size, cut, temperature, and housing. The most common frequency is 32768 Hz which is almost universally used in quartz-based clocks. Figure 1-20 shows, from left to right, a quartz crystal in a natural form, in a component form, and inside a casing with additional oscillator circuitry.

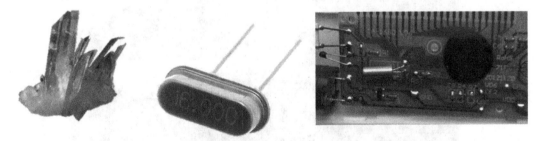

Figure 1-20. *A quartz crystal in a natural form (left), in a component form (middle), and in a circuit (right)*

Quartz-based clocks are usually accurate enough for general-purpose use. However, several factors such as manufacturing differences, casing, and operating environment (too cold, too hot) impact the operation of a quartz crystal. Usually, too low or high a temperature can slow down the clock. Imagine if an electronic device operating in the field is exposed to high temperatures; the clock can run slower than a clock working in normal favorable conditions. This difference caused by the clock running faster or slower is called drift. Drift is measured in parts per million (ppm) units.

In almost all quartz clocks, the frequency of the quartz crystal is 32,768 kHz due to its cut and size and how it is manufactured. This is a specific cut and size which looks like a tuning fork, due to which the frequency produced is always 32,768 Hertz. I decided to do a small experiment with my oscilloscope and an old clock lying around to demonstrate this fact.

Here are the results! Figure 1-21 shows a quartz crystal in a clock circuit producing exactly 32,768 Hertz at normal room temperature, shown on the oscilloscope screen.

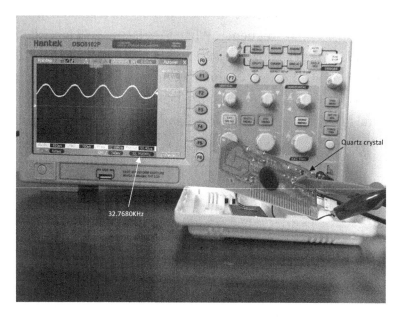

Figure 1-21. *Quartz crystal clock measured using an oscilloscope*

In Figure 1-21, the probes from the oscilloscope are connected to the quartz crystal component on the clock circuit, and the waveform is shown on the oscilloscope screen. Also, the frequency is displayed at the right bottom of the oscilloscope screen, which reads 32.7680KHz.

Clock Skew vs. Drift

Due to environmental factors such as temperature and manufacturing differences, quartz crystal clocks can slow down, resulting in skew and drift. The immediate difference between the time shown by two clocks is called their skew, whereas the rate at which two clocks count time differently is called drift. Note that the difference between physical clocks between nodes in a heterogeneous distributed system may be even more significant than homogenous distributed systems where hardware, OS, and architecture are the same for all nodes.

Generally, it is expected that roughly a drift of one second over 11 days can develop, which over time can lead to an observable and significant difference. Imagine two servers running in a data center with no clock synchronization mechanism and are only dependent on their internal quartz clock. In a month, they will be running two to three seconds apart from each other. All time-dependent operations will run three seconds apart, and over time this will continue to worsen. For example, a batch job that is supposed to start at 11 AM will begin at 11 + 3 seconds in a month. This situation can cause issues with time-dependent jobs, can cause security issues, and can impact time-sensitive operations, and software may fail or depict an arbitrary behavior. A much more accurate clock than a quartz clock is an atomic clock.

Atomic Clocks

Atomic clocks are based on the quantum mechanical properties of atoms. Atoms such as cesium or rubidium and mercury are used, and resonant frequencies (oscillations) of atoms are used to record accurate and precise times.

Our notion of time is based on astronomical observations such as changing seasons and the Earth's rotation. The higher the oscillation, the higher the frequency and the more precise the time. This is the principle on which atomic clocks work and produce highly precise time.

In 1967, the unit of time was defined as a second of "the duration of 9,192,631,770 periods of the radiation corresponding to the transition between the two hyperfine levels of the ground state of the caesium-133 atom." In other words, oscillation of cesium atoms between two energy states exactly 9,192,631,770 times under controlled environment defines a true second. An atomic clock is shown in Figure 1-22.

Figure 1-22. *Cesium-based atomic clocks: image from* https://nara. getarchive.net/media/cesium-beam-atomic-clocks-at-the-us-naval- observatory-provide-the-basis-for-29fa0c

Now imagine a scenario where we discover a clock skew and see that one clock is running behind ten seconds. We can usually and simply advance it to ten seconds to make the clock accurate again. It is not ideal but not as bad as the clock skew, where we may discover a clock to run ten seconds behind. What can we do in that case? Can we simply push it back to ten seconds? It is not a very good idea because we can then run into situations where it would appear that a message is received before we sent it.

To address clock skews and drifts, we can synchronize clocks with a trusted and accurate time source.

You might be wondering why there is such a requirement for more and more precise clocks and sources of time. Quartz clocks are good enough for day-to-day use; then we saw GPS as a more accurate time source, and then we saw atomic clocks that are even more accurate and can drift only a second in about 300 million years![1] But why do we need such highly accurate clocks? The answer is that for day-to-day use, it doesn't matter. If the time on my wristwatch is a few seconds different from other clocks, it's not a problem. If my post on a social media site has a timestamp that is a few seconds

---

[1] www.nist.gov/si-redefinition/second/second-present

apart from the exact time I posted it, perhaps that is not an issue. Of course, as long as the sequence is maintained, the timestamp is acceptable within a few seconds. But the situation changes in many other practical scenarios and distributed systems. For example, high-frequency trading systems require (by regulation MiFID II) that the mechanism format the timestamp on messages in the trading system in microseconds and be accurate within 100 microseconds. From a clock synchronization point of view, only 100 microseconds divergence is allowed from UTC. While such requirements are essential for the proper functioning and regulation of the trading systems, they also pose technical challenges. In such scenarios, the choice of source of accurate time, choice of synchronization algorithms, and handling of skews and drifts become of prime importance.

You can see specific MiFID requirements here as a reference:

```
https://ec.europa.eu/finance/securities/docs/isd/mifid/rts/160607-rts-25-
annex_en.pdf
```

There are other applications of atomic clocks in defense, geology, astronomy, navigation, and many others.

Recently, Sapphire clocks have been developed, which are much more precise than even cesium-based atomic clocks. It is so precise that it can lose or gain a second in three billion years.

Usually, there are two ways in which time is represented in computers. One is epoch time, also called Unix time, which is defined as the number of seconds elapsed since January 1, 1970. Another common timestamp format is ISO8601, which defines a date and time format standard.

Synchronization Algorithms for Physical Clocks

There are two methods to synchronize clocks:

1. External synchronization

2. Internal synchronization

In the external clock synchronization method, there is an external and authoritative source of time to which nodes in a distributed system synchronize with.

In the internal synchronization method, clocks in nodes (processes) are synchronized with one another.

NTP

The network time protocol (NTP) allows clients to synchronize with UTC. In NTP, servers are organized in so-called strata, where stratum 1 servers (primary time servers) are directly connected to an accurate time source in stratum 0, for example, GPS or atomic clock. Stratum 2 servers synchronize with stratum 1 servers over the network, and stratum 2 servers synchronize with stratum 3 servers. This type of architecture provides a reliable, secure, and scalable protocol. Reliability comes from the use of redundant servers and paths. Security is provided by utilizing appropriate authentication mechanisms, and scalability is characterized by NTP's ability to serve a large number of clients. While NTP is an efficient and robust protocol, inherent network latency, misconfigurations in the protocol setup, network misconfigurations that may block the NTP protocol, and several other factors can still cause clocks to drift.

GPS As a Time Source

A GPS receiver can be used as an accurate source of time. All 31 GPS satellites have atomic clocks on board, which produce precise time. These satellites broadcast their location and time, where GPS receivers receive and calculate time and position on earth after applying some corrections for environmental factors and time dilation. Remember, time runs slightly faster on GPS satellites than objects on the earth's surface due to relativity. Other relativity-related effects include time dilation, gravitational frequency shift, and eccentricity effects. All these errors are handled, and many other corrections are made before an accurate time is displayed on the GPS receiver. While the GPS as a source of precise time is highly accurate, the inherent latency introduced even after the existence of correct and accurate time at the GPS receiver in the network can lead to drift and skew of clocks over time. There is a need to introduce some clock synchronization algorithms to address this limitation.

A combination of atomic clocks and GPS is used in Google's spanner (Google's globally distributed database) for handling timing uncertainties.

However, note that even with all the efforts, the clocks cannot be perfectly synchronized, which is good enough for most applications. However, these very accurate clocks are still not enough to capture the causality relationship between events in a distributed system. The causality relationship between events and the fundamental monotonicity property can be accurately captured by logical clocks.

In distributed systems, even if each process has a local clock and is synchronized with some global clock source, there is still a chance that each local processor would see the time differently. The clocks can drift over time, the processors can experience bugs, or there can be an inherent drift, for example, quartz clocks or GPS systems, making it challenging to handle time in a distributed system.

Imagine a distributed system with some nodes in the orbit and some in other geographical locations on earth, and they all agree to use UTC. The physical clocks in satellites or ISS will run at a different rate, and skew is inevitable. The core limitation in depending on physical clocks is that even if trying to synchronize them perfectly, timestamps will be slightly apart. However, these physical clocks cannot (should not) be used to establish the order of events in a distributed system because it is difficult to accurately find out the global order of events based on timestamps in different nodes.

Physical clocks are not very suitable for distributed systems because they can drift apart. Even with one universal source, such as the atomic clock through NTP, they can still drift and desynchronize over time with the source. Even a difference of a second can sometimes cause a big issue. In addition, there can be software bugs in the implementation that can cause unintentional consequences. For example, let's look at a famous bug, the leap second bug that is a cause of significant disruption of Internet services.

UTC Time

UTC time is a time standard used around the world. There are two sources of time that are used to make up coordinated universal time (UTC):

- International atomic time (TAI)

  - TAI is based on around 400 atomic clocks around the world. A combined and weighted output from all these atomic clocks is produced. This is extremely accurate where they only deviate one second in around 100 million years!

- Astronomical time

  - This time is based on astronomical observations, that is, the rotation of the Earth.

While TAI is highly accurate, it doesn't consider the Earth's rotation, that is, the astronomically observed time that determines the true length of the day. Earth's rotation is not constant. It is occasionally faster and is slowing down overall. Therefore, days are not exactly 24 hours. The impact on Earth's rotation is due to celestial bodies such as the moon, tides, and other environmental factors. Therefore, UTC is kept in constant comparison with the astronomical time, and any difference is added to UTC. This difference is added in the form of leap second; before the difference between TAI and astronomical time reaches 0.9, a leap second is added to the UTC. This is the practice since 1972.

OK, this seems like a reasonable solution to keep both times synced; however, computers don't seem to handle this situation well. Unix systems use Unix time (epoch), simply the number of seconds elapsed since January 1, 1970. When a leap second is added, this is how the clock looks like: in a normal case, it is observed that after 23:59:59, there is 00:00:00. However, adding a leap second seems as if after 23:59:59, there is 23:59:60 and then 00:00:00. In other words, 23:59:59 happens twice. When Unix time deals with this addition of an extra second, it can produce arbitrary behavior. In the past, when a leap second is added, servers across the Internet experienced issues and services as critical as airline booking systems were disrupted.

A technique called "leap smear" has been developed, which allows for the gradual addition of a few milliseconds over a day to address this issue of sudden addition and problem associated with this sudden one-second additional.

OK, so far, we have seen that UTC and astronomical time are synced by adding a leap second. With the "leap second smear" technique, we can gradually add a leap second over time, which alleviates some of the issues associated with sudden additional leap second. There are also calls to abolish this ritual altogether. However, so far, we see adding a leap second as a reasonable solution, and it seems to work somewhat OK. We just add a leap second when the Earth's rotation slows down, but what if the Earth is spinning faster? In 2020, the Earth indeed spun faster, during the pandemic, for whatever reason. Now the question is, do we remove one second from UTC? In other words, introduce the negative leap second! This situation can pose some more challenges – perhaps even more demanding to address as compared to adding a leap second.

The question is, what to do about this, ignore this? What algorithm can help to remove one second and introduce a negative leap second?

So far, it is suggested that simply skip 23:59:59, that is, go from 23:59:58 to 00:00:00 directly. It is expected that this is easier to deal with as compared to adding a leap second. Perhaps, a solution is unnecessary because we may ignore the Earth spinning faster or slower altogether and abolish the leap second adjustment practice, either negative or positive. It is not ideal, but we might do that to avoid issues and ambiguity associated with handling leap seconds, especially adding leap seconds! At the time of writing, this is an open question.

Some more info are found here: `https://fanf.dreamwidth.org/133823.html` (negative leap second) and `www.eecis.udel.edu/~mills/leap.html`.

To avoid limitations and problems associated with physical clocks and synchronization, for distributed systems, we can use logical clocks, which have no correlation with physical clocks but are a way to order the events in a distributed system. Although, as we have seen, ordering of events and a causal relationship is an essential requirement in distributed systems, logical clocks play a vital role in ensuring this in distributed systems.

From a distributed system point of view, we learned earlier that the notion of global state is very important, which allows us to observe the state of a distributed system and helps to snapshot or checkpoint. Thus, time plays a vital role here because if time is not uniform across the system (each processor running at a different time), and we try to read states from all different processors and links in a system, it will result in an inconsistent state.

Types of Physical Clocks

Physical clocks can be divided into two categories:

1. Time-of-day clocks

2. Monotonic clocks

Time-of-day clocks are characterized by the representation of time since a fixed point in time. For example, Unix time that is calculated from January 1, 1970 is an example of a time-of-day clock. The time can be adjusted via synchronization to a time source and can move backward or forward. However, moving the time backward is not a good idea. Such a scenario can lead to situations where, for example, it would appear that a message is received before it was sent. This issue can happen due to the timestamp being adjusted and moving backward in time due to adjustments made by the synchronization algorithms, for example, NTP.

As the time always increases, time shouldn't go backward; we need monotonic clocks to handle such scenarios.

With physical clocks, it is almost impossible to provide causality. Even if time synchronization services are used, there is still a chance that the timestamp of one process differs from another just enough to impact the order of events adversely. Thus, the ordering of events is a fundamental requirement in distributed systems. To fully understand the nature of this ordering requirement, we use a formal notion of something called "happens-before relationship."

Just before we introduce the happens-before relationship and causality, let us clarify some basic math concepts first. This will help us to not only understand causality but will also help with concepts explained later in this book.

Set

A set is a collection of elements. It is denoted by a capital letter. All elements of the set are listed inside the brackets. If an element x is present in a set, then it is written as $x \in X$, which means x is in X or x belongs to X. Similarly, if an element x is not present in a set X, it is written as $x \notin X$. It does not matter which order the elements are in. Two sets are equal if they have the same elements. Equality is expressed as $X = Y$, meaning set X is equal to set Y. If two sets X and Y are not equal, it is written as $X \neq Y$. A set that does not have any elements is called an empty set and is denoted as { } or ϕ. An example of a set is

$$X = \{1,5,2,8,9\}$$

A set Y is a subset of set X if every element of Y is also an element of X, for example:

$$Y = \{2,8\}$$

Set Y is a subset of set X. This relationship is written as

$$Y \subseteq X$$

A union of two sets A and B contains all the elements in A and B, for example:

$$A = \{1,2,3\}$$

and

$$B = \{3,4,5\}$$

A union of sets A and B is

$$S = \{1,2,3,4,5\}$$

The cartesian product of two sets A and B is the set of ordered pairs (a, b) for each element in sets A and B. It is denoted as $A \times B$. It is a set of ordered pairs (a, b) for each $a \in A$ and $b \in B$.

An ordered pair is composed of two elements inside parentheses, for example, (1, 2) or (2, 1). Note here that the order of elements is important and matters in the case of ordered pairs, whereas in sets the order of elements does not matter. For example, (1, 2) is not the same as (2, 1), but {1,2} and {2,1} are the same or equal sets.

An example of a cartesian product, $A \times B$, for sets shown earlier is

{(1,3), (1,4), (1,5), (2,3), (2,4), (2,5), (3,3), (3,4), (3,5)}

Note that in the ordered pair, the first element is taken from set A and the second element from set B.

Relation

A relation (binary) between two sets A and B is a subset of the cartesian product $A \times B$.

The relationship between two elements is binary and can be written as a set of ordered pairs. We can express this as a R b (infix notation) or (a, b) \in R, meaning the ordered pair (a, b) is in relation R.

When a binary relation on a set S has properties of reflexivity, symmetry, and transitivity, it is called an **equivalence relation**.

When a binary relation on a set S has three properties of reflexivity, antisymmetry, and transitivity, then it is called a **partial ordering** on S.

Partial Order

It is a binary relation $\leq$ (less than or equal to – for comparison) between the elements of a set S. A binary relation on a set S, which is reflexive, antisymmetric, and transitive, is known as a partial ordering on S. We now define the three conditions.

Reflexivity

This property means that every element is related to itself. Mathematically, we can write it like this: $\forall a \in S, a \leq a$.

Antisymmetry

This means that two elements cannot be related in both directions. Mathematically, it can be written as $\forall a, b \in S, if\ a \leq b \wedge b \leq a, a = b$.

Transitivity

The transitive property indicates a comparative relationship where if $a < b$ and $b < c$, it implies that $a < c$. Mathematically, it can be written as $\forall a, b, c \in S$, $if\ a \leq b \wedge b \leq c\ then\ a \leq c$.

A set with a partial order is called a partially ordered set or poset. In terms of the happens-before relationship, the set S is a set of all events.

Irreflexive Partial Order

The irreflexive partial order or strict partial order is irreflexive, antisymmetric, and transitive.

Irreflexive

This property means that there is no element that is related to itself. Mathematically, we can write it like $\forall a \in S, a \nleq a$, or given a relation R on a set S, R is irreflexive if $\forall s \in S : (s, s) \notin R$.

Total Order

A total order or linear order is a partial order in which each pair of elements is comparable.

After this brief introduction to some math concepts, let us now look into what causality is and what is a happens-before relationship.

Happens-Before Relationship and Causality

We saw earlier that a node could perform some events. It can either do the local computation, send a message, or receive a message. All events happen in a sequential order on a single node, and it is easy to see what happened before the next event. It is a strict total order imposed on each node.

A happens-before relationship is an irreflexive partial order (strict partial order) with three properties: **irreflexivity**, **antisymmetry**, and **transitivity**.

Now imagine there are two events e and f that have happened. To ascertain if event e happened before event f, we use the following rules.

Event e happened before event f if and only if (iff) : e → f (right arrow used as a symbol for happens-before):

- If e and f occurred on the same process and e executed before f on this process, then we can deduce that e precedes f, that is, a sequential order.

- Event e is a message send event of some (unique) message m, and event f is the receipt of message m.

- If there exists an event g such that e→g and g→f, then e→f. This is called a transitive relationship.

We can visualize all these three rules in Figure 1-23.

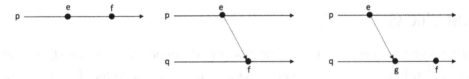

Figure 1-23. *Happens-before rules*

If *e* and *f* are partially ordered, we then say that e happened before *f*. If *e* and *f* are not partially ordered, then we say that *e* and *f* are concurrent. This also doesn't mean that *e* and *f* are executed independently exactly at the same time. It just means that *e* and *f* are not causally related. In other words, there is no sequence of messages which leads from one event to another. The concurrency is written as *e* ∥ *g*. Figure 1-24 shows an example scenario in detail.

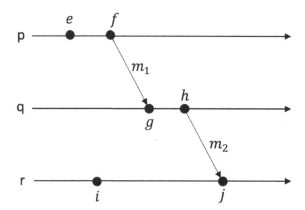

Figure 1-24. *Example happens-before relationship*

In Figure 1-24, the relations $e \rightarrow f$, $g \rightarrow h$, $i \rightarrow j$ are due to the order in which processes execute the events. The relations $f \rightarrow g$, $h \rightarrow j$ are due to messages m_1 and m_2. Moreover $e \rightarrow g$, $e \rightarrow h$, $e \rightarrow j$, $f \rightarrow h$, $f \rightarrow j$, $g \rightarrow j$ represent transitive relation. Finally, the concurrent events are $e \parallel i$, $f \parallel i$, $g \parallel i$, $h \parallel i$.

Logical Clocks

Logical clocks do not depend on physical clocks and can be used to define the order of events in a distributed system. Logical clocks only measure the order of events without any reference to external physical time.

Lamport Clocks

A Lamport clock is a logical counter that is maintained by each process in a distributed system, and with each occurrence of an event, it is incremented to provide a means of maintaining and observing a happens-before relationship between events occurring in the distributed system.

The key idea here is that each event is assigned a number which increments as the event occurs in the system. This number is also called the Lamport clock. A Lamport clock captures causality.

The algorithm for Lamport's clocks/logical clocks is described as follows:

- Every process maintains a local counter which is set to zero at initialization.

- With every event on a process, the counter is incremented by one by that process.

- When a message is sent, a process includes its current value of the counter.

- When a message is received, a process sets its counter value to `max(local + received) + 1`.

In a happens-before relationship where $e \rightarrow f$, we can say that possibly e caused f. This means that the happens-before relationship captures causality of the events.

More formally, the Lamport algorithm is shown in Listing 1-1.

Listing 1-1. Lamport clock

```
on init
t := 0

on event localcomputation do
t := t + 1
end

on event send(m) do
t := t + 1
send(m, t)
end

on event receive(m', t') do
t := max(t, t') + 1
end
```

Lamport clocks are consistent with causality. We can write this like

$$if\ e \rightarrow f \Rightarrow LC(e) < LC(f)$$

This means that if e happened before f, then it implies that the timestamp (Lamport clock – LC) of event e is less than the timestamp of event f.

There is a correctness criterion called the **clock condition** which is used to evaluate the logical clocks:

$$\forall a,b : a \rightarrow b \Rightarrow LC(a) < LC(b)$$

This is read as follows: for all a and b, a happened before b implies that the Lamport clock (timestamp) of a is less than the Lamport clock (timestamp) of b.

This means that if event A happens before event B, then it implies that the Lamport clock of event A is less than the Lamport clock of event B.

Now we can see a picture emerging. Without using physical clocks, we can now see how events in a distributed system can be assigned a number which can be used for ordering them by using Lamport clocks.

Now let's run this algorithm on a simple distributed system composed of three processes (nodes, computers) – P, Q, and R.

There are two key properties of this algorithm:

1.   If $a \rightarrow b$, then LC(a) < LC(b).

2.   But $LC(a) < LC(b)$ does not mean that $a \rightarrow b$.

This means that two events can have the same timestamp. As shown in Figure 1-25, on process lines P and R, notice event timestamp 1 as the same. Did you spot a problem here? In this scheme, the total order is not guaranteed because two events can get the same timestamp.

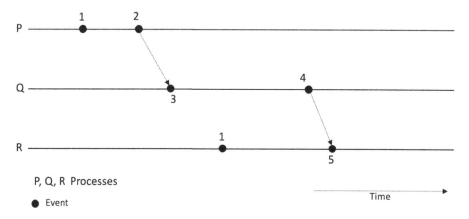

Figure 1-25. *Example run of a Lamport clock algorithm*

One obvious way to fix this is to use an identifier for the process with the timestamp. This way, the total order can be achieved.

Figure 1-26 shows executions with a totally ordered logical clock.

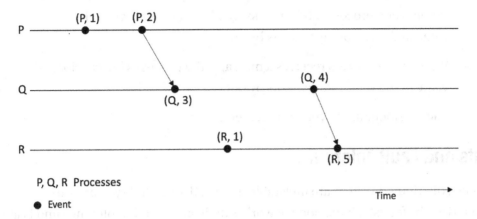

Figure 1-26. Example run of a Lamport clock with a total order

Knowing the order of events in a distributed system is very useful. The order of events allows us to find the causality between the events. The knowledge of causality in distributed systems helps to solve several problems. Some examples include but are not limited to consistency in replicated databases, figuring out causal dependency between different events, measuring the progress of executions in a distributed system, and measuring concurrency.

We can use it to build distributed state machines. If events are timestamped, we can also see when exactly an event has occurred and what happened before and what occurred after, which can help debug and investigate distributed systems' faults. This knowledge can be instrumental in building debuggers, snapshotting a point in time, pruning some data before a point in time, and many other use cases.

The limitation that $LC(a) < LC(b)$ does not mean that $a \rightarrow b$. This means that Lamport clocks cannot tell if two events are concurrent or not. This problem can be addressed using vector clocks.

Vector Clocks

It is a type of logical clock which allows detecting concurrent events in addition to determining partial ordering of events and detecting causality violations. Here is how it works:

- At the start, all vector clocks in a distributed system are set to zero, that is, [0,0,0,0,0].

- Whenever an internal event occurs at a process, the process's logical clock value in the vector increments by one.

- Whenever a process sends a message, the process's logical clock value in the vector increments by one.

- Whenever a process receives a message, the process's logical clock value in the vector increments by one.

- Each element in the vector increments.

Faults and Fault Tolerance

Faults in a distributed system are inevitable. In fact, distributed systems are characterized by faults. A large body of work is dedicated to fault tolerance and is at the core of the distributed systems research. To understand faults, let's look at a small example.

Imagine a simplest distributed system with two nodes, shown in Figure 1-27.

Figure 1-27. *A simplest distributed system*

Think about what faults can occur:

- The processor p1 or p2 may crash.

- Communication link can fail.

- Latency on the communication link.

- Slow processing at p1 or p2.

- P1 can pretend that it sent some message; in fact, it has not.

There can be several faults that occur in a distributed system:

- Process/program faults

- Communication/link faults

- Storage faults

There are several types of faults that have been formally defined in distributed systems literature. These types are categorized under the so-called fault model which basically tells us which kind of faults can occur.

We now define each one of these as follows.

Crash-Stop

In this scenario, a process can fail to stop a function at any point in time. This can happen when a hardware fault may have occurred in a node. Other nodes are unable to find out about the crash of the node in this model.

Fail-Stop

In this model, a process can fail by stopping execution of the algorithm. Other nodes in the distributed system can learn about this failure, usually by using failure detectors.

Omission Faults

Omission faults are where a message can be lost.

Send Omission

This is where a process fails to send a message.

Receive Omission

This is where a process fails to receive a message.

General Omission

This is where a process may exhibit either a send omission or a receive omission.

Covert Faults

This model captures a behavior where a failure might remain hidden or undetected.

Computation Faults

In this scenario, we capture the situation where a processor responds incorrectly.

Byzantine Faults

This model captures the arbitrary faults where a process may fail in arbitrarily many ways.

Byzantine Faults with Authentication

In this model, a process can exhibit arbitrary behavior; however, there is a verification of received messages to this process, which is possible by using authentication and digital signatures. This nonrepudiation and verification can make dealing with Byzantine faults a bit easier.

Byzantine Faults Without Authentication

In this model, a process can exhibit arbitrary behavior, but no message verification is possible to ascertain the validity of the messages.

Timing Faults

This is where a process can exhibit slow behavior or may run faster than other processes. This can initially look like a partially synchronous behavior, but a node that has not received a message for a very long time can be seen as one example of this type of fault. This covers scenarios where an expected message delivery is not in line with the expected delivery time or lies outside the specified time interval.

Failures can be detected using failure detectors where a process can be suspected of a failure. For example, a message not received for an extended period of time or that has gone past the threshold of timeout can be marked as a failed process.

More on failure detector in Chapter 3; now let's discover what a fault model is and fault classes.

In Figure 1-28, we can visualize various classes of faults, where Byzantine faults encompass all types of faults at varying degrees of complexity and can happen arbitrarily, whereas crash faults are the simplest type of faults.

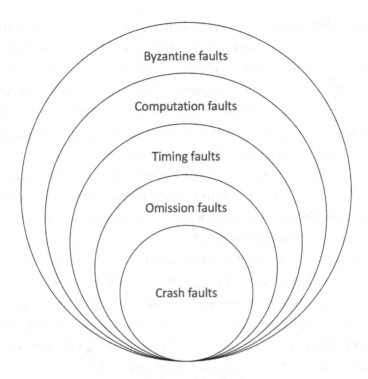

Figure 1-28. *Diagram of fault models and fault classes*

Fault classes allow us to see what faults can occur, whereas fault models help us to see what kind of faults the system can exhibit and what types of faults should be tolerated in our distributed algorithm.

A system or algorithm that can tolerate crash faults only is called a crash fault tolerant or CFT in short. In contrast, a system that can handle Byzantine faults is called the Byzantine fault–tolerant system or algorithm. Usually, this applies to consensus mechanisms categorized and developed with the goal of crash fault tolerance or Byzantine fault tolerance. We will see more about this in Chapter 3, where we discuss consensus algorithms.

Safety and Liveness

Remember we discussed in communication abstractions that broadcast protocols and point-to-point links have some properties. For example, a fair-loss property ensures that messages sent will eventually be delivered under fair-loss links. This type of property where something will eventually happen is considered a liveness property. Colloquially speaking, this means that something good will eventually occur.

Also, remember that under the finite duplication property for fair-loss links, we said that there are finite message duplications. This type of property where something can be measured and observed infinite time is called a safety property. Colloquially speaking, this means that something bad never happens. Of course, if you don't do anything, then nothing will ever happen, which theoretically satisfies the safety property; however, the system is not making any progress in this scenario. Therefore, the liveness property, which ensures the progress of the system, is also necessary.

These properties are used in many different distributed algorithms to reason about the correctness of the protocols. In addition, they are frequently used in describing the safety and liveness requirements and properties of consensus protocols. We will cover distributed consensus in detail in Chapter 3.

Safety and liveness are correctness properties of a distributed algorithm. For example, the safety and liveness of traffic signals at a crossing can be described as follows. The safety properties in this scenario are that, at a time, only one direction must be a green light, and no signal should have all lights turned on at the same time. Another safety property could be that the system should turn off no signals. And the liveness property is that, eventually, each signal must get the green light.

For example, in a partially synchronous system, to prove safety properties, it is assumed that the system is asynchronous, whereas to prove the liveness of the system, the partial synchrony assumption is used. The progress of liveness of the system is ensured in a partially synchronous system, for example, after GST when the system is synchronous for long enough to allow the algorithm to achieve its objective and terminate.

For a distributed system to be practical, safety and liveness properties must be specified and guaranteed.

Forms of Fault Tolerance

A correct program (distributed algorithm) satisfies both its safety and liveness properties. If a program tolerates a given class of faults and remains alive and safe, we call this type of fault tolerance masking. If a program can remain safe but not live, we call this type of fault tolerance fail-safe. Similarly, in the presence of faults, a program cannot remain safe (not safe) but remains live. Such behavior is called nonmasking. If a program is neither live nor safe in the presence of faults, it means that this program does not depict any form of fault tolerance.

CAP Theorem

The CAP theorem states that a distributed system can only deliver two of three desired features, that is, consistency, availability, and partition tolerance. Let's first define these terms, and then we'll investigate the theorem in more detail.

Consistency

The consistency property means that data should be consistent across all nodes in the distributed system, and the client connecting to the distributed system at the same time should see the same consistent data. This is commonly achieved using replication.

Availability

Availability means the distributed system responds to the client requests even in the presence of faults. This is achieved using fault tolerance techniques such as replication, partitioning, or sharding.

Partition Tolerance

A partition refers to a scenario where the communication link between two or more nodes breaks. A distributed system should be able to tolerate that and continue to operate correctly.

We know that partitions in a network are almost inevitable; sooner or later, there will be some communication disruption. This means that as network partitions are unavoidable, the choice really becomes to choose between availability and consistency. The question becomes, in the case of partitions, what we are willing to sacrifice, consistency or availability. It all depends on the use case. For example, in a financial application, it's best to sacrifice availability in favor of consistency, but perhaps on web search results, we could sacrifice a bit of consistency in favor of availability. It should be noted that when there are no network partitions, consistency and availability are both provided. But then again, if a network partition occurs, then what do we choose, availability or consistency?

A Venn diagram shown in Figure 1-29 can be used to visualize this concept.

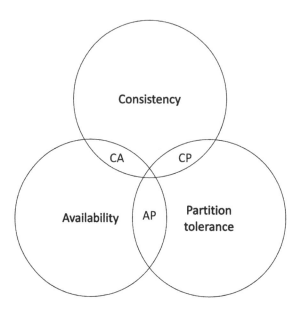

Figure 1-29. *CAP theorem*

The CAP theorem allows us to categorize databases (NoSQL DBs) based on the properties they support. For example, a CP database provides consistency and partition tolerance but sacrifices availability. In the case of a partition, the nonconsistent nodes are shut down until the network partition heals. An AP database sacrifices consistency but offers availability and partition tolerance. In the case of a network partition, there is a chance that nodes that have not been able to get the updates due to a network partition will continue to serve old data. This might be acceptable in some scenarios, such as a web search. When the partition heals, the out-of-sync nodes are synchronized with the latest updates. On the other hand, a CA database is not partition tolerant and can provide both consistency and availability only if the network is healthy. As we saw earlier, network partitions are inevitable; therefore, CA databases only exist in an ideal world where no network partitions occur.

While the CAP theorem is helpful, there are many other more precise impossibility results in distributed computing.

Let's now discuss what eventual consistency is. Eventual consistency refers to a situation where nodes may disagree or not update their local database, but, eventually, the state is agreed upon and updated.

One example of such a scenario could be when an electronic voting system captures voters' votes and writes them to a central vote registration system. However, it could happen that due to a network partition, the communication link in the central vote registration system is lost, and this voting machine is now not able to write data to the backend voting registration system. It could now keep receiving votes from the user and record them locally, and when the network partition heals, it can write the ballots back to the central vote registration system. During the network partition from the central vote registration system's point of view, the count of votes is different from what the voting machine can see. The machine can write back to the central vote registration system when the partition heals to achieve consistency. The consistency between the backend server storage and local storage is not achieved immediately, but, over time, this type of consistency is called eventual consistency.

A now established example of an eventually consistent system is Bitcoin. We will learn more about this in Chapter 4 and see how Bitcoin is eventually consistent.

The domain name system (DNS) is the most prevalent system that implements eventual consistency. When a name is updated, it is distributed as per a configured pattern, and, eventually, all clients see the update.

Through the lens of the CAP theorem, the distributed consensus is a CP system where availability is sacrificed in favor of consistency. As a result, the distributed consensus is used to provide strong consistency guarantees.

For example, if you have a five-node system and three nodes go down, then the whole system stalls until the other three nodes come up. This is so that a consistency guarantee can be maintained, even if the system is not available for some time.

If we look at Bitcoin, it appears that it is an AP system where consistency is sacrificed for some time due to forks, but, eventually, the consistency is achieved. Therefore, Bitcoin can also be considered a CP system where consistency is eventually strong.

Usually, strong consistency (also called linearizability) is for what distributed consensus is used for; however, eventual consistency in systems like Bitcoin is also acceptable.

Cryptography in Distributed Systems

Distributed systems operate under challenging conditions where they are exposed to adversaries, faults, and untrusted users. In such conditions, it becomes critical to protect the distributed system against all these threats. Therefore, appropriate security measures are put in place to thwart any attempts to disrupt the system.

The usual security services required in a distributed system include confidentiality, integrity, access control, and authentication. To this end, cryptography plays a vital role in distributed systems.

Cryptographic protocols provide security services in a distributed system by utilizing cryptographic primitives such as symmetric cryptography, asymmetric cryptography, and hash functions.

We will cover this topic in Chapter 2, where we study cryptography in general and its applications in distributed systems and blockchain. Chapter 2 will introduce several primitives that are useful in consensus protocols and blockchain for achieving data integrity and relevant security purposes.

Summary

We covered several topics in this chapter:

- A distributed system is a set of interconnected computers coordinating together via messages to achieve a common goal.

- Distributed systems face several challenges. The most prominent are (1) no common global knowledge, (2) no global time, (3) achieving consistency, and (4) failures.

- A distributed system model allows us to reason about the system and abstract away all unnecessary details.

- The leap second bug that is a cause of significant disruption of Internet services and several techniques has been developed to address this.

- Safety and liveness properties must be ensured in distributed systems.

- Crash fault–tolerant distributed algorithms only handle crash faults, whereas Byzantine fault–tolerant algorithms are designed to handle arbitrary faults.

- Logical clocks do not depend on physical clocks and can be used to define the order of events in a distributed system.

- In a distributed system, the same algorithm runs on all computers concurrently to achieve a common goal.

- The CAP theorem states that a distributed system can only deliver two of three desired features, that is, consistency, availability, and partition tolerance.

Bibliography

1. Safety and liveness properties were first formalized in a paper by Alpern, B. and Schneider, F.B., 1987. Recognizing safety and liveness. Distributed computing, 2(3), pp. 117–126.

2. Notion of timing and ordering of events was first introduced in 1978 in "Lamport, L., 2019. Time, clocks, and the ordering of events in a distributed system. In Concurrency: the Works of Leslie Lamport (pp. 179–196)."

3. Cachin, C., Guerraoui, R., and Rodrigues, L., 2011. Introduction to reliable and secure distributed programming. Springer Science & Business Media.

4. Brewer, E.A., 2000, July. Towards robust distributed systems. In PODC (Vol. 7, No. 10.1145, pp. 343477–343502).

5. Van Steen, M. and Tanenbaum, A., 2002. Distributed systems principles and paradigms. Network, 2, p. 28.

6. Coulouris, G., Dollimore, J., and Kindberg, T. Distributed Systems: Concepts and Design Edition 3. System, 2(11), p. 15.

7. Kleppmann, M., 2017. Designing data-intensive applications: The big ideas behind reliable, scalable, and maintainable systems. O'Reilly Media, Inc.

8. Kleppmann, M., Distributed Systems. Vancouver.

9. Sapphire clocks: `https://sciencemeetsbusiness.com.au/ sapphire-clock/`

10. Sapphire clocks: `https://spectrum.ieee.org/for-precision-the-sapphire-clock-outshines-even-the-best-atomic-clocks?utm_campaign=post-teaser&utm_content=7190c3vu`

11. Bashir, I., 2020. Mastering Blockchain: A deep dive into distributed ledgers, consensus protocols, smart contracts, DApps, cryptocurrencies, Ethereum, and more. Packt Publishing Ltd.

12. Baran, Paul. On Distributed Communications: I. Introduction to Distributed Communications Networks. Santa Monica, CA: RAND Corporation, 1964. `www.rand.org/pubs/research_memoranda/RM3420.html`. Also available in print form.

CHAPTER 2

Cryptography

This chapter will cover cryptography and its two main types, symmetric cryptography and public key cryptography. After exploring some fundamental ideas, we will dive deeper into symmetric key primitives and then public key primitives.

Moreover, we will examine hash functions, message authentication codes, digital signature schemes, and elliptic curve cryptography. Finally, we'll shed some light on some progressive ideas, proposals, and techniques, especially those which are used in blockchain consensus.

Introduction

Cryptography is the science of secret communication in the presence of adversaries. Historically, this subject was more of an art, but, now, it is a rigorous and formal science with formal definitions, assumptions, and security proofs.

There are three fundamental principles of cryptography: confidentiality, integrity, and authenticity. Confidentiality is the assurance that the information is available only to the authorized entities. Integrity assures that only authorized entities can modify the information. Finally, authenticity guarantees the message validity or identity of an entity. Authentication can be of two types, entity authentication or data origin authentication.

Entity authentication ensures that an entity claiming some identity (the claimant) is verifiably identifiable to another identity (the verifier) and that the entity is alive and participating. Different methods such as something you have (e.g., a hardware token), something you know (e.g., a password), and something you are (e.g., fingerprint) are used to achieve entity authentication in identification protocols. Entity authentication is of a fundamental concern in a secure distributed system. As a distributed system is dispersed and heterogenous, with multiple users, it can become an easy target for

© Imran Bashir 2022
I. Bashir, *Blockchain Consensus*, https://doi.org/10.1007/978-1-4842-8179-6_2

adversarial attacks. Especially in the case of blockchains and specifically consensus protocols running on blockchains, entity authentication is of prime importance to ensure protection against adversarial attacks. Authentication protocols are built using symmetric and public key cryptography.

Another related assurance is nonrepudiation, where an entity after performing an action cannot deny its action. Usually, this is achieved by digital signatures. In addition to two-party protocols, there also are multiparty nonrepudiation protocols that are suitable for multiple parties.

Data origin authentication or message authentication ensures that the source of information is authentic and verified. Message authentication codes (MACs) and digital signatures are used to provide data origin authentication.

A Typical Cryptosystem

A typical model of a cryptographic system is shown in Figure 2-1. We can define a cryptographic system as a combined manifestation of cryptographic primitives, protocols, and algorithms to accomplish specified security goals. Thus, a cryptosystem is composed of several components.

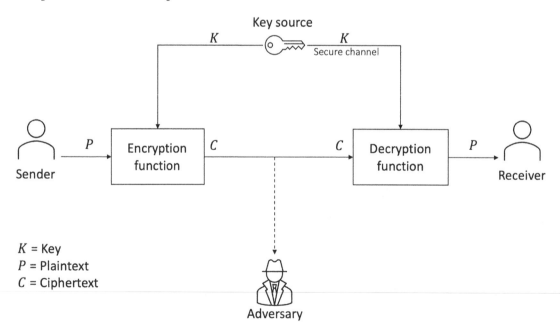

Figure 2-1. *A model of a cryptographic system or cryptographic scheme*

There are three key actors in this system: sender, receiver, and adversary. The sender wants to send a secret message to the receiver via an insecure channel in the presence of an adversary who is a malicious attacker wishing to learn about the message. Other elements are plaintext, ciphertext, keys, secure channel, encryption function, decryption function, and key source:

- A sender is the sending party of the message.

- A receiver is the intended recipient of the message.

- An encryption function is the encryption algorithm which transforms a plaintext into ciphertext by using an encryption key and plaintext as input.

- A decryption function is the decryption algorithm which converts ciphertext into plaintext by using a decryption key and ciphertext as input.

- Plaintext is the raw message which Alice wants to send to Bob in such a way that no one learns about the original message except the intended recipient. It is readable and accessible by Alice and any authorized entity.

- Ciphertext is the scrambled form of the plaintext, which unless decrypted is meaningless to anyone reading it.

- A key source is a key management system or some source of cryptographic keys from which keys are obtained or generated.

- A key is some value that is used to encrypt and/or decrypt data.

- A secure channel is some channel through which messages can pass unencrypted without the possibility of eavesdropping.

- An adversary is some malicious hacker (or eavesdropper, observer) who can read the encrypted data and tries to learn some information by cryptanalyzing it or by some other means.

Cryptographic Primitives

A cryptographic primitive is a fundamental method that delivers particular security services, for example, confidentiality or integrity. These cryptographic primitives are used to build security protocols, such as authentication protocols. Cryptographic primitives include symmetric primitives, asymmetric primitives, and keyless primitives. A high-level taxonomy of cryptographic primitives is shown in Figure 2-2.

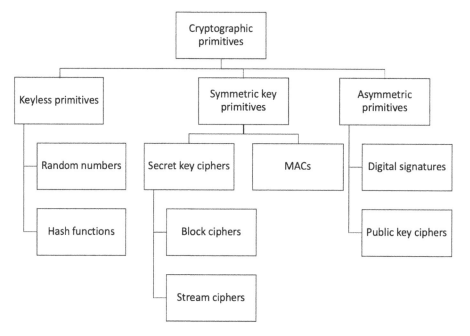

Figure 2-2. *Cryptographic primitives*

Now let's have a look at the symmetric primitives.

Symmetric Cryptography

Symmetric cryptosystems use the same key for encryption and decryption. The key must be kept secret and transferred over a secure channel before the data transfer between a sender and a receiver. For secure key transfers, key establishment protocols are used. Usually, public key cryptography is used to exchange keys, allowing for easier key management than symmetric key management, where it can become challenging to manage keys as the number of users grows.

The primary purpose of designing symmetric cryptography algorithms is to provide confidentiality, but we can also use them to provide other security services, such as data origin authentication.

There are two classes of symmetric cryptosystems, stream ciphers and block ciphers. Figure 2-3 shows how stream and block ciphers operate at a high level.

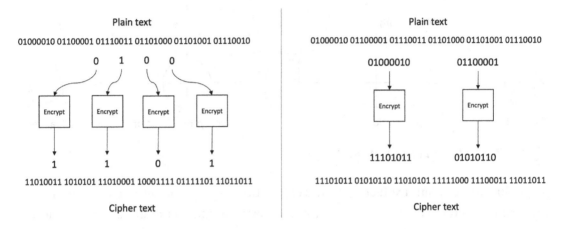

Figure 2-3. *Stream (left) vs. block ciphers (right)*

Stream Ciphers

These cryptosystems encrypt the plaintext one bit at a time. The algorithm takes a single bit of the plaintext as input, processes it, and produces a single bit of ciphertext. The processing involves the use of XOR operations to perform encryption and decryption. The model of stream ciphers is in Figure 2-4.

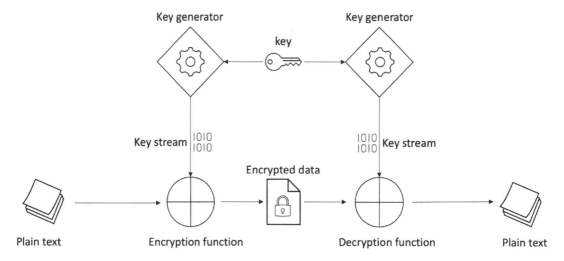

Figure 2-4. *Stream cipher model*

In this model, plaintext feeds into the encryption function bit by bit along with a keystream generated by the key generator. The key generator generates a pseudorandom keystream which is usually much smaller than the plaintext. Usually, the key length is 128 bits. The keystream and plaintext go through the XOR to produce the ciphertext. During decryption, the same process applies again, and plaintext is retrieved. Pseudorandom generation means that the bits generated are not random but appear random, hence the term pseudorandom. Keystreams are commonly generated using linear feedback shift registers (LFSRs). The input bit of LFSR is a linear function of its previous state, where the linear function is usually the XOR operation.

The key generator is a cryptographically secure pseudorandom number generator (CSPRNG or CPRNG). Being "pseudo," we can compute the number, and anyone computing it will have the same result, which implies that these PRNGs are also deterministic. If they are truly random and not deterministic, then once generated, the random number cannot be regenerated by anyone else, meaning the decryption won't be possible. So, they look random, but actually they are not and are computable. CPRNGs have a particular property that the numbers they generate are unpredictable.

There are two types of stream ciphers: synchronous stream ciphers and asynchronous stream ciphers. In synchronous stream ciphers, the keystream is dependent only on the key. In contrast, the keystream relies on the fixed number of previously transmitted encrypted bits and the key in asynchronous stream ciphers.

Stream ciphers are usually more suited for hardware devices; however, they can also be used in software environments. Many examples of stream ciphers exist, such as A5/1, used in GSM communications to provide confidentiality. However, Salsa20 and ChaCha are most used in software environments. Some other stream ciphers include Trivium, Rabbit, RC4, and SEAL.

Block Ciphers

Block ciphers encrypt the plaintext by dividing it into blocks of fixed length. Historically, block ciphers, such as DES, were built using Feistel mechanisms. Modern ciphers, such as AES, use a substitution-permutation network (SPN).

A simple model of a block cipher is shown in Figure 2-5.

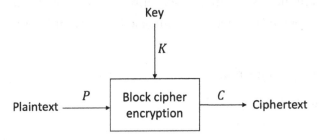

Figure 2-5. *Block cipher*

The model shown in Figure 2-5 comprises plaintext, encryption, and ciphertext. The encrypter takes the plaintext in fixed-length blocks and the secret key as input and produces the ciphertext blocks.

Block ciphers are primarily used for encryption but can be used to build hash functions, create stream ciphers, and build pseudorandom number generators and message authentication codes.

There are two necessary properties that encryption tries to achieve, confusion and diffusion. Confusion adds obscurity to the relationship between the encrypted text and the plaintext. It is achieved by using substitution, which is performed by lookup tables called S-boxes in modern encryption algorithms, such as AES.

Diffusion ensures that plaintext statistically spreads over the encrypted data. In other words, it ensures that even if a single bit changes in the plaintext, the ciphertext changes so much that the relationship between the plaintext and the ciphertext is hidden. In other words, it hides the statistical properties of the plaintext to thwart statistical analysis attacks. In addition, permutation boxes provide diffusion in modern encryption algorithms, such as AES. Thus, both confusion and diffusion are combined to create secure cipher algorithms.

The Data Encryption Standard (DES) was developed in the 1970s and was used widely in the 1980s and 1990s. Over time, due to technological advancements, the efficacy of DES started to decrease. It was mainly due to its smaller 56-bit key length. After some successful brute-force attacks in the late 1990s, such as deep crack and COPACOBANA, it became clear that the DES was no longer secure. As a result, triple DES was introduced, which encrypts three times in a row (triple encryption) to increase the key length to 112 bits essentially. It helped to protect against brute-force attacks, and indeed triple DES is still unbreakable today. However, NIST finally replaced DES with AES due to concerns over slow performance and 64-bit block size in 2001.

There are different modes in which block ciphers work. These modes enable block ciphers to not only provide confidentiality but also integrity and authenticity. Some of the modes include

- Electronic codebook mode
- Cipher block chaining mode
- Counter mode
- Cipher feedback (CFB) mode
- Galois/Counter Mode (GCM)
- Output feedback (OFB) mode

We will explain just three modes here.

Electronic Codebook

Electronic codebook (ECB) is a fundamental mode of operation in which the encrypted data results from applying the encryption algorithm to each block of plaintext, one by one.

This mode is the most straightforward, but we should not use it in practice as it is insecure and can reveal information.

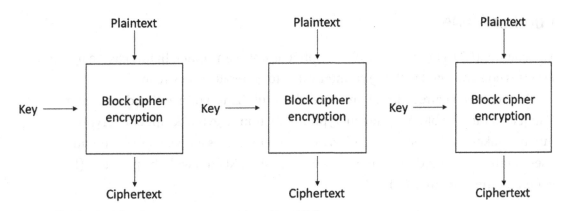

Figure 2-6. *Electronic codebook mode for block ciphers*

Figure 2-6 shows that we have plaintext P provided as an input to the block cipher encryption function and a key, which produces ciphertext C as output.

Cipher Block Chaining

In cipher block chaining (CBC) mode, each plaintext block is XORed with the previously encrypted block. CBC mode uses the IV to encrypt the first block. The IV must be randomly chosen. CBC mode operation is shown in Figure 2-7.

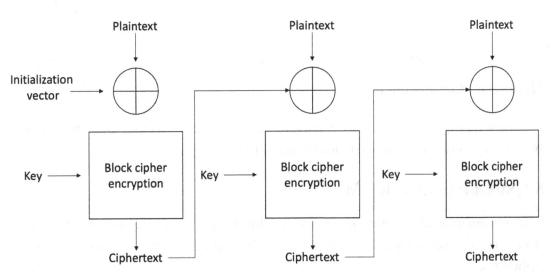

Figure 2-7. *Cipher block chaining mode*

Counter Mode

The counter (CTR) mode uses a block cipher as a stream cipher. In this case, a unique nonce is concatenated with the counter value to generate a keystream.

As shown in Figure 2-8, CTR mode works by utilizing a nonce N and a counter C that feed into the block cipher encryption function. The block cipher encryption function takes the secret key "KEY" as input and produces a keystream (a stream of pseudorandom or random characters), which, when XORed with the plaintext (P), generates the ciphertext (C).

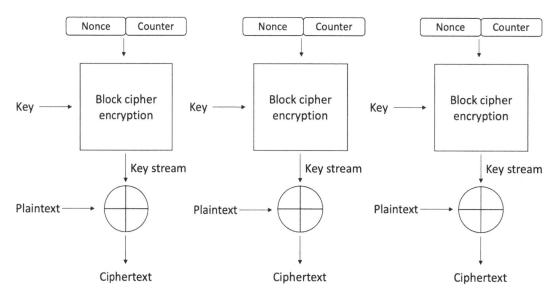

Figure 2-8.   *Counter mode*

There are other modes that we can use for different purposes other than encryption. We discuss some of these in the following section.

Keystream Generation Mode

In keystream generation mode, the encryption function generates a keystream. Stream ciphers use this keystream where it is XORed with the plaintext stream to produce the ciphertext.

Message Authentication Mode

A message authentication code (MAC) is produced from an encryption function in the message authentication mode. A MAC is a cryptographic checksum that provides the integrity service. Block ciphers in the cipher block chaining mode (CBC mode) are used to generate MACs. We can use a MAC to check if an unauthorized entity has modified a message. We achieve this by encrypting the message with a key using the MAC function. Then, the receivers check the message's MAC by encrypting the received message again with the key and comparing it with the received MAC. If they match, it means that no unauthorized entity has modified the message; thus, an integrity service is provided. If they don't match, then it means that some unauthorized entity has altered the message during transmission.

Any block cipher such as AES in CBC mode can generate a MAC. The MAC of the message is the output of the last round of the CBC operation. The length of the MAC output is the same as the block length of the block cipher used to generate the MAC. Even though MACs work like digital signatures, they cannot provide the nonrepudiation service due to their symmetric nature.

Cryptographic Hash Mode

Hash functions are primarily used to compress a message to a fixed-length digest. Block ciphers in cryptographic hash mode can also be used as a compression function to produce a hash.

Now we describe the Advanced Encryption Standard (AES) in detail.

Advanced Encryption Standard

AES was originally named Rijndael, after its inventors' names Joan Daemen and Vincent Rijmen. It was standardized as Advanced Encryption Standard (AES) by NIST in 2001 after an open competition.

In the original version of Rijndael, different key and block sizes of 128 bits, 192 bits, and 256 bits are allowed. However, only a 128-bit block size and key sizes of 128 bits, 192 bits, and 256 bits are allowed in AES.

AES processes an array of bytes of size 4 x 4 called state in multiple rounds depending on the key size. For example, if the key length is 128 bits, 10 rounds are required; for 192 bits, it needs 12 rounds; and for 256 bits, it needs 14 rounds.

After state initialization using the input plaintext, AES sequentially performs the following four operations to produce the ciphertext:

- **AddRoundKey**: First, the state array is XORed with a subkey derived from the master key.

- **SubBytes**: This step performs **byte substitution** where a fixed lookup table (S-box) is used to replace all bytes of the 4 x 4 state array.

- **ShiftRows**: This step shifts each row to the left in the state array in a cyclic and incremental manner. The first row is excluded, the second row is shifted left by one byte, the third row is shifted left by two bytes, and the fourth row is shifted left by three bytes or positions.

- **MixColumns**: Finally, all bytes are mixed in a linear fashion (i.e., linear transformation), where four bytes of the column are taken as input by this function, and four new bytes are produced as output which replaces the input column.

The abovementioned four steps form a single round of AES. In the final round, step 4 (MixColumns) is not performed. Instead, it is replaced with the AddRoundKey step to ensure that the first three steps cannot be simply reversed. This process is shown in Figure 2-9.

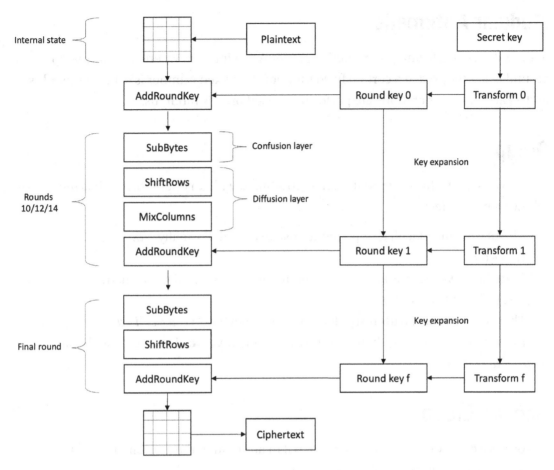

Figure 2-9. *AES block cipher*

Some Basic Mathematics

Before we dive into cryptography, it is important to understand some very basic mathematics and related terminology.

Prime

A prime is a number which is only divisible fully by itself and 1. For example, 23 is a prime number as it can only be divided precisely without leaving any remainder either by 23 or 1.

Modular Arithmetic

It is a system of performing arithmetic operations on integers where numbers wrap around when they reach a certain fixed number. This fixed number is called a modulus, and all arithmetic operations are performed based on this modulus.

Group

A group G is a set whose elements can be combined with an operation $\circ$. It has the following properties:

Closure means that all group operations are closed. Formally, $\forall a$, $b \in G : a \circ b = c \in G$.

Associativity means that all group operations are associative. Formally, $a \circ (b \circ c) = (a \circ b) \circ c : \forall a, b, c \in G$.

There exists a special **identity** element i such that $\forall a \in G : a \circ i = i \circ a = a$.

In each element $a \in G$, there is a corresponding **inverse** element a^{-1} such that $a \circ a^{-1} = a^{-1} \circ a = i$.

Abelian Group

A group is a commutative or abelian group if in addition to the abovementioned properties of groups, $\forall a, b \in G : a \circ b = b \circ a$.

Field

A field F is a set with two operations on F called addition and multiplication.

Finite Field (Galois Field)

A finite field is a field with a finite number of elements.

Prime Fields

A prime field is a finite field containing a prime number of elements.

Generator

A generator is a point on an elliptic curve.

Public Key Cryptography

Public key cryptographic systems use two different keys for encryption and decryption. The public key is known openly, and the private key must remain secret. In these systems, the sender uses the recipient's public key to encrypt data. The recipient decrypts the ciphertext by using the corresponding private key.

This model is shown in Figure 2-10.

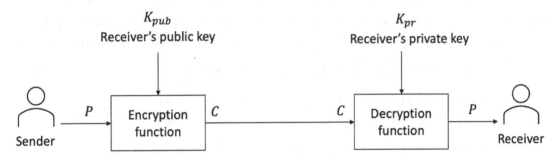

P = Plaintext
C = Ciphertext

Figure 2-10. *Public key cryptography–based cryptosystem*

A fundamental issue in symmetric key systems is that they need a secret key to be shared before the communication using a secure channel, which can be challenging to achieve. Another issue with symmetric key systems is key management. The number of keys grows exponentially as the number of users grows in the system. An n user network will need n(n-1)/2 keys where each user will store n-1 keys. In a 100-user network, each user will store 99 keys. The formula 100(100-1)/2 means there are 4950 keys in total, which is quite tricky to manage practically. Public key cryptography solves this issue of key distribution and key management.

A typical use of public key cryptography is to establish a shared secret key between two parties. This shared secret key is used by symmetric algorithms, such as AES, to encrypt the data. As they have already established a secret key, both parties can then encrypt and decrypt without ever transmitting the secret key on the wire. This way, the parties get the high security of public key cryptography with the speed of symmetric encryption. Asymmetric cryptography is not used much for bulk encryption due to slow performance; however, this is the norm for key establishment. Such systems where a symmetric key is used to encrypt the data and a secret key is encrypted using public key cryptography are called hybrid cryptosystems. For example, the Integrated Encryption Scheme is a hybrid encryption scheme. ECIES is the elliptic curve (EC) version of the IES scheme.

Diffie-Hellman Key Exchange

For key exchange, the pioneering and fundamental scheme is the Diffie-Hellman key exchange. It is an interactive protocol that runs between two parties. A basic and intuitive mathematical example of the Diffie-Hellman exchange is shown as follows:

1. Alice and Bob want to establish a shared secret key.

2. Both agree on two numbers, a prime number $P = 13$ and a generator of P, $G = 6$. In practice, however, P is very large.

3. Both randomly choose a large random integer (i.e., private keys).

   a. Alice's private key = 5, Bob's private key = 4

4. Both calculate public keys:

   a. Alice

$$6^5 \bmod 13$$
$$7776 \bmod 13 = 2$$
$$Public\ key = 2$$

   b. Bob

$$6^4 \bmod 13$$
$$1296 \bmod 13 = 9$$
$$Public\ key = 9$$

5. Bob sends public key 9 to Alice, and Alice sends public key 2 to Bob.

6. Both calculate the shared key using private keys 5 and 4.

    a. Alice

$$9^5 \ mod \ 13 = 3$$

    b. Bob

$$2^4 \ mod \ 13 = 3$$

7. A shared secret key is established.

Public key cryptosystems rely on one-way trap door functions. Trapdoor functions are easy to compute in one direction but difficult to compute in the opposite direction, unless there is a special value, called the trapdoor, available. This concept can be visualized in Figure 2-11.

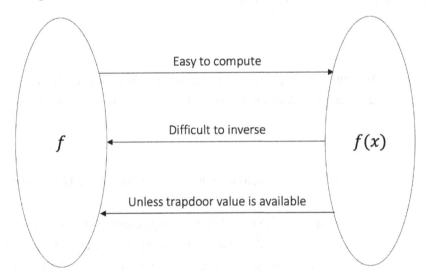

Figure 2-11. *Trapdoor function*

Different hard computational problems, such as a large integer factorization problem and a discrete logarithm problem, provide suitable one-way trapdoor functions. Cryptography schemes using integer factorization are based on the infeasibility of factoring large integers. A typical example that relies on such an assumption is RSA. Integer factorization is the decomposition of a composite number (formed by multiplying two smaller integers) into smaller integers (factors).

In cryptography, factors are restricted to prime numbers. We can demonstrate the problem with a simple example as follows.

For example, it is straightforward to see that 15 is the product of 5 and 3 as 5 x 3 = 15. What about a larger prime number, for example, 6887? It is comparatively difficult, but we get 71 and 97 as factors with some calculation. What if the number is huge, say 1024 bits, and prime? Then multiplying two such primes is easy to do but extremely hard to factor, making it a one-way function that we can use in cryptography.

A discrete logarithm problem is the basis for many different cryptography schemes such as the Diffie-Hellman key exchange and digital signature algorithms. It is based on a problem in modular arithmetic where it is easy to calculate the result of a modulo operation, but it is hard to find the exponent of the generator. This hardness creates a one-way function where it is computationally infeasible to find the input from the output.

A simple example can demonstrate the crux of this problem:

$$3^2 \ mod \ 10 = 9$$

Now, given 9, finding 2, the exponent of the generator 3, is extremely hard to do. Formally, we can say that given numbers a and n where n is a prime, the function

$$f(b) = a^b \ mod \ n$$

is a one-way function, because calculating $f(b)$ is easy, but given $f(b)$, finding b is hard.

Another method developed in the mid-1980s is elliptic curve cryptography. Elliptic curve cryptography has gained special attention due to its usage in blockchain platforms, such as Bitcoin and Ethereum. Protocols such as the Elliptic Curve Diffie-Hellman key exchange and elliptic curve digital signature algorithms are most prevalent in this space. ECC is fundamentally a discrete logarithm problem but founded upon elliptic curves over finite fields. A key advantage of ECC is that a smaller key size provides the same level of security as a larger key size in RSA. For example, a security level of a 1024-bit integer factorization scheme, such as RSA, can be achieved by only a 160-bit elliptic curve–based scheme, such as ECDSA.

Public key cryptosystems can be used for encryption, though it is very less common and not efficient for large datasets. It is also used for providing other security services and protocols, such as digital signatures, entity authentication, and key agreement.

Digital Signatures

Digital signatures are one of the most common uses of public key cryptography. Digital signatures provide nonrepudiation services. Most common examples include RSA-based digital signatures, digital signature algorithms, and ECDSA and Schnorr signatures.

Entity Authentication

Entity authentication or identification is another service that public key cryptosystems can provide. Usually, challenge-response mechanisms are in widespread use where a challenge sent by the verifier is required to be responded to correctly by the prover (claimant of identity) to ascertain the legitimacy of the claimant.

Key Agreement

Key agreement protocols are used to establish secret keys before an encrypted data transfer. The most common example of such protocols is the Diffie-Hellman key exchange protocol.

RSA

RSA is widely used for secure key transport and building digital signatures. Diffie and Hellman invented public key cryptography in 1976. Based on this idea, in 1978, the RSA public key cryptosystem was developed by Rivest, Shamir, and Adleman.

In this section, I will walk you through the steps of generating key pairs in RSA and how to encrypt and decrypt.

Key Pair Generation

1. Generate a modulus.

    a. Select p and q, two large prime numbers. Usually, 2^{1024} bits or more.

2. Multiply p and q to generate modulus n. $n = p.q.$ n becomes 2^{2048}.

3. Choose a random number with some special properties. Assume
    that we call this number *e*.

    a. This number *e* should have some special properties:

        i. It should be greater than 1.

        ii. It should be less than $\phi(n) = (p - 1)(q - 1)$.

        iii. $gcd(e, (p - 1)(q - 1) = 1$.

        iv. $e \in \{1, 2, \ldots, \phi(n) - 1\}$.

    Formally speaking, this number e should be the coprime (relatively
    prime) of $(p - 1)(q - 1)$, that is, no number other than 1 can
    be divided fully into e and $(p - 1)(q - 1)$. Coprimes have no
    common factors except 1, so the greatest common divisor (GCD) of
    coprimes is 1.

4. Public key generation

    a. The modulus n generated in step 1 and the special number e generated
       in step 2 is pair (n, e) that is the public key. This pair is public, so it can be
       shared with anyone; however, p and q must be kept secret.

5. Private key generation

    a. The private key, let's call it *d*, is calculated from two primes *p* and *q* from
       step 1 and the special number *e* from step 2. The private key is the inverse of
       e modulo $(p - 1)(q - 1)$, which we can write as

$$ed = 1 \, mod \, (p - 1)(q - 1)$$

$$ed = 1 \, mod \, \phi n$$

$$d = e^{-1} = 7 \, mod \, 20$$

In practice, the extended Euclidean algorithm is used to calculate *d* which takes *p*, *q*,
and e as input and outputs *d*. *d* must be kept secret.

Encryption and Decryption

Now, let's see how encryption and decryption operations are performed using RSA. RSA uses the following equation to produce ciphertext:

$$C = P^e \bmod n$$

This means that plaintext P is raised to the power of e and then reduced to modulo n. Decryption in RSA is provided in the following equation:

$$P = C^d \bmod n$$

This means that the receiver who has a public key pair (n, e) can decipher the data by raising C to the value of the private key d and then reducing to modulo n.

Example of Key Generation, Encryption, and Decryption

1. Let the plaintext be message m. $m = 5$, to be sent from Alice to Bob.

2. Let $p = 3$ and $q = 11$.

3. $n = pq = 3 \times 11 = 33$.

4. $e = 3$, because $(3 - 1)(11 - 1) = 20$ which is greater than 1 and less than 20 and $GCD(3, 20) = 1$.

5. The public key is pair $(n, e) = (33, 3)$.

6. The private key is $ed = 1 \bmod (p - 1)(q - 1)$.

$$d = e^{-1} \ 7 \bmod 20, (33,7)$$

7. Send public key (n, e) (33, 3) to Alice.

8. Alice does $5^3 = 125 \bmod 33 = 26$.

9. Alice sends 26 as the encrypted text to Bob.

10. Bob does $26^7 = 8031810176 = 8031810176 \bmod 33 = 5$ and retrieves the plaintext message 5.

Elliptic Curve Cryptography

Elliptic curve cryptography (ECC) is based on a concept in mathematics called elliptic curves. It is a set of points on a plane whose x, y coordinates satisfy a specific equation and some conditions. Typically, it is the Weierstrass form $y^2 = x^3 + ax + b$ where a and b are fixed.

Elliptic curves are groups. They are used in many different areas of mathematics, including number theory, complex analysis, and mathematical physics. When used in cryptography, a suitable elliptic curve's points over a finite field form a group structure which allows to build cryptography schemes based on a discrete logarithm problem.

A prime field is used in elliptic curve cryptography. *In a prime field, all arithmetic operations are performed modulo a prime number p.*

An elliptic curve is defined in the following equation:

$$y^2 = x^3 + ax + b \bmod p$$

Here, a and b belong to a finite field Zp or Fp (prime finite field), that is, $(a, b) \in Z$, and an imaginary point of infinity. The point of infinity ∞ is used to provide identity operations for points on the curve.

Furthermore, a condition shown below ensures that the curve is nonsingular, meaning the curve does not self-intersect or has vertices:

$$4a^3 + 27b^2 \neq 0 \bmod p$$

To construct the discrete logarithm problem based on elliptic curves, a large enough cyclic group is required. First, the group elements are identified as a set of points that satisfy the elliptic curve equation. After this, group operations need to be defined on these points. The fundamental group operations on elliptic curves are point addition and point doubling. Point addition is a process where two different points are added, and point doubling means that the same point is added to itself.

An elliptic curve can be visualized over real numbers as shown in Figure 2-12.

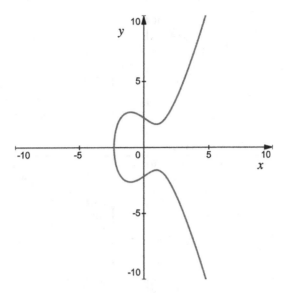

Figure 2-12. *An elliptic curve over real numbers* $y^2 = x^3 - 3x + 5$

We can visualize the curve and group operations, that is, addition and doubling, geometrically over real numbers, which helps to build intuition. In practice, however, the curve over prime field is used to build ECC-based schemes. Though, when we try to plot it, it appears quite random and not intuitive.

Point Addition

For adding two points, a line is drawn through points P and Q (the diagonal line in Figure 2-13) to obtain a third point. This point, when reflected, is point R, shown as P+Q in Figure 2-13.

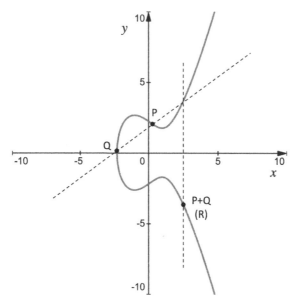

Figure 2-13. *Point addition*

Algebraically speaking, in point addition operation, two points P and Q are added to obtain the coordinates of the third point R on the curve:

$$P + Q = R$$

where $P = (x_1, y_1)$ and $Q = (x_2, y_2)$ and $R = (x_3, y_3)$.

For addition, we calculate the gradient between the points:

$$S = \frac{(y_2 - y_1)}{(x_2 - x_1)} \bmod p$$

where S depicts the line going through P and Q.

Now to obtain the new point R:

$$x_3 = s^2 - x_1 - x_2 \bmod p$$

$$y_3 = s(x_1 - x_2) - y_1 \bmod p$$

Point Doubling

In point doubling, P is added to itself. In other words, P and Q are the same point. As the point adds to itself, we can call this operation point doubling.

To double a point, a tangent line (the dotted diagonal line in Figure 2-14) is drawn through point P, which obtains a second point where the line intersects with the curve. This point is reflected to yield the result R, shown as 2P in Figure 2-14.

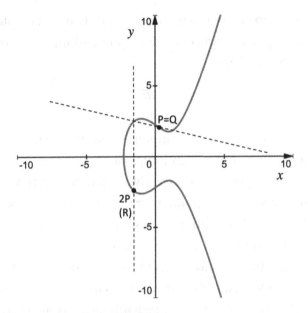

Figure 2-14. *Elliptic curve point doubling*

For doubling, we use

$$S = \frac{\left(3x_1^2 + a\right)}{2_{y1}} \bmod p$$

where S depicts the tangent line going through point P.

Now to obtain the point R:

$$x_3 = s^2 - x_1 - x_2 \bmod p$$

$$y_3 = s(x_1 - x_2) - y_1 \bmod p$$

Scalar Point Multiplication

This operation is used to multiply a point on the elliptic curve by a given integer, for example, an integer d and the point P. We get dP by repeatedly adding P, d times, as shown in the following:

$$P + P + \ldots + P = dP$$

This operation is used to generate a public key in ECC-based cryptosystems. It is a very computationally expensive process as both point addition and doubling are performed repeatedly to calculate:

$$Q = dP$$

where P is a point on the curve, d is a randomly chosen integer as the private key, and Q is the public key obtained after the multiplication.

Making point multiplication faster is an active area of research. While there are many algorithms for making scalar multiplication more quickly, we describe a quick example here using the double and add algorithm. It combines point addition and doubling operations to achieve performance.

For example, if using addition only, to get 9P we must do P + P + P + P + P + P + P + P + P, which can become impracticable very quickly if the number of Ps increases. We can use the double and add mechanism to make this faster. Here, we first convert nine into binary. Starting from the most significant bit (MSB), for each bit that is one (high), perform the double and addition operations, and for each zero, perform only the double operation. We do not perform any operation on the most significant bit. Nine is 1001 in binary, so for each bit we get (starting from left to right) P, 2P, 4P, 8P+P. This scheme produces 9P only with three double operations and one addition operation, instead of nine addition operations.

Elliptic Curve Discrete Logarithm Problem

Now consider that dP results in producing another point Q on the curve. Even if we know the points P and Q, it is computationally infeasible to reconstruct the sequence of all the double and addition operations that we did to calculate the number d. Even if someone knows P and Q, it is impossible for them to find d. This means that it is a one-way (trapdoor function) function. It is the basis of the elliptic curve discrete logarithm problem (ECDLP).

Consider an elliptic curve E, with two elements P and Q. The discrete logarithm problem is to find the integer d, where $1 < = d < = \# E$, such that

$$P + P + \ldots + P = dP = Q$$

Here, Q is the public key (a point generated on the curve, (x, y)), and d is the private key (another point on the curve). The public key is a random multiple of the generator point P, whereas the private key is the integer d that is used to generate the multiple. The Generator point or base point G is a point on the curve that generates a cyclic subgroup, which means that every point in the group can be reached by repeated addition of the base point.

#E represents the order of the group (elliptic curve), which means the number of points that are present in the cyclic subgroup of the elliptic curve. A cyclic group is formed by a combination of points on the elliptic curve and the point of infinity. Cofactor h is the number of points in the curve divided by the order of the subgroup.

The initial starting point P is a public parameter, and the public key Q is also published, whereas d, the private key, is kept secret. If d is not known, it is unfeasible to calculate with only the knowledge of Q and P, thus creating the hard problem on which ECDLP is built.

A key pair is linked with the specific domain parameters of an elliptic curve. Domain parameters are public values that are required to implement ECC schemes. These parameters are represented as a tuple $\{p, a, b, G, n, h\}$:

- P: Field (modulo prime)

- a, b: Fixed elliptic curve coefficients

- G: The generator point to generate a cyclic group

- n: Order of the group (curve)

- h: Cofactor

For example, Bitcoin uses the SECP256k1 curve with the equation $y^2 = x^3 + 7$ and domain parameters as defined here: `https://en.bitcoin.it/wiki/Secp256k1`.

The most used curves are NIST proposed curves, such as P-256. Other curves include Curve25519, Curve1174, and many more. Of course, it is advisable to choose a safe curve. An excellent resource of safe and unsafe curves along with explanations is maintained online here: `https://safecurves.cr.yp.to`.

Digital Signatures

Public key cryptography is used to create digital signatures. It is one of the most common applications of public key cryptography. In this section, we will discover how RSA, ECDSA, and Schnorr signatures work. Concepts such as aggregate signatures and multisignatures, also commonly used in blockchains, will be introduced.

Digital signatures provide a means of associating a message with an entity from which the message has originated. Digital signatures are used to provide data origin authentication and nonrepudiation.

Digital signatures are used in consensus algorithms and especially in blockchain networks to sign the transactions and messages sent by a user on the blockchain network. Blocks are sealed cryptographically using a digital signature so that the recipient can verify the authenticity of the transmitted block. Similarly, all transactions are signed as well. It is common in consensus algorithms that blocks are sealed and broadcast to the network that recipients (other nodes) receive, who verifies the signature to ascertain the block's authenticity. The blocks are inserted into the local blockchain after verification.

Digital signatures have three security properties: authenticity, unforgeability, and nonreusability.

Authenticity

This means that the digital signatures are verifiable by the receiving party.

Unforgeability (Nonrepudiation)

This property guarantees that only the message's sender can sign using the private key. Digital signatures must also protect against forgery. Forgery means an adversary fabricating a valid signature for a message without access to the legitimate signer's private key. In other words, unforgeability implies that no one else can produce the signed message produced by a genuine sender.

Nonreusability

This property necessitates that the digital signature cannot be separated from a message and used again for another message. In other words, the digital signature is firmly bound to the corresponding message and cannot be separated from its original message and attached to another.

The process of signing and verification using digital signatures is shown in Figure 2-15.

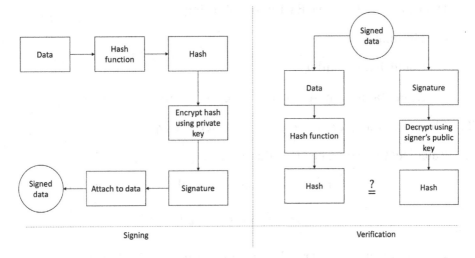

Figure 2-15. *Digital signing (left) and verification process (right)*

First, we produce the hash of the data for which we want to prove data origin authentication. Then we encrypt the hash using the prover's private key (signing key) to create a "signature" and attach it with the data. Finally, this signed object is sent to the verifier.

The verifier decrypts the encrypted hash of the data using the signer's (sender) public key to retrieve the original hash. The verifier then takes the data and hashes it again through the hash function to produce the hash. If both these hashes match, the verification is successful, proving that the signer indeed signed the data. It also proves the data origin authentication, along with nonrepudiation and data integrity properties.

Now we describe how ECDSA (elliptic curve digital signature algorithm) works.

ECDSA Signatures

ECDSA is a DSA based on elliptic curves. The DSA is a standard for digital signatures. It is based on modular exponentiation and the discrete logarithm problem. It is used on Bitcoin and Ethereum blockchain platforms to validate messages and provide data integrity services.

Now, we'll describe how ECDSA works.

To sign and verify using the ECDSA scheme, first a key pair needs to be generated:

1. Define an elliptic curve E with the following:

    - Modulus P

    - Coefficients a and b

    - A generator point A that forms a cyclic group of prime order q

2. Choose an integer d randomly such that $0 < d < q$.

3. Calculate the public key B so that $B = dA$.

    - The public parameters are a sextuple in the form shown here:

$$Kpb = (p, a, b, q, A, B)$$

    - The private key is a randomly chosen integer d in step 2:

$$Kpr = d$$

Now, the signature can be generated using the private and public keys.

4. An ephemeral key K_e is chosen, where $0 < K_e < q$. Also, ensure that K_e is random and that no two signatures end up with the same key; otherwise, the private key can be calculated.

5. A value R is calculated using $R = K_e A$, that is, by multiplying A (the generator point) and the random ephemeral key.

6. Initialize a variable r with the x coordinate value of point R so that $r = xR$.

7. The signature can now be calculated as follows:

$$s = \left(h(m) + d.r\right) K_{e^{-1}} \, mod \, q$$

Here, m is the message for which the signature is calculated, and $h(m)$ is the hash of the message m.

8. Signature verification is carried out as follows:

    •   A value w is calculated as $w = s^{-1}\ mod\ q$.

    •   A value $u1 = w.\ h(m)\ mod\ q$.

    •   A value $u2 = w.\ r\ mod\ q$.

    •   Calculate point P:

$$P = u1\ A + u2\ B$$

9. Verification is carried out as follows:

    • $r,\ s$ is accepted as a valid signature if the x coordinate of point P calculated in step 4 has the same value as the signature parameter $r\ mod\ q$; that is:

    $X_p = r\ mod\ q$ means a valid signature.

    $X_p \neq r\ mod\ q$ means an invalid signature.

This completes our introduction to digital signatures and especially ECDSA. ECDSA is quite commonly used in blockchain networks, including Bitcoin, Ethereum, and several enterprise chains. Now we describe some other digital signature variations.

Multisignatures

In this scheme, multiple unique keys held by their respective owners are used to sign a single message. In blockchain implementations, multisignature schemes allow multiple users to sign a transaction, which results in increased security. Moreover, in blockchain networks, these schemes can be used so that users can set the condition of at least one or more than one signature to authorize transactions.

For example, a 1-of-2 multisignature scheme can represent a joint account where either one of the joint account holders is required to authorize a transaction by signing it. In another variation, a 2-of-2 multisignature can be used where both joint account holders' signatures must authorize the transaction. This concept is generalized as m of n signatures, where m is the minimum number of expected signatures and n is the total number of signatures.

This process is shown in Figure 2-16.

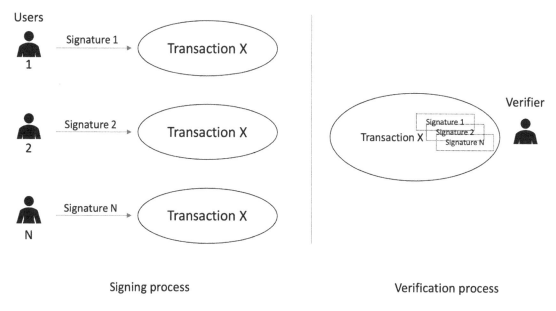

Figure 2-16. *Multisignature scheme*

Figure 2-16 shows the signing process on the left-hand side, where m is the number of different users, and holding m unique signatures signs a single transaction. When the validator or verifier receives it, all the signatures in it need to be individually verified.

Threshold Signatures

This scheme does not rely on users to sign the message with their individual keys; instead, it requires only one public key and one private key to produce the digital signature. In a multisignature scheme, the signed message contains digital signatures from all signers. It requires verification individually by the verification party, but the verifier must verify only one digital signature in threshold signatures. The key idea in this scheme is to split the private key into multiple parts, and each signer keeps its share of the private key. The signing process requires each user to use their respective share of the private key to sign the message. A particular communication protocol manages the communication between the signers.

In contrast with multisignatures, the threshold signatures result in smaller transaction sizes and are faster to verify. A downside, however, is that for threshold signatures to work, all signers must remain online. In multisignature schemes, the signatures can be delivered asynchronously. In other words, users can provide signatures whenever available. One downside is that there could be a situation where users may withhold their signature maliciously, resulting in a denial of service. We can also use threshold signatures to provide anonymity in a blockchain network, as individual signers are unidentifiable in multisignature schemes.

Figure 2-17 shows the signing process on the left-hand side, where an m number of different users, holding different parts (shares) of a digital signature, sign a single transaction. When the validator or verifier receives it, only one signature needs to be verified.

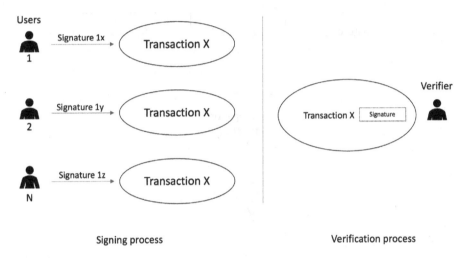

Figure 2-17. *Threshold signatures*

Aggregate Signatures

Aggregate signatures reduce the size of digital signatures. This scheme is beneficial in scenarios where multiple digital signatures are in use. The core idea is to aggregate multiple signatures into a single signature without increasing the size of the signature of a single message. It is simply a type of digital signature that supports aggregation.

The small aggregate signature is enough to prove to the verifier that all users signed their original messages. Thus, aggregate signatures are commonly used to reduce the size of messages in network and security protocols. For example, we can significantly reduce the size of digital certificate chains in Public Key Infrastructure (PKI) by compressing all signatures in the chain into a single signature. Boneh-Lynn-Shacham

(BLS) aggregate signatures are a typical example of the aggregate signature. BLS has also been used in various blockchains and especially in Ethereum 2.0.

Schnorr signatures are another type of signature based on elliptic curve cryptography that allows key and signature aggregation. Schnorr signatures are 64 bytes in size as compared to ECDSA, which is 71 bytes in signature size. ECDSA's private key size is 32 bytes and its public key is 33 bytes, whereas the Schnorr scheme's private and public keys are 32 bytes in size. Overall, Schnorr signatures are smaller and faster than ECDSA.

Figure 2-18 shows how the aggregate signatures work.

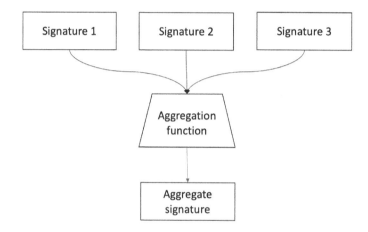

Figure 2-18. *Aggregate signatures*

Schnorr signatures are proposed to be used in Bitcoin under Bitcoin Improvement Proposal (BIP) 340.

Ring Signatures

Ring signature schemes are mechanisms where any member of a group of signers can sign a message on behalf of the entire group. Each member of the ring group keeps a public key and a private key. The key point here is that the identity of the actual signer who signed the message must remain unknown (computationally infeasible to determine) to an outside observer. It looks equally likely that anyone from the trusted group of signers could have signed the message, but it is not possible to figure out the individual user who signed the message. Thus, we can use ring signatures to provide an anonymity service.

Hash Functions

Hash functions are keyless primitives which create fixed-length digests of arbitrarily long input data. There are three security properties of hash functions.

Preimage Resistance

This property is also called a one-way property. It can be explained by using the simple equation:

$$h(x) = y$$

where h is the hash function, x is the input, and y is the output hash. The first security property requires that y cannot be reverse-computed to x. x is the preimage of y, thus the name preimage resistance. This property is depicted in Figure 2-19.

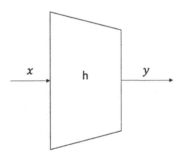

Figure 2-19. *Preimage resistance*

Second Preimage Resistance

This property is also known as the weak collision resistance property. This property ensures that given x and $h(x)$, it is almost impossible to find any other message m, where $m \neq x$ and hash of m = hash of x or $h(m) = h(x)$. This property is shown in Figure 2-20.

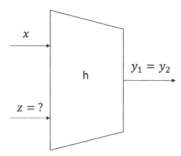

Figure 2-20. *Second preimage resistance*

Collision Resistance

The collision resistance property requires that two different input messages should not hash to the same output. In other words, $h(x) \neq h(z)$. Figure 2-21 shows a depiction of collision resistance.

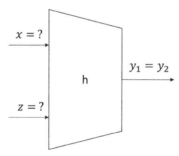

Figure 2-21. *Strong collision resistance*

In addition, there are two functional properties of hash functions:

- Compression of arbitrary size data into a fixed-length digest

- Easy to compute

Hash functions, due to their very nature, are always expected to have collisions, where two different messages hash to the same output, but in a good hash function, collisions must be computationally infeasible to find.

Moreover, hash functions should also have a property that a small change, even a single character change in the input text, should result in an entirely different hash output. This is known as the **avalanche effect**.

Hash functions are usually designed by using the iterated hash function method, where the input data is divided into equal block sizes and then they are processed iteratively through the compression functions.

Some prominent approaches to build hash functions using iterative methods are listed as follows:

- Merkle-Damgard construction

- Sponge construction

The most common hash function schemes are SHA-0, SHA-1, SHA-2, SHA-3, RIPEMD, and Whirlpool.

Design of Secure Hash Algorithms (SHA)

In this section, we will introduce the design of SHA-256 and SHA-3. Both are used in Bitcoin and Ethereum, respectively. However, Ethereum uses Keccak, the original algorithm presented to NIST, rather than NIST standard SHA-3. NIST, after some modifications, such as an increase in the number of rounds and simpler message padding, standardized Keccak as SHA-3.

Design of SHA-256

SHA-256 has an input message size limit of $2^{64} - 1$ bits. The block size is 512 bits, and it has a word size of 32 bits. The output is a 256-bit digest.

The compression function processes a 512-bit message block and a 256-bit intermediate hash value. There are two main components of this function: the compression function and a message schedule.

The algorithm works as follows, in nine steps.

Preprocessing

- Padding of the message is used to adjust the length of a block to 512 bits if it is smaller than the required block size of 512 bits.

- Parsing the message into message blocks, which ensures that the message and its padding are divided into equal blocks of 512 bits.

- Setting up the initial hash value, which consists of the eight 32-bit words obtained by taking the first 32 bits of the fractional parts of the square roots of the first eight prime numbers. These initial values are fixed and chosen to initialize the process. They provide a level of confidence that no backdoor exists in the algorithm.

Hash Computation

- Each message block is then processed in a sequence, and it requires 64 rounds to compute the full hash output. Each round uses slightly different constants to ensure that no two rounds are the same.

- The message schedule prepares.

- Eight working variables initialize.

- The compression function runs 64 times.

- The intermediate hash value is calculated.

- Finally, after repeating steps 5 through 8 until all blocks (chunks of data) in the input message are processed, the output hash is produced by concatenating intermediate hash values.

At a high level, SHA-256 can be visualized in Figure 2-22.

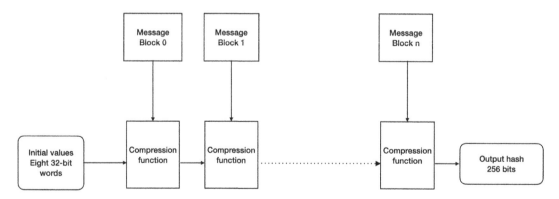

Figure 2-22. *SHA-256 high-level overview*

As shown in Figure 2-22, SHA-256 is a Merkle-Damgard construction that takes the input message and divides it into equally sized blocks of 512 bits. Initial hash values, or the initialization vector, which are composed of eight 32-bit words (i.e., 256 bits), are fed into the compression function with the first message. Subsequent blocks are fed into the compression function until all blocks are processed to produce the output hash.

The compression function of SHA-256 is shown in Figure 2-23.

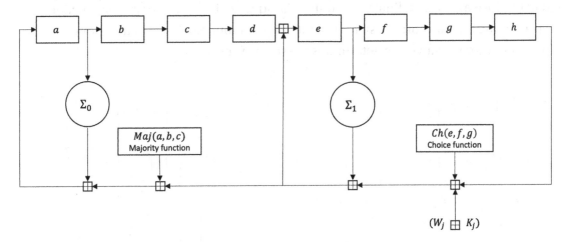

Figure 2-23.   *One round of the SHA-256 compression function*

In Figure 2-23, a, b, c, d, e, f, g, and h are the registers for eight working variables. Maj and Ch are functions which are applied bitwise. Σ_0 and Σ_1 perform bitwise rotation. The round constants are W_j and K_j, which are added in the main loop (compressor function) of the hash function, which runs 64 times.

Design of SHA-3 (Keccak)

The structure of SHA-3 is very different from that of SHA-1 and SHA-2. SHA-3 is based on unkeyed permutations instead of other typical hash function constructions that used keyed permutations. Keccak also does not use the Merkle-Damgard transformation, commonly used to handle arbitrary-length input messages in hash functions. Instead, a newer approach, called sponge and squeeze construction, is used in Keccak. It is a random permutation model.

Different variants of SHA-3 have been standardized, such as SHA3-224, SHA3-256, SHA3-384, SHA3-512, SHAKE128, and SHAKE256. In addition, SHAKE128 and SHAKE256 are extendable-output functions (XOFs), which allow the output to be extended to any desired length.

Figure 2-24 shows the sponge and squeeze model on which SHA-3 or Keccak is based. Analogous to a sponge, the data (m input data) is first "absorbed" into the sponge after applying padding. It is then changed into a subset of permutation state using XOR (exclusive OR), and, finally, the output is "squeezed" out of the sponge function representing the transformed state. The rate r is the input block size of the sponge function, whereas capacity c determines the security level.

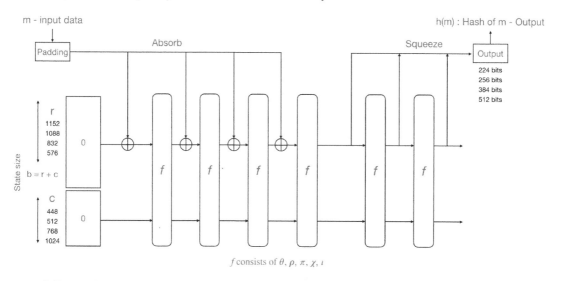

f : Permutation function operating on b bits
r : Bit rate of sponge function (block size)
c : Capacity bits

Figure 2-24. *The SHA-3 absorbing and squeezing function*

In Figure 2-24, state size b is calculated by adding bit rate r and capacity bits c. r and c can be any values if sizes of r + c are 25, 50, 100, 200, 400, 800, or 1600. The state is a three-dimensional bit matrix which is initially set to 0. The data m is entered into the absorb phase block by block via XOR ⊕ after applying padding.

Table 2-1 shows the value of bit rate r (block size) and capacity c required to achieve the desired output hash size under the most efficient setting of r + c = 1600.

Table 2-1. *Bit rate and capacity supported in SHA-3*

r (block size)	c (capacity)	Output hash size
1152	448	224
1088	512	256
832	768	384
576	1024	512

The function f is a permutation function. It contains five transformation operations named Theta, Rho, Pi, Chi, and Iota, which are described as follows:

θ–*Theta*: XOR bits in the state, used for mixing

ρ–*Rho*: Diffusion function performing rotation of bits

π–*Pi*: Diffusion function

χ–*Chi*: XOR each bit, bitwise combine

ι–*Iota*: Combination with round constants

The key idea is to apply these transformations to achieve the avalanche effect, which ensures that even a tiny change in the input results in a substantial change in the output. These five operations combined form a single round. In the SHA-3 standard, the number of rounds is 24 to achieve the desired level of security.

Message Authentication Codes

Message authentication codes (MACs) are used to provide authentication services in a cryptosystem. MACs are sometimes called keyed hash functions, and we can use them to provide message integrity and data origin authentication. MACs can be constructed using block ciphers or hash functions.

Figure 2-25 shows a MAC operation where a sender has appended an authentication tag T to the message M. MACs are symmetric cryptographic primitives that use a shared key between the sender and the receiver. The sender uses this key to generate the authentication tag, whereas the receiver uses the same key for verification. The MAC function takes the key and message M as input and produces the authentication tag T.

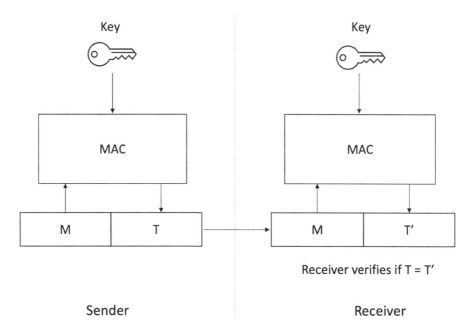

Figure 2-25. *Operation of a MAC function*

T and M are sent to the receiver who runs the same process and compares T with T', which the verifier has generated by applying the same MAC function, and if they match, the verification is successful.

Hash-Based MACs (HMACs)

Like the hash functions, hash-based MACs (HMACs) produce a fixed-length output and take an arbitrarily long message as the input. In this scheme, the sender signs a message using the MAC, and the receiver verifies it using the shared secret key. The key is hashed with the message using either the secret prefix or the secret suffix method. With the secret prefix method, the key is concatenated with the message, that is, the key comes first, and the message comes afterward, whereas with the secret suffix method, the key comes after the message, as shown in the following:

$$Secret\ prefix: M = MAC_k(x) = h(k \parallel x)$$

$$Secret\ suffix: M = MAC_k(x) = h(x \parallel k)$$

There are pros and cons to both methods. Some attacks on both schemes have occurred. HMAC construction schemes use *ipad* (inner padding) and *opad* (outer padding) for padding, which is considered secure with some assumptions.

Various significant applications of hash functions are used in peer-to-peer networks and blockchain networks, such as Merkle trees, Patricia tries, Merkle Patricia tries, and distributed hash tables.

Some latest advancements, such as verifiable delay functions, are discussed next.

Verifiable Delay Functions

Verifiable delay functions (VDFs) are cryptographic primitives that require a sequential number of steps (substantial time) to evaluate but are very quick and efficient to verify. The evaluation must be sequential, and even with parallelization, the evaluation must take the specified amount of time. However, the verification is efficient. VDFs have multiple applications in distributed networks, for example, they can be used as randomness beacons that publish random, unpredictable, and non-manipulable values at fixed intervals. Randomness beacons can be used to build random leader election algorithms. VDFs also have applications in multiparty computations, permissionless consensus, and timestamping of events.

Formally, VDFs can be defined as follows. There are three procedures involved in a VDF:

> *setup*$(\lambda, t) \rightarrow pp$ where λ is the security parameter and t is the time parameter, for example, a ten-minute delay.

> *evaluate*$(pp, x) \rightarrow y$, π where x is the input, pp is the public parameters, y is the output, and π is the proof. π can be optional depending on the construction.

> *verify*$(pp, x, y. \pi) \rightarrow \{true, false\}$ which outputs either true or false indicating the success or failure of the verification which checks the correctness of the output.

There are two security properties of VDFs, uniqueness and sequentiality. Uniqueness ensures that the output y produced by VDF is unique for every input x. The sequentiality property ensures that the delay parameter t is enforced.

Figure 2-26 shows the operation of VDFs.

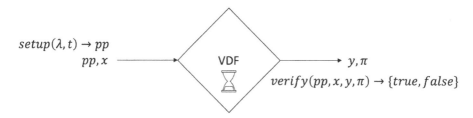

Figure 2-26. *Operation of a VDF*

There are many proposals on how to construct VDFs. Some approaches include hardware enclaves to store cryptographic keys inside the enclave and use those keys to generate VDFs. Using hash functions to iteratively hash the output again as input to form a hash chain is another way of constructing verifiable delay functions. Creating a hash chain using a hash function iteratively is a sequential process and takes time; thus, it can work as an evaluation function of the VDF. Another method gaining more popularity is the algebraic construction, where finite cyclic groups are used which are assumed to have unknown order.

VDFs have many innovative applications in blockchains, including constructing consensus algorithms, as a source of verifiable randomness and leader election. You will explore these applications in detail when we discuss relevant consensus protocols in Chapter 8.

Verifiable Random Functions

A verifiable random function (VRF) is a pseudorandom public key function that provides a proof that the output it has generated is correctly calculated. The owner of the private key generates the proof and output of the function which is verifiable publicly by a public key to ascertain that the value is indeed correctly calculated. VRFs have many applications in consensus algorithms and blockchains, for example, Cardano and Polkadot use them in the block production mechanism. They also have been used to provide verifiable randomness on chains, for example, in the case of chainlink.

Summary

- Cryptography is the science of secret communication.

- Symmetric key cryptography and asymmetric cryptography are the two main categories of cryptography.

- Elliptic curve cryptography has found major applications in blockchains and relevant consensus protocols, where commonly ECDSA is used for digitally signing blocks and transactions.

- Hash functions create a fixed-length message digest of an arbitrary-length input.

- MACs are message authentication codes used for message authentication.

- Digital signatures provide nonrepudiation, integrity, and authentication services.

- Authentication protocols are used in distributed systems to provide entity authentication.

- Hybrid encryption schemes combine public and symmetric key cryptography to achieve performance and security.

- Verifiable delay functions are functions that take time to evaluate but are quick to verify and have many applications in consensus protocols and blockchains.

- VRFs are public key–based functions which generate a verifiable correct output.

Bibliography

1. Paar, C. and Pelzl, J., 2009. Understanding cryptography: a textbook for students and practitioners. Springer Science & Business Media.

2. Martin, K.M., 2012. Everyday cryptography. Everyday Cryptography: Fundamental Principles and Applications. Print publication date: 2017 Print ISBN-13: 9780198788003, Published to Oxford Scholarship Online: July 2017, DOI:10.1093/oso/9780198788003.001.0001.

3. Multisignatures: This scheme was introduced in 1983 by Itakura et al. in their paper A Public-key Cryptosystem Suitable for Digital Multisignatures, vol. 71, Nec Research & Development (1983), pp. 474–480. Multisignatures are also sometimes called multiparty signatures in literature.

4. Bashir, I., 2020. Mastering Blockchain: A deep dive into distributed ledgers, consensus protocols, smart contracts, DApps, cryptocurrencies, Ethereum, and more. Packt Publishing Ltd.

5. Daniel J. Bernstein and Tanja Lange. SafeCurves: choosing safe curves for elliptic-curve cryptography. `https://safecurves.cr.yp.to`, accessed August 7, 2021.

6. VDF research: `https://vdfresearch.org`

7. Boneh, D., Bonneau, J., Bünz, B., and Fisch, B., 2018, August. Verifiable delay functions. In *Annual international cryptology conference* (pp. 757–788). Springer, Cham.

CHAPTER 3

Distributed Consensus

Consensus is a fundamental problem in distributed computing. This chapter will cover the fundamentals of the consensus problem and discuss some history covering the Byzantine generals problem, building blocks of consensus, and how we can solve this problem in distributed systems.

As fault tolerance is a fundamental requirement in distributed systems, several primitives introduce fault tolerance. Fault-tolerant broadcast algorithms allow for the development of fault-tolerant applications. Consensus enables processes to reach a common decision despite failures. Both topics are well researched in academia and the industry.

Before we dive into discussing consensus and agreement problems in detail, let's cover some building blocks in continuation of link abstractions from Chapter 1 that are closely related to consensus and agreement problems.

Broadcast Primitives

Earlier in Chapter 1, we learned about links that pass messages between a pair of processes in a point-to-point or one-to-one setting. This one-to-one communication (also called unicast) is quite common and used in the client-server architecture. For example, a web server making requests to a backend database can be seen as an example of this type of two-sided connection. There is one sender and one specific recipient, that is, the web server and backend database, respectively.

However, in many cases where multiple nodes are involved, the client-server type scheme is not adequate. Moreover, in many situations, one-to-one communication is not sufficient, and we need to use some mechanism that can send messages to multiple nodes or a group of nodes simultaneously. In such situations, we use broadcast protocols.

© Imran Bashir 2022
I. Bashir, *Blockchain Consensus*, https://doi.org/10.1007/978-1-4842-8179-6_3

Broadcast protocols allow a process to send a message simultaneously to all processes in a distributed system, including itself.

In this section, we will look at broadcast abstractions. There can be multiple senders and receivers involved. Broadcast abstractions ensure that the processes agree on the messages that they deliver.

Broadcast abstractions can be explained with a visualization in Figure 3-1.

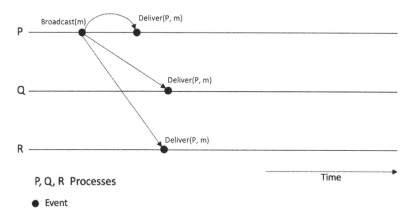

Figure 3-1. *A node broadcasting a message m and all three nodes delivering it*

Note that there is a difference between sending and receiving and broadcasting and delivering. Sending and receiving are used in the context of point-to-point links, and broadcast and delivery are used in broadcast abstractions where a message is broadcast to multiple/all nodes.

Point-to-point links discussed in Chapter 1 are associated with send and receive primitives where a node sends a message, and the recipient node receives them.

Broadcast abstractions with broadcast and deliver primitives depict a situation where a node sends a message to multiple/all nodes in the network and nodes receive them, but, here, the broadcast algorithm can store and buffer the message after receiving it and deliver it to the process later. It depends on the broadcast algorithm (also called middleware). For example, in total order broadcast, the message may be received by broadcast algorithms running on each process but can be buffered until the conditions meet to deliver the message to the application.

The diagram in Figure 3-2 shows this concept visually.

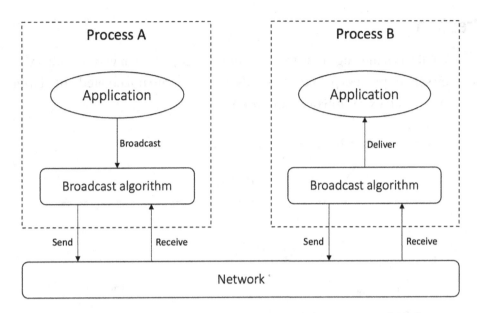

Figure 3-2. *Send and receive and broadcast and delivery*

The communication occurs within a group of nodes where the number of nodes might be static or dynamic. One process sends it, and all nodes in the group agree on it and deliver it. If a single processor or some processors become faulty, the remaining nodes carry on working. Broadcast messages are targeted to all processes.

Broadcast abstractions allow for the development of fault-tolerant applications. There are several types which I describe as follows.

Best-Effort Broadcast

In this abstraction, reliability is guaranteed only if the sender process does not fail. This is the weakest form of reliable broadcast. There are three properties that best-effort broadcast has.

Validity

If a message m is broadcast by a correct process p, then message m is eventually delivered by every correct process. This is a liveness property.

No Duplication

Every message is delivered only once.

No Creation

If a process delivers a message m with a sender process p, then m was previously broadcast by sender process p. In other words, messages are not created out of thin air. Figure 3-3 depicts an execution of best-effort broadcast.

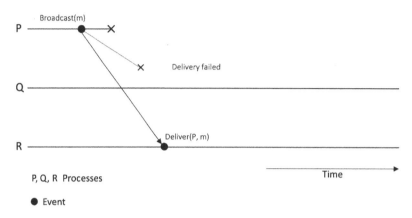

Figure 3-3. *Best-effort broadcast – an example scenario*

In Figure 3-3, notice that process p has broadcast the message but then crashed, and as per system properties, message delivery is not guaranteed in this case. Notice that process q did not deliver the message because our process p is no longer correct. However, process R delivered it. There is no delivery guarantee in this abstraction if the sender fails, as shown in Figure 3-3. In case some processes may deliver the messages, and some don't, it results in disagreement. As you can imagine, this abstraction may not be quite useful in some stricter scenarios. We need some more robust protocol than this. To address such limitations, a reliable broadcast abstraction is used.

Reliable Broadcast

A reliable broadcast abstraction introduces an additional liveness property called agreement. **No duplication** and **no creation** properties remain the same as the best-effort broadcast abstraction. The **validity** property is slightly weakened. Formally, validity and agreement properties can be stated as follows.

Validity

If a message m is broadcast by a correct process p, then p itself eventually delivers m.

Agreement

If a message m is delivered by a correct process, then every correct process delivers m.

Remarks

In case the sender process crashes while broadcasting and has not been able to send to all processes, the agreement property ensures that no process delivers it. It is possible that some processes may have received the message, but reliable broadcast ensures that no process will deliver it unless there's an agreement on the delivery. In other words, if the sender process crashes, the reliable broadcast ensures that either all correct nodes eventually deliver the message or no nodes deliver the message at all.

If the sender process fails, this property ensures that all correct nodes get the message or none of the correct nodes receives the message. This property is achieved by correct processes retransmitting any dropped messages, which result in the eventual delivery of the message.

This solution seems reasonable enough, but there might be situations in which the broadcaster process may have been able to deliver to itself but then crashed before it could send to other processes. This means that all correct processes will agree not to deliver the message because they have not received it, but the original broadcaster delivers it. Such situations can cause safety issues.

To address this limitation, uniform reliable broadcast, which provides a stronger guarantee, is used.

Uniform Reliable Broadcast

In uniform reliable broadcast, while all other properties such as validity, no duplication, and no creation remain the same as best-effort broadcast, there's a stronger notion of the agreement property that we saw in the reliable broadcast abstraction. It is introduced to ensure that agreement is achieved even in the scenarios where the sender process might fail. This property is called the uniform agreement property.

Uniform Agreement

If a message m is delivered by a process p, every correct process eventually delivers m. p can be either a correct or a failed process.

In all the preceding discussed abstractions, there's a crucial element missing which is required in many distributed services. For example, imagine a scenario of an online chat app. If a user sends a message saying "England has won the cricket match," and another user replies "congratulations," and a third user says "But I wanted Ireland to win," the expected sequence in which the messages are supposed to appear in the chat app is

- **User 1**: England has won the cricket match
- **User 2**: congratulations
- **User 3**: But I wanted Ireland to win

However, if there is no order imposed on the message delivery, it might appear that even if User 1's message was sent first, it may turn out that in the app (to the end user) the messages might appear like this:

- **User 2**: congratulations
- **User 3**: But I wanted Ireland to win
- **User 1**: England has won the cricket match

Now this is not the expected order; the "congratulations" message without the context of winning the match would appear confusing. This is the problem that is solved by imposing an order guarantee on the broadcast abstractions.

Note   We discussed causality and happens-before relationships in Chapter 1; if you need a refresher, refer to that chapter.

Now we will discuss four abstractions that deliver messages with an order guarantee with varying degrees of strictness: FIFO reliable broadcast, causal reliable broadcast, total order reliable broadcast, and FIFO total order broadcast.

FIFO Reliable Broadcast

This abstraction imposes a first-in, first-out (FIFO) delivery order on reliable broadcast. This means that messages broadcast are delivered in the same that they were sent by the sender process.

In this abstraction, all properties remain the same as reliable broadcast; however, a new property for FIFO delivery is introduced.

FIFO Delivery

If a process has broadcast two messages m1 and m2, respectively, then any correct process does not deliver m2 before m1. In other words, if m1 is broadcast before m2 by the same process, then no correct process delivers m2 unless it has delivered m1 first. This guarantee is however only in the case when m1 and m2 are broadcast by the same process; if two different processes have broadcast messages, then there is no guarantee in which order they will be delivered.

In practice, TCP is an example of FIFO delivery. If you need FIFO delivery in your use case, you can simply use TCP.

Causal Reliable Broadcast

This abstraction imposes a causal delivery order on reliable broadcast. This means that if a message broadcast happens before broadcast of another message, then every process delivers these two messages in the same order. In scenarios where two messages might have been broadcast concurrently, then a process can deliver them in any order.

Total Order Reliable Broadcast or Atomic Reliable Broadcast

This abstraction is usually just called **total order broadcast** or **atomic broadcast**. There are four properties that total order broadcast has, which are described as follows.

Validity

If a correct process p broadcasts a message m, then some correct process eventually delivers m.

Agreement

If a message m is delivered by a correct process p, then all correct processes eventually deliver m.

Integrity

For any message m, each process delivers m at most once and only if m was previously broadcast. In literature, this property is sometimes divided into two separate properties: **no duplication** where no message is delivered more than once and **no creation** which states that a delivered message must be broadcast by the sender process. In other words, no messages are created out of thin air.

Total Order

In this property, if a message m1 is delivered before m2 in a process, then m1 is delivered before m2 in all processes.

FIFO Total Order Broadcast

This abstraction combines both FIFO broadcast and total order broadcast.

The total order can be achieved using a single leader known as the sequencer approach and using Lamport clocks, but none of these are fault-tolerant approaches. What if the leader goes down then there is no sequencing and in case of Lamport clocks if any of the nodes fail then the total order cannot be guaranteed? Introducing fault tolerance in total order broadcast to automatically choose a new leader is the problem that is studied and addressed using consensus protocols. A consensus protocol, at a fundamental level, addresses the problem of choosing a new leader in case of failure. This is the key motivation behind consensus protocols. We will see more about this and details on total order broadcast and its relationship with state machine replication, fault tolerance, and consensus protocols later in this chapter.

So far, the abstractions that we have discussed can work with a smaller set of processes. Imagine a distributed system is spread across multiple continents and there are 1000s of nodes participating in it. Can the abstractions presented so far be efficient enough to withstand the communication complexity that arises with 1000s of heterogenous and dispersed nodes in a distributed system? The answer is no, and in order to address such requirements, probabilistic protocols are developed. Also, imagine a scenario where a single node is responsible for sending messages to 1000 nodes. Even if we manage to send a message to 1000 nodes with some hardware support or some other method, the problem becomes complex to handle when that single sender node receives the acknowledgements from 1000 nodes. This problem is called **ack implosion**. The question is how we can avoid such issues.

Imagine another situation where using reliable links a node has sent a message to all nodes individually, but while in transit to some nodes, some messages were dropped. At this point, the sender process fails and consequently no retransmission occurred. As a result, those nodes that did not receive messages will now never receive messages because the sender process has crashed. How can we improve reliability in this scenario? We can devise a scheme where if one node receives a message for the first time, it broadcasts it again to other nodes through reliable channels. This way, all correct nodes will receive all the messages, even if some nodes crash. This is called **eager reliable broadcast**. Eager reliable broadcast is reliable; however, it can incur $O(n)$ steps and $O(n)^2$ messages for n number of nodes.

Figure 3-4 visualizes the eager reliable protocol.

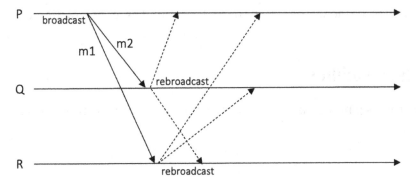

Figure 3-4. *Eager reliable broadcast*

There are also other algorithms which we can call *nature-inspired* algorithms. For example, consider how an infectious disease might spread or a rumor might spread. One person infects a few others, and then those others infect others, and quickly the infection rate increases. Now imagine if a broadcast protocol is designed on such principle, then it can be very effective at disseminating information (messages) throughout the network quickly. As these protocols are basically randomized protocols, they do not guarantee that all nodes will receive a message, but there is usually a very high probability that all nodes eventually get all messages. Probabilistic protocols or gossip protocols are commonly used in peer-to-peer networks. There are many protocols that have been designed based on this type of dissemination.

Figure 3-5 illustrates how a gossip protocol works. The idea here is that when a node receives a message for the first time, it forwards it to some randomly chosen other nodes. This technique is useful for broadcasting messages to many nodes, and the message eventually reaches all nodes with high probability.

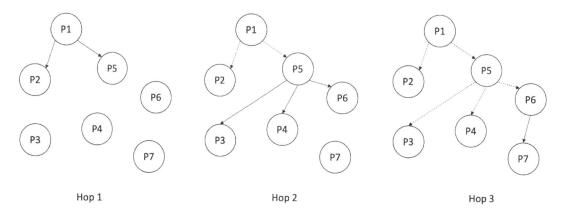

Figure 3-5. *Gossip protocol*

A probabilistic broadcast abstraction can be defined as an abstraction which has two properties.

Probabilistic Validity

If a correct process p broadcasts a message m, then every correct process eventually delivers it with probability 1.

Integrity

Any message is delivered at most once, and the message delivered has been previously broadcast by a process – in other words, no duplicate message and no message creation out of thin air.

Relationship Between Broadcasts and Consensus

Best-effort broadcast is the weakest broadcast model. By adding additional properties and requirements, we can achieve stronger broadcast models, as shown in Figure 3-6.

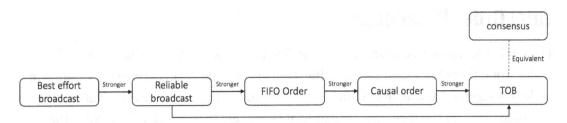

Figure 3-6. *Broadcast relationship – from weakest to strongest – and consensus equivalency*

With this, we complete our discussion on broadcast protocols. Let's now move on to the agreement abstraction, which is one of the most fundamental problems in distributed computing.

First, I'll explain what an agreement is, and then we'll build upon this fundamental idea and present the consensus problem.

Agreement

In a distributed system, the agreement between the processes is a fundamental requirement. There are many scenarios where processes need to agree for the distributed system to achieve its goals. For example, in broadcast abstractions, an agreement is needed between processes for the delivery of messages.

There are various agreement problems, and we will cover the most prominent of them in the following and then focus more on consensus.

We have already covered reliable broadcast and total order broadcast. In this section, I will explain some additional points briefly on reliable broadcast and total order broadcast; then, we'll explore the Byzantine agreement and consensus.

Reliable Broadcast

The reliable broadcast assures reliability even if the sender process fails. In other words, reliability is guaranteed whether the sender is correct or not.

Total Order Broadcast

The total order broadcast guarantees reliability and the same order of delivery at all nodes. Total order broadcast can be achieved using a single leader approach where one node is designated as a leader. All messages go through this leader which establishes a common order for the messages. The messages are sent to the leader first, which then broadcasts them using the FIFO broadcast mechanism. However, in this case, the issue is that if the leader crashes, then no messages can be delivered. The question then becomes how we can change the failed leader while ensuring the safety of the algorithm.

If the elected leader that establishes the common delivery order fails, the nodes must elect a new leader. The problem now becomes to choose a new honest leader and agree on the new leader's choice. Again, now nodes must achieve an agreement, and the problem now becomes an agreement on a new leader instead of an agreement on the delivery order. In either case, nodes must run some agreement protocol.

Also, earlier, we discovered that Lamport clocks, using the software event counter and the process identifier, can achieve a total order. Combined with FIFO links and timestamps in a total order, Lamport clocks to achieve a total order make intuitive sense, but this can be challenging in practical terms. For example, if a node goes down, then the entire protocol halts.

Both single leader (sequencer/orderer approach and Lamport clocks) are not fault tolerant. We will shortly see what we can do about this. Total order broadcast and consensus are different problems but are related to each other. If you solve consensus, then you can solve the total order and vice versa.

Total order broadcast is also called atomic broadcast because it ensures that either the messages are delivered to all processes or not at all. This atomicity (all or nothing) of total order broadcast is what makes it an atomic broadcast protocol, hence the name atomic broadcast.

The Byzantine Agreement Problem

The Byzantine agreement problem can be defined in three different ways: the Byzantine generals problem, the interactive consistency problem, and the consensus problem.

The Basic Byzantine Generals Problem or BGP

There is a designated process called the source process with an initial value. The goal of the problem is to reach an agreement with other processes about the initial value of the source process. There are three conditions that need to be met:

- **Agreement**: All honest processes agree on the same value.

- **Validity**: If the source process is honest, the decided (agreed-upon) value by all honest processes is the same value as the initial value of the source process.

- **Termination**: Each honest process must eventually decide on a value.

This problem is fundamentally a broadcast primitive in which the designated process starts with an initial value (input), and other processes do not have an input (initial value). When the algorithm terminates, all processes agree on (output) the same value. The crux of the solution for the Byzantine generals problem (BGP) is that the sender process reliably sends its input to all processes so that all processes output (decide) the same value.

The Interactive Consistency Problem

In this interactive consistency problem, each process has an initial value, and all correct processes must agree on a set of values (vector) where each process has a corresponding value. The requirements are listed as follows:

- **Agreement**: All honest processes agree on the same array of values (vector).

- **Validity**: If a correct process decides on a vector V and a process P1 is correct and takes as input a value V1 from the vector, then V1 corresponds to P1 in the vector V.

- **Termination**: Every correct process eventually decides.

The Consensus Problem

In the consensus problem, each process has an initial value, and all correct processes agree on a single value:

- **Agreement**: All processes agree on the same value; no two processes decide on different values.

- **Validity**: A decided value must be a proposed value of a process.

- **Integrity:** A process decides at most only once.

- **Termination**: Every honest process eventually decides on a value.

Validity and agreement are safety properties, whereas termination is a liveness property.

Figure 3-7 shows how consensus looks like visually. There is not much in the diagram, but it depicts visually and helps to build a mental model of how consensus looks like.

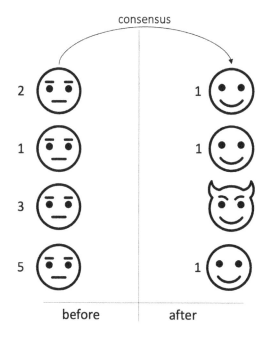

Figure 3-7. *Consensus – how it looks visually*

There are many variations of the consensus problem depending upon the system model and failure models.

The abovementioned consensus problem is called uniform consensus where the agreement property is strict and does not allow a crashed process to decide differently.

Another variant of consensus is **non-uniform consensus**. In non-uniform consensus, the agreement property is *weakened* to allow a crashed process to decide on a different value.

We can write the *agreement* property of **uniform consensus** as

- **Agreement**: No two honest processes decide on different values.

Now if we make the validity property *stronger* in addition to weakening the agreement property, we achieve **Byzantine-tolerant consensus**. In this case, the validity property becomes

- **Validity**: A decided value of an honest process must be a proposed value of an honest process.

The first variation where the validity property is weak and the agreement is also weak can be categorized as **crash fault–tolerant consensus**.

An algorithm that satisfies all these safety and liveness properties is called a correct algorithm. Solving a consensus problem is not difficult in failure-free synchronous systems; however, the problem becomes difficult in systems that are failure-prone. Failures and asynchrony make solving consensus a complex problem.

Binary consensus is a simple type of consensus where the input is restricted, and as a result, the decision value is restricted to a single bit, either zero or one. **Multivalued consensus** is a type of consensus where the objective is to agree on multiple values, that is, a series of values over time.

While binary consensus may not seem like a very useful construct in the first instance, a solution to a binary consensus problem leads to a solution for multivalued consensus; hence, it is an important area for research.

The definitions of properties of consensus may change slightly depending on the application. For example, usually in blockchain consensus protocols the validity property is defined differently from established definitions and may settle for a weaker variant. For example, in Tendermint consensus the validity property simply states, *"a decided value is valid i.e. it satisfies the predefined predicate denoted valid( )"*. This can be an application-specific condition. For example, in blockchain context it could be required that a new block added to the Bitcoin blockchain must have a valid block header that passes node validation checks. In other variations, the valid( ) predicate requirement and the condition "if all honest processes propose the same value, then all decide on that same value" can be combined. This is a combination of validity predicate and traditional validity condition. There are variations and different definitions. Some are strict, and some are not so strict, depending on the application. We will cover blockchain consensus and relevant consensus protocols throughout this book and will define and redefine these requirements in the context of the consensus algorithm and fault models being discussed.

A consensus protocol is **crash fault tolerant (CFT)** if it can tolerate benign faults up to a certain threshold. A consensus protocol is **Byzantine fault tolerant (BFT)** if it can tolerate arbitrary faults. In order to achieve crash fault tolerance, the underlying distributed network must satisfy the condition N >= 2F+1, where N is the number of nodes in the network, and F is the number of faulty nodes. If the network satisfies this condition, only then it will be able to continue to work correctly and achieve consensus. If Byzantine faults are required to be tolerated, then the condition becomes N>=3F+1. We will cover this more formally when we discuss impossibility results later in this chapter. But remember these conditions as lower tight bounds.

A consensus problem applies to other problems in distributed computing too. Problems like total order broadcast, leader election problem, and terminating reliable broadcast require an agreement on a common value. These problems can be considered consensus variants.

System Models

To study consensus and agreement problems and develop solutions, there are some underlying assumptions that we make about the behavior of the distributed system. We learned many of these abstractions regarding node and network behavior in Chapter 1. Here, we summarize those assumptions and move on to discuss the consensus problem in more detail. The reason for describing system models here is twofold: first, to summarize what we learned in the chapter regarding the behavior of the nodes and networks and, second, to put this knowledge in the context of studying consensus and agreement problems. For a detailed study, you can refer to Chapter 1.

Distributed System

A distributed system is a set of processes that communicate using message passing. Consensus algorithms are designed based on assumptions made about timing and synchrony behavior of the distributed system. These assumptions are captured under the timing model or synchrony assumptions, which we describe next.

Timing Model/Synchrony

Synchrony assumptions capture the timing assumption about a distributed system. The relative speed of processors and communication is also taken into consideration. There are several synchrony models. We briefly describe those as follows:

- Synchronous systems where there is a known upper bound on the processor and communication delay which always holds.

- Asynchronous systems where there are assumptions made about timing. There is no bound on the processor or communication delay. This is a useful notion because protocols designed with this assumption are also automatically resilient in synchronous and other models, which are more favorable. In other words, a program proven correct in an asynchronous model is automatically correct in a synchronous model.

- Partial synchrony which can be defined in several ways:

  - There is an unknown upper bound which always holds.

  - There is a known upper bound that eventually holds after some GST.

  - There are guaranteed periods of synchrony, which are long enough that a decision can be made, and an algorithm can terminate.

  - There is an unknown upper bound which eventually holds after some GST.

  - Weak synchrony introduced with practical Byzantine fault tolerance (PBFT) assumes that the network latency doesn't grow infinitely more than the timeout.

  - A system can be asynchronous initially but is synchronous after GST.

Usually, in practice a partially synchronous assumption is made regarding the timing behavior of the distributed system. This choice is especially true in blockchain protocols, where most consensus protocols are designed for eventually synchronous/partially synchronous models, for example, PBFT for blockchain. Of course, some are designed for the asynchronous model, such as HoneyBadger. We will cover blockchain consensus in Chapter 5 and then throughout this book. For now, I will focus on the distributed consensus problem in general and from a traditional point of view.

Also, note that an asynchronous message-passing model with Byzantine faults expresses conditions of a typical distributed system based on the Internet today. Especially, this is quite true in public blockchain platforms such as Bitcoin or Ethereum.

Process Failures

Failure models allow us to make assumptions about which failures can occur and how we can address them. Failure models describe the conditions under which the failure may or may not occur. There are various classes, such as crash failures, where processes can crash-stop or crash-fail, or omission failures where a processor can omit sending or receiving a message.

Another type of omission fault is called the dynamic omission fault. In this model, a system can lose a maximum number of messages in each round. However, the channels on which the message losses occur may change from round to round.

Timing failures are those where processes do not comply with the synchrony assumptions. The processes may exhibit Byzantine behavior where the processes can behave arbitrarily or maliciously. In the Byzantine model, the corrupted processor can duplicate, drop a message, and actively try to sabotage the entire system. We also define an adversary model here where we make some assumptions about an adversary who can adversely affect the distributed system and corrupt the processors.

In authenticated Byzantine failures, it is possible to identify the source of the message via identification and detect the forged messages, usually via digital signatures. Failures that occur under this assumption are called authenticated Byzantine failures.

Messages can be authenticated or non-authenticated. Authenticated messages usually use digital signatures to allow forgery detection and message tampering. The agreement problem becomes comparatively easier to solve with authenticated messages because recipients can detect the message forgery and reject the unsigned or incorrectly signed messages or messages coming from unauthenticated processes. On the other hand, distributed systems with non-authenticated messages are difficult to deal with as there is no way to verify the authenticity of the messages. Non-authenticated messages are also called oral messages or unsigned messages. Even though it is difficult, it is indeed a common assumption about solving consensus or agreement problems. However, digital signatures are ubiquitous in blockchain systems, and the model under which blockchain consensus works is almost always authenticated Byzantine.

Channel Reliability

It is often assumed that the channel is reliable. Reliable channels guarantee that if a correct process p has sent a message m to a correct process q, then q will eventually receive m. In practice, this is usually the TCP/IP protocol that provides reliability.

Lossy channels are another assumption that captures the notion of channels where messages can be lost. This can happen due to poor network conditions, delays, denial-of-service attacks, hacking attacks in general, slow network, a misconfiguration in the network configuration, noise, buffer overflows, network congestion, and physical disconnections. There might be many other reasons, but I just described the most common ones.

There are two variations of fair-loss channels. There is an upper bound k on the number of lost messages in one variation, and in another, known as fair-loss channels, there is no such upper bound. The first variation is easier to handle where the algorithm can retransmit the message k+1 times, ensuring that at least one copy is received. In the latter variation, the fair-loss channels, if the sender keeps resending a message, eventually it is delivered, provided that both the sender and the receiver are correct. We discussed this in greater detail in Chapter 1.

History

Consensus problems have been studied for decades in distributed computing. Achieving consensus under faults was first proposed by Lamport et al. in their paper "SIFT: Design and analysis of a fault-tolerant computer for aircraft control."

Later, a Byzantine fault–tolerant protocol under a synchronous setting was first proposed by Lamport et al. in their seminal paper "Reaching Agreement in the Presence of Faults."

The impossibility of reaching an agreement even if a single process crash-fails was proven by Fischer, Lynch, and Paterson. This discovery is infamously known as the FLP impossibility result.

Ben-Or proposed asynchronous Byzantine fault tolerance using randomization to circumvent FLP. In addition, partial synchrony was presented in DLS 88 for BFT.

Two Generals' Problem

The Two Generals' Paradox or Two Generals' Problem was formulated by Gray et al. in 1978. In this thought experiment, two generals are sharing a common goal to capture a hill. The condition is that if both of those generals act simultaneously and attack the hill together at the same time, then success is guaranteed. If either one of the generals attacks alone, they will lose the battle. It is also assumed that both generals are camped some distance apart, and they can communicate only via messengers (runners). However, these messengers are not reliable and can get lost or captured. If one general sends a message to another general to attack, for example, "Attack at 0400 hours," then it is possible that the message doesn't reach the other general. Suppose the message doesn't reach the second general. In that case, it is impossible to differentiate whether the first general sent a message or not or the messenger got captured on its way to the second general. The general who has sent the message cannot assume that his message got through because unless he receives an explicit acknowledgment from the second general, he cannot be sure. Now the question is what protocol we can come up with to reach an agreement on a plan to attack. The situation is tricky because there is no common knowledge between the generals, and the only way to know is via messengers, which are unreliable.

Both generals have two options. Either they can go ahead regardless of any acknowledgment received from the other general, or they don't and wait until a response is received (acknowledgment) from the other general. In the first case, the risk is that the general goes ahead without a response from the other general and might end up alone in the attack and gets defeated. In the latter case, the general will not act until a response is received. In this case, the first general waiting for an acknowledgment is safe because he will only attack if the response is received. So now it becomes the second general's responsibility to decide whether to attack and be alone or wait for an acknowledgment from the first general that he has received the acknowledgment. One solution that comes to mind is that perhaps if generals send a lot of messengers, then there is a probability that at least one might get through, but there is also a chance that all messengers are captured, and no message goes through. For example, if general 1 sends many messages to general 2 and all messengers are lost, then general 2 doesn't know about the attack, and if general 1 goes ahead and attacks, then the battle is lost.

The Two Generals' Problem is depicted in Figure 3-8.

Figure 3-8. *Two Generals' Problem*

In Figure 3-8, two generals must agree on the time to attack; otherwise, no win.

The issue is that no general can ever be sure about the commitment from the other general. If general 1 always attacks even if no acknowledgment is received from general 2, then general 1 risks being alone in the attack if all messengers are lost. This is the case because general 2 knows nothing about the attack. If general 1 attacks only if a positive acknowledgment is received from general 2, then general 1 is safe. General 2 is in the same situation as general 1 because now he is waiting for general 1's acknowledgment. General 2 might consider himself safe as he knows that general 1 will only attack if general 2's response is received by general 1. General 2 is now waiting for the acknowledgment from general 1. They are both thinking about whether the other general received their message or not, hence the paradox!

From a distributed system perspective, this experiment depicts a situation where two processes have no common knowledge, and the only way they can find out about the state of each other is via messages.

Byzantine Generals Problem

The Byzantine generals problem was proposed by Lamport in 1982. In this thought experiment, an imaginary scenario is presented in which three or more army units are camped around a city, and the collective aim of the units is to capture the city. Each army unit is led by a general, and they communicate via messengers. The city can only be captured if all army units attack simultaneously.

The requirement here is to reach an agreement to attack so that all armies can attack at the same time and as a result capture the city.

The problems this setting can face are

- Messages can be lost, that is, messengers can be captured or lost.

- Any general can be a traitor who can send misleading messages to other generals, can withhold the messages, may not send messages to all generals, may tamper with the messages before relaying them to other generals, or can send contradictory messages, all with an aim to subvert the agreement process between the generals.

- The honest generals also don't know who the traitors are, but traitors can collude together.

The challenge here is whether in this situation an agreement can be reached and what protocol can solve this problem, if any. Figure 3-9 shows this problem.

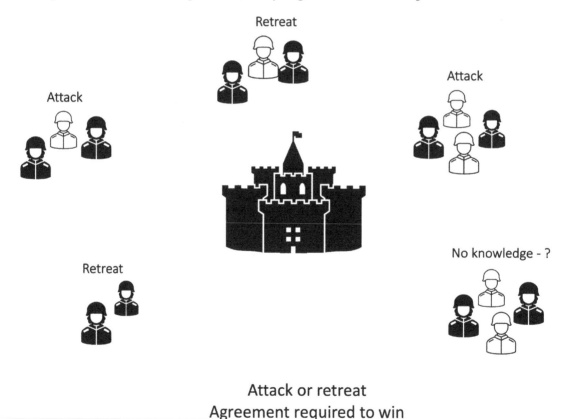

Figure 3-9. *Byzantine generals problem – showing each army unit receiving misleading, correct, or no messages at all*

It turns out that this problem is impossible to solve. It has been proven that this problem can be solved only if fewer than one-third of generals are traitors. For example, if there are 3t + 1 generals, only up to t can be malicious. This is a proven lower bound on the Byzantine fault tolerance. We will see this more formally under the section "Impossibility Results" where we discuss FLP, CFT lower bounds, and BFT lower bounds.

In distributed systems, we can have an analog where generals represent processes (nodes), traitors represent Byzantine processes, honest generals represent correct processes, messengers represent communication links, loss of a message is a captured messenger, and no time limit on the messenger to reach generals represents asynchrony. I think you get the picture now!

Replication

In this section, we will discuss replication. Replication is used to maintain an exact copy of the data in multiple nodes. This technique has several advantages. One key advantage is fault tolerance. One example of the simplest replication is RAID in storage systems. For example, in RAID-1, there are two disks, and they are exact replicas (mirror) of each other. If one is unavailable, the copy is available, resulting in fault tolerance and high availability. In distributed systems, replication is used for various reasons and, unlike RAID, is between multiple nodes instead of just between two disks within a server.

Also, if data remains unchanged, then replication is easy. You can just make a one-off copy of the data and store it on another disk or node. The challenging part is how to keep replication consistent when the data is subject to constant change.

There are several advantages:

- High availability due to fault tolerance, for example, if one replica goes down, another is available to serve clients.

- Load distribution due to each replica node being an independent node, and clients can send requests to different nodes (or can be managed via load balancers to route requests to less busy replicas – load balancing). The load can be distributed among different replicas to achieve higher performance.

- Data consistency means that the same copy of data is available across all nodes, which helps with the integrity of the overall system.

- Better performance, which is achieved via load balancing, where nodes that are less busy can take up the requests in case other nodes are near or full capacity. There are several techniques for this, which are beyond the scope of this book; however, usually load balancers are used which route requests from clients usually in a round-robin fashion to replicas. This way, the load is distributed across multiple replicas instead of one node getting all the hits and as a result becoming less responsive due to CPU load.

- Data locality, where, especially in a geographically distributed network, the nodes that are local to a client can serve the requests instead of scenarios where there might be only one node in some remote data center and all clients either geographically close or far make requests to only that single server. The clients that are physically nearer to the server will get their response quicker as compared to clients that are physically located cities or continents apart. For example, in file download services, a mirror that is, for example, available in Ireland will be able to serve the download requests much faster than a server that might be in Australia. The network latency alone makes such setting vulnerable to performance hit.

There are some shortcomings as well:

- High cost, due to multiple replica nodes required, the setup might be expensive.

- Maintaining data consistency among replicas is hard.

Replication can be achieved by using two methods. One is the state transfer, where a state is sent from one node to another replica. The other approach is state machine replication. Each replica is a state machine that runs commands deterministically in the same sequence as other replicas, resulting in a consistent state across replicas. Usually, in this case, a primary server receives the commands, which then broadcasts them to other replicas that apply those commands.

There are two common techniques for achieving replication. We define them as follows.

Active Replication

In this scheme, the client commands are ordered via an ordering protocol and forwarded to replicas that execute those commands deterministically. The intuition here is that if all commands are applied in the same order at all replicas, then each replica will produce the same state update. This way, all replicas can be kept consistent with each other. The key challenge here is to develop a scheme for ordering the commands and that all nodes execute the same commands in the same order. Also, each replica starts in the same state and is a copy of the original state machine. Active replication is also known as **state machine replication**.

Passive Replication

In the passive replication approach, there is one replica that is designated as primary. This primary replica is responsible for executing the commands and sending (broadcast) the updates to each replica, including itself. All replicas then apply the state update in the order received. Unlike active replication, the processing is not required to be deterministic, and any anomalies are usually resolved by the designated primary replica and produce deterministic state updates. This approach is also called **primary backup replication**. In short, there is only a single copy of the state machine in the system kept by the primary replica, and the rest of the replicas only maintain the state.

Pros and Cons

There are pros and cons of both approaches. Active replication can result in wastage of resources if the operations are intensive. In the case of passive replication, large updates can consume a large amount of network bandwidth. Furthermore, in passive replication, as there is one primary replica, if it fails, the performance and availability of the system are impacted.

In the passive approach, client write requests are preprocessed by the primary and transformed into state update commands, which apply to all replicas in the same order. Each replica is a copy of the state machine in active replication, whereas, in passive replication, only the primary is a single copy of the state machine.

Note that even though there is a distinction between active and passive replication at a fundamental level, they both are generic approaches to making a state machine fault-tolerant.

Let's now see how primary backup replication works. I am assuming a fail-stop model here.

Primary Backup Replication

Primary backup replication is the most common type of replication scheme. There is one replica that is designated primary, and the rest of the nodes are backups. A correct process bearing the lowest identifier is designated as a primary replica. A client sends requests to the designated primary, which forwards the request(s) to all backups. The primary replies to the client only after it has received responses from the backups. When the client makes a write request, the primary sends the request to all replicas, and after receiving the response from the backups, it makes the update to itself (deliver to itself).

The algorithm works as follows:

1. The client sends a write request to the primary.

2. The primary broadcasts it to the backup replicas.

3. Backup replicas send an acknowledgment (response) to the primary replica.

4. The primary waits until it has received all responses from backup replicas.

5. Once it has received all responses, it delivers the request to itself. This is called the commit point.

6. After this, the primary sends the response back to the client.

In the case of read operation

1. The client sends a request to the primary.

2. The primary responds.

Figure 3-10 illustrates this concept.

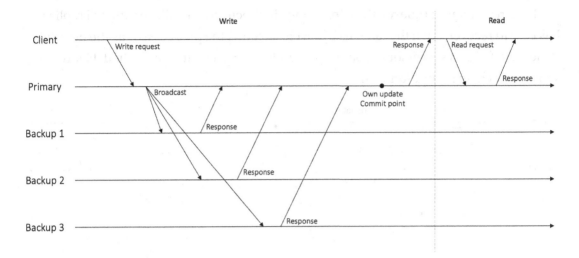

Figure 3-10. *Primary backup replication*

How are failures handled? If the primary fails, one of the backups will take over.

Now, this looks like a suitable protocol for achieving fault tolerance, but what if the primary fails? Primary failure can lead to downtime as recovery can take time. Also, reading from the primary can produce incorrect results because, in scenarios where the client makes a read request to the primary before the commit point, the primary will not produce the result, even though all replicas have that update delivered to them. One solution might be to deal with reads as updates, but this technique is relatively inefficient. Also, the primary is doing all the work, that is, sending to other replicas, receiving responses, committing, and then replying to the client. Also, the primary must wait until all responses are received from the replicas for it to be able to respond to the client. A better solution, as compared to the primary backup replica solution, is chain replication. Here, the core idea is that one of the backup servers will reply to read the requests, and another will process the update commands.

Chain Replication

Chain replication organizes replicas in a chain with a head and a tail. The head is the server with the maximum number, whereas the tail is the one with the lowest number. Write requests or update commands are sent to the head, which sends the request using reliable FIFO links to the next replica on the chain, and the next replica then forwards it to the next until the update reaches the last (tail) server. The tail server then responds to the client. The head replica orders the requests coming in from the clients.

For a read request (query), the client sends it directly to the tail, and the tail replies. It is easy to recover when the tail fails by just reselecting the predecessor as the new tail. If the head fails, its successor becomes the new head and clients are notified. Figure 3-11 shows how chain replication works.

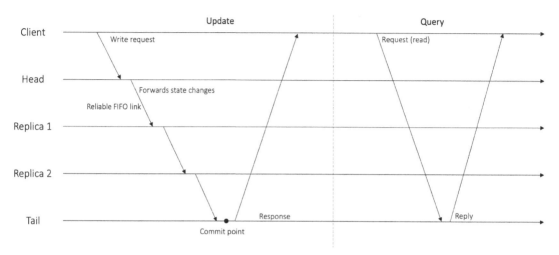

Figure 3-11. *Chain replication*

Chain replication provides high availability, high throughput, and strong consistency. It can tolerate up to $n - 1$ failures.

State Machine Replication

The state machine methodology was introduced by Leslie Lamport in his seminal paper "Time, Clocks, and the Ordering of Events in a Distributed System" in 1978. It is a de facto standard for achieving fault tolerance in distributed systems.

Let's first define what a state machine is. A state machine executes a sequence of commands. It stores the state of the system. This stored state transitions to the next state through a state transition function as a result of executing commands. Commands are deterministic, and the resultant state and output are only determined by the input commands which the machine has executed.

The simple algorithm in Listing 3-1 describes a state machine node.

Listing 3-1. State machine

```
state := initial
log := lastcommand
while (true) {
on event receivecommand()
     {
     appendtolog(command)
     output := statetransition(command, state)
     sendtoclient(output)
     }
}
```

In this pseudocode, the state machine starts with an initial state. When a command is received from the client, it appends that to the log. After that, it executes the command through the transition function and updates the state and produces an output. This output is sent to the client as a response.

Figure 3-12 illustrates this concept.

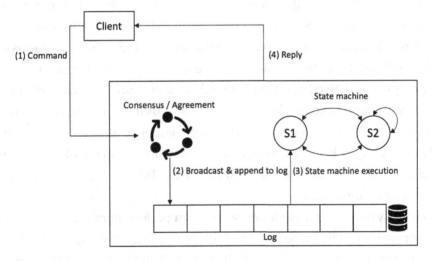

Figure 3-12. *State machine replica*

The key idea behind state machine replication is that if the system is modelled as a state machine, then replica consistency can be achieved by simply achieving an agreement on the order of operations. If the same commands are applied to all nodes in the same order, then a general approach to keep all replicas consistent with each other is achieved. However, the challenge here is to figure out how to achieve a common global order of the commands.

In order to achieve an agreement on the order of operations, we can use agreement protocols such as Byzantine agreement protocols or reliable broadcast protocols. We discussed the total order broadcast abstraction earlier in this chapter. We can also use consensus algorithms such as Paxos or PBFT to achieve this. Remember that in total order broadcast, each process delivers the same message in the same order. This property immediately solves our problem of achieving an agreement on the order of operations, which is the core insight behind state machine replication. Total order broadcast ensures that commands from different clients are delivered in the same order. If commands are delivered in the same order, they will be executed in the same order and as state machine is deterministic, all replicas will end up in the same state.

Each replica is a state machine which transitions its state to the next deterministically as a result of executing the input command. The state on each replica is maintained as a set of (key, value) pairs. The output of commands is transitioned from the current state to the next. Determinism is important because this ensures that each command execution produces the same output. Each replica starts in the same initial state. Total order broadcast delivers the same command to each replica in the global order, which results in each replica executing the same sequence of commands and transitioning to the same state. This achieves the same state at each replica.

This principle is also used in blockchains where a total order is achieved on the sequence of transactions and blocks via some consensus mechanism, and each node executes and stores those transactions in the same sequence as other replicas and as proposed by proof of work winner, leader. We will explore this in detail in Chapter 5. Traditional protocols such as Practical Byzantine Fault Tolerance (PBFT) and RAFT are state machine replication protocols.

SMR is usually used to achieve increased system performance and fault tolerance. System performance can increase because multiple replicas host copies of data, and more resources are available due to multiple replicas. Fault tolerance increases due to the simple fact that as data is replicated on each replica, even if some replicas are not available, the system will continue to operate and respond to client queries and updates.

Now let's look at SMR properties formally.

Same Initial State

The replicas always start in the same initial state. It could just be an empty database.

Deterministic Operations

All correct replicas deterministically produce the same output and state for the same input and state.

Coordination

All correct replicas process the same commands in the same order.

The coordination property requires the use of agreement protocols such as total order broadcast or some consensus algorithms.

There are also two *safety* and *liveness* properties which we describe as follows.

Safety

All correct replicas execute the same commands. This is the **agreement** property. There are two general approaches to achieve an agreement. We can use either a total order broadcast or a consensus protocol. A total order broadcast protocol needs to run only once per state machine replication, whereas a consensus mechanism is instantiated for each period of the sequence of commands.

Liveness

All correct commands are eventually executed by correct replicas. This is also called the **completion** property.

Safety ensures consistency, whereas liveness ensures availability and progress.

Figure 3-13 demonstrates how SMR generally works.

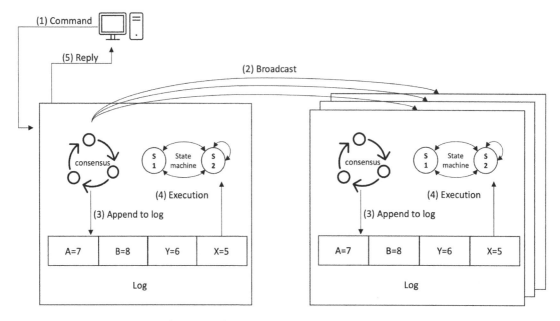

Figure 3-13. *State machine replication*

In Figure 3-13, we can see how the process works:

1. The client submits the command x = 5 to replica 1.

2. Replica 1 sends this command to replica 2 and replica 3.

3. All replicas append the command to their logs.

4. Each state machine on all replicas executes the command.

5. Replica 1 responds back to the client with the reply/result.

The replicated log on the replicas ensures that commands are executed by the state machine in the same order on each replica. The consensus mechanism (in the top-left corner of the image) ensures that an agreement is achieved on the order of commands and as a result written into the log as such. This involves reaching an agreement on the sequence of commands with other replicas. This replicated system will make progress if majority of the replicas are up.

Consensus and state machine replication are related in the sense that distributed consensus establishes the global common order of state machine commands, whereas the state machine executes these commands according to the global order determined by the consensus (agreement) algorithm, and thus each node (state machine) reaches the same state.

A crash fault–tolerant SMR requires at least 2f+1 replicas, whereas a BFT SMR requires 3f+1 replicas, where f is the number of failed replicas.

State machine replication achieves consistency among replicas. There are various replica consistency models. We'll briefly explore them here.

Linearizability

Another stronger property that a state machine replication protocol may implement is called linearizability. Linearizability is also called atomic consistency, and it means that command execution appears as if executed on a single copy of the state machine, even if there are multiple replicas. The critical requirement of linearizability is that the state read is always up to date, and no stale data is ever read.

Consistency models allow developers to understand the behavior of the replicated storage system. When interacting with a replicated system, the application developers experience the same behavior as interacting with a single system. Such transparency allows developers to use the same single server convention of writing application logic. If a replicated system possesses such transparency, then it is said to be linearizable.

In literature, linearizability is also called strong consistency, atomic consistency, or immediate consistency.

Sequential Consistency

In this type of consistency, all nodes see the same order of commands as other nodes.

Linearizability and sequential consistency are two classes of **strong consistency**.

Eventual Consistency

Under the eventual consistency model, there is an eventual guarantee that each replica will be in the same state if there are no more updates. However, this implies that there is no timing guarantee because updates may never stop. Therefore, this is not quite a reliable model. Another stronger scheme is called strong eventual consistency which has two properties. Firstly, updates applied to one honest replica are eventually applied to every nonfaulty replica. Secondly, regardless of the order in which the updates have been processed, if two replicas have processed the same set of updates, they end up in the same state. The first property is called eventual delivery, whereas the second property is named convergence.

There are several advantages of this approach. It allows replicas to progress without network connectivity until the connectivity is restored, and eventually replicas converge to the same state. Eventual consistency can work with weaker models of broadcast, instead of total order broadcast.

Eventual consistency has several categories such as last write wins. The technique here is to apply updates with the most recent timestamp and discard any other updates writing to the same key (updating the same data) with lower timestamps. This means that we accept some data loss in favor of eventually converging state at all replicas.

SMR Using Weaker Broadcast Abstractions

SMR makes use of total order broadcast for achieving a global order of commands in the system. Here, the question arises whether we can use weaker types of broadcast abstractions to build state machine replication. The answer is yes; however, a property called "commutativity" is required along with some other properties. Updates are commutative if the order of two updates does not matter, for example, in arithmetic, $A + B = B + A$, the order of A and B doesn't matter; it will achieve the same result. Similarly, we say that commands x and y commute, if in every state s of the state machine executing x before y or y executing before x results in the same state update and x and y returns the same response when executed. In this, we say x and y commute.

The key insight here is that if replica state updates are commutative, then replicas can process the commands in any order and still would end up in the same state. Of course, you must build commutative mechanics into the protocol. Table 3-1 shows different broadcasts and relevant properties along with assumptions regarding a state update.[1]

---

[1] This table has been adapted from wonderful lectures on distributed computing by Dr. Martin Kleppmann.

Table 3-1. *Broadcasts and requirements to build replication*

Type of Broadcast	Key Property	State Update Requirement
Total order	All messages delivered in the same order at all replicas	Deterministic
Causal broadcast	Delivers messages in causal order, but concurrent messages could be delivered in any order	Deterministic, concurrent updates commutativity
Reliable broadcast	No ordering guarantee with no duplicate messages	Deterministic, all updates commutativity
Best-effort broadcast	Best effort, no delivery guarantee	Deterministic, commutative, idempotent, and tolerates message loss

Now let's explore some fundamental results in distributed computing which underpins distributed protocols and algorithms.

Fundamental Results

In distributed computing, there are many fundamental results that have been reported by researchers. These fundamental results provide the foundation on which the distributed computing paradigm stands. Most interesting of these are impossibility results.

Impossibility Results

Impossibility results provide us an understanding of whether a problem is solvable or not and the minimum resources required to do so. If a problem is unsolvable, then these results provide a clear understanding why a specific problem is unsolvable. If an impossibility result is proven, then no further research is necessary on that, and researchers can focus their attention on other problems or to circumvent these results somehow. These results show us that certain problems are unsolvable unless sufficient resources are provided. In other words, they show that certain problems cannot be computed if resources are insufficient. There are problems that are outright unsolvable, and some are solvable only if given enough resources. The requirement of minimum available resources to solve a problem is known as **lower bound results**.

In order to prove that some problems cannot be solved, it is essential to define a system model and the class of allowable algorithms. Some problems are solvable under one model but not in others. For example, consensus is unsolvable under asynchronous network assumptions but is solvable under synchronous and in partially synchronous networks.

One of the most fundamental results in distributed computing is how many nodes/processes are required to tolerate crash only and Byzantine faults.

Minimum Number of Processes

It has been proven that a certain minimum number of processes is required to solve consensus. If there is no failure, then consensus (agreement) is achievable in both synchronous and asynchronous models. Consensus is not possible in asynchronous systems, but in synchronous systems under a crash failure model and Byzantine failure model, consensus can be achieved. However, there is a lower bound on the ratio of fault processes. Consensus can only be achieved if less than one-third of the processors are Byzantine.

Lamport showed that when faulty nodes do not exceed one-third, then honest nodes can always reach consensus.

Crash Failure

To achieve crash fault tolerance, the tight lower bound is $N => 2F + 1$, where F is the number of failed nodes. This means that a minimum of three processes are required, if one crash-fails to achieve crash fault tolerance. Consensus is impossible to solve if $n <= 2f$ in crash fault–tolerant settings.

Byzantine Failure

To achieve Byzantine fault tolerance, the tight lower bound is $N >= 3F + 1$, where F is the number of failed nodes. This means that a minimum of four nodes are required, if one fails arbitrarily to achieve Byzantine fault tolerance.

No algorithm can solve a consensus problem if $n<=3f$, where n are nodes and f are Byzantine nodes. There is a proven tight lower bound of $3F+1$ on the number of faulty processors.

Minimum Connectivity

The minimum network connectivity to tolerate failures is at least 2f+1.

Minimum Rounds

The minimum number of rounds required is f+1, where f can fail. This is because one round more than the number of failures ought to have one round failure-free, thus allowing consensus.

FLP Impossibility

The FLP impossibility result states that it is impossible to solve consensus deterministically in a message-passing asynchronous system in which at most one process may fail by crashing. In other words, in a system comprising n nodes with unbounded delays there is no algorithm that can solve consensus. Either there will be executions in which no agreement is achieved or there will be an execution which does not terminate (infinite execution).

The key issue on which the FLP impossibility result is based is that in an asynchronous system, it is impossible to differentiate between a crashed process and a process that is simply slow or has sent a message on a slow link, and it's just taking time to reach the recipient.

FLP is one of the most fundamental unsolvability results in distributed computing. FLP is named after the authors MICHAEL J. FISCHER, NANCY A. LYNCH AND MICHAEL S. PATERSON who reported this result in 1982 in their paper "Impossibility of Distributed Consensus with One Faulty Process."

A configuration of global state C is univalent if all executions starting from C output the same value, that is, there is only one possible output. The configuration is 0-valent if it results in deciding 0 and 1-valent if it results in deciding 1. A configuration of global state C is bivalent if there are two executions starting from C that output different values.

We can visualize this in Figure 3-14.

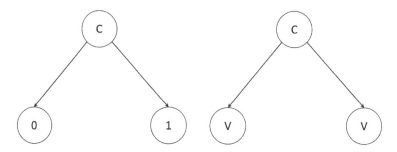

Figure 3-14. *Univalent and bivalent configuration*

The key idea behind FLP is that a bivalent configuration can always transition to some bivalent configuration. As there is an initial bivalent configuration, it follows that there is a nonterminating execution, leading to only bivalent configurations.

We can understand this through a scenario. Suppose you have two different sets of nodes, say set A and set B, each with five nodes. In a five-node network with no failures, the majority (i.e., three out of five) in each set will lead to the consensus. Suppose that in set A the five nodes have a proposed value of 1 {11111}, then we know that in an honest environment the decision will be value 1 by all nodes. Similarly in set B, if the initial value is 0 at all nodes {00000}, then all nodes will agree to the value 0 in a fault-free environment. We can say the configuration, that is, global state, is 1-valent and 0-valent in set A and set B, respectively. However, now imagine a situation where not all nodes are 0 or 1, but some are 0 and some have a value of 1. Imagine in set A, three nodes are 1, and two have a value of 0, that is, {11100}. Similarly in set B, two nodes are 1 and three nodes are holding value 0, that is, {11000}. Note that these sets now only have one difference of a single node with value 1 in set A and value 0 in set B, that is, the middle node (third element) in the set. Consensus of 1 is reached in set A due to three out of five majority, whereas consensus 0 is reached in set B due to three out of five majority. Let's call these two sets, configurations or global states. So now we have two configurations, one reaching consensus of 1 and the other 0. So far so good, but imagine now that one node fails, and it is that middle node which is the only difference between these two sets.

If the middle node is failed from both sets A and B, they become {1100} each, which means that both sets are now indistinguishable from each other implying that they both can reach the same consensus of either 0 or 1 depending on the availability of the third element (middle node). This also means that one of these sets can reach both consensus decisions, 0 or 1, depending on the availability of node 3.

Now imagine that the default value of all nodes is 0, and now with a failed (removed) node, set A {11100} will end up reaching consensus of 0 if the middle node is failed, and it will have consensus of 1 if no node fails. This is an ambiguous situation, called a bivalent configuration where consensus 0 is reached if the middle node holding value 1 is unavailable but will reach consensus of 1 if no node fails. The situation is now that sets (nodes) can reach consensus of either 0 or 1 and the outcome is unpredictable.

It is proven that this ambiguous situation of bivalent initial configuration can always exist in case of even a single failure, and secondly it can always lead to another ambiguous situation. In other words, an initial bivalent configuration can always transition to another bivalent configuration, hence the impossibility of consensus as no convergence on a univalent (either 0-valent or 1-valent) is possible.

There are two observations which lead to FLP impossibility results. First, there always exists at least one bivalent initial configuration in any consensus algorithm working in the presence of faults. Second, a bivalent configuration can always transition to another bivalent configuration.

The FLP result concludes that in asynchronous systems, first there is a global state (configuration) where the algorithm cannot decide, and there always will be a scenario where the system is inconclusive. In other words, there is always an admissible run which always remains in an indecisive state under asynchrony.

State machine replication under asynchrony is also prone to FLP impossibility limitation. Blockchain networks are also subject to FLP impossibility results. Bitcoin, Ethereum, and other blockchain networks would have not been possible to build if FLP impossibility wasn't circumvented by introducing some level of synchrony.

Many efforts have been proposed to somehow circumvent the FLP impossibility. This circumvention revolves around the use of oracles. The idea is to make an oracle available to the distributed system to help solve a problem. An **oracle** can be defined as a service or a black box that processes (nodes) can query to get some information to help them decide a course of action. In the following, we introduce some common oracles that provide enough information to distributed algorithms to solve a problem, which might be unsolvable otherwise. We can use oracles to facilitate solving consensus problems in distributed systems.

The key ideas behind the circumvention of FLP impossibility are based around sacrificing asynchrony and determinism. Of course, as we have learned, deterministic consensus is not possible under asynchrony even if one process crash-fails; therefore, the trick is to slightly sacrifice either asynchrony or determinism, just enough to get to a point to reach a decision and terminate.

151

Now we discuss some techniques:

- Random oracles

- Failure detectors

- Synchrony assumptions

- Hybrid models

Synchrony Assumptions

Under the synchrony assumption, assumptions about timing are introduced in the model. Remember, we discussed partial synchrony earlier in this chapter and the first chapter. Partial synchrony is a technique that allows solving consensus by circumventing FLP impossibility. Under the partial synchrony model, asynchrony is somewhat forfeited to introduce some timing assumptions that allow for solving the consensus problem. Similarly, under the eventual synchrony model, assumptions are made that the system is eventually synchronous after an unknown time called global stabilization time (GST). Another timing assumption is the weak synchrony which assumes that the delays remain under a certain threshold and do not grow forever. Such timing assumptions allow a consensus algorithm to decide and terminate by assuming some notion of time (synchrony).

Random Oracles

Random oracles allow for the development of randomized algorithms. This is where determinism is somewhat sacrificed in favor of reaching an agreement probabilistically. The advantage of this approach is that there are no assumptions made about timing, but the downside is that randomized algorithms are not very efficient. In randomized consensus algorithms, one of the safety or liveness properties is changed to a nondeterministic probabilistic version. For example, the liveness property becomes

- **Liveness**: Each correct process eventually decides with high probability.

This addresses FLP impossibility in the sense that FLP impossibility means in practice that there are executions in the consensus that do not terminate. If the termination is made probabilistic, it can "circumvent" the impossibility of consensus:

- **Agreement**: All correct processes eventually agree on a value with probability 1.

Usually, however, the liveness property is made probabilistic instead of safety properties of agreement, validity, and integrity. Sacrificing a safety property in favor of a liveness (termination) property is usually not advisable.

The core technique in randomized algorithms is something known as "coin flip." Coin tossing or coin flips can be divided into two types.

A local coin is where the state of the processor advances from the current state to the next, which is chosen as per the probability distribution of the algorithm. This is usually implemented as a random bit generator, which returns zero or one (head or tail) with equal probability.

Shared coin or global coin algorithms make use of these local coins to build a global coin. The requirement here is to provide the same coin value to all honest processes and achieve an agreement.

Local coin algorithms terminate in an exponential number of communication steps, whereas shared coin algorithms terminate in a constant number of steps.

There are pros and cons of sacrificing determinism and employing randomization. One of the key advantages is that there are no timing assumptions required. However, the downside is that the number of rounds is considerably higher, and cryptography required to introduce randomization could be computationally expensive.

Randomized algorithms for Byzantine consensus first appeared in Ben-Or and Rabin's work in 1983, which we will discuss along with some others in Chapter 6.

Hybrid Models

In a hybrid model approach to circumvent FLP impossibility, a combination of randomization and failure detectors is used.

Wormholes are extensions in a system model with stronger properties as compared to other parts of the system. Usually, it is a secure, tamper-proof, and fail-silent trusted hardware which provides a way for processes to correctly execute some crucial steps of the protocol. Various wormholes have been introduced in the literature such as attested append-only memory, which forces replicas to commit to a verifiable sequence of operations. The trusted timely computing base (TTCB) was the first wormhole introduced for consensus supported by wormholes.

Failure Detectors

This intuition behind failure detectors is that if somehow we can get a hint about the failure of a process, then we can circumvent FLP impossibility. Remember the FLP impossibility result suggests that it is impossible to distinguish between a crashed process and simply a very slow one. There is no way to find out, so if somehow we can get an indication that some process has failed, then it would be easier to handle the situation. In this setting, asynchrony is somewhat sacrificed because failure detectors work based on heartbeats and timeout assumptions. Failure detectors are added as an extension to the asynchronous systems.

A failure detector can be defined as a distributed oracle at each process that gives hints about (suspects) whether a process is alive or has crashed. In a way, failure detectors encapsulate timeout and partial synchrony assumptions as a separate module. There are two categories of properties that define failure detectors:

- **Completeness** implies that a failure detector will eventually detect faulty processes. This is a liveness property.

- **Accuracy** implies that a failure detector will never suspect a correct process as failed. This is a safety property.

Based on the preceding two properties, eight classes of failure detectors have been proposed by Chandra and Toueg in their seminal paper "Unreliable Failure Detectors for Reliable Distributed Systems." It is also possible to solve consensus by introducing a weak unreliable failure detector. This work was also proposed by Chandra and Toueg.

The ability of a failure detector to accurately suspect failure or liveness depends on the system model. A failure detector is usually implemented using a heartbeat mechanism where heartbeat messages are exchanged between processes, and if these messages are not received by some processes for some time, then failure can be suspected. Another method is to implement a timeout mechanism which is based on worst-case message round-trip time. If a message is not received by a process in the expected timeframe, then timeout occurs, and the process is suspected failed. After this, if a message is received from the suspected process, then the timeout value is increased, and the process is no longer suspected failed. A failure detector using a heartbeat mechanism is shown in Figure 3-15.

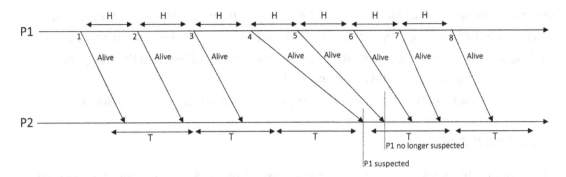

Figure 3-15. *Failure detector using heartbeats*

In Figure 3-15, process P1 sends a regular heartbeat message "Alive" to process P2. There are two parameters in the failure detector: a heartbeat interval H and a timeout value T. Process P1 is suspected if P2 does not receive any heartbeat messages from P1 for a time period longer than T. In the diagram, message 4 did not arrive within the timeout value T; therefore, P2 now suspects P1 of failure, due to timeout. If P2 starts to receive any message (either heartbeat or any other protocol, application message) from P1, then P2 no longer suspects process P1. This is shown from message 5 onward in the diagram. Timer T starts again (resets) as soon as P2 receives a message from P1.

Failure detectors are practical only under synchronous and partially synchronous system models. In asynchronous systems, failure detectors cannot achieve completeness and accuracy at the same time. However, we may achieve completeness independently by immediately (and naively) suspecting all processes have crashed. After that, if some process fails, then the suspicion will be true, fulfilling the completeness property. Similarly, accuracy can be achieved by just not suspecting any processes, which of course is quite useless, but presumably achieves accuracy. In other words, perfect failure detectors are possible in synchronous systems, whereas no perfect failure detector is possible in asynchronous systems. In a way, we encapsulate partial synchrony and timeouts in failure detectors to achieve failure detection capability in our system.

Another advantage of failure detectors is that all the timeout mechanics are localized within the failure detector module, and the program is free to perform other tasks. In the case where no failure detector module is present, the program ends up waiting infinitely long for an expected incoming message from a crashed process. We can understand this with a comparison. For example, a blocking receive operation *"Wait for message m from process p"* becomes *(wait for message m from process p) or (suspect p of failure)*. Now you can see the blocking program becomes nonblocking, and there is now no infinite waiting; if the p is suspected, then it's added to the suspected list, and the program continues its operation, whatever that might be.

Now let's look at the properties of strong and weak completeness and accuracy.

Strong Completeness

This property requires that eventually every crashed process is permanently suspected by every correct process.

Weak Completeness

The property requires that eventually each crashed process is permanently suspected by some correct process.

Strong Accuracy

This property denotes that a process is never suspected until it crashes (before it crashes) by any correct process.

Weak Accuracy

This property describes that some correct process is never suspected by any correct process.

Eventual Strong Accuracy

This property suggests that after some time, correct processes do not suspect any correct processes any longer.

Eventual Weak Accuracy

This property implies that after some time, some correct process is not suspected anymore by any correct process.

We can visualize strong and weak completeness in the diagram shown in Figure 3-16.

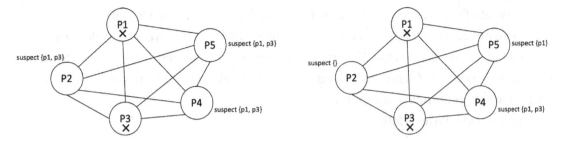

Figure 3-16. *Strong completeness vs. weak completeness*

Now we discuss eight classes of failure detectors. There are four classes of failure detectors which provide strong completeness. The first two failure detectors work under synchronous systems, namely, perfect detector P and strong detector S. The other two work under partially synchronous models, namely, eventually perfect detector (diamond P) and eventually strong detector (diamond S).

We describe these classes now, first with strong completeness.

Perfect Failure Detector P

This type of failure detector satisfies strong completeness and strong accuracy properties. P cannot be implemented in asynchronous systems. This is because strong completeness and accuracy cannot be achieved for P in asynchronous systems.

Strong Failure Detector S

This failure detector has weak accuracy and strong completeness.

Eventually Perfect Failure Detector – Diamond P

This class of FDs satisfies strong completeness and eventual strong accuracy.

Eventually Strong Failure Detector – Diamond S

This class of FDs satisfies strong completeness and eventual weak accuracy.

There are also four classes of failure detectors which provide weak completeness. Detector Q and weak detector W work under synchronous models. Two other detectors, eventually detector Q (diamond Q) and eventually weak detector (diamond W), work under partial synchrony assumptions.

We describe these as follows.

Weak Failure Detector W

This type satisfies weak completeness and weak accuracy properties.

Eventually Weak Failure Detector (Diamond W)

This type satisfies weak completeness and eventual weak accuracy properties.

Detector Q or V

This type satisfies weak completeness and strong accuracy.

Eventually Detector Q (Diamond Q) or Diamond V

This type satisfies weak completeness and eventual strong accuracy.

Figure 3-17 shows all this in summary.

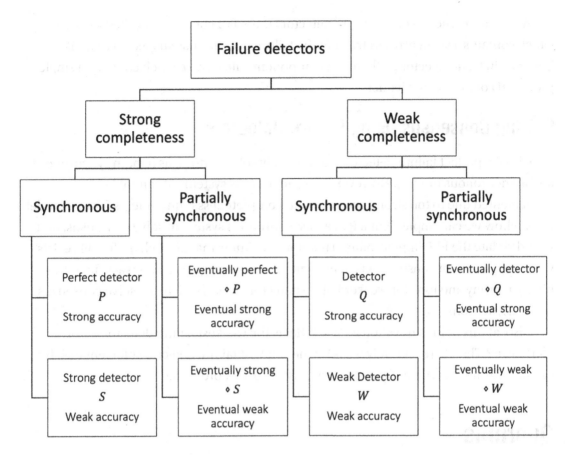

Figure 3-17. *Failure detector classes*

The properties of failure detectors fundamentally revolve around the idea of how fast and correctly a failure detector detects faults while avoiding false positives. A perfect failure detector will always correctly detect failed processes, whereas a weak failure detector may only be able to detect very few or almost no faults accurately.

Leader Elector Failure Detector

Sometimes, we are not interested in finding out if processes have failed but just that if a single process is correct. In this approach of failure detection, instead of suspecting other processes a single process is considered a leader. This failure detector can be seen as a leader election algorithm called the Omega Ω failure detector. Initially, the leader elector can be unreliable and may elect a faulty process or can cause different processes to trust different leaders. We can define this FD as a failure detector where eventually every nonfaulty process elects the same nonfaulty leader process.

As we saw earlier, in other failure detectors there is a component called *suspect* which contains a set of process IDs that the failure detector has suspected as faulty; however, in leader elector Ω, there is a component called *trust* which contains a single process ID of the elected leader.

Solving Consensus Using Failure Detectors

If we have a perfect failure detector, we can easily solve consensus in both synchronous and asynchronous models. However, in asynchronous systems, P cannot be implemented due to too strong accuracy and completeness requirements for this model. If somehow we can implement a P in an asynchronous system to solve consensus, that would violate the FLP impossibility. Therefore, we know that no such perfect FD exists which can solve consensus in a purely asynchronous system. We must sacrifice a little bit asynchrony and look for weaker failure detector classes which can solve consensus under asynchrony.

Also, at this point a question arises: What is the weakest failure detector to solve consensus? The $\diamond W$ (eventually weak) is the weakest failure detector sufficient to solve consensus under asynchrony with a majority of correct processes.

Quorums

A quorum can be defined as any set of majority of processes. The concept is related to voting among a set of objects. Quorum systems are important to ensuring the consistency, availability, efficiency, and fault tolerance in replicated systems.

A quorum can also be thought of as a set of minimum number of processes (votes) required to decide about an operation in a distributed system. A quorum-based methodology ensures consistency in a distributed system. We just learned under the "Replication" section that replication allows to build a fault-tolerant consistent distributed system. Here, the question arises about how many replicas are required to decide to finally commit an update or abort.

Mathematically, a quorum is defined as follows:

A quorum is a non-empty subset of $\pi = \{1, 2, 3, \ldots n\}$.

A quorum system is defined as a set Q of non-empty subsets of π which satisfies the following property:

Quorum intersection: $\forall A, B \in Q : A \cap B \neq \phi$

This means that any two quorums must intersect at one or more processes. This is also known as the pigeonhole principle. Moreover, this is called the **consistency** property.

There must always be at least one quorum available that is not failed. This is the **quorum availability** property.

Quorum systems are usually used in scenarios where a process, after broadcasting its request, awaits until it has received a response from all processes that belong to a quorum. This way, we can address the consistency requirements of a problem. Quorums are usually used to achieve crash and Byzantine fault tolerance. In consensus algorithms, for example, a certain size of a quorum is needed to guarantee safety and liveness. In other words, algorithms based on quorums satisfy safety and liveness only if a quorum of correct processes can be established.

Crash Fault–Tolerant Quorums

To achieve crash fault tolerance in N number of crash-stop processes, Quorum Q is set with at least $\left\lfloor \dfrac{n}{2} \right\rfloor + 1$ processes.
For example, if n = 7, then $\left\lfloor \dfrac{7}{2} \right\rfloor + 1 = \lfloor 3.5 \rfloor + 1 = 3 + 1 = 4$

This means that in a network of seven nodes, at least four nodes (a quorum of four nodes) should be nonfaulty and available to achieve crash fault tolerance.

For example, if you have n replicas, out of which f may crash-stop, what Quorum Q size is required to achieve liveness?

For liveness, there must be a nonfaulty Quorum Q available where Q <= n – f.

For safety, there must be any two quorums that must intersect at one or more processes.

Lamport used quorums under the name of amoeba in 1978.

Byzantine Quorums

Byzantine failures are difficult to handle. Imagine if there are N nodes, out of which f number of nodes turn Byzantine. Now these f nodes can behave arbitrarily, and there can be a case where they can vote in favor of a value and against it. They can make different statements to different nodes on purpose. Such a situation can cause even correct nodes to have divergent states and can also lead to dead locks.

A Byzantine quorum that can tolerate f faults has more than $(n + f)/2$ processes. There is always an intersection of at least one correct process between two Byzantine fault–tolerating quorums. The progress is guaranteed in Byzantine settings if $N > 3f$. In other words, Byzantine fault tolerance requires that $f < n/3$.

For example:

$$n = 7, f = 1$$

$$(n + f)/2$$

$$(7 + 1)/2 = 4$$

$$ceiling\ (7 + 1 + 1/2) = 4$$

Each Byzantine quorum contains more than $n - f/2$ honest processes. $7 - 1/2 = > 3$, so there is at least one correct process in the intersection of two Byzantine quorums.

Read and Write Quorums

Quorum-based protocols fundamentally rely on voting to determine whether a read or write operation can be performed or not. There are read quorums and write quorums. A read quorum is the minimum number of replicas required to achieve an agreement on a read operation. Similarly, a write quorum is the minimum number of replicas required to achieve an agreement on a write operation.

Where Are We Now

Based on the last more than 40 years of research in classical distributed consensus and modern blockchain era protocols, we can divide consensus into two broad families.

Classical Consensus

Classical consensus or traditional distributed consensus has been a topic of research for around 40 years now. Starting with the SIFT project and Lamport's and many other researchers' contributions, we now have a large body of work that deals with the classical distributed consensus. Protocols such as Paxos, PBFT, and RAFT are now a norm for implementation in various practical systems.

Nakamoto and Post-Nakamoto Consensus

On the other hand, we have a family of protocols which we can call the Nakamoto consensus family as this family was introduced for the first time by Satoshi Nakamoto, with Bitcoin.

From a blockchain perspective, both traditional and Nakamoto-style protocols are in use. Almost all the permissioned blockchains use variants of PBFT classical algorithms. On the other hand, permissionless public blockchains like Ethereum and Bitcoin make use of Nakamoto-style (PoW) consensus algorithms. There are other classes such as proof of stake and other variants, but they all were introduced after the introduction of Bitcoin's proof of work in 2008.

We will cover Nakamoto and post-Nakamoto-style algorithms in detail in Chapter 4.

Summary

In this chapter, we covered the main concepts of agreement, broadcast, replication, and consensus:

- Consensus is a fundamental problem in distributed computing.

- Consensus and atomic broadcast are equivalent problems. If you solve one, the other is solved too.

- There are several broadcast primitives such as best-effort broadcast, reliable broadcast, eager reliable broadcast, and total order broadcast with varying degrees of strictness regarding the delivery guarantees.

- There are also probabilistic broadcast protocols that deliver messages with some high probability inspired by dissemination of gossip among the public.

- Replication and state machine replication are techniques to provide fault tolerance in distributed systems.

- Quorum systems are important for ensuring the consistency, availability, efficiency, and fault tolerance in replicated systems.

- The last half century of research has produced two main classes of consensus, that is, classical permissioned consensus and Nakamoto nonpermissioned consensus.

- Various impossibility results have been proven in the last many decades of research by researchers. Results such as FLP impossibility, requirement of a minimum number of processes, and network links have been proposed and proven. These fundamental results allow researchers to focus on other problems because if something has been proven impossible, there is no value in spending time and effort on trying to solve it.

- Other research includes failure detectors which provide a means to detect failures in a distributed system and allow processes to respond accordingly to make progress. Augmenting a distributed system with oracles such as failure detectors, synchrony assumptions, randomized protocols, and hybrid protocols is a means to circumvent the FLP impossibility result.

In the next chapter, we will cover blockchain and describe what it is and how we can see it in the light of what we have learned so far in this book.

Bibliography

1. Chandra, T.D. and Toueg, S., 1996. Unreliable failure detectors for reliable distributed systems. Journal of the ACM (JACM), 43(2), pp. 225–267.

2. Ordering of events first introduced in "The Implementation of Reliable Distributed Multiprocess Systems" – Lamport, L., 1978. The implementation of reliable distributed multiprocess systems. *Computer Networks (1976)*, 2(2), pp. 95–114.

3. Pease, M., Shostak, R., and Lamport, L., 1980. Reaching agreement
    in the presence of faults. Journal of the ACM (JACM), 27(2),
    pp. 228–234.

4. Kshemkalyani, A.D. and Singhal, M., 2011. Distributed computing:
    principles, algorithms, and systems. Cambridge University Press.

5. What is the weakest failure detector to solve consensus? This
    question was answered in Chandra, T.D., Hadzilacos, V.,
    and Toueg, S., 1996. The weakest failure detector for solving
    consensus. Journal of the ACM (JACM), 43(4), pp. 685–722.

6. Wormholes were introduced in Neves, N.F., Correia, M., and
    Verissimo, P., 2005. Solving vector consensus with a wormhole.
    IEEE Transactions on Parallel and Distributed Systems, 16(12),
    pp. 1120–1131.

7. An excellent survey is Correia, M., Veronese, G.S., Neves, N.F.,
    and Verissimo, P., 2011. Byzantine consensus in asynchronous
    message-passing systems: a survey. International Journal of
    Critical Computer-Based Systems, 2(2), pp. 141–161.

CHAPTER 4

Blockchain

In this chapter, we'll learn what a blockchain is and its various elements and see the blockchain through the lens of distributed computing. Also, we will present formal definitions and properties of the blockchain. In addition, we will also introduce Bitcoin and Ethereum. Finally, I will introduce some blockchain use cases.

Blockchains are fascinating because they touch many disciplines, including distributed computing, networking, cryptography, economics, game theory, programming languages, and computer science.

Blockchains are appealing to people from so many different areas, including but not limited to the subjects mentioned earlier. With use cases in almost every walk of life, blockchains have captured the public's imagination and, indeed, many academics and industry professionals.

The blockchain emerged in 2008 with Bitcoin, a peer-to-peer, decentralized, electronic cash scheme that does not need any trusted third party to provide trust guarantees associated with money.

What Is Blockchain

There are many definitions of a blockchain on the Internet and many different books. While all those definitions are correct, and some are excellent, I will try to define the blockchain in my own words.

First, we'll define it from a layman's perspective and then from a purely technical standpoint.

Layman's Definition

A blockchain is a shared record-keeping system where each participant keeps a copy of the chronologically ordered records. Participants can add new records only if they collectively agree to do so.

© Imran Bashir 2022
I. Bashir, *Blockchain Consensus*, https://doi.org/10.1007/978-1-4842-8179-6_4

Technical Definition

A blockchain is a peer-to-peer, cryptographically secure, append-only, immutable, and tamper-resistant shared distributed ledger composed of temporally ordered and publicly verifiable transactions. Users can only add new records (transactions and blocks) in a blockchain through consensus among peers on the network.

Background

The origins of the blockchain can be found in early systems developed for the digital timestamping of documents. Also, the long-standing problem of creating secure electronic cash with desirable features such as anonymity and accountability has inspired blockchain development.

Some of the key ideas that contributed to the development of the blockchain are discussed as follows.

Two fundamental issues need to be dealt with to create practical digital cash:

- Accountability to prevent double-spends

- Anonymity to provide privacy to the users

The question is how to resolve accountability and double-spend issues. The schemes described in the following tried to address these issues and managed to achieve these properties; however, the usability was difficult, and they relied on trusted third parties.

Digital Cash Creation Attempts

There are several attempts to create digital cash in the past. For example, David Chaum invented blind signatures and used secret sharing mechanisms to create digital cash. Blind signatures enabled signing without revealing what is being signed, which provided anonymity, and secret sharing allowed detection of double-spending.

B-money is another electronic cash scheme that was invented in 1998 by Wei Dai. This original idea mentions many ideas that can be considered direct precursors to Bitcoin. It was a novel idea; however, it required trusted servers. It also introduced possible solutions to cooperate between untraceable pseudonymous entities with a medium of exchange and a method to enforce contracts. The idea of each server depositing a certain amount in a special account and using this for penalties and rewards is very close to the concept that we know as proof of stake today. Similarly, the idea of solving a previously unsolved computational problem is what we know today as proof of work.

Another electronic cash proposal is **BitGold**, introduced by Nick Szabo. Bitgold can be seen as a direct precursor of Bitcoin. The Bitgold proposal emphasized no dependence on trusted third parties and proof of work by solving a "challenge string."

On the other hand, progress and development in cryptography and computer technology generally resulted in several advances and innovative applications. Some of these advances related to the blockchain are digital timestamping of documents, email spam protection, and reusable proof of work.

The work on timestamping of digital documents to create an ordered chain of documents (hashes) by using a timestamping service was first proposed by Haber and Stornetta. This idea is closely related to the chain of blocks in a blockchain. However, the timestamping service is centralized and needs to be trusted.

The origins of proof of work based on hash functions used in Bitcoin can be found in previous work by Dwork and Naor to use proof of work to thwart email spam. Adam Back invented the Hashcash proof of work scheme for email spam control. Moreover, Hal Finney introduced reusable proof of work for token money, which used Hashcash to mint a new PoW token.

Another technology that contributed to the development of Bitcoin is cryptography. Cryptographic primitives and tools like hash functions, Merkle trees, and public key cryptography all played a vital role in the development of Bitcoin. We covered cryptography in Chapter 2 in detail.

Figure 4-1 illustrates this fusion of different techniques.

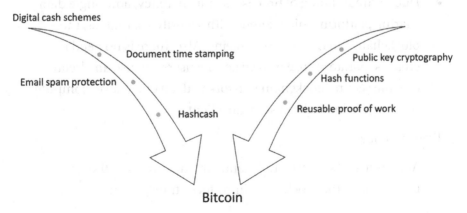

Figure 4-1. Technologies leading to Bitcoin

The First Blockchain?

When Bitcoin was revealed, the blockchain was introduced as a base operating layer for Bitcoin cryptocurrency. Still operational today, this is the first public blockchain. Soon after, the innovation started, and many different blockchains emerged – some for a specific purpose, some for cryptocurrencies, and quite a few for enterprise use cases. In the next section, we will look at different types of blockchain.

Benefits of Blockchain

Multiple benefits of blockchain technology are envisaged, and a lot has been accomplished since the invention of Bitcoin. Especially with the advent of Ethereum, a programmable platform is available where smart contracts can implement any logic, which resulted in increased utility and paved the path for further adoption. Today, one of the most talked-about applications of the blockchain, decentralized finance, or DeFi for short, is seen as a significant disruptor of the current financial system. Non-fungible tokens (NFTs) are another application that has gained explosive popularity. NFTs on the blockchain enable tokenization of assets. Currently, there is almost 60 billion USD worth of value locked in the DeFi ecosystem. This huge investment is a testament that the blockchain has now become part of our economy. You can track this metric at `https://defipulse.com/`.

Now I list some of the most prominent benefits of the blockchain:

- Cost saving

  - Due to streamlining of processes, transparency, and single data sharing platform which comes with security guarantees, the blockchain can result in cost saving. Also, there is no need to create separate secure infrastructure; users can use an already existing secure blockchain network with an entry-level computer running the blockchain software client.

- Transparency

  - As all transactions are public and anyone can verify the transactions, the blockchain introduces transparency.

- Auditability

  - Due to immutable history of records, blockchains provide a natural platform for auditing purposes.

- Speed and efficiency

  - As all parties involved in a transaction are part of the same network, the speed of transaction dealing between multiple parties is increased. However, note that the transactions per second in a public blockchain are quite low, for example, three to seven in Bitcoin; however, in consortium blockchains, it's much better, and with parties directly interacting with each other, it increases the overall efficiency of the transaction.

- Security

  - Blockchains are based on cryptographic protocols which ensure integrity and authenticity of the blockchain, thus providing a secure platform for transactions.

There are many use cases in different industries:

- Supply chain

- Government

- Medicine/health

- Finance

- IoT – Internet of Things

- Trading

- Identity

- Insurance

Next, we discuss the different types of blockchain.

Types of Blockchain

There are several types of blockchains. The original blockchain introduced with Bitcoin is a public blockchain:

- Public blockchain or permissionless blockchain
- Permissioned blockchain
  - Private blockchain
  - Consortium or enterprise blockchain
- Application-specific blockchain
- Heterogeneous multichain

A **public blockchain**, as the name suggests, is a **permissionless blockchain**. There is no restriction on participating in the network. All that is required is to download a software client and run it to become part of the network. Usually, these types of blockchains are used for cryptocurrencies, such as Bitcoin and Ethereum.

There are two types of **permissioned blockchains**. **Private blockchains** are in control of only one organization and are usually run within an organization. On the other hand, **consortium blockchains** or **enterprise blockchains** are permissioned blockchains where multiple organizations participate in the blockchain's governance. Enterprises commonly use consortium chains for specific enterprise use cases.

We can also further classify chains that stakeholders may have only developed for a single purpose. We can call them **application-specific blockchains**. For example, a blockchain developed only for a single type of cryptocurrency. In a way, Bitcoin is an application-specific blockchain, with only one application, Bitcoin cryptocurrency. Similarly, suppose an organization runs a private blockchain for a specific purpose, such as an audit function. In that case, it can also be classified as an application-specific blockchain, as it has only been developed for a single specific purpose.

However, in practice, blockchains serve as a generic platform that guarantees a consistent, secure, tamper-resistant, and ordered ledger of records, making it suitable for a wide variety of applications. Also, depending on the design, multiple applications can run on a single blockchain. For example, Ethereum can run different programs called smart contracts on it, making it a general-purpose blockchain platform. A blockchain that has been developed for a specific single use case can be called application-specific blockchain, or ASBC for short.

Blockchains are also shared data platforms where multiple organizations can share data in a tamper-resistant manner, ensuring data integrity. However, this sharing can be achieved if there is only one standard blockchain, but many different blockchains have emerged since the advent of Ethereum. This variety has resulted in a problem where one blockchain runs a different protocol and cannot share its data with another blockchain. This disconnect creates a situation where each blockchain is a silo. To solve this issue, the organization that wants to join a consortium network must either use the software client specific to that blockchain or somehow devise a complex interoperability mechanism. This problem is well understood, and a lot of work is underway regarding novel interoperability protocols. Also, new types of blockchains, such as **heterogeneous multichains** and sharding-based approaches, are emerging. One prime example is Polkadot, a replicated sharded state machine where heterogenous chains can talk to each other through a so-called relay chain. Another effort is Ethereum 2.0, where sharded chains serve as a mechanism to provide scalability and cross-shard interoperability. Cardano is another blockchain that is on course to provide scalability and interoperability between chains. With all these platforms and the pace of the work in progress to realize these ideas, we can envisage that in the next eight to ten years, these blockchains and others will be running just like we have the Internet today with seamless data sharing between different chains. The chains that facilitate such a level of natural interoperability, giving rise to an ecosystem of multiple interoperating, general-purpose enterprise chains and ASBCs, are called **heterogeneous multichains**.

Now let's clarify an ambiguity. You might have heard the term "distributed ledger," which is sometimes used to represent a blockchain. While both terms, blockchain and distributed ledger, are used interchangeably, there's a difference. The distributed ledger is an overarching term describing a ledger with distributed properties. Blockchains fall under this umbrella. A blockchain is a distributed ledger, but not all distributed ledgers are a blockchain. For example, some distributed ledgers do not use blocks composed of transactions in their blockchain construction. Instead, they treat transaction records individually and store them as such. Usually, however, in most distributed ledgers, blocks are used as containers for a batch of transactions and several other elements such as block header, which also contains several components. Such use of blocks to bundle transactions makes them a blockchain.

Blockchain Is a Distributed System

A blockchain is a distributed system. As such, it should be defined and reasoned about in the light of distributed computing. Furthermore, this formal description allows for better reasoning.

We discussed the CAP theorem in Chapter 1. Therefore, we can analyze the blockchain through the CAP theorem to ascertain what type of system it is.

CAP and Permissionless Blockchain

Permissionless blockchains are AP (availability and partition tolerance) blockchains because consistency is somewhat sacrificed in favor of availability. We could argue that eventual consistency is achieved, but as consistency (agreement) is sacrificed in favor of availability, we can say that permissionless or public blockchains are AP systems. For example, Ethereum and Bitcoin are AP systems. This is the case due to the proof of work (PoW) type of probabilistic consensus.

CAP and Permissioned Blockchain

Permissioned blockchains are CP (consistency and partition tolerance) systems because availability is sacrificed in favor of consistency. This is the case because almost all permissioned blockchains use traditional BFT protocols, where if a threshold of nodes is faulty, then the whole system stalls until the faults are resolved, and then the system continues to operate. For example, in a five-node network, if three nodes go down, the system doesn't progress unless the other nodes come back online. Similarly, in the case of partitioning between subsets of two and three nodes, the system doesn't make progress unless the partition heals. This is the case due to the use of traditional BFT algorithms, such as PBFT. The requests coming from the clients are processed only if there's a majority of honest nodes. In other words, if the system falls below 3f+1 in the case of Byzantine fault tolerance, the system immediately degrades to nonfunctional.

We can visualize both these concepts in Figure 4-2.

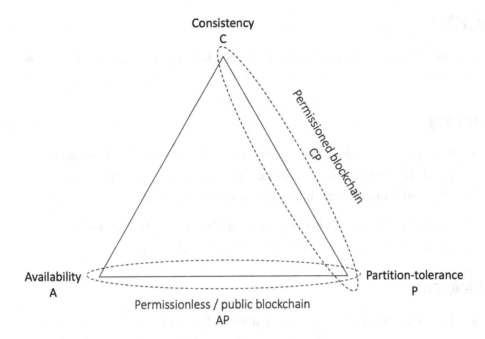

Figure 4-2. *CAP theorem and blockchain*

Next, we describe blockchain ledger abstraction which is an abstract view of a blockchain.

Blockchain Ledger Abstraction

Blockchain abstraction or sometimes called ledger abstraction can be defined with the help of operations it can perform and several properties.

There are at a high level three operations that processes in a blockchain network can perform:

`Get(), append(), verify()`

When `get()` is invoked, it returns a copy of the current canonical state of the blockchain (ledger).

When `append()` is invoked, it creates and appends a new record *r* to the blockchain.

When `verify()` is invoked, it verifies and returns the validity status of the record *r* or blockchain *b*.

Properties

There are several properties associated with a blockchain, which are described as follows.

Consistency

- All replicas hold the same up-to-date copy of the data. In the case of public blockchains, it is usually eventual consistency, and in the case of permissioned blockchains, it is strong consistency.

- Formally, if a record r is seen first by a process p before another record r2, then every honest process sees r before r2.

Fault Tolerant

- Blockchains are fault-tolerant distributed systems. A blockchain network can withstand Byzantine or crash faults up to a threshold.

- In BFT-based blockchains (usually with a PBFT variant implemented in blockchains), the lower bound is $3F + 1$, where F is the number of faults.

- In CFT-based blockchains (usually with RAFT implementation in consortium chains), the lower bound is $2F + 1$, where F is the number of faults.

- In proof of work–based blockchains, it is the <50% of the hash power.

Finality

- Finality occurs when a transaction is considered irrevocable and permanent. This event can be a certain number of blocks, a time interval, or a step (phase) in the execution of a consensus algorithm. For example, in Bitcoin it is usually six blocks after which a transaction is considered irrevocable, and in permissioned blockchains using BFT protocols, the moment the transaction is committed, it is considered irrevocably final.

Immutability

- Blockchains are immutable, which means that once a record has made it to the ledger, it can never be removed.

Append Only

- New records can only be appended to the blockchain. New records cannot be inserted in between previously existing records. For example, a new block can only be added after the last final block, not in between other blocks.

- Formally, if a block b' is inserted after a block b, then a new block b" can only be inserted after b' and not before b' or b.

Tamper Resistant/Proof

- It is practically impossible to remove or rearrange finalized blocks in a blockchain.

- It is arguable whether a blockchain is tamper resistant or tamper-proof, but for all practical purposes, the probability that some adversary can remove or rearrange blocks or transactions becomes almost zero. This guarantee is good enough for all practical purposes.

Validity

- Only valid transactions and blocks are appended to the blockchain

Termination Guarantee of Blockchain Operations: get(), append(), verify()

- Eventually, all the operations will terminate with a result.

Order

- If a block x happens before block y and block y happens before block z, then block x happens before block z and forms a transitive relationship.

- In practice, this is a chronologically ordered chain of blocks.

- It is an ordered ledger.

Verifiable

- All transactions and blocks in a blockchain are verifiable and adhere to a validity predicate specific to the blockchain. Anyone can verify the validity of a transaction.

Consensus-specific properties are discussed in more detail in Chapter 5.

Some other properties include programmability (smart contract support), encrypted ledger and anonymity for confidentiality and user privacy, and unanimity for allowing unanimous decisions on appending new blocks.

A blockchain can also be seen as a state machine replication protocol. A blockchain and a state machine appear to be the same; however, there's a subtle difference. In a state machine, only the latest state is stored in the log, whereas in a blockchain state machine, the entire history is stored and available when queried.

Bitcoin and blockchains have outpaced the growth of the Internet. Thousands of users are using Bitcoin daily. On average, about 200,000 transactions are processed on Bitcoin daily. On Ethereum, roughly more than a million transactions are processed daily, and the interest is growing. Contrary to a reasonable belief held by some, I think it is not correct to say that the Bitcoin experiment has failed. It has accomplished what it set out to achieve, peer-to-peer digital cash. That's what it is and is being used as a digital cash platform today. Bitcoin also stimulated further innovation, and platforms like Ethereum and now the latest blockchains like Polkadot and Cardano have emerged. With such a level of growth, in the next eight to ten years, I believe almost all financial services will run on a blockchain, including some central bank digital currencies.

How Blockchain Works

At times, there are subtle differences in the way a blockchain works at a micro level; however, at a high level all blockchains principally work the same. In the following, I list seven key steps that show how a blockchain works:

1. A transaction occurs between two or more users.

2. The transaction is broadcast to the network.

3. The transaction is validated and added to the transaction pools.

4. A proposed block is created by adding transactions to it by miners.

5. Miners race to solve the proof of work to win the right to insert their block into the blockchain, or a consensus mechanism runs to agree on the transactions. Usually, miners run a proof of work type of consensus mechanism to win the right to add a block. In consortium or private chains, usually a variant of traditional Byzantine or crash fault–tolerant algorithm runs, which by voting achieves the agreement on a block which is then inserted into the blockchain.

6. If a miner wins the right, it inserts the block in its local chain and broadcasts that block to the network.

7. Other nodes accept it if valid, and the process starts again.

This process can be visualized in Figure 4-3.

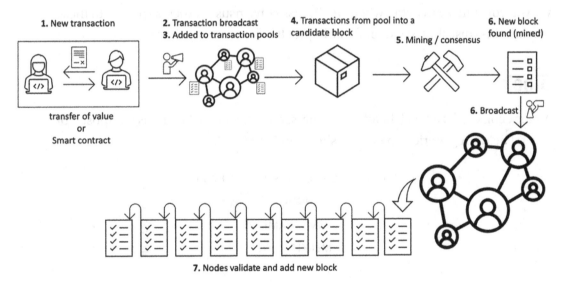

Figure 4-3. *How a blockchain works*

Anatomy of a Blockchain

A blockchain is composed of blocks, where each block is linked to its previous block except the first genesis block. The blockchain term was used by Satoshi Nakamoto in his Bitcoin code for the first time. Even though now it is used as one word, in his original Bitcoin code it was written as two separate words, "block chain." It can be visualized as a chain of blocks, as shown in Figure 4-4.

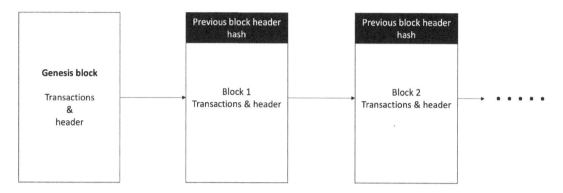

Figure 4-4. *Generic structure of a blockchain*

Other structures such as DAGs, hash graphs, and Merkle trees are now used in some distributed ledgers instead of the usual block-based model in modern blockchains. For example, Avalanche uses DAGs for storage instead of a linear block-based structure. We will cover these in detail when we discuss consensus protocols specific to these blockchains (distributed ledgers) in Chapter 8.

Block

A block consists of a block header and transactions. A block header is composed of several fields. A generic depiction is shown in Figure 4-5.

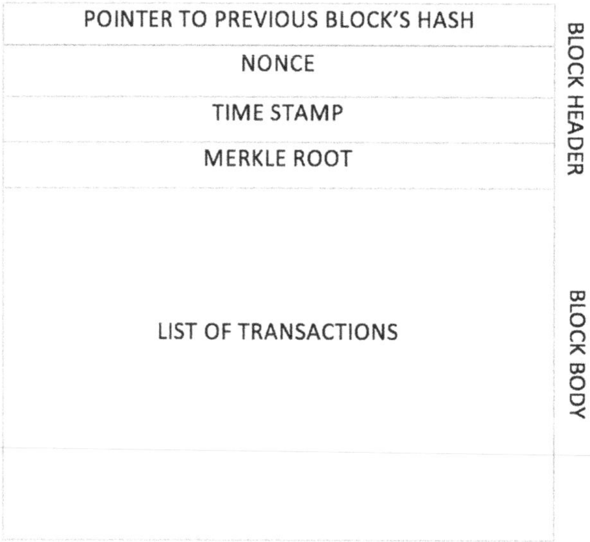

POINTER TO PREVIOUS BLOCK'S HASH	
NONCE	BLOCK HEADER
TIME STAMP	
MERKLE ROOT	
LIST OF TRANSACTIONS	BLOCK BODY

Figure 4-5. *Generic block structure*

Later in this chapter, in the section on blockchains, where I introduce Bitcoin and other blockchains, I will discuss a more detailed design of blocks specific to that blockchain. However, the structure is fundamentally like a block header and transactions, pointing to the previous block by including the hash of the last header block in the current block header, thus creating a verifiable linked list.

Platforms

In this section, we will describe two major blockchain platforms, Bitcoin and Ethereum.

Bitcoin

Bitcoin was invented in 2008 as the first blockchain by Satoshi Nakamoto. However, it is believed to be a pseudonym as the identity of Satoshi Nakamoto is shrouded in mystery. After the introduction of Bitcoin, Satoshi remained active for some time but left the community abruptly. Since then, no contact has been made by him.

We discussed the prehistory and attempts to create digital cash and document timestamping system before in this chapter. In this section, I will jump straight into technical details.

Bitcoin is a peer-to-peer electronic cash system that solved the double-spending problem without requiring a trusted third party. Furthermore, Bitcoin has this fantastic property called "inclusive accountability," which means that anyone on the Bitcoin network can verify claims of possession of electronic cash, that is, the Bitcoin. This property makes Bitcoin a transparent and verifiable electronic cash system.

The Bitcoin network is composed of nodes. There are three types of nodes in a Bitcoin network: miner nodes, full nodes, and light nodes. Miner nodes perform mining and keep a full copy of the chain. Bitcoin is a loosely coupled network composed of nodes. All nodes communicate with each other using a peer-to-peer gossip protocol.

Bitcoin Node and Architecture

In practical terms, a node in a distributed system runs the distributed algorithm. Similarly, in Bitcoin, a node runs the software client called Bitcoin Core. It can run on several types of hardware, including Intel and ARM processors. Also, the supported operating systems are Mac OS, Linux, and Windows.

There are primarily three different types of nodes in the Bitcoin network. Full nodes keep the entire history of the blockchain. Miner nodes keep the whole history and participate in mining to add new blocks to the blockchain. Finally, light nodes do not keep a copy of the entire blockchain. Instead, they only download the block headers and use a method called simple payment verification to validate the authenticity of the transactions. The Bitcoin node architecture is shown in Figure 4-6.

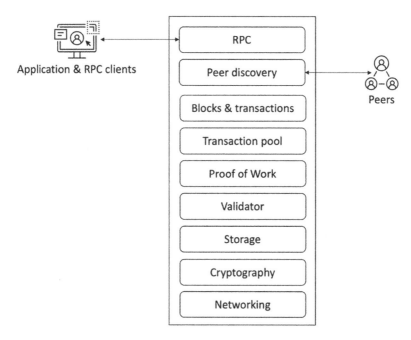

Figure 4-6. *Bitcoin node architecture*

When a node starts up, it discovers other nodes using a process called node discovery. In this process, the node first connects to the seed nodes, which are trusted bootstrap nodes maintained by the core developers. After this initial connection, further connections are made. At one point, there are x connections alive with other peers. There is also spam protection built in the Bitcoin protocol, where a points-based reputation system scores the nodes based on the connection attempts it is trying to make. If a node sends excessive messages to another node, its reputation score goes above a threshold of 100 points, and it gets blocked for 24 hours. The node discovery and handshake between nodes rely on several protocol messages. A list is shown in the following with their explanations. In Figure 4-7, you can visualize how node handshake and message exchange occurs.

Some of the most used protocol messages and an explanation of them are listed as follows:

- **Version:** This is the first message that a node sends out to the network, advertising its version and block count. The remote node then replies with the same information, and the connection is then established.

- **Verack:** This is the response of the version message accepting the connection request.

- **Inv:** This is used by nodes to advertise their knowledge of blocks and transactions.

- **Getdata:** This is a response to inv, requesting a single block or transaction identified by its hash.

- **Getblocks:** This returns an inv packet containing the list of all blocks starting after the last known hash or 500 blocks.

- **Getheaders:** This is used to request block headers in a specified range.

- **Tx:** This is used to send a transaction as a response to the getdata protocol message.

- **Block:** This sends a block in response to the getdata protocol message.

- **Headers:** This packet returns up to 2000 block headers as a reply to the getheaders request.

- **Getaddr:** This is sent as a request to get information about known peers.

- **Addr:** This provides information about nodes on the network. It contains the number of addresses and address list in the form of an IP address and port number.

- **Ping:** This message is used to confirm if the TCP/IP network connection is active.

- **Pong:** This message is the response to a ping message confirming that the network connection is live.

We can see these messages in use in Figure 4-7.

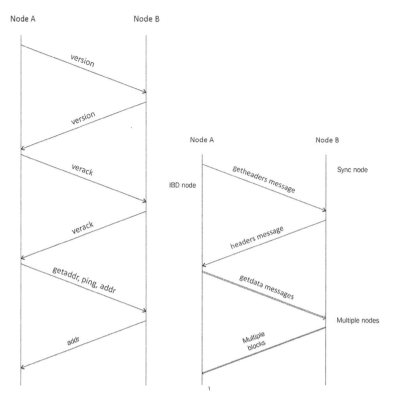

Figure 4-7. *Node discovery and handshake diagram + header and block synchronization*

Cryptography in Bitcoin

Cryptography plays a vital role in the Bitcoin blockchain. The entire security of the Bitcoin blockchain is indeed based on cryptography. Although we discussed cryptography in Chapter 2, I will now describe which cryptographic protocols are used in Bitcoin and how.

Public Keys and Private Keys

Private keys prove the ownership of bitcoins and users use them to authorize a payment by signing the transactions with the private key.

The SHA-256 hash function is used in a proof of work algorithm. There is also a Base58 encoder in the Bitcoin client, which is used to encode the addresses in a readable format in Bitcoin.

Wallets in Bitcoin are used to store cryptographic keys. Wallets sign transactions using private keys. Private keys are generated by randomly choosing a 256-bit number provided by the wallet. A Bitcoin client includes a standard wallet called nondeterministic wallet.

Addresses and Accounts

Users are represented by accounts in Bitcoin. The Bitcoin address generation process is shown in Figure 4-8.

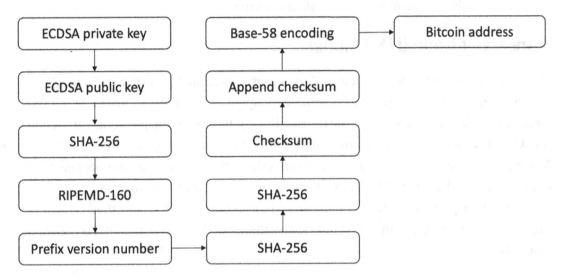

Figure 4-8. *Bitcoin address generation*

1. In the first step, we have a randomly generated ECDSA private key.

2. The public key is derived from the ECDSA private key.

3. The public key is hashed using the SHA-256 cryptographic hash function.

4. The hash generated in step 3 is hashed using the RIPEMD-160 hash function.

5. The version number is prefixed to the RIPEMD-160 hash generated in step 4.

6. The result produced in step 5 is hashed using the SHA-256 cryptographic hash function.

7. SHA-256 is applied again.

8. The first 4 bytes of the result produced from step 7 is the address checksum.

9. This checksum is appended to the RIPEMD-160 hash generated in step 4.

10. The resultant byte string is encoded into a Base58-encoded string by applying the Base58 encoding function.

11. Finally, the result is a typical Bitcoin address.

Transactions and UTXO Model

Transactions are the fundamental unit of operation in Bitcoin. Every transaction is composed of at least one input and output. An unspent transaction output (UTXO) is the basic unit of bitcoin transactions. The transaction inputs refer to the previous transaction's UTXOs. The transaction output represents the transfer of ownership of unspent values. The account balance in bitcoin for an account is the sum of all unspent outputs belonging to that account. Therefore, UTXO always must have equal inputs and outputs.

A bitcoin transaction consumes inputs and creates outputs with specified values. Every input is an output from a previous transaction. This transaction model is shown in Figure 4-9.

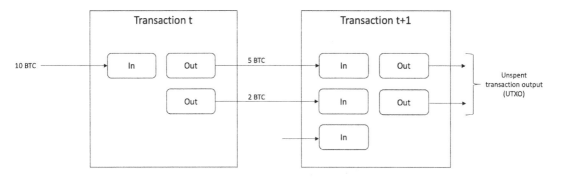

Figure 4-9. *Bitcoin transaction UTXO model*

The Bitcoin transaction life cycle is described as follows:

- A user creates a transaction.

- The transaction is signed by the owner(s) using the private key.

- The transaction is broadcast to the network using the gossip protocol.

- All nodes verify the transaction and place it in their transaction pools.

- Miner nodes bundle up these transactions into a candidate block.

- Mining starts and one of the miners that solves the proof of work problem wins the right to announce its block and earn bitcoins as a reward.

- Once the block is broadcast to the network, it is propagated across the entire Bitcoin network.

- After six confirmations (six blocks), the transaction is considered irrevocably final; however, it is possible to accept transactions even after the first confirmation.

A transaction is made up of several fields. Table 4-1 shows all fields and their description.

Table 4-1. *Bitcoin transaction*

Field	Description	Size
Version no	Currently 1	4 bytes
Flag	Witness data indicator	Optional 2-byte array
In-counter	Number of inputs	1–9 bytes
List of inputs	Inputs	Many inputs
Out-counter	Number of outputs	1–9 bytes
List of outputs	Outputs list	Many outputs
Witnesses	List of witnesses	Variable
lock_time	Block height or timestamp until transaction is pending	4 bytes

Transactions are of two types. On-chain transactions are native to the Bitcoin network, and off-chain transactions are performed outside the blockchain network. On-chain transactions occur on the blockchain network and are validated on-chain by network participants, whereas off-chain transactions use payment channels or sidechains to perform transactions. On-chain transactions are slower, have privacy issues, and are not scalable. Off-chain mechanisms aim to solve these issues. One prime example is the Bitcoin lightning network, which provides faster payments.

Bitcoin Script and Miniscript

A Bitcoin script is a non-Turing complete, stack-based language which is used to describe how bitcoins should be transferred. The scripts are evaluated from left to right in a LIFO stack. Scripts are composed of two components, elements and operations, as shown in Figure 4-10. Elements represent data such as digital signatures, and operations are the actions that are performed by the script. Operations are coded as opcodes. Opcodes include operational categories such as flow control, stack operations, bitwise logical operations, arithmetic, cryptography operations, and lock time.

Some common opcodes are listed as follows:

- **OP_CHECKSIG:** Takes a signature and a public key and verifies the transaction's ECDSA signature. If correct, then 1 is returned, otherwise 0.

- **OP_DUP:** Takes the top item on the stack and duplicates it.

- **OP_HASH160:** Calculates the SHA-256 and then RIPEMD 160-bit hash of the input.

- **OP_EQUAL:** Checks the equality of the top two items on the stack. Outputs TRUE if equal, otherwise FALSE, on the stack.

- **OP_VERIFY:** Checks if the top item on the stack is false; if it is, the script terminates and outputs failure.

- **OP_EQUALVERIFY:** First runs OP_EQUAL and then OP_VERIFY.

- **OP_RETURN:** Terminates the script, outputs fail, and marks the transaction invalid.

- **OP_ADD:** Takes two inputs and performs sum operation.

A script is a combination of a locking script called `ScriptPubKey` and an unlocking script called `ScriptSig`, as shown in Figure 4-10. Outputs are locked by `ScriptPubKey`, which contains the unlocking conditions for the output. In other words, locking means giving bitcoins to someone, and unlocking means consuming the received bitcoins.

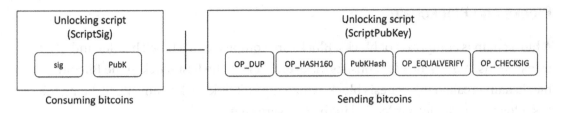

Figure 4-10. *Bitcoin script (unlocking + locking) diagram*

There are several types of scripts in Bitcoin. The most common is Pay-to-Public-Key-Hash (P2PKH), which is used to send a transaction to a bitcoin address. The format of this script is shown as follows:

ScriptPubKey: OP_DUP OP_HASH160 <pubKeyHash> OP_EQUALVERIFY OP_CHECKSIG

ScriptSig: <sig> <pubKey>

Both ScriptPubKey and ScriptSig are combined and executed, as shown in Figure 4-11.

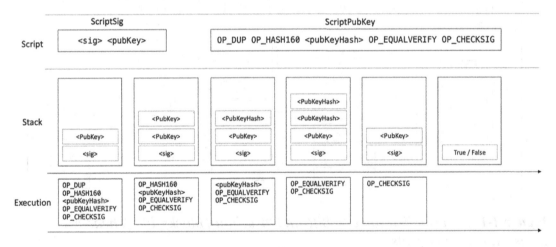

Figure 4-11. *Bitcoin P2PKH script execution*

While the bitcoin script is the original method of transferring payments, and it works well, it is not much flexible. There is a language developed for bitcoin which supports development of smart contracts. The language is called **Ivy**. A solution to make writing scripts easier and in a more structured way is the bitcoin **miniscript**.

Blocks and Blockchain

A blockchain is composed of blocks. Blocks are composed of a block header and transactions. A block header consists of several fields. The first block in the Bitcoin blockchain is called the genesis block, which doesn't link back to any block, being the first block. It is usually hardcoded in the software clients.

We can see a complete visualization of blocks, block headers, transactions, and scripts in Figure 4-12.

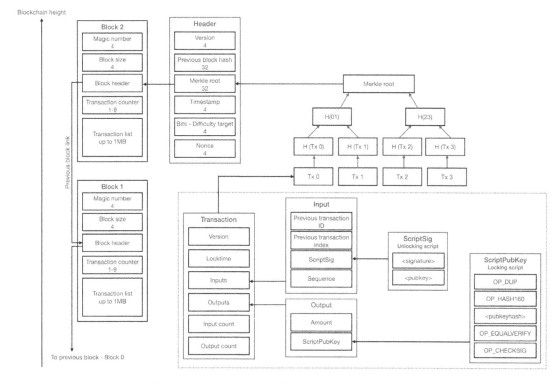

Figure 4-12. *A visualization of a Bitcoin blockchain, blocks, block headers, transactions, and scripts*

The FLM[1] impossibility states that Byzantine consensus is not possible if an adversary can control more than $\frac{n}{3}$ nodes. In the case of the PKI setup, this lower bound does not hold. It turns out that Bitcoin circumvents FLM impossibility. In proof of work environments, a Byzantine agreement is possible without the PKI [2] setup.

---

[1] After the authors' names: Fischer, Lynch, and Merritt – `https://groups.csail.mit.edu/tds/papers/Lynch/FischerLynchMerritt-dc.pdf`

[2] Public Key Infrastructure.

Mining

Mining is the process by which new coins are added to the Bitcoin blockchain. This process secures the network and incentivizes the users who spend resources to protect the network. More details on the specifics are in Chapter 5; however, now I will touch upon the mining hardware. When Bitcoin was introduced, it was easy to mine with CPUs, which quickly increased the difficulty, leading to miners using GPUs. Shortly after the successful adoption of GPUs, FPGAs emerged as a mechanism to further speed up SHA-256 hashing. Soon, these were outperformed by ASICs, and now ASICs are a prevalent mechanism to mine Bitcoin. However, solo mining where individual users use mining hardware to mine is also not much profitable due to exorbitant mining difficulty. Instead, mining farms comprising thousands of ASICs are commonly used now. Also, mining pools are common where multiple users collectively solve the hash puzzle to earn rewards proportionate to their contribution.

Bitcoin As a Platform

Other than electronic cash, Bitcoin as a platform can be used for several use cases. For example, it can be used as a timestamping service or a general ledger to store some information permanently. In addition, we can use the OP_RETURN instruction to store data, which can store up to 80 bytes of arbitrary data. Other use cases such as smart property, smart assets, and blocks as a source of randomness also transpired.

The desire to use Bitcoin for different purposes also resulted in techniques to enhance Bitcoin, resulting in colored coins, rootstock, Omni layer, and counterparty projects. While Bitcoin did what it intended to do and a lot more in the form of innovations mentioned earlier, the fundamental limitation in Bitcoin protocols meant that all flexible new protocols would have to be built on top of Bitcoin. There is no inherent flexibility in Bitcoin to perform all these different tasks. Therefore, there was a need felt to do more than just cryptocurrency on Blockchain. This ambition motivated the invention of Ethereum, the first general-purpose blockchain platform that supported smart contracts.

Ethereum

Ethereum was introduced in 2014 in a whitepaper by Vitalik Buterin. Ethereum introduced a platform on which users can run arbitrary code in the form of smart contracts. To thwart the denial-of-service attacks caused by infinite loops in code, the concept of metered execution was also introduced. Metered executions require that for every operation performed on the blockchain, a fee is charged, which is paid in Ether, the native currency of the Ethereum blockchain. With smart contracts, Ethereum opened a whole new world of generic platforms where the operations are no longer limited to only bitcoin-style value transfer transactions, but users can execute any type of diverse business logic on-chain due to Ethereum's Turing complete design. Ethereum is currently the most used blockchain platform for smart contracts.

Today's Internet is centralized, which is dominated by large companies. The Internet that we use today is called Web 2. Ethereum is developed with the vision of Web3, where anyone can participate in the network without any reliance on a third party. In the Web 2 model, big service providers currently provide services in return for personal data; however, in Web3, anyone can participate without giving up their personal information in exchange for services. However, with decentralized applications (DApps), anyone can provide any service which any user on the network can use, and no one can block your access to the service.

Ethereum Network

An Ethereum network is composed of loosely coupled nodes which exchange messages via a gossip protocol.

A high-level visualization of the Ethereum network is shown in Figure 4-13.

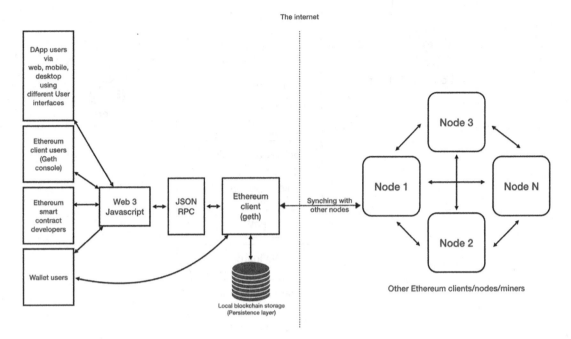

Figure 4-13. *Ethereum network high-level overview*

Nodes run client software which is an implementation of the Ethereum blockchain protocol described in the yellow paper to enable any user to participate on the network. A node is composed of different components, as shown in Figure 4-14.

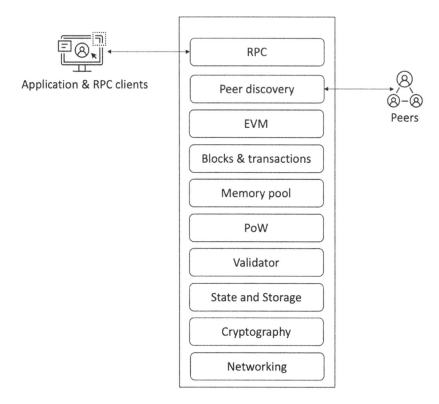

Figure 4-14. *Ethereum node architecture*

There are three main types of nodes in the Ethereum network:

- Full node

- Light node

- Archive node

Full nodes store the entire chain data and validate blocks, transactions, and states. Light nodes only store the block headers and verify the data against state roots present in the block headers. Light nodes are suitable for resource-constrained devices, such as mobile devices. Archive nodes include everything that is in a full node but also builds an archive of historical states. Miner nodes are a full node but also perform mining operation and participate in proof of work consensus.

A new Ethereum node joining the network uses hardcoded bootstrap nodes as an initial entry point into the network from where the further discovery of other nodes begins.

RLPx is a TCP-based transport protocol. It enables secure communication between Ethereum nodes by using the Elliptic Curve Integrated Encryption Scheme (ECIES) for handshaking and key exchange.

DEVP2P or the wire protocol negotiates an application session between two Ethereum nodes that have been discovered and have established a secure channel using RLPx.

After discovering and establishing a secure transport channel and negotiating an application session, the nodes exchange messages using "capability protocols," for example, eth (versions 62, 63, and 64), Light Ethereum Subprotocol (LES), Whisper, and Swarm. These capability protocols or application subprotocols enable different application-level communications, for example, eth for block synchronization.

The node discovery protocol and other relevant protocols are shown in Figure 4-15.

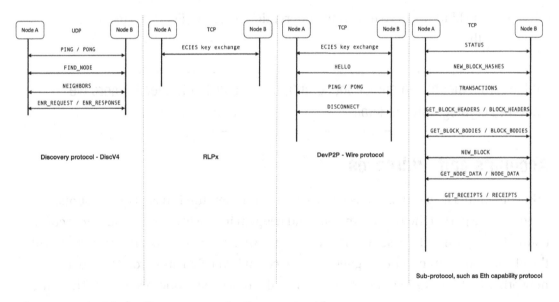

Figure 4-15. *Node discovery and other protocols*

Cryptography in Ethereum

Like any other blockchain, Ethereum's security relies on cryptography. Ethereum uses cryptography throughout the blockchain and node design:

- AES CTR is used in RLP handshake and subsequent P2P messaging. It is also used in a keystore as AES CTR 128-bit cipher.

- Digital signatures in Ethereum clients use the SECP256K1 curve. It is used in ECDSA signatures for transaction signing, ECDH key exchanges, and for generating a shared key before the RLP P2P handshake.

- SCRYPT and PBKDF2 are used as key derivation functions in the keystore.

- The KECCAK-256 hash function is used in the proof of work algorithm for mining and solidity language.

- The Elliptic Curve Integrated Encryption Scheme (ECIES) is used in Ethereum.

If the terms mentioned earlier sound unfamiliar, refer to Chapter 2 where we covered cryptography in detail.

Accounts and Addresses

A Bitcoin model is based on transactions, whereas Ethereum is based on accounts. Accounts are part of the Ethereum state and keep an intrinsic balance and transaction count. 160-bit long addresses identify accounts. An account is how a user interacts with the blockchain. A transaction signed by an account is verified and broadcast to the network, which results in a state transition on the blockchain once executed. There are two types of accounts, contract accounts (CAs) and externally owned accounts (EOAs). EOAs are associated with a human user, whereas CAs have no intrinsic association with a user.

A world state is a mapping between addresses and account states. An account state consists of the fields shown in Table 4-2.

Table 4-2. *Account state*

Element	Description
Nonce	Number of transactions originated from an address or, in the case of smart contracts, the number of contracts created by an account
Balance	Number of Wei owned by this address
StorageRoot	256-bit hash of the root node of the Merkle Patricia trie, which encodes the storage contents of the account
codeHash	Hash of the associated EVM code (bytecode)

Transactions and Executions

Transactions in Ethereum are signed instructions which once executed result in a message call or contract creation (new account with associated code) on the blockchain. Fundamentally, there are two types of transactions, **message call** and **contract creation**, but over time for easier understanding, three types are now usually defined:

- Value transfer transactions

- Contract creation transactions

- Contract execution transactions

A transaction consists of several fields. Each transaction is part of the transaction trie, the root of which is stored in the block header in the block. When a transaction is executed, a receipt is returned which can be used as a verification for the transaction execution.

A transaction, either a message call or a contract creation, includes the common fields shown in Table 4-3.

Table 4-3. *Transaction structure*

Element	Description
Nonce	Number of transactions sent by the sender
gasPrice	Number of Wei to be paid per unit of gas for the execution of the transaction
gasLimit	Maximum amount of gas that is expected to be used for executing a transaction. It is paid up front and cannot be increased later
to	The 160-bit address of the message call's (value transfer, contract execution) recipient or for a contract creation transaction
value	Number of Wei to be transferred to the message call's recipient. In the case of contract creation, it is the endowment (number of Wei) for the newly created contract account (smart contract)
V, R, S	Values corresponding to the signature of the transaction used to determine the sender of the transaction
init	(In the case of contract creation transaction) An unlimited size byte array specifying the EVM code for the contract account (smart contract) initialization procedure
data	(In the case of message call transaction) An unlimited size byte array specifying the input data of the message call

A transaction takes several steps in the Ethereum blockchain. A high-level transaction flow is described as follows:

1. First, a transaction is created. It can either be a contract creation transaction or a message call.

2. The transaction is signed using ECDSA, verified, and broadcast to the network.

3. The transaction is propagated via a gossip protocol and picked up by miners and other nodes to populate their transaction pools.

4. Miners create a candidate block by adding transactions to it and start the mining process.

5. A miner who solves the proof of work announces its block to the network.

6. Other nodes receive the block, validate it, and append it to their blockchain.

Blocks and Blockchain

Blocks in Ethereum are composed of a block header and transactions. A blockchain consists of blocks, which contain transactions.

Like any other blockchain, blocks are the main building blocks of Ethereum. An Ethereum block consists of the block header, the list of transactions, and the list of ommer block headers. A block header also consists of several elements. All these elements in a block are shown in Tables 4-4 and 4-5 with a description.

Table 4-4. *Block structure*

Element	Description
Block header	Header of the block
List of transactions	Series of transactions included in the block
List of ommer block headers	List of uncle or ommer headers. An uncle block is a child of a parent but doesn't have any child blocks. They are valid but stale blocks which do not make it to the main chain but do earn a reward for their participation

The block header structure is described in Table 4-5.

Table 4-5. *Block header structure*

Element	Type	Description
Parent hash	Hash	Keccak 256-bit hash of the parent block's header
Ommers hash	Hash	Keccak 256-bit hash of the list of ommers
Beneficiary	Address	160-bit recipient address for mining reward
State root	Hash	Keccak 256-bit hash of the root node of the transaction trie
Transaction root	Hash	Keccak 256-bit hash of the root node of the transaction trie
Receipts root	Hash	Keccak 256-bit hash of the root node of the transaction receipts trie, which contains receipts of all transactions included in the block
Logs bloom	Variable	Bloom filter composed logger address and log topics
Difficulty	Integer	Difficulty level of the current block
Number	Integer	Total number of all previous blocks

(continued)

Table 4-5. (*continued*)

Element	Type	Description
Gas limit	Integer	Limit set on the gas consumption per block
Gas used	Integer	Total gas consumed by all transactions included in the block
Timestamp	Integer	Unix epoch timestamp
Extra	Variable	An optional free field for storing extra data
MixHash	Integer	Computational effort proof
Nonce	Integer	Combined with MixHash to prove computational effort
basefeepergas	Integer	(Post EIP-1559) Records the protocol calculated fee required for a transaction to be included in the block

Ethereum uses a new data structure called Merkle Patricia trie to store and organize transactions and relevant data. It is a combination of Patricia and Merkle trees with novel properties.

There are four tries used in Ethereum to organize data such as transactions, state, receipts, and contract storage.

Transaction Trie

Each Ethereum block contains the root of a transaction trie, which is composed of transactions.

World State Trie

A state trie is a key-value mapping from user addresses to an account state. Also called the world state trie, this trie has its root referred in the block. A state trie is composed of account states.

Transaction Receipts Trie

Transaction receipts store results of transaction execution and include information such as status, logs, and events. Each block contains a transaction receipts trie. A transaction receipts trie consists of transaction receipts.

Account Storage Trie

This trie has its root as a storage root in the account state. It stores smart contract code and relevant data.

Figure 4-16 shows all tries including the block structure.

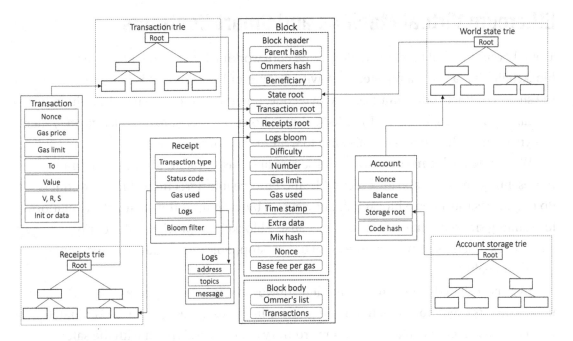

Figure 4-16. *Block and tries*

Transactions within the blocks are executed using the Ethereum virtual machine, which we describe next.

Mining in Ethereum

In contrast with Bitcoin, mining in Ethereum is ASIC (application-specific integrated circuit) resistant.

ASIC-based, special-purpose, efficient, and extremely fast hardware is built for performing Bitcoin mining. These devices have only one specific job, and that is to run hash function SHA-256 repeatedly and extremely fast.

Ethereum uses proof of work; however, the consensus is memory-hard, which makes building ASICs difficult due to large memory requirements. The protocol is called ETHASH, which generates a large direct acyclic graph (DAG) to be used by miners.

DAG grows and shrinks according to the network difficulty level; however, over time, it has increased up to roughly about 4 GB in size. As this DAG consumes large memory, building ASICs with such large memory is prohibitively hard, thus making ETHASH an ASIC-resistant algorithm. We will explain ETHASH in more detail in Chapter 8.

Ethereum Virtual Machine and Smart Contracts

The Ethereum virtual machine (EVM) is the core working horse of the Ethereum blockchain. It is a 256-bit register stack with a depth of 1024 items. It is designed to run the smart contract code compiled into bytecode. Smart contracts are usually written in a domain-specific language (DSL) called Solidity; however, there are other languages, such as Vyper, which developers can also use to write smart contract code.

We can define a **smart contract** as a secure and unstoppable computer program representing an automatically executable and enforceable agreement. Smart contracts do not necessarily need a blockchain; however, a blockchain is the most natural platform for running smart contracts. This is so because a blockchain provides all security guarantees that make smart contracts secure, unstoppable, automatically executable, and enforceable.

EVM is designed to be Turing complete; however, it is bound by a gas limit, which means that its execution is metered and paid for in the so-called gas fee denominated in ether. This mechanism allows for any arbitrary code execution but with the safety that the execution will halt when the gas runs out, preventing infinite executions due to loops or malicious code. EVM executes bytecode composed of **opcodes** that cost gas on a per-operation basis. There are around 150 opcodes categorized into several groups: arithmetic opcodes, memory manipulating opcodes, and program flow–related opcodes. A complete list is available in the Ethereum yellow paper.

The consensus in Ethereum is proof of work based, which we will cover in detail in Chapter 8.

The Ethereum 1.0 blockchain will continue to evolve according to its road map and will eventually become a shard in phase 1 of Ethereum 2.0.

With this, we complete our brief discussion on the two most prominent and pioneering blockchain platforms. More modern blockchain platforms, such as Polkadot, Cardano, Solana, Avalanche, and Ethereum 2.0, will be introduced when we discuss their respective consensus protocols in Chapter 8.

Summary

- A blockchain is a peer-to-peer, cryptographically secure, append-only, immutable, and tamper-proof shared distributed ledger composed of temporally ordered and publicly verifiable transactions.

- Origins of the blockchain can be found in previous attempts to create digital cash and digital timestamping of documents.

- A blockchain is a distributed system.

- Blockchains are primarily of two types, permissioned and public.

- Blockchains have many cross-industry use cases, including but by no means limited to government, finance, medical, supply chain, and technology.

- Blockchains provide several benefits, such as cost saving, transparency, and data sharing.

- Various technologies such as public key cryptography, hash functions, and Merkle trees have provided foundations for building security of the blockchain.

- From the CAP theorem's perspective, permissioned blockchains are CP systems, whereas public chains are AP systems.

- A blockchain ledger abstraction has several properties along with get(), append(), and verify() operations.

- Bitcoin is the first blockchain invented by Satoshi Nakamoto.

- Ethereum is the first smart contract blockchain platform proposed by Vitalik Buterin.

- Bitcoin and Ethereum are the most prominent platforms.

- Ethereum will become a shard of Ethereum 2.0.

- Modern blockchain platforms are focusing on the heterogenous multichain architecture where multiple chains interoperate and form an ecosystem of blockchains cooperating and interoperating together, which serve multiple use cases.

Bibliography

1. Bashir, I., 2020. Mastering blockchain: a deep dive into distributed ledgers, consensus protocols, smart contracts, DApps, cryptocurrencies, Ethereum, and more.

2. Wood, G., 2014. Ethereum: A secure decentralised generalised transaction ledger. Ethereum project yellow paper, 151(2014), pp. 1–32.

3. Raynal, M., 2018. Fault-Tolerant Message-Passing Distributed Systems (p. 459). Springer.

4. Nakamoto, S., 2008. Bitcoin: A peer-to-peer electronic cash system.

5. Bitgold: https://unenumerated.blogspot.com/2005/12/bit-gold.html

6. David Chaum's blind signatures paper is available here: https://sceweb.sce.uhcl.edu/yang/teaching/csci5234WebSecurityFall2011/Chaum-blind-signatures.PDF

7. Haber, S. and Stornetta, W.S., 1990, August. How to time-stamp a digital document. In *Conference on the Theory and Application of Cryptography* (pp. 437–455). Springer, Berlin, Heidelberg.

8. B-money published here: www.weidai.com/bmoney.txt

9. Dwork and Naor email spam combatting was published in Pricing via Processing or Combatting Junk Mail: www.iacr.org/cryptodb/data/paper.php?pubkey=1268

10. Hashcash for email spam combatting published in `www.hashcash.org/papers/hashcash.pdf`

11. Reusable proof of work by Hal Finney published here: `https://cryptome.org/rpow.htm`

12. Gupta, S., Hellings, J., and Sadoghi, M., 2021. Fault-Tolerant Distributed Transactions on Blockchain. *Synthesis Lectures on Data Management, 16*(1), pp. 1–268.

13. A complete list of Bitcoin opcodes is available here: `https://en.bitcoin.it/wiki/Script`

14. Documentation on Ivy is available here: `https://docs.ivylang.org/bitcoin/`

15. More details on the miniscript are available here: `http://bitcoin.sipa.be/miniscript/`

16. More on FLM impossibility here: `https://decentralizedthoughts.github.io/2019-08-02-byzantine-agreement-is-impossible-for-$n-slash-leq-3-f$-is-the-adversary-can-easily-simulate/`

17. Fischer, M.J., Lynch, N.A., and Merritt, M., 1986. Easy impossibility proofs for distributed consensus problems. *Distributed Computing, 1*(1), pp. 26–39.

CHAPTER 5

Blockchain Consensus

Blockchain consensus is the core element of a blockchain, which ensures the integrity and consistency of the blockchain data. Blockchain being a distributed system, in the first instance, it may appear that we can apply traditional distributed consensus protocols, such as Paxos or PBFT, to address the agreement and total order requirements in a blockchain. However, this can only work in consortium chains where participants are known and limited in number. In public chains, traditional consensus protocols cannot work due to the permissionless environment. However, in 2008 a new class of consensus algorithms emerged, which relied on proof of work to ensure random leader election by solving a mathematical puzzle. The elected leader wins the right to append to the blockchain. This is the so-called Nakamoto consensus protocol. This algorithm for the very first time solved the problem of consensus in a permissionless public environment with many anonymous participants.

We have already discussed distributed consensus from a traditional perspective in Chapter 3. In this chapter, we will cover what blockchain consensus is, how the traditional protocols can be applied to a blockchain, how proof of work works, how it was developed, and what the blockchain consensus requirements are, and we will analyze blockchain consensus such as proof of work through the lens of distributed consensus. Also, we'll see how the requirements of consensus may change depending upon the type of blockchain in use. For example, for public blockchains proof of work might be a better idea, whereas for permissioned blockchains BFT-style protocols may work better.

© Imran Bashir 2022
I. Bashir, *Blockchain Consensus*, https://doi.org/10.1007/978-1-4842-8179-6_5

Background

Distributed consensus has always been a fundamental problem in distributed systems. Similarly, in blockchain it plays a vital role in ensuring the integrity of the blockchain. There are two broad classes of algorithms that have emerged as a result of the last almost 45 years of research on distributed consensus:

1. Leader-based traditional distributed consensus or permissioned consensus

2. Nakamoto and post-Nakamoto consensus or permissionless consensus

Leader-based protocols work on the principle of voting where nodes in a distributed system vote to perform an operation. These protocols are usually deterministic and have been researched since the 1970s. Some such protocols include Paxos, PBFT, and RAFT. Another different type of class emerged in 2008 with Bitcoin, which relied on the proof of work type of crypto puzzle. This type of protocol is probabilistic where a participant wins the right to append a new block to the blockchain by solving the proof of work.

Usually, in the blockchain world, Byzantine fault–tolerant protocols are used, especially because these blockchains are expected to either run publicly or in a consortium environment where malicious attacks are a reality. Perhaps not so much on consortium chains where the participants are known, but still due to the nature of the enterprise applications that run on these platforms, it's best to consider a Byzantine fault–tolerant model. Applications related to finance, health, egovernance, and many other use cases run on consortium chains; therefore, it is necessary to ensure protection against any arbitrary faults including even active adversaries.

There are pros and cons of both approaches. Traditional BFT protocols or their variants in the blockchain provide stronger consistency as compared to proof of work–type algorithms, which can only offer eventual consistency. However, proof of work consensus is much more scalable as compared to traditional BFT protocols. See a comparison in Table 5-1 between BFT and PoW consensus.

Table 5-1. *Traditional BFT vs. Nakamoto consensus*

Property	Traditional BFT	Nakamoto
Agreement	Deterministic	Eventual
Termination	Deterministic	Probabilistic
Energy consumption	Low	Very high
Sybil resistance	No	Yes
Finality	Immediate	Probabilistic
Consistency	Stronger	Weaker (eventual)
Communication pattern	Broadcast	Epidemic
Throughput (TPS)	Higher	Low
Scalability	Lower (10–100 nodes)	Higher (1000s of nodes)
Forking	None	Possible
Identity	Known	Anonymous (pseudonymous)
Network	Peer to peer	Peer to peer
Order	Temporal	Temporal
Formal rigor (correctness proofs, etc.)	Yes	Mostly nonexistent
Fault tolerance	1/3, <=33%	<=25% computing power* >50% computing power
Number of clients	Many	Many

Another point to keep in mind is the distinction between a broadcast problem and a consensus problem. Consensus is a decision problem, whereas broadcast is a delivery problem. The properties of both are the same but with slightly different definitions. These properties include agreement, validity, integrity, and termination. In essence, broadcast and consensus are interrelated and deeply connected problems as it is possible to implement one from the other.

We will be focusing more on a consensus problem instead of a broadcast problem.

Blockchain Consensus

A blockchain consensus protocol is a mechanism that allows participants in a blockchain system to agree on a sequence of transactions even in the presence of faults. In other words, consensus algorithms ensure that all parties agree on a single source of truth even if some parties are faulty.

There are some properties that are associated with blockchain consensus. The properties are almost the same as standard distributed consensus but with a slight variation.

As a standard, there are safety and liveness properties. The safety and liveness properties change depending on the type of blockchain. First, we define the safety and liveness properties for a permissioned/consortium blockchain and then for a public blockchain.

Traditional BFT

There are several properties that we can define for traditional BFT consensus, which are commonly used in a permissioned blockchain. There are various variants, for example, Tendermint, that are used in a blockchain. We covered traditional BFT in detail in Chapter 3; however, in this section we will redefine that in the context of a blockchain and especially permissioned blockchain. Most of the properties remain the same as public permissionless consensus; however, the key difference is between deterministic and probabilistic termination and agreement.

Agreement

No two honest processes decide on a different block. In other words, no two honest processes commit different blocks at the same height.

Validity

If an honest process decides on a block b, then b satisfies the application-specific validity predicate *valid ()*. Also, the block b agreed must be proposed by some honest node.

Termination

Every honest process decides. After GST, every honest process continuously commits blocks.

Agreement and validity are safety properties, whereas termination is a liveness property.

Integrity

A process must decide at most once in a consensus round.

Other properties can include the following.

Chain Progress (Liveness)

A blockchain must keep growing by continuously appending new blocks to it after GST.

Instant Irrevocability

Once a transaction has made it to the block and the block is finalized, the transaction cannot be removed.

Consensus Finality

Finality is deterministic and immediate. Transactions are final as soon as they've made it to the block, and blocks are final as soon as they've been appended to the blockchain.

While there are many blockchain consensus algorithms now, Nakamoto consensus is the first blockchain protocol introduced with Bitcoin, which has several novel properties. Indeed, it is not a classical Byzantine algorithm with deterministic properties; instead, it has probabilistic features.

Nakamoto Consensus

The Nakamoto or PoW consensus can be characterized with several properties. It is commonly used in public blockchains, for example, Bitcoin.

Agreement

Eventually, no two honest processes decide on a different block.

Validity

If an honest process decides on a block b, then b satisfies the application-specific validity predicate valid (). Also, the transactions within the block satisfy the application-specific validity predicate valid(). In other words, only valid and correct transactions make it to the block, and only correct and valid blocks make it to the blockchain. Only valid transactions and blocks are accepted by the nodes. Also, mining nodes (miners) will only accept the valid transactions. In addition, the decided value must be proposed by some honest process.

Termination

Every honest process eventually decides.

Agreement and validity are safety properties, whereas termination is a liveness property.

Note   In public blockchain networks, an economic incentive is usually associated with the consensus properties so that participants who are working toward ensuring the safety and liveness of the network are economically incentivized to do so.

Remember we discussed randomized algorithms earlier in Chapter 3, where termination is guaranteed probabilistically. Randomized protocols are used to circumvent FLP impossibility. Usually, the termination property is made probabilistic to achieve an agreement to circumvent FLP impossibility. However, with the Bitcoin blockchain, the agreement property is made probabilistic instead of termination. Here, the safety property is somewhat sacrificed because in the Bitcoin blockchain, it is allowed that temporarily a fork can occur, and when the fork is resolved, some previously finalized transactions are rolled back. This is due to the longest chain rule.

There are a few other properties which we describe now.

Consensus Finality

With two correct processes p1 and p2, if p1 appends a block b to its local blockchain before another block b', then no other correct node appends b' before b.

For a proof of work blockchain point of view, we can further carve out some properties.

Chain Progress (Liveness)

A blockchain must keep growing steadily by new blocks continuously being appended to it every n interval. N can be a predefined time interval defined by the protocol.

Consistent/Consistency

The blockchain must eventually heal a forked chain to arrive at a single longest chain. In other words, everyone must see the same history.

Eventual Irrevocability

The probability of a transaction being rolled back decreases with more blocks appended to the blockchain. This is a crucial property from end users' point of view as this property gives confidence to the users that after their transaction has been made part of a block and it's been finalized and accepted, then new blocks being added to the blockchain further ensure that the transaction is permanently and irrevocably part of the blockchain.

Table 5-1 shows some key differences between traditional BFT and Nakamoto consensus.

Now we turn our attention to system models, which are necessary to describe as they capture the assumption that we make about the environment in which blockchain consensus protocols will operate.

System Model

Blockchain consensus protocols assume a system model under which they guarantee the safety and liveness properties. Here, I describe two system models, which are generally applicable to public and permissioned blockchain systems, respectively.

Public Blockchain System Model (Permissionless)

A blockchain is a distributed system where nodes communicate via message passing. The broadcast protocol is usually probabilistic in the case of a public blockchain where transactions (messages) are disseminated by utilizing a gossip-style protocol.

Usually, the network model is asynchronous as there is no bound on the processor delay or communication delay, especially because a public blockchain system is most likely to be heterogenous and geographically dispersed. Nodes do not know each other, nor do they know how many total nodes are there in the system. Nodes can arbitrarily join and drop off the network. Anyone can join by simply running the protocol software on the network.

Consortium Blockchain System Model (Permissioned)

In this model, blockchain nodes communicate via message passing. A broadcast protocol is usually a one-to-all communication within the consensus protocol. For example, in PBFT the leader broadcasts its proposal in one go to all replicas, instead of sending it to a few, and then those other nodes send it to other nodes, as we saw in gossip dissemination. Moreover, the network model is partially synchronous. More precisely, blockchain consensus protocols are modelled under an eventually synchronous model where after an unknown GST the system is guaranteed to make progress.

Now let's turn our attention to the first blockchain consensus protocol and explore how it works: the proof of work protocol or Nakamoto consensus.

First Blockchain Consensus

The proof of work consensus algorithm or Nakamoto consensus was first introduced with the Bitcoin blockchain in 2008. It is fundamentally a leader election algorithm where a mandatory and random waiting time is imposed between leader elections. This also serves as a Sybil attack mechanism. One of the weaknesses in traditional distributed consensus protocols is that they need each participant to be known and identifiable in the protocol. For example, in PBFT all participants must be known and identifiable. This limitation (albeit useful in consortium chains) makes BFT-style protocols somewhat unsuitable for public chains. This is so because an attacker can create multiple identities and can use those multiple nodes/identities to vote in their favor. This is the so-called Sybil attack. If somehow we can make creating and then using that identity on a blockchain an expensive operation, then such a setup can thwart any Sybil attack attempts and will prevent an attacker from taking over the network by creating multiple fake identities.

The term Sybil attack is coined after a book named *Sybil* published in 1973, where the main character in the book named Sybil Dorsett has multiple personality disorder.

The first proof of work was introduced by Dwork and Naor in 1992 [1]. This work was done to combat junk emails whereby associating a computational cost, that is, pricing functions, with sending emails results in creating a type of access control mechanism where access to resources can only be obtained by computing a moderately hard function which prevents excessive use. Proof of work has also been proposed in Adam Back's Hashcash proposal [10].

The key intuition behind proof of work in a blockchain is to universally slow down the proposals for all participants, which achieves two goals. First, it allows all participants to converge on a common consistent view, and, second, it makes Sybil attacks very expensive, which helps with the integrity of the blockchain.

It has been observed that it is impossible (impossibility results) to achieve an agreement in a network where participants are anonymous even if there is only one Byzantine node [2]. This is due to the Sybil attack, which can create arbitrarily many identities to game the system in attackers' favor by voting many times. If there is a way to prevent such attacks, only then there is some guarantee that the system will work as expected; otherwise, the attacker can create arbitrarily many identities to attack the system. This problem was solved practically by proof of work consensus or Nakamoto consensus [3]. Before Bitcoin, the use of moderately hard puzzles to assign identities in an anonymous network was first suggested by Aspnes [4]. However, the solution that Aspnes introduced requires authenticated channels, whereas in Bitcoin unauthenticated communication is used, and puzzles are noninteractive and publicly verifiable.

So even in the presence of the abovementioned impossibility results in classical literature, Nakamoto consensus emerged, which for the first time showed that consensus can be achieved in a permissionless model.

Remember we discussed random oracles in Chapter 3. In proof of work, hash functions are used to instantiate random oracles. Since the output of hash functions is sufficiently long and random, an adversary cannot predict future hashes or can cause hash collisions. These properties make SHA-256 a good choice to use it as a hash function in the proof of work mechanism.

The key requirement in a blockchain is to totally order the transactions. If all participants are known and the scale is limited to a few nodes, then we can use traditional consensus like BFT; however, with thousands of unknown nodes, traditional BFT cannot be used. The proof of work consensus mechanism addresses this issue.

There is a scalability vs. performance trade-off [6] that comes up when comparing traditional BFT with PoW, as shown in Figure 5-1.

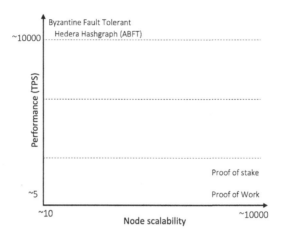

Figure 5-1. *Performance vs. scalability*

The proof of work or Nakamoto consensus protocol is a Byzantine fault–tolerant protocol because it can tolerate arbitrary faults. It can be seen as an **eventual Byzantine agreement** mechanism.

How PoW Works

Let's first define some of the requirements of PoW. Indeed, proof of work was originally introduced in Bitcoin without any rigorous documentation or proofs of correctness. Here, for clarity and easier understanding, we will list some of the requirements (almost retrospectively) and see if PoW fulfills those requirements and how:

- **Consistency**: New blocks are replicated to all nodes.

- **Linked with previous block**: A log is maintained in such a way that each new entry is linked with the previous entry forming a chain.

- **Permissionless and open participation**: Nodes can join without any access control and can leave without notice.

- Partition tolerance.

- Geographically dispersed.

- Thousands of nodes allowed where anyone anywhere in the world can download a client and become part of the network by running the client.

- Highly adversarial environment, so Byzantine fault tolerance is of prime importance.

- Heterogenous where a number of different types of computers and hardware devices can join.

- Asynchronous in the sense that there is no bound on the CPU or communication delays, just an eventual guarantee that messages are expected to reach all nodes with high probability.

The question is, how do you design a consensus protocol for such a difficult environment? Yet, Bitcoin PoW has stood the test of time, and apart from some limited and carefully orchestrated attacks and some inadvertent bugs, largely the Bitcoin network has been running without any issues for the last 13 years. How? I'll explain now.

Pedagogical Explanation of PoW

Imagine a scenario where a node has proposed a block and has broadcast it to the network. The nodes that receive it can do either of two things. Either they can accept the block and append it to a local blockchain, or they can reject it if the block is not valid. Now also imagine the block is indeed valid, then the receiving nodes can simply accept it and agree on the proposed block. Imagine there is only a proposer node ever in the entire system, and that node is honest and trustworthy. This means that there is no real consensus required; the proposer node simply proposes new blocks, and nodes agree to it, resulting in an eventual total order of blocks containing transactions. But this is a centralized system with a trusted third party that, if it stays honest, as a leader, can drive the whole system because everyone trusts it. What if it turned malicious, then it's a problem?

Perhaps, we can allow other nodes to propose as well, to take away control from that single node, which is not trustworthy. Imagine that we now have two nodes proposing valid blocks and broadcasting them on the network. Now there is a problem; some of the receiving nodes will add one block and then the other. Some wouldn't know which one to accept or which to reject. Proposals are made at the same time, and now nodes don't know which block to insert; perhaps, they will insert both. Now some nodes have inserted blocks from proposer 1 and the others from proposer 2 only and some from both. As you can imagine, there is no consensus here.

Imagine another scenario where two nodes simultaneously announce a block; now the receiving nodes will receive two blocks, and instead of one chain, there are now two chains. In other words, there are two logs and histories of events. Two nodes proposed a block at the same time; all nodes added two blocks. Now it is no longer a single chain, it is a tree, with two branches. This is called a fork. In other words, if nodes learn about two different blocks pointing to the same parent at the same time, then the blockchain forks into two chains.

Now in order to resolve this, we can allow nodes to pick the longest chain of blocks at that time that they know of and add the new block to that chain and ignore the other branch. If it so happens that there are two or more branches somehow with the same height (same length), then just pick up randomly one of the chains and add the new block to it. This way, we can resolve this fork. Now all nodes, knowing this rule that only the longest chain is allowed to have new blocks, will keep building the longest chain. In the case of two or more same height chains, then just randomly add the block to any of these. So far, so good! This scheme appears to work. A node decides to add the new block into a randomly chosen chain and propagates that decision to others, and other nodes add that same block to their chains. Over time, the longest chain takes over, and the shorter chain is ignored because no new blocks are added to it, because it's not the longest chain.

But now there is another problem. Imagine a situation where a node randomly chooses one chain after a fork, adds a block to it, propagates that decision to others, other nodes add as well, and, at this point, some nodes due to latency don't hear about the decision. Some nodes add the block they heard from another node to one of its chains, another one does the opposite, and this cycle repeats. Now you can clearly see that there are two chains, both getting new blocks. There is no consensus. There is a livelock situation where nodes can keep adding to both chains.

At this point, let's think about what the fundamental reason is and why this livelock is occurring. The reason is that blocks are generating too fast, and other nodes receive many different blocks from different nodes, some quickly, some delayed. This asynchrony results in a livelock. The solution? Slow it down! Give nodes time to converge to one chain! Let's see how.

We can introduce a random waiting period, which will make miners to arbitrarily sleep for some time and then mine. The key insight here is that the livelock (continuous fork) problem can be resolved by introducing a variable speed timer at each node. When a node adds a new block to its chain, it stops its timer and sends it to other nodes. Other nodes are waiting for their timers to expire, but during that waiting time, if they hear about this new block from another node, they simply stop their timers and add this new block and reset the timers and start waiting again. This way, there will only be one block added to the chain, instead of two. If the timers are long enough, then chances of forking and livelocking decrease significantly. Another thing to note here is that if there are many nodes in the system, then there is a higher chance that some timer will expire soon, and as we keep adding more and more nodes, the probability of such occurrences increases because timers are random and there are many nodes now. In order to avoid the same livelock situations, we need to increase the sleeping time of these timers as we add more nodes, so that the probability of adding a block by nodes quickly is decreased to such a level that only one node will eventually succeed to add a new block to their chain and will announce that to the network. Also, the waiting period ensures with high probability that forks will be resolved during this waiting time. It is enough time to ensure complete propagation of a new valid block so that no other block for the same height can be proposed.

Bitcoin chooses this timeout period based on the rate of block generation of 2016 blocks, which is roughly two weeks. As the block generation should be roughly a single block every ten minutes, if the protocol observes that the block generation has been faster in the last two weeks, then it increases the timeout value, resulting in slower generation of blocks. If the protocols observe that the block generation has been slower, then it decreases the timeout value. Now one problem in this timeout mechanism is that if a single node turns malicious and always manages to somehow make its timer expire earlier than other nodes, this node will end up creating a block every time. Now the requirement becomes to build a timer which is resistant to such cheating. One way of doing this is to build a trusted mechanism with some cryptographic security guarantees to act as a secure enclave in which the timer code runs. This way, due to cryptographic guarantees, the malicious node may not be able to trick the time into always expiring first.

This technique is used in the PoET (proof of elapsed time) algorithm used in Hyperledger Intel Sawtooth blockchain. We will discuss this in Chapter 8.

Another way, the original way, Nakamoto designed the algorithm is to make computers do a computationally complex task which takes time to solve – just enough to be able to solve it almost every ten minutes. Also, the task is formulated in such a way that nodes cannot cheat, except to try to solve the problem. Any deviation from the method of solving the problem will not help, as the only way to solve the problem is to try every possible answer and match it with the expected answer. If the answer matches with the expected answer, then the problem is solved; otherwise, the computer will have to try the next answer and keep doing that in a brute-force manner until the answer is found. This is a brilliant insight by Satoshi Nakamoto which ensures with high probability that computers cannot cheat, and timers only expire almost every ten minutes, giving one of the nodes the right to add its block to the blockchain. This is the so-called proof of work, meaning a node has done enough work to demonstrate that it has spent enough computational power to solve the math problem to earn the right to insert a new block to the blockchain.

Proof of work is based on cryptographic hash functions. It requires that for a block to be valid, its hash must be less than a specific value. This means that the hash of the block must start with a certain number of zeroes. The only way to find such a hash is to repeatedly try each possible hash and see if it matches the criterion; if not, then try again until one node finds such a hash. This means that in order to find a valid hash, it takes roughly ten minutes, thus introducing just enough delay which results in resolving forks and convergence on one chain while minimizing the chance of one node winning the right to create a new block every time.

Now it is easy to see that proof of work is a mechanism to introduce waiting time between block creation and ensuring that only one leader eventually emerges, which can insert the new block to the chain.

So, it turns out that PoW is not, precisely speaking, a consensus algorithm; it is a consensus facilitation algorithm which, due to slowing down block generations, allows nodes to converge to a common blockchain.

Now as we understand the intuition behind the proof of work mechanism, next we will describe how exactly the proof of work algorithm works in Bitcoin.

PoW Formula

The PoW consensus process can be described with the help of a formula:

$$SHAd256(nonce \,\|\, Block\ header) \leq target$$

where *SHAd256* represents a SHA-256 hash twice. In other words, double SHA-256 means the hash of the hash of the input. A block header consists of Version, hashPrevBlock, hashMerkleRoot, Time, Bits (difficulty target), and Nonce. Nonce is an arbitrary number that is repeatedly changed and fed into the proof of work algorithm to see if it results in a value which is less than or equal to the difficulty target.

The target value is calculated from the mining difficulty which changes every 2016 blocks, which is equivalent to roughly two weeks. If miners are mining too fast – let's say every eight minutes, they manage to generate a block instead of ten minutes – it means there is too much hash power; therefore, as a regulation mechanism, the difficulty goes up. If miners are producing blocks over the course of the previous 2016 blocks too slowly, say 1 block every 12 minutes, then it is slower than expected; therefore, the difficulty is regulated down. Let's go through some formulas.

First, Bitcoin's difficulty formula calculates the new difficulty for the next 2016 blocks based on the rate of block generation of the previous 2016 blocks. The formula is

$$New\ difficulty = \frac{(previous\ difficulty \times 2016 \times 10\ minutes)}{(time\ took\ to\ mine\ most\ recent\ 2016\ blocks)}$$

This formula basically regulates the blockchain to produce new blocks roughly at a mean rate of ten minutes.

Now in order to calculate the target, first calculate the difficulty using the following formula:

$$difficulty = \frac{(possible\ target)}{(current\ target)}$$

Finally, the target is calculated using the following formula:

$$target = \frac{(possible\ target)}{(difficulty)}$$

Now that we have established how the target value is calculated, let's see what miners do and how they find a hash which satisfies the preceding equation, that is, the value obtained after hashing the block is less than the target value. In other words, the block hash must match a specific pattern where the hash starts with a certain number of zeroes. This is also known as the partial hash inversion problem. This problem is to find a partial preimage to the double SHA-256 hash function, which can only be found (if ever) by trying different inputs one by one until one of the inputs works.

Fundamentally, Bitcoin mining is the process of finding a nonce that, when concatenated with a block and hashed twice using the SHA-256 hash function, produces a number which starts with a specific number of zeroes.

So, what do miners do?

Task of Miners

In the Bitcoin blockchain network, when new transactions are executed by a user they are broadcast to all nodes on the network via a peer-to-peer gossip protocol. These transactions end up in transaction pools of nodes. Miners perform several tasks:

- Miners maintain transaction pools. They listen for incoming transactions and keep those in their pools.

- They also listen for new blocks and append any new valid blocks to their chain. This is of course not only the task for a miner, other nonmining nodes also simply synchronize the blocks.

- Create a candidate block by picking up transactions from the transaction pool.

- Find a nonce by trying every nonce which when concatenated with the block and the previous hash results in a number which is less than the target as per formula 3 earlier.

- Broadcast the newly mined block to the network.

- Fetch the reward by receiving Coinbase on the address that the miner wants to send the reward to.

Let's see what a candidate block contains and how it is created.

A potentially valid candidate block and eventually a valid block contain several elements, which are listed in Table 5-2.

Table 5-2. *Block elements*

Size	Description	Data Type	Explanation
4	Version	Integer	Block version
32	prev_block	Character	The hash value of the previous block Header
32	merkle_root	Character	Merkle root hash of all transaction in block
4	timestamp	Unsigned integer	Time of block creation in Unix time format
4	bits	Unsigned integer	Network difficulty target for the block
4	nonce	Unsigned integer	Nonce for this block
1+	txn_count	Variable integer	Total number of transactions
variable	txns	tx[]	Transactions

The diagram in Figure 5-2 shows how transactions from a transaction pool (bottom left of the figure) are picked up and a Merkle tree is created, the root of which is included in the candidate block. Finally, double (SHA-256) is computed for the block for a comparison against the target.

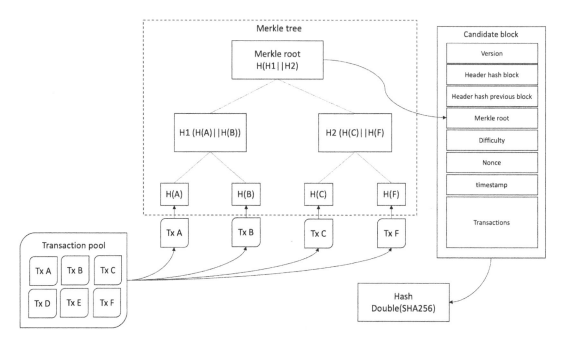

Figure 5-2. *Transaction pool transactions to the Merkle tree and candidate block*

A nonce is a number from 1 to $2^{32} - 1$, that is, a 32-bit unsigned integer which gets included in the block. Using this nonce in each iteration of checking if the resultant number is less than the target is what's called a mining. If the resultant number is less than the target, then it's a block mined and it's valid, which is then broadcast to the network.

The nonce field in a block being an unsigned integer, there are only 2^{32} nonces to try. As such, miners can run out of them quite quickly. In other words, it means that there are roughly four billion nonces to try which miners can quickly perform given the powerful mining hardware available. It also is very easy even for a normal computer to quickly check.

This of course can create an issue where no one is able to find the required nonce which produces the required hash. Even if miners try again, they will try the same thing again with the same results. At this stage, we can use other attributes of the block and use them as a variable and keep modifying the block until the hash of the block is less than the target, that is, *SHAd256(Block header || nonce) < Target.*

Now after going through all these iterations, what if the valid nonce is not found? At this point, miners will have to increase the search space somehow. For this, they can modify the block somewhat to get a different hash. They can do several things:

- Drop the transactions, add new transactions, or pick up a new set of transactions. This modification will recalculate the Merkle root, and hence the header, and as a result, the hash will be different.

- Modify the timestamp slightly (in the range of two hours; otherwise, it's an invalid block). It can be done simply by adding just a second, which will result in a different header and consequently a different hash.

- Modify Coinbase via unused *ScriptSig*, where you can put any arbitrary data. This will change the Merkle root and hence the header and consequently the hash.

And miners can keep modifying with different variations until they reach SHAd256(*Block header* || *nonce*) < *target*, which means that they've found a valid nonce that solves the proof of work.

The discovery of the valid hash is based on the concept known as *partial hash inversion*.

Proof of work has some key properties. Formally, we list them as follows.

Properties of PoW

Proof of work has five properties: completeness, computationally complex, dynamic cost adjustment, quick verification, and progress free.

Completeness

This property implies that proofs produced by the prover are verifiable and acceptable by the verifier.

Computationally Complex – Difficult to Compute – Slow Creation

The creation of proof of work is slow but not intractable. Creating proofs requires spending considerable computational resources and takes a considerable amount of time.

Auto-adjustable Cost – Dynamic Cost

This is the elegance of this protocol. First, PoW is difficult to compute. It takes considerable effort to generate proof of work. Roughly, it is more than quintillions of hashes that are checked per second on the Bitcoin network to solve the proof of work. Second, the parameters are adjustable, which means that even if blocks are produced faster or slower, no matter how much hash power is put in place or how much is removed from the network, the block generation rate roughly remains ten minutes per block. In the early days when the difficulty was one, blocks were still generated one per minute; now in 2022, even if the difficulty is roughly 25 tera hashes per second, still the protocol readjusts itself, and the block generation rate is still one per ten minutes. This is amazing and a testament to the robust design of the protocol. So, in summary if the block generation in a period of 2016 blocks is taking more than ten minutes per block, then in the next 2016 block period the difficulty will be readjusted to low. If the block generation is faster and taking less than ten minutes per block, for example, in case some bleeding-edge hardware is introduced for hashing in the network, then the difficulty will go up for the next 2016 blocks. This is how a state of balance is maintained in the network. Also note that many blocks are produced very quickly under ten minutes; some take a lot longer than that, but the average is ten minutes. This is due to the probabilistic nature of the protocol.

Quick and Efficient Verification – Quick Verification

This property implies that proofs are very quick and efficient to verify. It should not be computationally complex to verify the proof. In the case of Bitcoin, it is simply running a SHA-256 hash function twice on the block with the nonce produced by the miner, and if $SHAd256(nonce \| block\ header) \leq target$, then the block is valid. It only takes as long as it takes to generate SHA-256 hash and then compare, which both are very compute-efficient processes. The key idea here is that it should be computationally complex to generate a block with a valid nonce; however, it should be easy for other nodes to verify its validity.

Progress Free

This property implies that the chance of solving the proof of work is proportional to the hash power contributed; however, it is still a chance, not a 100% guarantee that a miner with the highest hash power will always win. In other words, miners with more hash power get only proportional advantage, and miners with less power get proportional compensation too and get lucky sometimes to find blocks before even miners with more hash power.

In practice, this means that every miner is in fact working on a different candidate block to solve the proof of work. Miners are not working on the same block; they are not trying to find a valid nonce for the same hash. This is because of several differences, such as transactions, version number, Coinbase differences, and other metadata differences, which when hashed result in a totally different hash (SHA-256 twice). This means that every miner is solving a different problem and solving a different part of the double SHA-256 or conveniently written as *SHAd256* search space.

The progress free property can be visualized in Figure 5-3. As shown in Figure 5-3, miners are all working on their own candidate block, which is different from other blocks due to differences mentioned earlier. So, every nonce that the miners concatenate with the block data to get the hash will result in a hash that no other miner is aware of. This gives some advantage to a miner with less power, where it can happen that the block which this small miner is trying to find a valid nonce for manages to find the nonce that solves PoW before a miner with more hash power finds the valid nonce for their block.

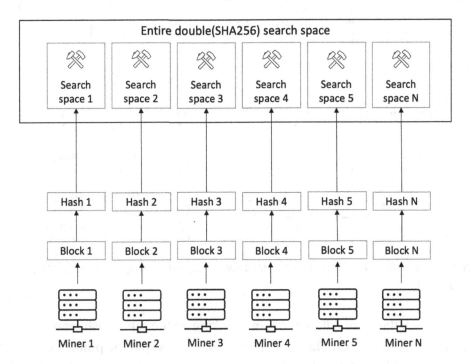

Figure 5-3. *Progress free property – each miner working on a different part of double (SHA-256) search space*

This is another elegant property of PoW which ensures that miners with more hash power may have some advantage, but it also means that a miner with less hash power can be lucky in finding the nonce that works before the large miners. The key point is miners are not working on the same block! If it were the same block every time, the most powerful miner would've won. This is called the progress free property of Bitcoin PoW.

It is however possible that many miners collaboratively work on the same block (same search space), hence dividing up the work between themselves. Imagine the search space is 1 to 100 for a block, it may be divided in 10 different parts, then all miners can collectively work on a single block. This divides up the work, and all miners can contribute and earn their share of the reward. This is called **pool mining**. Unlike **solo mining** where only one miner tries and the entire effort can be lost if it doesn't find the nonce and tries again for the next block, in pool mining individual contribution is not wasted.

This concept can be visualized in Figure 5-4.

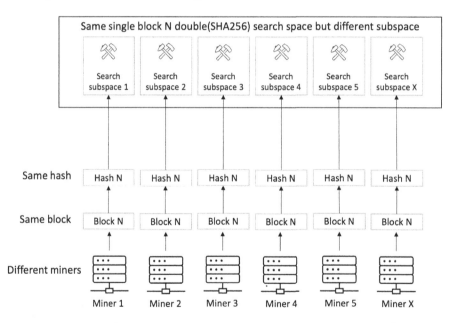

Figure 5-4. *Mining pool – many miners working on a single block (shad256 search space)*

In Figure 5-4, there are different miners working on the same hash search space produced by the same block. This way, the pool operators split the proof of work into different pieces and distribute them to the miners in the pool. All miners work and put in the effort, and eventually one miner finds the block which is broadcast normally to the Bitcoin network. The pool operator receives the block reward which is split between the miners in proportion to the effort put in by the miners.

Probabilistic Aspects of Dynamic Parameters

Now let's shed some light on the probabilistic aspects related to the property (dynamic and auto-adjustable parameters), where I will explain what the average of ten minutes means and what parameterization means.

In probability theory, a Bernoulli trial is an action that has two possible outcomes, either success or failure. The probability of success or failure is fixed between trials. For example, in coin flips the probability of heads or tails is 50%. The outcome is also independent. It is not the case that having three heads in a row will lead to a definite head for the fourth time too. Similarly, in Bitcoin mining, the outcome of success or failure, as shown in the following, remains independent and almost like coin flips roughly 50% probabilistic. We can see this in the following formula.

Success and failure in mining can be written like the following two formulas:

$$Success = SHAd256\left(nonce \| block\ header\ \right) < target$$

$$Failure = SHAd256\left(nonce \| block\ header\ \right) \geq target$$

PoW is almost like roll dicing, for example, if I have rolled the dice a few times, I cannot know when the next six will occur; it might be that I get six in the first attempt, may never get six, or get six after several rolls. Similarly, whether a single nonce has been tried to find the valid nonce or trillions and trillions of nonces have been tried, the mean time until a miner finds the valid nonce remains probabilistic. It doesn't matter whether 100 million nonces have been tried or only one; the probability of finding the valid nonce remains the same. So trying millions of nonces doesn't make it more likely to find the valid nonce; even trying once or only a few times could find the valid nonce.

A Bernoulli trial iterated enough to achieve a continuous result instead of discrete is called a Poisson process. Formally, we can say that a Poisson process is a sequence of discrete events, where events occur independently at a known constant average rate, but the exact timing of events is random.

For example, movements in a stock price are a Poisson process. A Poisson process has some properties:

- Events are independent of each other, that is, no influence of an outcome on some other.

- The rate of events per time period is constant.

- Two events cannot occur simultaneously.

The average time between events is known, but they are randomly spaced (stochastic). In Bitcoin, of course, we know the time between two block generation events is known, that is, roughly ten minutes, but the generations are randomly spaced.

The mean time for a new block is ten minutes on average. We can use a simple formula to find out the meantime of finding the next block for a particular miner.

$$Next\ block\ mean\ time\,(specific) = \frac{10\ minutes}{fraction\ of\ hash\ power\ controlled\ by\ the\ miner}$$

Probability of an Attacker Catching Up

In this section, we answer the question of what the probability is of an attacker to mine enough blocks to take over the chain. Suppose an attacker has some mining power, say q. A seller waits for z confirmation (z blocks) before accepting the payment, and the honest chain hash rate is denoted by p.

The probability of an attacker catching up q_z can be calculated as shown follows:

$$q_z = \left\{ 1\,if\ p \leq q\,\_\left(\frac{q}{p}\right)^z\,if\ p > q \right\}$$

where

$$q = attacker's\ hash\ rate$$

$$p = honest\ hash\ rate$$

$$z = blocks\ to\ catch\,up$$

This means that if the honest hash rate is less than the attacker's hash rate, then the probability of an attacker catching up is one, and if the honest hash rate is more than the attacker's hash rate, then the probability of catching up is $\left(\dfrac{q}{p}\right)^{z}$.

In the next section, we formally write the proof of work algorithm.

PoW Algorithm

Formally, we can write the entire proof of work algorithm as follows:

```
1:   nonce := 0
2:   hashTarget := nBits
3:   hash := null
4:   while (true) {
5:     SHA256(SHA256(blockheader || nonce))
6:         if (hash ≤ hashTarget) {
7:               append to blockchain
8:       else
9:               nonce := nonce + 1
10:  }
11: }
```

In the preceding algorithm, the nonce is initialized as zero. The hash target which is the difficulty target of the network is taken from the *nBits* field of the candidate block header. The hash is initialized to null. After that, an infinite loop runs, which first concatenates the block header and the nonce and runs SHA-256 twice on it to produce the hash. Next, if the produced hash is less than the target hash, then it is accepted and appended to the blockchain; otherwise, the nonce is incremented and the process starts again. If no nonce is found, then the algorithm tries the next block.

This process can be visualized in Figure 5-5.

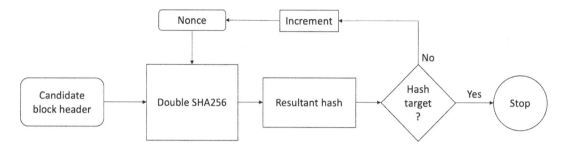

Figure 5-5. *Proof of work*

In Figure 5-5, the previous block hash, transactions, and nonce are fed into a hash function to produce a hash which is checked against the target value. If it is less than the target value, then it's a valid hash and the process stops; otherwise, the nonce is incremented, and the entire process repeats until the resultant hash is less than the target, where the process stops.

Game Theory and Proof of Work

Game theory is the study of behaviors in strategic interactive situations where an individual's best course of action depends on the choice of others. Game theory models represent real-life situations in an abstract manner. Game theory is useful in many different fields, such as economics, biology, social science, finance, politics, computer science, and many more. For example, in economics, product launch decisions made by businesses are influenced by their competitor's choice of product and marketing strategy. In computer networks, networked computers may compete for resources such as bandwidth. A Nash equilibrium is used to study political competition. In politics, politicians' policies are influenced by announcements and promises made by their opponents.

A game can be defined as a description of all strategic actions that a player may take but without describing the likely outcome.

There are some entities in a game which are listed as follows:

- **Players**: Strategic rational decision makers in a game

- **Actions**: Set of actions available to a player

- **Payoffs**: A payout to be received by a player for a particular outcome

Games represent different strategic situations. There are some classical games such as Bach or Stravinsky, prisoner's dilemma, Hawk-Dove, and matching pennies. In games, players are not aware of the actions of other players when making their own decisions; such games are called **simultaneous move games**.

Games can be analyzed by creating a table where all possible actions of players and payoffs are listed. This table is known as the **strategic form** of the game or **payoff matrix**.

A **Nash equilibrium** is a fundamental and powerful concept in game theory. In a Nash equilibrium, each rational player chooses the best course of action in response to the choice made by other players. Each player is aware of other players' equilibrium strategies, and no player can make any gains by changing only their own strategy. In short, any deviation from the strategy does not result in any gain for the deviant.

Prisoner's Dilemma

In this simultaneous move game, two suspects of a crime are put into separate cells without any way to communicate. If they both confess, then they both will be imprisoned for three years each. If one of them confesses and acts as a witness against the other, then charges against him will be dropped; however, the other suspect will get four years in prison. If none of them confesses, then both will be sentenced to only one year in prison. Now you can see that if both suspects cooperate and don't confess, then it results in the best outcome for both. However, there is a big incentive of going free for both to not cooperate and act as a witness against the other. This game results in gains for both if they cooperate and don't confess and results in only one year in prison each. Let's name these characters Alice and Bob for ease and see what possible outcomes there are in this game.

There are four possible outcomes of this game:

1. Alice does not confess, and Bob does not confess.

2. Alice confesses, and Bob does not confess.

3. Alice does not confess, and Bob confesses.

4. Alice confesses, and Bob confesses.

If Alice and Bob can somehow communicate, then they can jointly decide to not confess, which will result in only a one-year sentence each. However, the dominant strategy here is to confess rather than don't confess.

A **dominant strategy** is a strategy that results in the largest payoff regardless of the behaviors of other players in the game.

We can represent this in a payoff matrix form as shown in Figure 5-6.

	Don't confess	Confess
Don't confess	Alice: 1 , Bob: 1	Alice: 4 , Bob: 0
Confess	Alice: 0 , Bob: 4	Alice: 3 , Bob: 3

Figure 5-6. *Prisoner's dilemma payoff matrix*

Alice and Bob are both aware of this matrix and know that they both have this matrix to choose from. Alice and Bob are players, "confess" and "don't confess" are actions, and payoffs are prison sentences.

Regardless of what Alice does or Bob does, the other player still confesses. Alice's strategy is that if Bob confesses, she should confess too because a one-year prison sentence is better than three. If Bob does not confess, she should still confess because she will go free. The same strategy is employed by Bob. The dominant strategy here is to confess, regardless of what the other player does.

Both players confess and go to prison for three years each. This is because even if Bob had somehow managed to tell Alice about his no confession strategy, Alice would have still confessed and became a witness to avoid prison altogether. Similar is the case from Alice's perspective. Therefore, the best outcome for both becomes "confession" in a Nash equilibrium. This is written as {*confess, confess*}.

In the prisoner's dilemma, there is a benefit of cooperation for both players, but the possible incentive of going free for each player entices contest. When all players in a game are rational, the best choice is to be in a Nash equilibrium.

Game theory models are highly abstract; therefore, they can be used in many different situations, once developed for a particular situation. For example, the prisoner's dilemma model can be used in many other areas. In network communications where wireless network devices compete for bandwidth, energy supply, etc., there is a need to regulate node behavior in such a way that all devices on the network can work in harmony. Imagine a network where two cell towers working on the same frequency in close vicinity can affect each other's performance. One way to counter this problem is to run both towers at low energy so that they don't interfere with each other, but that will decrease the bandwidth of both the towers. If one tower increases its energy and the other don't, then the one that doesn't loses and runs on lower bandwidth. So, the dominant strategy here becomes to run towers at maximum power regardless of what the other tower does, so that they achieve maximum possible gain. This result is like the prisoner's dilemma where confession is the best strategy. Here, maximum power is the best strategy.

Now in the light of the preceding explained concepts, we can analyze the Bitcoin protocol from a game theoretic perspective.

PoW and Game Theory

We can think of Bitcoin as a distributed system with selfish players; nodes might be trying to gain incentives without contributing or trying to gain more incentives than their fair share.

The Bitcoin protocol is a **Nash equilibrium** because no deviation from the protocol's equilibrium strategy can result in a gain for the deviant. The protocol is designed in such a way that any deviation from the protocol is punished, and normal (good) behavior is economically incentivized. The dominant strategy in Bitcoin is to mine according to the protocol rules as there is no other strategy that would result in a better outcome. Each participant is better off by just sticking to the rules of the network.

If the other miners don't switch their strategy, an attacker has no incentive to switch their own strategy. Neither player can increase their payoffs by switching to a different strategy if the other player doesn't switch their strategy. This means that in Bitcoin if all other miners are honest, an adversary has no incentive to change their strategy and try to perform malicious mining.

Incentive mechanisms such as block reward and transaction fees in Bitcoin discourage malicious behavior. These incentives encourage participants to behave according to the protocol, which not only results in the creation of new bitcoins, that is, network progress is guaranteed, but also the security of the network is maintained.

Since 2009, the Bitcoin network has attracted so much investment in the form of mining farms and Bitcoin businesses, exchanges, and services that network participants will benefit more by protecting the network rather than destroying it. They gain by protecting the network. Even attackers cannot gain much. Imagine if some adversary managed to find a way to move all coins owned by Satoshi Nakamoto into another account. There probably is no incentive for an attacker to do so, because the moment it happens, the Bitcoin almost certainly will become worthless, because this event would imply that the very cryptography that protects the network has been broken (assuming that real Satoshi is not alive or has lost his private keys irrecoverably).

I have a feeling that Satoshi is not moving his coins because that can cause Bitcoin to lose its value drastically.

Similarly, even if an adversary somehow gains 51% of the network hash power, taking over the entire network may not be beneficial anymore. Why? Because the best course of action in such a situation for the adversary is to keep mining silently with some reasonable hash power to gain economic incentives (earn bitcoins) just like others on the network, instead of utilizing the entire 51% hash power announcing the attack to the world. That would just diminish the Bitcoin value almost entirely, and any gains by the attacker would be worthless. Therefore, attackers do not have incentive to take over the Bitcoin network, perhaps apart from some mishaps that occurred due to human errors and compromised keys. This is the elegance and beauty of Bitcoin that even attackers do not gain by attacking the network. All participants gain by just playing by the rules. The dominant strategy for miners is to be honest.

For the very first time in distributed computing, a network is created which does not rely on any trusted third party and is permissionless, yet it doesn't let any attacker take over the network. Here, I remember something, which is not directly relevant to Bitcoin, but helps to feel what many distributed computing experts might feel about Bitcoin when they first realize how elegant it is.

It could not be true but it was true.

—Mikhael Gromov

www.ams.org/notices/201003/201003FullIssue.pdf

With the advent of Bitcoin and novel combination of cryptography, distributed computing, and economics, a new field of study has emerged, called Cryptoeconomics or Cryptonomics. This is depicted in Figure 5-7.

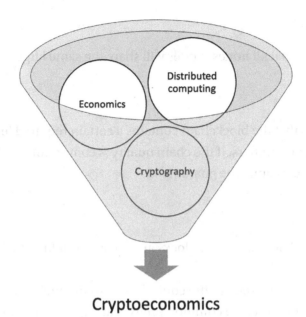

Cryptoeconomics

Figure 5-7. *Fusion of distributed computing, economics, and cryptography – Bitcoin*

We can also think of the fork resolution mechanism as a **Schelling point** solution. This is a game theory concept where a focal point or also called Schelling point is a solution that people choose by default in the absence of communication. Similarly, in the proof of work fork resolution mechanism, due to the longest (strongest) chain rule, nodes tend to choose the longest chain as a canonical chain to add the block that they've received without any communication or direction from other nodes. This concept of cooperating without communication was introduced by Thomas Schelling in his book *The Strategy of Conflict*.

Similarities Between PoW and Traditional BFT

Fundamentally, all consensus algorithms strive toward achieving safety and liveness properties. Either deterministic or probabilistic, basically all consensus algorithms have three main properties: agreement, validity, and termination. We have introduced these terms before. The question arises in Nakamoto consensus of whether we can redefine these properties in a way which is closer to the blockchain world. The answer is yes; agreement, validity, and liveness properties can be mapped to Nakamoto consensus-specific properties of common prefix, chain quality, and chain growth, respectively. These terms were first introduced in https://eprint.iacr.org/2014/765.pdf [7].

Common Prefix

This property implies that all honest nodes will share the same large common prefix.

Chain Quality

This property means that the blockchain contains a certain required level of correct blocks created by honest miners. If the chain quality is compromised, then the validity property of the protocol cannot be guaranteed.

Chain Growth

This property means that new correct blocks are constantly added to the blockchain regularly.

These properties can be seen as the equivalent of traditional consensus properties in the Nakamoto world. Here, the common prefix is an agreement property, the chain quality is a validity property, and chain growth can be seen as a liveness property.

PoW As State Machine Replication

A proof of work blockchain can be seen as a state machine replication mechanism where first a leader is elected who proposes a sequence of transactions batched in a block. Second, the finalized (mined) block is broadcast to other nodes via a gossip protocol, which is accepted and appended into their local blockchains, achieving log replication. We can think of it as if the leader is proposing an order and all nodes updating their log (local blockchain) based on this order of transactions set in the block.

Let's first see the leader election algorithm and replication algorithm in detail.

Leader Election Algorithm

A node that solves the proof of work puzzle is elected to finalize and broadcast its candidate block. The leader in proof of work is elected as a function of computational power of the mining node. There is no voting required from other nodes as opposed to other traditional BFT protocols. Also, unlike traditional BFT protocols, the leader is rotated every block. This approach has been used in later blockchain BFT protocols as well where the leader is rotated every block to thwart any attempts to sabotage (compromise) the leader. Also, in traditional BFT protocols, usually the primary or leader is only changed when the primary fails, but in PoW a leader is elected every block. Leader election in PoW is based on computational power; However, several techniques have been used in other permissioned blockchains, from simply randomly choosing a leader or simple rotation formula to complex means such as verifiable random functions. We will cover these techniques in Chapter 8 in detail.

The leader election formula is simply the same PoW formula that we have already covered in the section "How PoW Works." A soon as any miner solves the proof of work, it immediately is elected as a leader and earns the right to broadcast its newly mined block. At this point, the miner is also awarded 6.25 BTC. This reward halves every four years.

At the leader election stage, the miner node has successfully solved the PoW puzzle, and now the log replication can start.

Log Replication

The log replication or block replication to achieve consistency among nodes is achieved by broadcasting the newly mined block to other nodes via a gossip dissemination protocol. The key differences between a normal log and a blockchain log are as follows:

- It is append-only and immutable.

- Each new batch of transactions (block) has a hash of the previous block, thus linking it in a so-called proof of work chain or hash chain or chain of blocks or blockchain.

- The blocks (content in the log) are verifiable from the previous block.

- Each block contains transactions and a block header. This structure was discussed in detail in Chapter 4.

When a new block is broadcast, it is validated and verified by each honest node on the network before it is appended to the blockchain. Log replication after leader election can be divided into three steps.

New Block Propagation

A block is broadcast using the gossip protocol. We can visualize the block propagation mechanism in Figure 5-8. Notice that node 1 has sent a message, for example, a new block, to node 2, which is then sent to nodes 4, 14, and 13 by node 2. A similar pattern can be seen in the network for other nodes too.

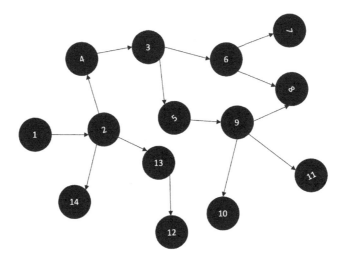

Figure 5-8. *Gossip protocol in Bitcoin*

This type of propagation ensures that eventually all nodes get the message with high probability. Moreover, this pattern does not overwhelm a single node with the requirement of broadcasting a message to all nodes.

Block Validation

Block validation can be seen as the state transition function (STF). This **block validation function** has the following high-level rules:

- The block is syntactically correct.

- The block header hash is less than the network difficulty target.

- The block timestamp is not more than two hours in future.

- The block size is correct.

- All transactions are valid within the block.

- It is referring to the previous hash.

The protocol specifies very precise rules, details of which can be found at https:// en.bitcoin.it/wiki/Protocol_rules; however, the preceding list is a high-level list of block validation checks a node performs.

Append to the Blockchain

The block is finally inserted into the blockchain by the nodes. When appending to the blockchain, it may happen that those nodes may have received two valid blocks. In that case, a fork will occur, and nodes will have to decide which chain to append the block to.

We can visualize this concept in Figure 5-9.

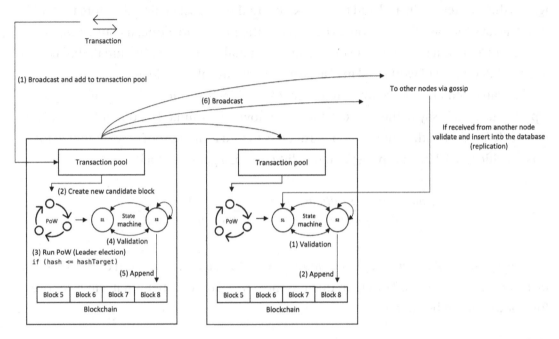

Figure 5-9. *Proof of work as state machine replication*

As shown in Figure 5-9, proof of work as a state machine replication consists of two main operations: leader election through proof of work and then replication via a gossip protocol and receiving node's block validation and insertion mechanism. After proof of work on a node, if the proof of work is valid, then the block is treated the same as if it has been received from another node and eventually inserted into the local blockchain database after validation.

A component that chooses which chain is conclusive in case of a conflict is called a fork handler which embodies fork resolution rules on how to handle a fork.

Fork Resolution

Fork resolution can be seen as a fault tolerance mechanism in Bitcoin. Fork resolution rules ensure that only the chain that has the most work done to produce it is the one that is always picked up by the nodes when inserting a new block. When a valid block arrives for the same height, then the fork resolution mechanism allows the node to ignore the shorter chain and add the block only to the longest chain. Also note that this is not always the case that the longest chain has the most work done; it could happen that a shorter chain may have the most computational hash power behind it, that is, the accumulated proof of work, and in that case, that chain will be selected.

We can calculate the accumulated proof of work by first calculating the difficulty of a particular block, say B, then we can use the following formula. The difficulty of a block can be defined as finding how much harder it is to find a valid proof of work nonce for this specific block B in comparison to the difficulty of a genesis block.

$$\frac{Genesis\ block's\ difficulty\ target}{B's\ difficulty\ target} = \frac{\left(\left(2^{16}\right) \times 256^2\right)}{B's\ difficulty\ target}$$

We can say that the accumulated proof of work for a chain is the sum of the difficulty of all blocks in the chain. The chain that has most proof of work behind it will be chosen for a new block to be appended.

The longest chain rule was originally simply the chain with the highest number of blocks. However, this simple rule was modified later, and the "longest" chain became the chain with the most work done to create it, that is, the strongest chain.

In practice, there is a *chainwork* value in the block which helps to identify the chain with the most work, that is, the correct "longest" or "strongest" chain.

For example, we use

```
bitcoin-cli getblockheader
00000000000000000000811608a01b388b167d9c94c0c0870377657d524ff0003
```

For block 687731, we get

```
{
    "result": {
        "hash":
        "0000000000000000000811608a01b388b167d9c94c0c0870377657d524ff0003",
        "confirmations": 1,
        "height": 687731,
        "version": 547356676,
        "versionHex": "20a00004",
        "merkleroot":
        "73f4a59b854ed2d6597b56e6bc499a7e0b8651376e63e0825dbcca3b9dde61ae",
        "time": 1623786185,
        "mediantime": 1623781371,
        "nonce": 2840970250,
        "bits": "170e1ef9",
        "difficulty": 19932791027262.74,
        "chainwork": "000000000000000000000000000000000000000001eb7091803
        0b922df7533fd4",
        "nTx": 2722,
        "previousblockhash":
        "0000000000000000000f341e0046c6d82979fdfa09ab324a0e8ffbabd22815d"
    },
    "error": null,
    "id": null
}
```

Notice the chainwork value when converted to a decimal results in an extremely large number, 6663869462529529036756. This is the amount of work behind this head of the chain.

There are several types of forks that can occur in the Bitcoin blockchain:

- Regular fork

- Hard fork

- Soft fork

- Byzantine fork

Regular fork

A fork can naturally occur in the Bitcoin blockchain when two miners competing to solve the proof of work happen to solve it almost at the same time. As a result, two new blocks are added to the blockchain. Miners will keep working on the longest chain that they are aware of, and soon the shorter chain with so-called orphan blocks will be ignored.

The diagram in Figure 5-10 shows how consensus finality is impacted by forks.

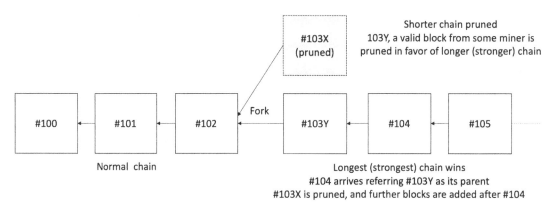

Figure 5-10. *Impact of forking on consensus finality*

Due to the forking possibility, consensus is probabilistic. When the fork is resolved, previously accepted transactions are rolled back, and the longest (strongest) chain prevails.

The probability of these regular forks is quite low. A split of one block can occur almost every two weeks and is quickly resolved when the next block arrives, referring to the previous one as a parent. The probability of occurrence of a two-block split is exponentially lower, which is almost once in 90 years. The probability of occurrence of a four-block temporary fork is once in almost 700,000,000 years.

Hard fork

A hard fork occurs due to changes in the protocol, which are incompatible with the existing rules. This essentially creates two chains, one running on the old rules and the new one on new rules.

We can visualize how a hard fork behaves in Figure 5-11.

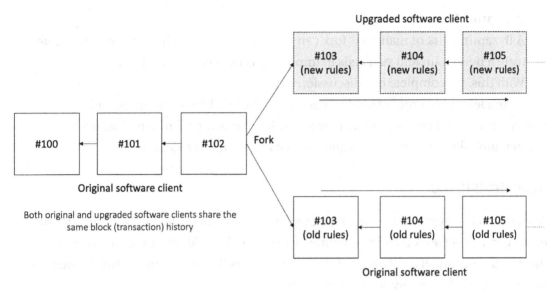

Figure 5-11. *Hard fork*

Soft fork

A soft fork occurs when changes in the protocol are backward compatible. It means that there is no need to update all the clients; even if not all the clients are upgraded, the chain is still one. However, any clients that do not upgrade won't be able to operate using the new rules. In other words, old clients will still be able to accept the new blocks.

This concept can be visualized in the diagram in Figure 5-12.

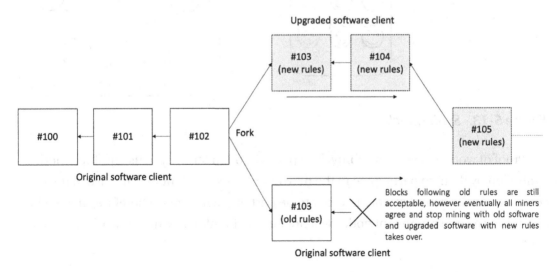

Figure 5-12. *Soft fork*

Byzantine fork

A Byzantine fork or malicious fork can occur in scenarios where an adversary may try to create a new chain and succeeds in imposing its own version of the chain.

With this, we complete our discussion on forks.

A core feature of proof of work consensus is the Sybil resistance mechanism which ensures that creating many new identities and using them is prohibitively computationally complex. Let's explore this concept in more detail.

Sybil Resistance

A Sybil attack occurs when an attacker creates multiple identities, all belonging to them to subvert the network relying on voting by using all those identities to cast vote in their favor. Imagine if an attacker creates more nodes than the entire network, then the attacker can skew the network in their favor.

A Sybil attack can be visualized in Figure 5-13, where an attacker is controlling more Sybil nodes than the network.

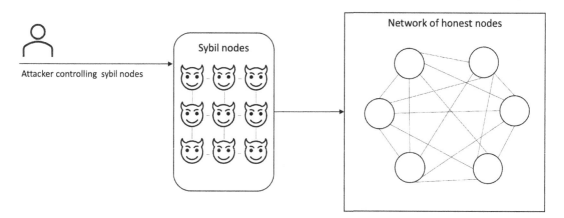

Figure 5-13. *Sybil attack*

Proof of work makes it prohibitively expensive for an attacker to use multiple nodes controlled by them to participate in the network because each node will have to do computationally complex work in order to be part of the network. Therefore, an attacker controlling a large number of nodes will not be able to influence the network.

Significance of Block Timestamp

The Bitcoin network with its heterogenous geographically dispersed nodes running on the Internet appears to be an asynchronous network. This appears to be the case because there is no upper bound on the processor speeds and no upper bound on the message delay. Usually, in traditional BFT consensus protocols, there is no reliance on a global physical clock, and network assumptions are usually partially synchronous networks. However, in Bitcoin all blocks have a timestamp field, which is populated by the local node which mined the block. This is part of the block validation process where a block is accepted only if its timestamp is less than or equal to the median of the last 11 blocks. Also, timestamps are vital for maintaining block frequency, difficulty retargeting, and network difficulty calculations. From this point of view, we can think of the Bitcoin network as loosely synchronous, where loose clock synchrony is required for the network to make progress and ensure liveness.

Note that the Bitcoin network is not partially synchronous because we defined partially synchronous and its variations earlier, and the Bitcoin network doesn't seem to fit in any of those definitions. It is synchronous in the sense that blocks have a timestamp generated from the local node on which the block was produced; however, from a processor delay perspective, it is almost asynchronous. Also, in the block validation mechanism, one of the rules requires that a block is produced within roughly the last two hours (median of the previous 11 blocks), making Bitcoin an "almost synchronous" system. This is so because timestamps are essential for the proper functioning of the Bitcoin system; however, due to large communication and processor delay tolerance, it can be thought of as a loosely synchronous system.

On the other hand, as timestamps are required only for proper functioning of the limited part of the system, that is, the difficulty calculations, and block validation and are not a requirement for achieving consensus (i.e., by choosing a leader by solving proof of work – mining), then from that point of view it is an asynchronous system, given that processor and communication delays have no defined upper bounds, except that messages will reach nodes eventually with a probabilistic guarantee of a gossip protocol.

In Bitcoin blocks, timestamps are not 100% accurate but enough to secure the proof of work mechanism. Originally, Satoshi envisioned a combination of a system clock, a median of other servers' clocks, and NTP servers for clock adjustment. However, NTP was never implemented, and the median of other nodes' clock remained as the primary source for clock adjustment in the network.

Block timestamps not only serve to provide some variation for the block hash, which is useful in proof of work, but also helps to protect against blockchain manipulation where an adversary could try to inject an invalid block in the chain. When a Bitcoin node connects to another node, it receives the timestamp in UTC format from it. The receiving node then calculates the offset of the received time from the local system clock and stores it. The network adjusted time is then calculated as the local UTC system clock plus the median offset from all connected nodes.

There are two rules regarding timestamps in Bitcoin blocks. A valid timestamp must be greater than the median timestamp of the previous 11 blocks. It should also be less than the median timestamp calculated based on the time received from other connected nodes (i.e., network adjusted time) plus two hours. However, this network time adjustment must never be more than 70 minutes from the local system clock.

The conclusion is that Bitcoin is in fact secure only under a synchronous network model. More precisely, it is a lockstep-free synchrony where there exists some known finite time bound, but execution is not in lockstep.

A Caveat

The order of transaction is not consensus driven. Each miner picks up a transaction in a hardcoded order within the client, and indeed there have been some attacks that can result in transaction censorship or ignoring or reordering. Consensus is achieved in fact on the block, and that is also not through voting; once a miner has solved PoW, it just simply wins the right to append a new block to the chain. Of course, it will be validated by other nodes when they receive it, but there is no real agreement or voting mechanism after the mined block has been broadcast by the successful miner. There is no voting or consensus which agrees on this new block; the miner who is the elected leader and because they solved PoW has won the right to add a new block. Other nodes just accept it if it passes the *valid()* predicate.

So, the caveat here is that when a candidate block is created by picking up transactions from the transaction pool, they are picked up in a certain order which a miner can influence. For example, some miners may choose not to include transactions without any fee and only include those which are paying fee. Fair for the miner perhaps, but unfair for the user and the overall Bitcoin system! However, eventually all transactions will be added, even those without a fee, but they might be considered only after some considerable time has elapsed since their inclusion in the transaction pool. If they've aged, then they'll be eventually included. Moreover, under the assumption that usually there is a majority of honest miners always in the network, the transactions are expected to be picked up in a reasonable amount of time in line with the protocol specification.

Let us now see what is that order.

The transactions are picked up from the transaction pool based on its priority, which is calculated using the following formula [8]:

$$priority = \frac{sum(input\ value\ in\ base\ units \times input\ age)}{size\ in\ bytes}$$

$$p = \frac{\Sigma(v_i \times a_i)}{s}$$

It is of concern that the ordering of transactions is not fair and leads to front running and other relevant attacks. We will discuss fair ordering in Chapter 10.

PoW As a Solution to Byzantine Generals Problem

This has been described by Satoshi Nakamoto himself in a post [5]. I will describe the logic here in a concise way.

Remember in the Byzantine generals problem, the problem is to agree on an attack time in the presence of treacherous generals and the possibility of captured messengers. In the case of proof of work, we can consider miners as generals where the understanding between generals is that any general can announce the attack time and the attack time heard first is accepted as the authoritative time to attack. The problem however is that if two generals propose different times almost simultaneously, it could happen due to messaging delays where some generals receive one of the attack times first, and some others receive the other attack time first, resulting in disagreement. In order to solve this problem, each general who receives an attack time starts to solve a complex math puzzle. When a general solves this math puzzle (proof of work), it broadcasts that to the network. When other generals receive it, they switch to this new time.

All generals are allowed to propose a time, but only one of the proposed times will eventually be accepted as valid by all generals.

For a proposed time to be valid, the condition is that each general must solve a mathematical puzzle and attach it with the proposed time message; if other generals receive this message and see that the solution to the math puzzle is valid, they accept that time. This mathematical puzzle serves two purposes; first, it is a proof that the general is honest as they have solved the math puzzle, and, second, it stops the generals from proposing too many times in quick succession, which will result in disagreement and confusion between the generals. We can see that this mechanism can be seen as a solution to the Byzantine generals problem; however, with a compromise, that temporary disagreement is acceptable.

Bitcoin PoW is a probabilistic consensus algorithm. The big question now arises whether deterministic consensus can be achieved when the number of nodes is unknown and in the presence of Byzantine nodes.

Now let's revisit the validity, agreement, and termination properties defined at the start of this chapter in the light of what we have learned so far about the proof of work algorithm.

We can see clearly now that PoW is not a classical deterministic Byzantine consensus algorithm. It is a protocol with probabilistic properties.

Let's revisit the properties now.

Agreement

An agreement property is probabilistic. This is the case because it can happen that two different miners produce a valid block almost simultaneously, and some nodes add a block from one miner and some other nodes from another. Eventually, however, the longest (strongest) chain rule will ensure that the chain with less proof of work behind it is pruned and the longest chain prevails. This will result in previously accepted transactions to be rolled back; thus, the agreement is probabilistic.

Validity – Predicate Based

This is a deterministic property agreement where honest nodes only accept those blocks which are valid. Formally, we can say that if a correct process p eventually decides on b, then v must satisfy the application-specific valid() predicate. We discussed the validity predicate, that is, the block validation criteria, in detail earlier in the chapter.

Termination

Termination is a probabilistic property. It is only achieved eventually due to the possibility of natural forks. This is because in the case of forks, the fork must be resolved in order to finally terminate a consensus process on the block. As there is a possibility that a previously accepted block is rolled back in favor of the heaviest/longest chain, the termination can only be guaranteed probabilistically. Usually, in order to ensure with high probability the finality of the transactions, in practice six confirmations are traditionally required. This means that the block is at least six blocks deeper in the chain, which means that the possibility of a rollback is so low that it can never happen or happen once in a millennia.

With this, we complete our discussion on proof of work.

PoW Concerns

There are several concerns regarding PoW, including attacks and extreme energy consumption.

In the next section, we discuss some of the attacks that can be carried out against the proof of work consensus, which adversely affects the Bitcoin network.

51% Attack

A 51% attack on Bitcoin can occur when more than 50% of the mining hash power is controlled by an adversary.

Table 5-3 shows a list of actions that an adversary can possibly try to take after taking over more than 50% hash power of the network.

Table 5-3. *List of actions by adversary*

Attack	Possibility	Explanation
Censor transactions	Yes	Can ignore transactions
Coin stealing	No	Controlled by a private key
Double-spend	Yes	Can create a private off-chain fork and exclude the block which contains previously spent transaction
Change protocol	No	A protocol cannot be changed as valid nodes will simply ignore the invalid blocks

Note that some attacks are still impossible, while the most detrimental to a system are possible, such as double-spend.

Selfish Mining

This type of attack occurs when a miner who has found a block keeps it a secret instead of announcing it and keeps building on top of it privately. Imagine the attacker has managed to create another block. Now the attacker has two blocks in their private forked chain. At this point, the attacker waits for someone else to find a block. When the attacker sees this new block, they release their two-block chain. Because other miners are honest and abiding by the longest chain rule, they will accept this new chain being the longest. Now the block that was mined by someone else is orphaned despite spending resources on it, but that work is wasted. The attacker could also wait for a longer chain to be created, albeit mostly by luck, but if the attacker manages to create such a private fork which is longer than the honest chain, then the attacker can release that as soon as some other block is announced. Now when the nodes see this new longest chain, according to the rules, they will start mining on top of this new longer chain and orphaning the other chains, which could just be one block shorter than the attacker's chain. All the work that has gone into creating the honest chain is now wasted, and the attacker gets the rewards, instead of other miners who did the work on the honest chain.

Race Attack

This attack can occur in a situation where the adversary can make a payment to one beneficiary and then a second one to themselves or someone else. Now if the first payment is accepted by the recipient after zero confirmations, then it could happen that the second transaction is mined and accepted in the next block, and the first transaction could remain unmined. As a result, the first recipient may never get their payment.

Finney Attack

The Finney attack can occur when a recipient of a payment accepts the payment with zero confirmations. It is a type of double-spend attack where an attacker creates two transactions. The first of these transactions is a payment to the recipient (victim) and the second to themselves. However, the attacker does not broadcast the first transaction; instead, they include the second transaction in a block and mine it. Now at this point, the attacker releases the first transaction and pays for the goods. The merchant does not wait here for the confirmations and accepts the payment. Now the attacker broadcasts the premined block with the second transaction that pays to themselves. This invalidates the first transaction as the second transaction takes precedence over the first one.

Vector76 Attack

This attack is a combination of Finney and race attacks. This attack is powerful enough to reverse a transaction even if it has one confirmation.

Eclipse Attack

This attack attempts to obscure a node's correct view of the network, which can lead to disruption to service, double-spend attacks, and waste of resources. There are several solutions to fix the issue, which have been implemented in Bitcoin. More details can be found here: `https://cs-people.bu.edu/heilman/eclipse/`.

ESG Impact

ESG metrics represent an overall picture of environmental, social, and governance concerns. These metrics are used as a measure to assess a company's exposure to environmental, social, and governance risks. They are used by investors to make investment decisions. Investors may not invest where ESG risks are higher and may prefer companies where ESG risk is low.

Proof of work has been criticized for consuming too much energy. It is true that currently at the time of writing, the total energy consumption of the Bitcoin blockchain is more than the entire country of Pakistan [9].

There are environmental, social, and governance concerns (ESG concerns) that have been the cause of low interest from savvy mainstream investors. Nonetheless, Bitcoin largely can be seen as a success despite its ESG concerns.

Not only has Bitcoin been criticized for its high energy consumption but often seen as a vehicle for criminal activities, where Bitcoin has been accepted as a mode of payment for illicit drugs and other criminal activities.

A centralization problem is also a concern where some powerful miners with mining farms take up most of the hash rate of the Bitcoin network. The ASICs that are used to build these mining farms are produced only by a few manufacturers, which means that this is also a highly centralized space. Moreover, a crackdown [13] on Bitcoin mining could also result in more centralization, where only the most powerful miners may be able to withstand this crackdown and survive, resulting in only a few surviving and powerful miners at the end.

There are however points in favor of Bitcoin. Bitcoin can be used as a cross-border remittance mechanism for migrant families. It can also be used as a mode of payment in struggling economies. It can serve the unbanked population, which is estimated to be 1.7 billion [12]. Bitcoin serves as a vehicle for financial inclusion.

We could think of scenarios where the heat produced by Bitcoin mining farms may be used to heat up water and eventually homes. Even electricity could be generated and fed back into the electricity grid by using thermoelectric generators due to thermoelectric effect. Of course, economics and engineering need to be worked out; however, this idea can work.

> *Thermoelectric power generator, any of a class of solid-state devices that either convert heat directly into electricity or transform electrical energy into thermal power for heating or cooling. Such devices are based on thermoelectric effects involving interactions between the flow of heat and of electricity through solid bodies. [11]*
>
> —*Encyclopaedia Britannica*, March 1, 2007, `www.britannica.com/technology/thermoelectric-power-generator`

Payment systems and in fact any system require electricity to run. Bitcoin is criticized of consuming too much energy; however, this is the price paid for the strength of the system. The network difficulty rate is so high now that even many attackers colluding together won't be able to generate enough hash power to launch a 51% attack. So yes, electricity is consumed, but in return there are benefits. In addition to the security of Bitcoin, there are other benefits such as

- Bitcoin can be used in suppressed regimes.

- Borderless payments.

- Bank the unbanked.

- Smooth cross-border remittance.

- Alternative payment system which doesn't have any intermediary.

- Payments without a middleman.

In summary, Bitcoin, despite its energy consumption and not living up to its original philosophy of One CPU = One Vote, still can be seen as a successful project with many benefits.

Variants of PoW

There are two types of proof of work algorithms depending on the hardware it is intended to run on:

- CPU-bound PoW

- Memory-bound PoW

CPU-Bound PoW

These puzzles run at the speed of the processor. CPU-bound PoW refers to a type of PoW where the processing required to find the solution to the cryptographic hash puzzle is directly proportional to the calculation speed of the CPU or hardware such as ASICs. Because ASICs have dominated Bitcoin PoW and provide somewhat undue advantage to the miners who can afford to use ASICs, this CPU-bound PoW is seen as shifting toward centralization. Moreover, mining pools with extraordinary hash power can shift the balance of power toward them. Therefore, memory-bound PoW algorithms have been introduced, which are ASIC resistant and are based on memory-oriented design instead of CPU.

Memory-Bound PoW

Memory-bound PoW algorithms rely on system RAM to provide PoW. Here, the performance is bound by the access speed of the memory or the size of the memory. This reliance on memory also makes these PoW algorithms ASIC resistant. Equihash is one of the most prominent memory-bound PoW algorithms.

There are other improvements and variations of proof of work, which we will introduce in Chapter 8.

Summary

In this chapter, we covered blockchain consensus:

- Proof of work is the first blockchain consensus introduced with Bitcoin, which is also a solution to the Byzantine generals problem.

- Blockchain consensus can be divided into two categories, the Nakamoto consensus and the traditional BFT based.

- Traditional BFT is deterministic, whereas Nakamoto consensus is probabilistic.

- Proof of work in Bitcoin is a Sybil resistance mechanism, a double-spending prevention mechanism, and a solution to the Byzantine generals problem.

- Proof of work can be seen in the light of game theory where the protocol is a Nash equilibrium, and the dominant strategy for all players is to be honest.

- Proof of work is effectively a Byzantine fault–tolerant protocol.

- Proof of work is a state machine replication protocol where a mined block is announced and replicated to other nodes via a gossip protocol.

- Proof of work consumes high energy, and there are ESG concerns; however, there are benefits as well.

Bibliography

1. Proof of work originally introduced in: Cynthia Dwork and Moni Naor. Pricing via processing or combatting junk mail. In Ernest F. Brickell, editor, Advances in Cryptology – CRYPTO '92, 12th Annual International Cryptology Conference, Santa Barbara, California, USA, August 16–20, 1992, Proceedings, volume 740 of Lecture Notes in Computer Science, pages 139–147. Springer, 1992.

2. Okun, Michael. Distributed computing among unacquainted processors in the presence of Byzantine failures. Hebrew University of Jerusalem, 2005.

3. https://bitcoin.org/bitcoin.pdf

4. www.cs.yale.edu/publications/techreports/tr1332.pdf

5. https://satoshi.nakamotoinstitute.org/emails/cryptography/11/

6. https://hal.inria.fr/hal-01445797/document

7. These terms were first introduced in https://eprint.iacr.org/2014/765.pdf

8. https://en.bitcoin.it/wiki/Miner_fees#Priority_transactions

9. Digiconomist: https://digiconomist.net/bitcoin-energy-consumption/

10. www.hashcash.org

11. Strohl, G. Ralph and Harpster, Joseph W. "Thermoelectric power generator." Encyclopedia Britannica, Mar. 1, 2007, www.britannica.com/technology/thermoelectric-power-generator. Accessed June 25, 2021.

12. https://globalfindex.worldbank.org/sites/globalfindex/files/chapters/2017%20Findex%20full%20report_chapter2.pdf

13. www.coindesk.com/bitcoin-slips-37k-china-vicecrackdown-mining

14. Introduction to the Distributed Systems channel by Chris Colohan: www.distributedsystemscourse.com

15. Bitcoin blockchain consensus: https://youtu.be/f1ZJPEKeTEY

CHAPTER 6

Early Protocols

In this chapter, I introduce early protocols. First, we start with a background on distributed transactions and relevant protocols, such as the two-phase commit. After that, we'll continue our journey, look at the agreement protocols, and conclude the chapter with some fundamental results in distributed computing. This chapter introduces early consensus algorithms such as those presented in the works of Lamport et al., Ben-Or et al., and Toueg et.al. It is helpful to understand these fundamental ideas before continuing our voyage toward more complex and modern protocols.

Introduction

In my view, the 1980s was the golden age for innovation and discovery in distributed computing. Many fundamental problems, algorithms, and results such as the Byzantine generals problem, FLP impossibility result, partial synchrony, and techniques to circumvent FLP impossibility were discovered during the late 1970s and 1980s. Starting from Lamport's phenomenal paper "Time, Clocks, and the Ordering of Events in a Distributed System" to the Byzantine generals problem and then Schneider's state machine replication paper, one after another, there were most significant contributions made to the consensus problem and generally in distributed computing.

Consensus can be defined as a protocol for achieving agreement. A high-level list of major contributions is described as follows.

In his seminal paper in 1978, "Time, Clocks, and Ordering of Events in a Distributed System", Lamport described how to order events using synchronized clocks in the absence of faults. Then in 1980, the paper "Reaching Agreement in the Presence of Faults" posed the question if agreement can be reached in an unreliable distributed system. It was proven that agreement is achievable if the number of faulty nodes in a distributed system is less than one-third of the total number of processes, i.e. n>=3f+1, where n is the number of total nodes and f is the number of faulty processors. In the paper "The Byzantine Generals Problem" in 1982, Lamport et al. showed that agreement

259

© Imran Bashir 2022
I. Bashir, *Blockchain Consensus*, https://doi.org/10.1007/978-1-4842-8179-6_6

is solvable using oral messages if more than two-thirds of the generals are loyal. In 1982, the paper "The Byzantine generals strike again" by Danny Dolev showed that unanimity is achievable if less than one-third of the total number of processors are faulty and more than one-half of the network's connectivity is available.

Unanimity is a requirement where if all initial values of the processes are the same, say v, then all processes decide on that value v. This is strong unanimity. However, a weaker variant called weak unanimity only requires this condition to hold if all processes are correct; in other words, no processes are faulty.

The paper also provided the first proof that the distributed system must have $3f + 1$ nodes to tolerate f faults. However, the celebrated FLP result appeared a little later which proved that deterministic asynchronous consensus is not possible even if a single process is crash faulty. FLP impossibility implies that safety and liveness of a consensus protocol cannot be guaranteed in an asynchronous network.

Lamport's algorithm was for a synchronous setting and assumed that eventually all the messages will be delivered. Moreover, it wasn't fault tolerant because a single failure will halt the algorithm.

After the FLP impossibility result appeared, attempts started to circumvent it and solve the consensus problem nevertheless. The intuition behind circumventing FLP is to relax some stricter requirements of timing and determinism.

Ben-Or proposed the earliest algorithms to sacrifice some level of determinism to circumvent FLP. As FLP impossibility implies that under asynchrony, there will always be an execution that does not terminate, one way of avoiding that is to try and make termination probabilistic. So that instead of deterministic termination, probabilistic termination is used. The intuition behind these algorithms is to use the "common coin" approach, where a process randomly chooses its values if it doesn't receive messages from other nodes. In other words, a process is allowed to select a value to vote on if it doesn't receive a majority of votes on the value from the rest of the processes. This means that eventually more than half of the nodes will end up voting for the same value. However, this algorithm's communication complexity increases exponentially with the number of nodes. Later, another approach that achieved consensus in a fixed number of rounds was proposed by Rabin. These proposals required $5f + 1$ and $10f + 1$ rounds, respectively, as compared to the $3f + 1$ lower bound commonly known today.

Consensus protocols that relax timing (synchrony) requirements aim to provide safety under all circumstances and liveness only when the network is synchronous. A significant breakthrough was the work of Dwork, Lynch, and Stockmeyer, which for the first time introduced a more realistic idea of partial synchrony. This model is more practical as it captures how real distributed systems behave. More precisely, distributed systems can be asynchronous for arbitrary periods but will eventually return to synchrony long enough for the system to make a decision and terminate. This paper introduced various combinations of processor and network synchrony and asynchrony and proved the lower bounds for such scenarios.

Note   We discussed partial synchrony in detail in Chapter 3.

Table 6-1 shows the summary of results from the DLS88 paper showing a minimum number of processors for which a fault-tolerant consensus protocol exists.

Table 6-1. *Minimum number of processors for which a fault-tolerant consensus protocol exists*

Type of Fault	Synchronous	Asynchronous	Partially Synch Comms and Processor
Fail-stop	f	NA	2f + 1
Omission	f	NA	2f + 1
Authenticated Byzantine	f	NA	3f + 1
Byzantine	3f + 1	NA	3f + 1

This paper introduced the DLS algorithm which solved consensus under partial synchrony.

Some major results are listed as follows, starting from the 1980s:

- Lamport showed in LPS 82 that under a synchronous setting, n > 2f with authentication and n > 3f are at least required with oral messages.

- The FLP result in 1982 showed that even with a single crash failure, consensus is impossible under asynchrony, and at least n > 3f are required for safety.

- Ben-Or in 1983 proposed a randomized solution under asynchrony.

Now let's go through distributed transaction which is a major concept in distributed systems.

Distributed Transactions

A distributed transaction is a sequence of events spread across multiple processes. A transaction either concludes with a commit or abort. If committed, all events are executed, and the output is generated, and if aborted, the transaction halts without complete execution. A transaction is atomic if it executes and commits fully; otherwise, it rolls back with no effect. In other words, atomic transactions either execute in full or not at all.

There are four properties that a transaction must satisfy, commonly known as the ACID consistency model:

- **Atomicity**: Either the transaction events fully execute or not at all.

- **Consistency**: If a transaction commits, it results in a valid (consistent) state of the system. It satisfies some invariants.

- **Isolation**: Unless the transaction is committed, no effects are visible.

- **Durability**: A transaction once committed has a permanent effect.

One point to note here is that consistency is guaranteed much easily in monolithic architectures. In contrast, consistency is not immediate in distributed architectures, and distributed architectures rely on so-called eventual consistency. Eventual consistency means that all nodes in a system eventually (at some point in time in future) synchronize and agree on a consistent state of the system. ACID properties must hold even if some nodes (processes) fail.

Atomicity, isolation, and durability are easier to achieve in monolithic architectures, but achieving these properties in distributed settings becomes more challenging.

A two-phase commit protocol is used to achieve atomicity across multiple processes. Replicas should be consistent with one another. Atomic commit protocols are in fact a kind of consensus mechanism because in transaction commit protocols nodes must come to an agreement to either commit if all is well or roll back in case something goes wrong. Imagine if a transaction is expected to be committed on all nodes in a distributed system (a network), then either it must commit on all or none to maintain replica consistency. We cannot have a situation where a transaction succeeds on some nodes and not on others, leading to an inconsistent distributed system. This is where atomic commit comes in. It can be seen fundamentally as a consensus algorithm because this protocol requires an agreement between all nodes in a network. However, there are fundamental differences between atomic commit and consensus. In consensus, one or more nodes propose a value, and nodes decide on one of the values using the consensus algorithm. This is usually achieved by majority consensus. In contrast, in an atomic commit protocol, all nodes are required to vote whether they commit or abort the transaction. In consensus algorithms, there can be multiple values proposed out of which one can be agreed upon, whereas in atomic commit the protocol must commit if all nodes vote to commit; otherwise, even if one node doesn't agree, then the transaction must be aborted by all nodes. A major distinction between atomic commit and consensus is that in consensus algorithms, faults (crashed nodes) are tolerated due to the quorum availability rule, whereas in atomic commit even if one node fails, the transaction must abort on all nodes. To handle crashed nodes, a complete and strongly accurate failure detector is used, which is implemented using a timeout mechanism.

In addition to the ACID consistency model, another common consistency model used in databases is the BASE model. BASE stands for basically available (BA), soft state (S), and eventually consistent (E). The databases using the BASE consistency model ensure availability by replicating data across nodes in the system. As the model does not provide immediate consistency, the data values could change over time, which results in eventual consistency. In the BASE model, consistency is only achieved eventually. However, it offers high availability, which is useful in many online services where immediate and strong consistency requirements are somewhat loose, like social networks and online video platforms. From a CAP theorem perspective, the BASE model sacrifices consistency and favors high availability.

Now we discuss the two-phase commit which is a famous commit protocol, achieving atomicity.

Two-Phase Commit

A two-phase commit (2PC) is an atomic commit protocol to achieve atomicity. It was first published in a paper by Lampson and Sturgis in 1979. A two-phase commit enables updating multiple databases in a single transaction and committing/aborting atomically.

As the name suggests, it works in two phases. The first phase is the vote collection phase in which a coordinator node collects votes from each node participating in the transaction. Each participant node either votes yes or no to either commit the transaction or abort the transaction. When all votes are collected, the coordinator (transaction manager) starts the second phase, called the decision phase. In the decision phase, the coordinator commits the transaction if it has received all yes votes from other nodes; otherwise, it aborts the transaction. Any node that had voted yes to commit the transaction waits until it receives the final decision from the coordinator node. If it receives no from the coordinator, it will abort the transaction; otherwise, it will commit the transaction. Nodes that voted no immediately terminate the transaction without waiting to receive a decision from the coordinator. When a transaction is aborted, any changes made are rolled back. The changes are made permanent after committing at nodes that said yes when they receive a commit decision from the coordinator. Any changes made by the transaction are not permanent, and any locks are released after a write operation is performed. All participants send the acknowledgment back to the coordinator after they've received the decision from the coordinator. As a failure handling mechanism, a logging scheme is used in two-phase commits. In this scheme, all messages are written to a local stable storage before they are sent out to the recipients in the network. When the coordinator fails (crashes), it writes its decision to the local disk in the log, and when it recovers, it sends its decision to other nodes. If no decision was made before the crash, then it simply aborts the transaction. When a node fails (other than the coordinator node), the coordinator waits until it times out, and a decision is made to abort the transaction for all.

Figure 6-1 shows the two-phase commit protocol in action. Here, the client (application) starts the transaction as usual and performs a usual read/write operation on the database nodes, that is, on the transaction participant nodes. After a normal transaction execution on each participant, when the client is ready to commit the transaction, the coordinator starts the first phase, that is, the prepare phase. It sends the prepare request to all nodes and asks them whether they can commit or not. If the participants reply with a yes, it means that they are willing and ready to commit the transaction, then the coordinator starts the second phase called the commit phase. This is when the coordinator sends out the commit decision, and the transaction is finally committed, and a commit actually takes place. If any of the participant nodes replies to the prepare request with a no, then the coordinator sends out the abort request in phase two, and all nodes abort accordingly. Note that after the first phase, there is a decision point where the coordinator decides whether to commit or abort. The action after the decision phase is either commit or abort, based on the yes or no received from the participants.

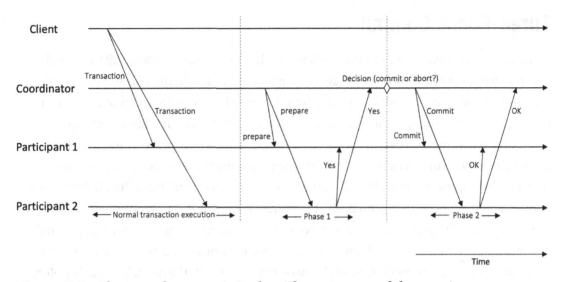

Figure 6-1. *The two-phase commit algorithm – a successful scenario*

The two-phase commit is a blocking algorithm because if the coordinator goes down after the "prepare" phase but before sending out its decision, other nodes have no way of finding out what has been decided by the coordinator. Now they are stuck in an uncertain state where they have agreed earlier to commit by saying yes/ok in the prepare phase but are now waiting to hear the final decision from the coordinator. Nodes cannot either commit or abort on their own after responding yes in the prepare phase because it will violate the atomicity property. The protocol in this situation blocks until the coordinator recovers. This means that the two-phase commit algorithm is not fault tolerant if the coordinator or a participant fails. In other words, 2PC is not partition tolerant.

More precisely, if the coordinator crashes just after the prepare phase before sending the decision, other nodes then have no idea what decision is made by the coordinator. At this stage, participants cannot commit or abort, and the protocol is blocked until the coordinator comes back online and participants receive the decision. The coordinator is a single point of failure in this protocol. There are ways to overcome this problem using a consensus mechanism or total order broadcast protocol. The commit protocol can use consensus to elect a new coordinator.

Also, note that if we remove the second phase and hence no rolling back, it becomes a one-phase commit, that is, the primary/backup replication. Sounds familiar? We discussed this in Chapter 3.

Three-Phase Commit

As we saw in the two-phase commit, it is not fault tolerant and blocks until the failed coordinator recovers. If the coordinator or a participant fails in the commit phase, the protocol cannot recover reliably. Even when the coordinator is replaced or recovers, it cannot proceed to process the transaction reliably from where the failure occurred. The three-phase commit solves this problem by introducing a new pre-commit intermediate phase. After receiving a yes from all the participants, the coordinator moves to this intermediate phase. Unlike 2PC, here, the coordinator does not immediately broadcast commit; instead, it sends a pre-commit first, which indicates the intention to commit the transaction. When participants receive the pre-commit message, they reply with the ack messages. When the coordinator receives this ack from all participants, it sends the commit message and proceeds as in the two-phase commit. If a participant fails before sending back a message, the coordinator can still decide to commit the transaction. If the coordinator crashes, the participants can still agree to abort or commit the transaction. This is so because no actual commit or abort has taken place yet. The participants now have another chance to decide by checking that if they have seen a pre-commit from the coordinator, they commit the transaction accordingly. Otherwise, the participants abort the transaction, as no commit message has been seen from the coordinator.

This process can be visualized in Figure 6-2.

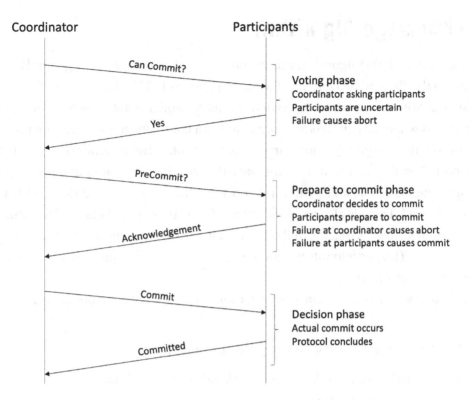

Figure 6-2. *Three-phase commit protocol*

Roughly speaking, commit protocols can be seen as agreement protocols because participants need to decide whether to accept the value proposed by the coordinator or not. Of course, it is a simple protocol and not fault tolerant, but it does achieve an agreement among parties; hence, it can be seen as a consensus mechanism. Moreover, we can say that validity is achieved because a participant proposes a final agreed-upon value. Also, termination is guaranteed because every participant makes progress. If there are no failures, eventually all participants respond to the coordinator, and the protocol moves forward and, finally, both phases end. Strictly speaking, however, distributed commit protocols are not consensus protocols.

Now, after this introduction to the most straightforward consensus protocols or distributed commit protocols (depending on how you look at them), let us focus on some early fault-tolerant consensus protocols that provide the foundation of what we see today as consensus protocols in various distributed systems and blockchains.

Oral Message Algorithm

The oral message (OM) algorithm was proposed to solve the Byzantine generals problem in the "Byzantine Generals Problem" paper in 1982 by Lamport et.al. This recursive algorithm runs under the synchronous network model. It assumes a collection of N generals where all generals are connected as a complete graph. One general is the "commander" responsible for starting the protocol. Other generals (N – 1) called "lieutenants" orally pass around the message they receive. The commander knows that at most f generals will be faulty (traitors) and starts the consensus algorithm with a known value of f. There is also a default value, either "retreat" or "attack." The intuition behind this algorithm is that you tell others what message you received on receiving every message. The participants accept the majority decision, which ensures the safety property of the algorithm.

There are two *interactive consistency* requirements that need to be met called IC1 and IC2:

1. **IC1**: All loyal lieutenants obey the same order.

2. **IC2**: If the commanding general is loyal, then every loyal lieutenant obeys its order.

Some assumptions about the system model are

1. The absence of message can be detected. This is due to synchronous communication.

2. Every sent message is delivered correctly.

3. The receiver of the message knows who sent it.

An oral message is a message whose contents are under complete control of the sender. The sender can send any possible message.

There is no solution to the Byzantine generals problem unless more than two-thirds of generals are loyal. For example, if there are three generals and one is a traitor, then there is no solution to BGP if oral messages are used. Formally

- **Lemma 1**: There is no solution to the Byzantine generals problem for $3m + 1$ generals with $> m$ traitors.

In other words, if $n <= 3m$, then a Byzantine agreement is not possible. The algorithm is recursive.

Algorithm
Base case: OM(0)

1. The commander broadcasts a proposed value to every lieutenant.

2. Every lieutenant accepts the received value. If no value is received, then it uses the DEFAULT value, either set to retreat or attack, at the start of the algorithm.

With traitor(s): OM(m), where m > 0

1. The commander sends the proposed value to every lieutenant.

2. Every lieutenant runs OM(m-1) and acts as the commander to send the value received in step 1 to all the other lieutenants.

3. Each lieutenant maintains a vector from which it uses the majority value out of the values received.

The base case and OM(1) case are depicted in Figure 6-3.

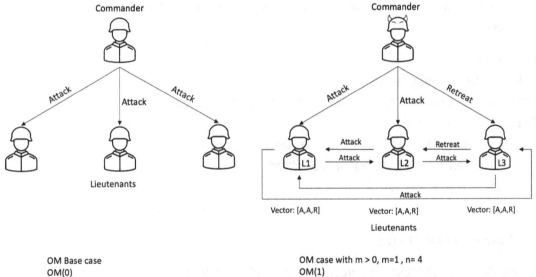

OM Base case
OM(0)
Commander : sends order – attack
Lieutenants : Follow the order if received

OM case with m > 0, m=1 , n= 4
OM(1)
Commander : sends conflicting orders – attack & retreat
Lieutenants : runs OM(0) as commander

Figure 6-3. *OM base case vs. OM(1) case, where the commander is the traitor*

We can also visualize the case where a lieutenant is the traitor as shown in Figure 6-4.

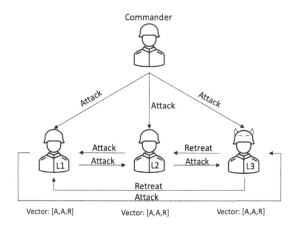

Figure 6-4. *OM case with M=1 where a lieutenant is a traitor*

We can formally describe the algorithm as shown in the following code:

Base case

```
OM(0)- base case
DEFAULT := Default value
Commander C broadcasts its proposed value to all Lieutenants
For i = 1 : N - 1 do
    Li stores the value from C in an array as Vi
    Vi = DEFAULT if no value received
    Li accepts Vi
End for
```

Case with f > 0, OM(m)

```
Commander C broadcast its value to all lieutenants
For I = 1 : n-1 do
    Li stores the value from commander as vi
    Vi = default if no value received from the commander
    Li runs OM(m-1) now as commander to send the value vi to other N - 2
Lieutenants
End for
```

```
For I = 1 : N - 1 do
    For j = 1 : N - 1 AND j ≠ i do
        Li stores the value received from Lj as vj
        Vj = default if no value received
    End for
Li chooses majority from {v1, v2, v3,  , , , Vn-1}
End for
```

As you may have noticed, this algorithm, while it works, is not very efficient due to the number of messages required to be passed around. More precisely, from a communication complexity perspective, this algorithm is exponential in the number of traitors. If there are no traitors, as in the base case, then its constant, $O(1)$, otherwise its $O(m^n)$, which means that it grows exponentially with the number of traitors, which makes it impractical for a large number of n.

Using the space-time diagram, we can visualize the base case as shown in Figure 6-5.

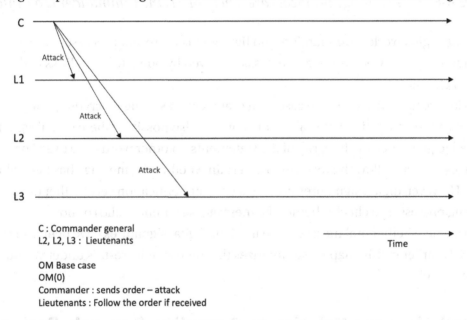

Figure 6-5. *Oral message protocol – base case – with no traitors*

We can also visualize the m > 0 case where the commander is the traitor sending conflicting messages to lieutenants in Figure 6-6.

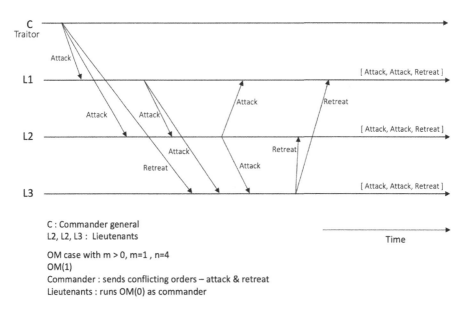

Figure 6-6. *Oral message protocol case where m =1, the commander is a traitor*

In the digital world, commanders and lieutenants represent processes, and the communication between these processes is achieved by point-to-point links and physical channels.

So far, we have discussed the case with oral messages using no cryptography; however, another solution with signed messages is also possible where digital signatures are used to guarantee the integrity of the statements. In other words, the use of oral messages does not allow the receiver to ascertain whether the message has been altered or not. However, digital signatures provide a data authentication service that enables receiving processes to check whether the message is genuine (valid) or not.

Based on whether oral messages are used, or digital signatures have been used, Table 6-1, earlier in this chapter, summarizes the impossibility results under various system models.

Signed Message Solution to Byzantine Generals Problem

The main issue with the oral message algorithm is that it needs $3t + 1$ (also denoted as $3f + 1$) nodes to tolerate t (also denoted as f) failures, which is expensive in terms of computational resources required. It is also difficult because traitors can lie about what other nodes said. The time complexity of this algorithm is $O(n^m)$.

There is a signed solution to BGP which was proposed in the same BGP paper by Lamport, Shostak, and Pease. It uses digital signatures to sign the messages. Here are the additional assumptions under this model:

1. The signature of a loyal general cannot be forged, and any modification of the general's messages is detectable.

2. Anyone can verify the authenticity of the general's signature.

Under this model, each lieutenant maintains a vector of signed orders received. Then, the commander sends the signed messages to the lieutenants.

Generally, the algorithm works like this:

A lieutenant receives an order from either a commander or other lieutenants and saves it in the vector that he maintains after verifying the message's authenticity. If there are less than m signatures on the order, the lieutenant adds a signature to the order (message) and relays this message to other lieutenants who have not seen it yet. When a lieutenant does not receive any newer messages, he chooses the value from the vector as a decision consensus value.

The lieutenants can detect that the commander is a traitor by using signed messages because the commander's signature appears on two different messages. Our assumptions under this model are that signatures are unforgeable, and anyone can verify the signature's authenticity. This implies that the commander is a traitor because only he could have signed two different messages.

Formally, the algorithm is described as follows.

Algorithm: For n generals and m traitor generals where $n > 0$. In this algorithm, each lieutenant i keeps a set V_i of properly signed messages it has received so far. When the commander is honest, then the set V_i contains only a single element.

Algorithm SM(m)

Initialization:

$Vi = \{ \}$, that is, empty

1. Commander C sends the signed message (value) to every lieutenant.

2. For each i

    a. If lieutenant i receives a message of the form $v : 0$ from the commander and has not yet received any message (order) from the commander, that is, V_i is empty, then

         i.   Set $V_i = \{v\}$.

        ii. It sends the message $v : 0 : i$ to every other lieutenant.

    b. If lieutenant i receives a message like $v : 0 : j_1. \ldots j_k$ and v is not in the set, V_i, then

         i. $V_i = V_i + \{v\}$, that is, add v to V_i.

        ii. If $k < m$, then send message $v : 0 : j_1 \ldots j_k : i$ to every lieutenant other than $j_1 \ldots j_k$.

3.   For each i

    a. When no more messages received by lieutenant i, then it obeys the order (message) via the function *choice* (V_i), which obtains a single order from a set of orders. *Choice*$(V) = retreat$ if set V is empty or it consists of more than one element. If there is only a single element v in set V, then *choice*$(V) = v$.

Here, $v : i$ is the value v signed by general i, and $v : i : j$ is the message $v : i$ counter signed by general j. Each general i maintains a set V_i which contains all orders received. The diagram in Figure 6-7 visualizes a traitor commander scenario.

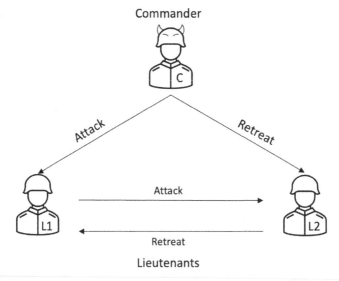

Figure 6-7. *Example of a signed message protocol with SM(1) – traitor commander*

With signed messages, it's easy to detect if a commander is a traitor because its signature would appear on two different orders, and by the assumption of unforgeable signature, we know that only the commander could have signed the message.

Formally, for any m, the algorithm $SM(m)$ solves the Byzantine generals problem if there are at most m traitors. The lieutenants maintain a vector of values and run a choice function to retrieve the order *choice {attack, retreat}*. Timeouts are used to ascertain if no more messages will arrive. Also, in step 2, lieutenant i ignores any message v that is already in the set V_i.

This algorithm has message complexity $O(n^{m+1})$, and it requires $m + 1$ number of rounds. This protocol works for $N \geq m + 2$.

In contrast with the oral message protocol, the signed message protocol is more resilient against faults; here, if at least two generals are loyal in three generals, the problem is solvable. In the oral message, even if there is a single traitor in three generals, the problem is unsolvable.

DLS Protocols Under Partial Synchrony

After the FLP impossibility result, one of the ways that researchers introduced to circumvent the FLP impossibility is to use the partial synchrony network model. There are some important concepts presented in this paper, such as rotating coordinators, consensus, termination under partial synchrony, and implementation of the round-based mechanism. We discussed various models, including partial synchrony, in Chapter 3.

The paper describes four algorithms for crash-stop, omissions, Byzantine, and authenticated Byzantine faults under partial synchrony. The key idea in these algorithms is that the agreement and validity are always satisfied, whereas termination is guaranteed when the system stabilizes, that is, has good episodes of synchrony.

A basic round model is introduced where protocol execution is divided into rounds of message exchange and local computations. Each round comprises a send step, a receive step, and a computation step. In addition, the basic round model assumes a round, called the global stabilization round, during which or after correct processes receive all messages sent from correct processes.

In this section, algorithm 2 is presented, a consensus algorithm for Byzantine faults with authentication. It assumes a network model with partially synchronous communications and processors that can be Byzantine. This model is also adopted for most, if not all, blockchain networks.

The algorithm achieves strong unanimity for a set V with an arbitrary value under Byzantine faults with authentication.

The algorithm progresses in phases. Each phase k consists of four consecutive rounds, from $4k - 3$ to $4k$. Each phase has a unique coordinator c which leads the phase. A simple formula $k = i \, (mod \, n)$ is used to select the coordinator from all processes, where k is the phase, i is the process number, and n is the total number of processes.

Each process maintains some variables:

- A local variable PROPER, which contains a set of values that the process knows to be proper.

- A local variable ACCEPTABLE, which contains value v that process p has found to be acceptable. Note that a value v is acceptable to process p if p does not have a lock on any value except possibly v. Also, value v is proper.

- A local variable LOCK which keeps the locked value. A process may lock a value in a phase if it believes that some process may decide on this value. Initially, no value is locked. A phase number is associated with every lock. In addition, a proof of acceptability of the locked value is also associated with every lock. Proof of acceptability is in the form of a set of signed messages sent by $n - t$ processes, indicating that the locked value is acceptable and proper, that is, it is in their PROPER sets at the start of the given phase.

Algorithm $N \geq 3t + 1$ – Byzantine faults with authentication
Trying phase k
Rounds:
Round 1: Round 4k – 3

Each process including the current coordinator sends an authenticated list of all its acceptable values to the current coordinator. Processes use the message format $E(list, k)$, where E is an authentication function, k is the phase, and *list* is all acceptable values.

Round 2: Round 4k – 2

The current coordinator chooses a value to propose. If a value is to be proposed by the coordinator, the coordinator must have received at least $n - t$ responses from the processes suggesting that this value is acceptable and proper at phase k. If there is more than one possible value that the coordinator may propose, then it will choose one arbitrarily.

The coordinator broadcasts a message of the form $E(lock, v, k, proof)$, where the *proof* is composed of the set of signed messages $E(list, k)$ received from the $n - t$ processes that found v acceptable and proper.

Round 3: Round 4k – 1

If any process receives an $E(lock, v, k, proof)$ message, it validates the proof to ascertain that $n - t$ processors do find v acceptable and proper at phase k. If the proof is valid, it locks v, associating the phase number k and the message $E(lock, v, k, proof)$ with the lock, and sends an acknowledgment to the current coordinator. In this case, the processes release any earlier lock placed on v. If the coordinator receives acknowledgments from at least $2t + 1$ processors, then it decides on the value v.

Round 4: Round 4k

This is where locks are released. Processes broadcast messages of the form $E(lock\ v, h, proof)$, indicating that they have a lock on value v with associated phase h and the associated proof and that a coordinator sent the message at phase h, which caused the lock to be placed. If any process has a lock on some value v with associated phase h and receives a properly signed message $E(lock, w, h', proof)$ with $w \neq v$ and $h' \geq h$, then the process releases its lock on v. This means that if a most recent properly signed message is received by a process indicating a lock on some value which is different from its locally locked value and the phase number is either higher or equal to the current phase number, then it will release the lock from the local locked value.

Notes

Assuming that the processes are correct, two different values cannot be locked in the same phase because the correct coordinator will never send conflicting messages which may suggest locks on two different values.

This algorithm achieves consistency, strong unanimity, and termination under partial synchrony, with Byzantine faults and authentication, where $n \geq 3t + 1$. Authenticated Byzantine means that failures are arbitrary, but messages can be signed with unforgeable digital signatures.

Consistency means no two different processes decide differently. Termination means every process eventually decides. Unanimity has two flavors, strong unanimity and weak unanimity. Strong unanimity requires that if all processes have the same initial value v and if any correct process decides, then it only decides on v. Weak unanimity means that if all processes have the same initial value v and all processes are correct, then if any process decides, it decides on v. In other words, strong unanimity means that if all initial values are the same, for example, v, then v is the only common decision. Under weak unanimity, this condition is expected to hold only if all processes are correct.

Ben-Or Algorithms

The Ben-Or protocol was introduced in 1983. It is named after its author Michael Ben-Or. This was the first protocol that solved the consensus problem with probabilistic termination under a model with a strong adversary. The Ben-Or algorithm proposed how to circumvent an FLP result and achieve consensus under asynchrony. There are two algorithms proposed in the paper. The first algorithm tolerates $t < n/2$ crash failures, and the second algorithm tolerates $t < n/5$ for Byzantine failures. In other words, with $N > 2t$ it tolerates crash faults and achieves an agreement, and with $N > 5t$ the protocol tolerates Byzantine faults and reaches an agreement. The protocol achieves consensus under the conditions described earlier, but the expected running time of the protocol is exponential. In other words, it requires exponential running time to terminate in the worst case because it can require multiple rounds to terminate. It can however terminate in constant time if the value of t is very small, that is, $O(\sqrt{n})$.

This protocol works in asynchronous rounds. A round simulates time because all messages are tagged with a round number, and because of this, processes can figure out which messages belong to which round even if they arrive asynchronously. A process ignores any messages for previous rounds and holds messages for future rounds in a buffer. Each round has two phases or subrounds. The first is the proposal (suggestion) phase, where each process p transmits its value v and waits until it receives from other $n - t$ processes. In the second phase, called the decision (ratification) phase, the protocol checks if a majority is observed and takes that value; otherwise, it flips a coin. If a certain threshold of processes sees the same majority value, then the decision is finalized. In case some other value is detected as a majority, then the processor switches to that value. Eventually, the protocol manages to terminate because at some point all processes will flip the coin correctly and reach the majority value. You may have noticed that this protocol only considers binary decision values, either a 0 or 1. Another important aspect to keep in mind is that the protocol cannot wait indefinitely for all processes to respond because they could be unavailable (offline).

This algorithm works only for binary consensus. There are two variables that need to be managed in the algorithm, a value which is either 0 or 1 and phase (p), which represents the stage where the algorithm is currently at. The algorithm proceeds in rounds, and each round has two subrounds or phases.

Note that each process has its own coin. This class of algorithms that utilize such coin scheme is called local coin algorithms. Local coin tossing is implemented using a random number generator that outputs binary numbers. Each process tosses its own coin and outputs 0 or 1, each with probability ½. The coin is tossed by a process to pick a new local value if a majority was not found.

The algorithm for benign faults/crash faults only – non-Byzantine:

Each process p executes the following algorithm:

Process p: Initial value x = 0 or 1
0: set r = 1
--First subround or phase - proposal phase
1: Broadcast (1, r, x) to all processes including itself
2: Wait until messages of type (1,r,*) are received from n - t processes.
    2(a): If > n /2 messages received have the same value v, then
--second subround or phase - decision phase
    2(b): Broadcast the message (2, r, v, D) to all processes
    including itself.
    2(c): else broadcast the message (2, r, ?) to all processes
    including itself.
3: Wait until messages of type (2, r, *) arrive from n - t processes.
    3(a): If there is 1 D type messages (2, r, v, D), then vote v i.e
    set x = v
    3(b): If there are > t, D type messages then decide v.
    3(c): Else set x = 0 or 1 each with probability 1/2 by   doing the
    coinflip
4: Start the next round by setting r = r + 1 and go to 1.

Here, r is the round number; x is the initial preference or value proposed by the process; 1 is the first subround, round, or phase of the main round; 2 is the second subround, round, or phase of the main round; * can be 0 or 1; ? represents no majority observed; N is the number of nodes (processes); D is an indication of approval (ratification) – in other words, it is an indication that the process has observed a majority of the same value – t is the number of faulty nodes; v is the value; and coinflip() is a uniform random number generator that generates either 0 or 1.

We can visualize this protocol in the diagram shown in Figure 6-8.

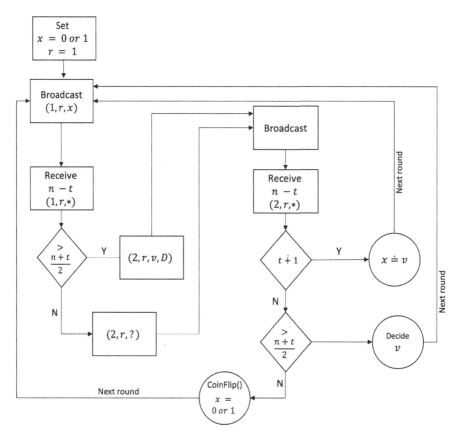

Figure 6-8. *Ben-Or crash fault tolerant only agreement protocol – (non-Byzantine)*

If $n > 2t$, the protocol guarantees with probability 1 that all processes will eventually decide on the same value, and if all processes start with the value v, then within one round all processes will decide on v. Moreover, if in some round a process decides on v after receiving more than t D type messages, then all other processes will decide on v within the next round.

The protocol described earlier works for crash faults; for tolerating Byzantine faults, slight modifications are required, which we describe next.

The Ben-Or algorithm for Byzantine faults:

Each process p executes the following algorithm:

Process p: Initial value x = 0 or 1
0: set r = 1
--First subround or phase - proposal phase
1: Broadcast (1, r, x) to all processes including itself
2: Wait until messages of type (1,r,*) are received from N - t processes.
> **2(a):** If more than (N + t)/2 messages have the same value v, then
--second subround or phase - decision phase
> **2(b):** Broadcast the message (2, r, v, D) to all processes including itself.
> **2(c):** else Broadcast the message (2, r, ?) to all processes including itself.
3: Wait until messages of type (2, r, *) arrive from n - t processes.
> **3(a):** If there are at least t + 1 D type messages (2, r, v, D), then vote v i.e set x = v
> **3(b):** If there are more than (n + t)/2 D type messages then decide v.
> **3(c):** Else set x to 0 or 1 each with probability 1/2 by   doing the coinflip
4: Start the next round by setting r = r + 1 and go to 1.

Here, r is the round number; x is the initial preference or value proposed by the process; 1 is the first subround, round, or phase of the main round; 2 is the second subround, round, or phase of the main round; * can be 0 or 1; ? represents no majority observed; N is the number of nodes (processes); D is an indication of approval (ratification) – in other words, it is an indication that the process has observed a majority of the same value – t is the number of faulty nodes; v is the value; and coinflip() is a uniform random number generator that generates either 0 or 1.

We can visualize this protocol in Figure 6-9.

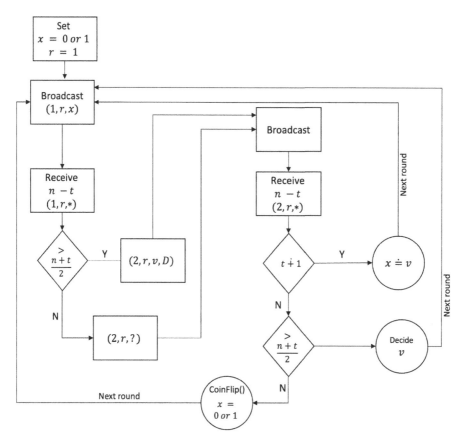

Figure 6-9. *Ben-Or Byzantine agreement protocol*

In the first subround or phase of the protocol, every process broadcasts its proposed preferred value and awaits $n - t$ messages. If more than $\frac{n+t}{2}$ processes agree, then a majority is achieved, and the preferred value is set accordingly.

In the second subround or phase of the protocol, if a majority is observed in the first subround, then an indication of majority is broadcast $(2, r, v, D)$; otherwise, if no majority (?) was observed in the first subround, then no majority is broadcast. The protocol then waits for $n - t$ confirmations. If at least $t + 1$ confirmations of a majority of either 0 or 1 are observed, then the preferred value is set accordingly. Here, only the preferred value is set, but no decision is made. A decision is made by p if more than $\frac{n+t}{2}$ confirmations are received, only then the value is decided. If neither $t + 1$ confirmations nor $\frac{n+t}{2}$ confirmations are received, then the coin is flipped to choose a uniform random value, either 0 or 1.

Note that, by waiting for $n - t$ messages, the Byzantine fault case where Byzantine processes maliciously decide not to vote is handled. This is because in the presence of t faults, at least n is honest. In the second subround, $t + 1$ confirmations of a majority value mean that at least one honest process has observed a majority. In the case of $\frac{n+t}{2}$, it means a value has been observed by a majority.

So, in summary, if $n > 5t$, this protocol guarantees with probability 1 that all processes will eventually decide on the same value, and if all processes start with the value v, then within one round all processes will decide on v. Moreover, if in some round an honest process decides on v after receiving more than $\frac{(n+t)}{2}$ D type messages, then all other processes will decide on v within the next round.

Note that I have used t to denote faulty processes, which is in line with the original paper on the subject. However, in literature f is also widely used to denote faults, either Byzantine or crash. So, t + 1 or f + 1 means the same thing, as t and f denote the same thing.

Now the question arises as to how this protocol achieves an agreement, validity, and termination. Let's try to answer these questions.

An agreement is possible because at most one value can be in a majority in the first phase (subround) of the main round. If some process observes the $t + 1$ D type message (ratification message of the form (2, r, v, D)), then every process observes at least one ratification message of the form (2, r, v, D). Finally, if every process sees a ratification message of the form (2, r, v, D), then every process votes for value v (accepts value v) in the first subround (phase) of r + 1 and decides on v in the second subround (phase) unless it has decided already.

Validity is possible because if all processes vote for (accept) their common value v in a round, then all processes broadcast (2, r, v, D) and decide in the second subround of the round. Also, note that the preferred value of only one of the processes is broadcast in the first subround of the round.

The reason why Ben-Or terminates is because eventually the majority of the nonfaulty processes will flip a coin to achieve the same random value. This majority value is then observed by the honest processes, which then propagate the D type message (ratification message) with the majority value. Eventually, honest processes will receive the D type message (ratification message), and the protocol will terminate.

Also, note that the reason why two subrounds are required is because in the first phase the number of preferred value proposals is reduced to at most one, and then in the second subround, a simple majority vote is sufficient to make the decision. It is possible to design a consensus algorithm with only one round, but that will require a minimum number of processes to be $3f + 1$. With two rounds under asynchrony, the $2f + 1$ lower bound is met.

The Ben-Or algorithms described earlier do not use any cryptographic primitives and assume strong adversary. However, a lot of work has also been carried out where an asynchronous Byzantine agreement is studied under the availability of cryptographic primitives. Of course, under this model the adversary is assumed to be always computationally bounded. Some prominent early protocols under this model are described earlier, such as the signed message protocol and the DLS protocol for the authenticated Byzantine failure model. There are other algorithms that process coin tosses cooperatively or, in other words, use global or shared coin tossing mechanisms. A shared coin or global coin is a pseudorandom coin that produces the same result at all processes in the same round. This attribute immediately implies that convergence is much faster in the case of shared coin–based mechanisms. A similar technique was first used in Rabin's algorithm [14] utilizing cryptographic techniques which reduced the expected time to the constant number of rounds.

After this basic introduction to early consensus protocols, I'll now introduce early replication protocols, which of course are fundamentally based on consensus, but can be classified as replication protocols rather than just consensus algorithms.

We saw earlier, in Chapter 3, that replication allows multiple replicas to achieve consistency in a distributed system. It is a method to provide high availability in a distributed system. There are different models including primary backup replication and active replication. You can refer to Chapter 3 to read more about state machine replication and other techniques.

Consensus Using Failure Detectors

We discussed failure detectors and its different classes earlier in Chapter 3. Here, we present the outline of an algorithm called the *Chandra-Toueg consensus protocol* to solve consensus using an eventually strong $\diamond S$ failure detector, which is the weakest failure detector for solving consensus [10]. Recall that an eventually strong failure detector satisfies strong completeness and eventual weak accuracy properties.

This protocol considers an asynchronous network model with $f < \left\lceil \dfrac{n}{2} \right\rceil$, that is, with at least $\left\lceil \dfrac{n+1}{2} \right\rceil$ correct processes. Less than $n/2$ failed process assumption allows processes to wait to receive majority responses regardless of what the failure detector is suspecting.

The protocol works in rounds under asynchrony with a rotating coordinator. The protocol uses reliable broadcast which ensures that any message broadcast is either not received (delivered) at all by any process or exactly once by all honest processes.

The algorithm works as follows.

Each process maintains some variables:

- Estimate of the decision value – proposed value

- State

- Process's current round number

- Last round in which the process updated its estimate (preference)

Until the state is decided, the processes go through multiple incrementing asynchronous rounds each divided into four phases or subrounds, and coordinators are rotated until a decision is reached. Coordinators are chosen in a round-robin fashion using the formula $(r \bmod n) + 1$, where r is the current round number, and n is the total number of processes:

1. All processes send their estimate (preference) to the current coordinator using a message of type (process id, current round number, estimate, round number when the sender updated its estimate).

2. The current coordinator waits to collect a majority $\left\lceil \dfrac{n+1}{2} \right\rceil$ estimates and chooses the proposed value with the most recent (largest) value of the last updated round as its estimate and then proposes the new estimate to all processes.

3. Each process waits for the new proposal (estimate) from the current coordinator or for the failure detector to suspect the current coordinator. If it receives a new estimate, it updates its preference, updates the last round variable to the current round, and sends the ack message to the current coordinator. Otherwise, it sends *nack*, suspecting that the current coordinator has crashed.

4. The current coordinator waits for the $\left\lceil \frac{n+1}{2} \right\rceil$ – that is, a majority of replies from processes, either *ack* or *nack*. If the current coordinator receives a majority of acks, meaning $\left\lceil \frac{n+1}{2} \right\rceil$ has accepted its estimate, then the estimate is locked, and the coordinator does a reliable broadcast of the decide message (decided value).

- Finally, any undecided process that delivers a value via the reliable broadcast accepts and decides on that value.

Note that there are other algorithms in the paper [10] as well, but I have described here only the one that solves consensus using an eventually strong failure detector.

Now let's see how agreement, validity, and termination requirements are met.

The **agreement** is satisfied. Let's think about a scenario where it is possible that two coordinators broadcast, and some processes end up accepting a value from the first coordinator and some from the other. This will violate the agreement because, here, two processes are deciding differently, that is, two different values are both chosen. However, this cannot occur because for the first coordinator to send a decision, it must have received enough acknowledgments (acks) from the majority of the processes. All subsequent coordinators looking for the majority will see an overlap with the previous one. The estimate will be the most recent one. As such, any two coordinators broadcasting the decision are sending out the same decision.

Validity is also satisfied because every estimate is some process's input value. The protocol design does not allow generating any new estimates.

The protocol eventually **terminates** because the failure detector, an eventually strong failure detector, will eventually stop suspecting some correct process, which will eventually become the coordinator. With the new coordinator, in some round, all correct processes will wait to receive this new coordinator's estimate and will respond with enough ack messages. When the coordinator collects the majority of ack messages, it will send its decided estimate to all, and all processes will terminate. Note that if some process ends up waiting for a response from an already terminated process, it will also eventually get the message by retransmission through other correct nodes and eventually decide and terminate. For example, suppose a process gets stuck waiting for messages from a crashed coordinator. Eventually, due to the strong completeness property of the eventually strong failure detector, the failed coordinator will be suspected, ensuring progress.

Summary

This chapter covered early protocols that provide a solid foundation for most of the consensus research done today. With the advent of blockchains, many of these protocols inspired the development of new blockchain age protocols, especially for permissioned blockchains. For example, Tendermint is based on the DLS protocol, that is, algorithm 2 from the DLS paper.

We did not discuss every algorithm in this chapter, but this chapter should provide readers with a solid foundation to build on further. To circumvent FLP impossibility, randomness can be introduced into the system by either assuming the randomized model or local coin flips at the processes. The first proposal that assumes a randomized model (also called fair scheduling, randomized scheduling) mechanism is by Bracha and Toueg [17]. Algorithms based on the second approach where processes are provided with a local coin flip operation were first proposed by Ben-Or [2], which is the first randomized consensus protocol. The first approach to achieve the expected constant number of rounds by using the shared coin (global coin) approach implemented using digital signatures and a trusted dealer is published in Rabin [14]. Protocols utilizing failure detectors were proposed by Chandra and Toueg [15]. An excellent survey of randomized protocols for asynchronous consensus is by Aspnes [16].

Randomized protocols are a way to circumvent an FLP result, but can we refute the FLP impossibility result altogether? Sounds impossible, but we'll see in Chapter 9 that refuting the FLP result might be possible.

In the next chapter, we will cover classical protocols such as PBFT, which is seen as a natural progression from the viewstamped replication (VR) protocol, which we will also introduce in the next chapter. While VR dealt with crash faults only, PBFT also dealt with Byzantine faults. We'll cover other protocols, too, such as Paxos, which is the foundation of most if not all consensus protocols. Almost all consensus algorithms utilize the fundamental ideas presented in Paxos in one way or another.

Bibliography

1. Impossibility of distributed consensus with one faulty process J. Assoc. Computer. Mach., 32 (No. 2) (1985), pp. 374–382.

2. M. Ben-Or: Another advantage of free choice: Completely asynchronous agreement protocols.

3.   L. Lamport, R. Shostak, M. Pease, the Byzantine Generals problem, ACM Transactions on Programming Languages and Systems, vol. 4 (no. 3) (1982), pp. 382–401, July 1982.

4.   Lampson, Butler, and Howard E. Sturgis. "Crash recovery in a distributed data storage system." (1979).

5.   Skeen, D., 1981, April. Nonblocking commit protocols. In Proceedings of the 1981 ACM SIGMOD international conference on Management of data (pp. 133–142).

6.   Dwork, C., Lynch, N., and Stockmeyer, L., 1988. Consensus in the presence of partial synchrony. Journal of the ACM (JACM), 35(2), pp. 288-323.

7.   G. Bracha, "Asynchronous Byzantine agreement protocols," Inf. Comput., 1987.

8.   S. Toueg, "Randomized Byzantine agreements," in PODC, 1984.

9.   G. Bracha and S. Toueg, "Resilient consensus protocols," in PODC, 1983.

10.   Chandra, T.D. and Toueg, S., 1996. Unreliable failure detectors for reliable distributed systems. Journal of the ACM (JACM), 43(2), pp. 225-267.

11.   Martin Kleppmann's lectures on distributed computing – Kleppmann, M., 2018. Distributed systems. www.cl.cam.ac.uk/teaching/2021/ConcDisSys/dist-sys-notes.pdf

12.   Distributed Algorithms: A Verbose Tour – by Fourre Sigs.

13.   Lindsey Kuper – lectures on distributed systems: https://youtube.com/playlist?list=PLNPUF5QyWU8PydLG2cIJrCv nn5I_exhYx

14.   Rabin, M.O., 1983, November. Randomized Byzantine generals. In 24th annual symposium on foundations of computer science (sfcs 1983) (pp. 403–409). IEEE.

15. Chandra, T.D. and Toueg, S., 1996. Unreliable failure detectors for reliable distributed systems. Journal of the ACM (JACM), 43(2), pp. 225–267.

16. Aspnes, J., 2003. Randomized protocols for asynchronous consensus. *Distributed Computing, 16*(2), pp. 165–175.

17. Bracha, G. and Toueg, S., 1985. Asynchronous consensus and broadcast protocols. *Journal of the ACM (JACM)*, 32(4), pp. 824–840.

CHAPTER 7

Classical Consensus

Consensus and replication protocols that appeared in the 1980s have made profound contributions in consensus protocol research. Early replication protocols like viewstamped replication provided deep insights into how fault-tolerant replication can be designed and implemented. Around the same time, Paxos was introduced, which offered a practical protocol with rigorous formal specification and analysis. In 1999, the first practical Byzantine fault–tolerant protocol was introduced. This chapter covers these classical protocols in detail, their design, how they work, and how they provide safety and liveness guarantees. Moreover, some ideas on how and if we can use them in the blockchain are also presented. Additionally, recently developed protocols such as RAFT are also discussed, which builds on previous classical protocols to construct an easy-to-understand consensus protocol.

Viewstamped Replication

A viewstamped replication approach to replicate among peers was introduced by Brian Oki and Barbara Liskov in 1988. This is one of the most fundamental mechanisms to achieve replication to guarantee consistency (consistent view) over replicated data. It works in the presence of crash faults and network partitions; however, it is assumed that eventually nodes recover from crashes, and network partitions are healed. It is also a consensus algorithm because to achieve consistency over replicated data, nodes must agree on a replicated state.

Viewstamped replication has two primary purposes. One is to provide a distributed system which is coherent enough that the clients see that as if they are communicating with a single server. The other one is to provide state machine replication. State machine replication requires that all replicas start in the same initial state and operations are deterministic. With these requirements (assumptions), we can easily see that if all replicas execute the same sequence of operations, then they will end up in the same

© Imran Bashir 2022
I. Bashir, *Blockchain Consensus*, https://doi.org/10.1007/978-1-4842-8179-6_7

state. Of course, the challenge here is to ensure that operations execute in the same order at all replicas even in the event of failures. So, in summary the protocol provides fault tolerance and consistency. It is based on a primary backup copy technique.

There are three subprotocols in the viewstamped replication (VR) protocol:

- **Normal operation protocol**: Handles client requests and achieves replication under normal conditions

- **View change protocol**: Handles primary failure and starts a new view with a new primary

- **Replica recovery protocol**: Handles rejoining of a failed replica that has now recovered

VR is inspired by the two-phase commit protocol, but unlike the two-phase commit, it's a failure-resilient protocol and does not block if the primary (coordinator in 2PC terminology) or replicas fail. The protocol is reliable and ensures availability if no more than f replicas are faulty. It uses replica groups of 2f + 1 and tolerates crash failures under asynchrony with f+1 quorum sizes.

Every replica maintains a state which contains information such as configuration, replica number, current view, current status – normal or view change or recovering, assigned op number to the latest request, log containing entries which contain the requests received so far with their op numbers, and the client table which consists of the most recent client request, with status if it has been executed or not and associated result for that request.

Let's see how the normal operation works in VR. First, let's see the list of variables and their meanings:

- **op**: Client operation

- **c**: Client ID

- **s**: Number assigned to the request

- **v**: View number known to the client

- **m**: Message received from the client

- **n**: The op number assigned to the request

- **i**: Nonprimary replica

- **x**: Result

Protocol Steps

1. A client sends a request message of the form <REQUEST op, c, s, v> message to the primary replica.

2. When received by the primary

   a. It increments the op number.

   b. It adds the request message at the end of the log.

   c. It sends a <PREPARE m, v, n> to other replicas.

3. When replicas receive the prepare message, they do the following:

   a. The prepare message is only accepted if all previous requests preceding the op number in the prepare message have entries in their log.

   b. Otherwise, they wait until the missing entries are updated – via state transfer.

   c. They append the request to their log.

   d. They send the <PREPAREOK v, n, i> message to the primary replica.

4. The primary waits for f PREPAREOK messages from other replicas; when received, it

   a. Considers the operation to be committed

   b. Executes any pending operations

   c. Executes the latest operation

   d. Sends the message <REPLY v, s, x> to the client

5. After the commit, the primary replica informs other replicas about the commit.

6. Other replicas execute it after appending it in their log but only after executing any pending operations.

This process is visualized in Figure 7-1.

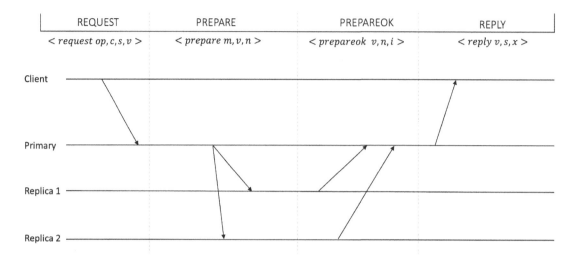

Figure 7-1. *VR protocol – normal operation*

When the primary fails, the view change protocol initiates. Failure is indicated by timeout at replicas:

- **v**: View number

- **l**: Replica's log/new log

- **k**: The op number of the latest known committed request that the replica is aware of

- **I**: Replica identifier

View Change

A view change protocol works as follows:

1. When a replica suspects the primary of failure, it

    a. Increments its view number

    b. Changes its status to view change

    c. Sends a <DOVIEWCHANGE v, l, k, i> message to the primary of the next view

2. When the new primary gets f+1 of the DOVIEWCHANGE message, it

    a. Chooses the most recent log in the message and picks that as its new log

    b. Sets the op number to that of the latest entry in the new log

    c. Changes its status to normal

    d. Sends the <STARTVIEW v, l, k> message to other replicas, indicating the completion of the view change process

3. Now the new primary

    a. Sequentially executes any unexecuted committed operations

    b. Sends a reply to the client

    c. Starts accepting new client requests

4. Other replicas upon receiving the startview message

    a. Replace their log with the one in the message

    b. Set their op number to the one in the latest entry in the log

    c. Set their view number to what is in the message

    d. Change their status to normal

    e. Send PREPAREOK for uncommitted messages

The view change protocol repeats if even a new primary fails.
Figure 7-2 visualizes this process.

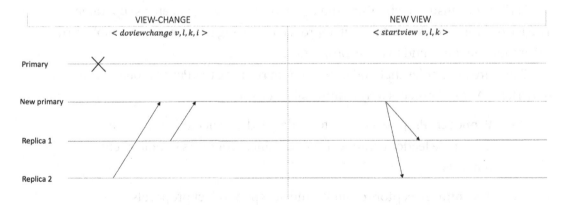

Figure 7-2. *View change in VR*

The key safety requirement here is that all committed operations make it to the next views with their order preserved.

VR is not discussed with all intricate details on purpose, as we focus more on mainstream protocols. Still, it should give you an idea about the fundamental concepts introduced in VR, which play an essential role in almost all replication and consensus protocols, especially PBFT, Paxos, and RAFT. When you read the following sections, you will see how PBFT is an evolved form of VR and other similarities between VR and different protocols introduced in this chapter. When you read the section on RAFT, you will find good resemblance between VR and RAFT.

Let's look at Paxos first, undoubtedly the most influential and fundamental consensus protocol.

Paxos

Leslie Lamport discovered Paxos. It was proposed first in 1988 and then later more formally in 1998. It is the most fundamental distributed consensus algorithm which allows consensus over a value under unreliable communications. In other words, Paxos is used to build a reliable system that works correctly, even in the presence of faults. Paxos made state machine replication more practical to implement. A version of Paxos called multi-Paxos is commonly used to implement a replicated state machine. It runs under a message-passing model with asynchrony. It tolerates fewer than $n/2$ crash faults, that is, it meets the lower bound of $2f + 1$.

Earlier consensus mechanisms did not handle safety and liveness separately. The Paxos protocol takes a different approach to solving the consensus problem by separating the safety and liveness properties.

There are three roles that nodes in a system running the Paxos protocol can undertake. A single process may assume all three roles:

- **Proposer**: Proposes values to be decided. An elected proposer acts as a single leader to propose a new value. Proposers handle client requests.

- **Acceptor**: Acceptors evaluate and accept or reject proposals proposed by the proposers according to several rules and conditions.

- **Learner**: Learns the decision, that is, the agreed-upon value.

There are also some rules associated with Paxos nodes. Paxos nodes must be persistent, that is, they must store what their action is and must remember what they've accepted. Nodes must also know how many acceptors make a majority.

Paxos can be seen as similar to the two-phase commit protocol. A two-phase commit (2PC) is a standard atomic commitment protocol to ensure that the transactions are committed in distributed databases only if all participants agree to commit. Even if a single node does not agree to commit the transaction, it is rolled back completely.

Similarly, in Paxos, the proposer sends a proposal to the acceptors in the first phase. Then, the proposer broadcasts a request to commit to the acceptors if and when they accept the proposal. Once the acceptors commit and report back to the proposer, the proposal is deemed final, and the protocol concludes. In contrast with the two-phase commit, Paxos introduced ordering, that is, sequencing, to achieve the total order of the proposals. In addition, it also introduced a majority quorum–based acceptance of the proposals rather than expecting all nodes to agree. This scheme allows the protocol to make progress even if some nodes fail. Both improvements ensure the safety and liveness of the Paxos algorithm.

The protocol is composed of two phases, the prepare phase and the accept phase. At the end of the prepare phase, a majority of acceptors have promised a specific proposal number. At the end of the accept phase, a majority of acceptors have accepted a proposed value, and consensus is reached.

The algorithm works as follows:

Phase 1 – prepare phase

- The proposer receives a request to reach consensus on a value by a client.

- The proposer sends a message *prepare(n)* to a majority or all acceptors. At this stage, no value is proposed for a decision yet. The majority of acceptors is enough under the assumption that all acceptors in the majority will respond. Here, the n represents the proposal number which must be globally unique and must be greater than any proposal number this proposer has used before. For example, n can be a timestamp in nanoseconds or some other incrementing value. If a timeout occurs, then the proposer will retry with a higher n. In other words, if the proposer is unable to make progress due to a lack of responses from the acceptors, it can retry with a higher proposal number.

- When an acceptor receives this *prepare(n)* message, it makes a "promise." It performs the following:

  - If no previous promise has been made by responding to the prepare message, then the acceptor now promises to ignore any request less than the proposal number n. It records n and replies with message *promise(n)*.

  - If the acceptor has previously promised, that is, already responded to another prepare message with some proposal number lower than n, the acceptor performs the following:

  - If the acceptor has not received any accept messages already from a proposer in the accept phase, it stores the higher proposal number n and then sends a promise message to the proposer.

  - If the acceptor has received an accept message earlier with some other lower proposal number, it must have already accepted a proposed value from some proposer. This previous full proposal is now sent along with the promise message to the proposer, indicating that the acceptor has already accepted a value.

Phase 2 – accept phase

Phase 2 starts when the proposer has received enough responses, that is, promise messages, from the majority of the acceptors for a specific n:

- The proposer waits until it gets responses from the majority of the acceptors for n.

- When responses are received, the proposer evaluates what value v to be sent in the accept message. It performs the following:

  - If the proposer received one or more promise messages with full proposals, it chooses the value v in the proposal with the highest proposal number.

  - If no promise messages received by the proposer include a full proposal, the proposer can choose any value it wants.

- The proposer now sends an accept message – a full proposal of the form *accept(n, v)* – to the acceptors, where n is the promised proposal number and v is the actual proposed value.

- When an acceptor receives this *accept(n, v)* message, it does the following:

  - If the acceptor has promised not to accept this proposal number previously, it will ignore the message.

  - Otherwise, if it has responded to the corresponding prepare request with the same *n*, that is, *prepare(n)*, only then it replies with *accepted(n, v)* indicating acceptance of the proposal.

  - Finally, the acceptor sends *accepted(n, v)* to all learners.

- If a majority of acceptors accept the value *v* in the proposal, then *v* becomes the decided value of the protocol i.e., consensus is reached.

Sometimes, there is a distinction made between the accept phase and a third phase called the learning phase where learners learn about the decided value from the acceptors. We have not shown that separately in the preceding algorithm, as learning is considered part of the second phase. As soon as a proposal is accepted in the accept phase, the acceptor informs the learners. Figure 7-3 does show a third phase called the learn phase, but it is just for visualizing the protocol in a simpler way; learning is in fact part of phase 2, the accept phase.

We have used the term majority indicating that a majority of acceptors have responded to or accepted a message. Majority comes from a quorum. In the majority quorum, every quorum has $\frac{n}{2}+1$ nodes. Also note that in order to tolerate f faulty acceptors, at least a set consisting of $2f + 1$ acceptors is required. We discussed quorum systems in Chapter 3.

The protocol is illustrated in Figure 7-3.

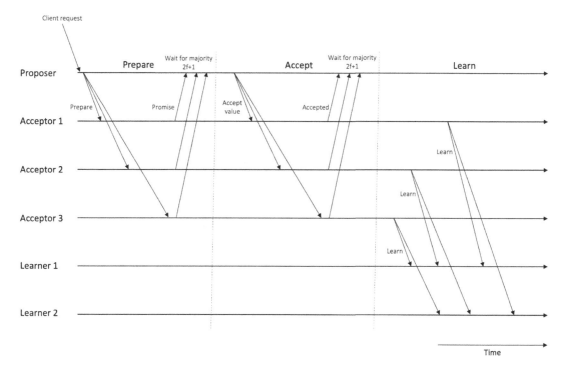

Figure 7-3. *A normal run of Paxos*

Note that the Paxos algorithm once reached a single consensus will not proceed to another consensus. Another run of Paxos is needed to reach another consensus. Moreover, Paxos cannot make progress if half or more than half of the nodes are faulty because in such a case a majority cannot be achieved, which is essential for making progress. It is safe because once a value is agreed, it is never changed. Even though Paxos is guaranteed to be safe, liveness of the protocol is not guaranteed. The assumption here is that a large portion of the network is correct (nonfaulty) for adequately enough time, and then the protocol reaches consensus; otherwise, the protocol may never terminate.

Usually, learners learn the decision value directly from the acceptors; however, it is possible that in a large network learners may learn values from each other by relaying what some of them (a small group) have learned directly from acceptors. Alternatively, learners can poll the acceptors at intervals to check if there's a decision. There can also be an elected learner node which is notified by the acceptors, and this elected learner disseminates the decision to other learners.

Now let's consider some failure scenarios.

Failure Scenarios

Imagine if an acceptor fails in the first phase, that is, the prepare phase, then it won't send the promise message back to the proposer. However, if a majority quorum can respond back, the proposer will receive the responses, and the protocol will make progress. If an acceptor fails in the second phase, that is, the accept phase, then the acceptor will not send the accepted message back to the proposer. Here again, if the majority of the acceptors is correct and available, the proposer and learners will receive enough responses to proceed.

What if the proposer failed either in the prepare phase or the accept phase? If a proposer fails before sending any prepare messages, there is no impact; some other proposer will run, and the protocol will continue. If a proposer fails in phase 1, after sending the prepare messages, then acceptors will not receive any accept messages, because promise messages did not make it to the proposer. In this case, some other proposer will propose with a higher proposal number, and the protocol will progress. The old prepare will become history. If a proposer fails during the accept phase after sending the accept message which was received by at least one acceptor, some other proposer will send a prepare message with a higher proposal number, and the acceptor will respond to the proposer with a promise message that an earlier value is already accepted. At this point, the proposer will switch to proposing the same earlier value bearing the highest accepted proposal number, that is, send an accept message with the same earlier value.

Another scenario could be if there are two proposers trying to propose their value at the same time. Imagine there are two proposers who have sent their prepare messages to the acceptors. In this case, any acceptor who had accepted a larger proposal number previously from P1 would ignore the proposal if the proposal number proposed by the proposer P2 is lower than what acceptors had accepted before. If there is an acceptor A3 who has not seen any value before, it would accept the proposal number from P2 even if it is lower than the proposal number that the other acceptors have received and accepted from P1 before because the acceptor A3 has no idea what other acceptors are doing. The acceptor will then respond as normal back to P2. However, as proposers wait for a majority of acceptors to respond, P2 will not receive promise messages from a majority, because A3 only is not a majority. On the other hand, P1 will receive promise messages from the majority, because A1 and A2 (other proposers) are in the majority and will respond back to P1. When P2 doesn't hear from a majority, it times out and can retry with a higher proposal number.

Now imagine a scenario where with P1 the acceptors have already reached a consensus, but there is another proposer P2 which doesn't know that and sends a prepare message with a higher than before proposal number. The acceptors at this point, after receiving the higher proposal number message from P2, will check if they have accepted any message at all before; if yes, the acceptors will respond back to P2 with the promise message of the form promise(nfromp2,(nfromp1, vfromp1)) containing the previous highest proposal number they have accepted, along with the previous accepted value. Otherwise, they will respond normally back to P2 with a promise message. When P2 receives this message, promise(nfromp2,(nfromp1, vfromp1)), it will check the message, and value v will become vfromp1 if nfromp1 is the highest previous proposal number. Otherwise, P2 will choose any value v it wants. In summary, if P2 has received promise messages indicating that another value has already been chosen, it will propose the previously chosen value with the highest proposal number. At this stage, P2 will send an accept message with its n and v already chosen (vfromp1). Now acceptors are happy because they see the highest n and will respond back with an accepted message as normal and will inform learners too. Note that the previously chosen value is still the value proposed by P2, just with the highest proposal number n now.

There are scenarios where the protocol could get into a livelock state and progress can halt. A scenario could be where two different proposers are competing with proposals. This situation is also known as "dueling proposers." In such cases, the liveness of Paxos cannot be guaranteed.

Imagine we have two proposers, P1 and P2. We have three acceptors, A1, A2, and A3. Now, P1 sends the prepare messages to the majority of acceptors, A1 and A2. A1 and A2 reply with promise messages to P1. Imagine now the other proposer, P2, also proposes and sends a prepare message with a higher proposal number to A2 and A3. A3 and A2 send the promise back to P2 because, by protocol rules, acceptors will promise back to the prepare message if the prepare message comes with a higher proposal number than what the acceptors have seen before. In phase 2, when P1 sends the accept message, A1 will accept it and reply with accepted, but A2 will ignore this message because it has already promised a higher proposal number from P2. In this case, P1 will eventually time out, waiting for a majority response from acceptors because the majority will now never respond. Now, P1 will try again with a higher proposal number and send the prepare message to A1 and A2. Assume both A1 and A2 have responded with promise messages. Now suppose P2 sends an accept message to get its value chosen to A2 and A3. A3 will respond with an accepted message, but A2 will not respond to P2 because it has already promised another higher proposal number from P1. Now, P2 will time out, waiting for the majority response from the acceptors. P2 now will try again with a higher proposal number. This cycle can repeat again and again, and consensus will never be reached because there is never a majority response from the acceptors to any proposers.

This issue is typically handled by electing a single proposer as the leader to administer all clients' incoming requests. This way, there is no competition among different proposers, and this livelock situation cannot occur. However, electing a leader is also not straightforward. A unique leader election is equivalent to solving consensus. For leader election, an instance of Paxos will have to run, that election consensus may get a livelock too, and we are in the same situation again. One possibility is to use a different type of election mechanism, for example, the bully algorithm. Some other leader election algorithms are presented in works of Aguilera et.al. We may use some other kind of consensus mechanism to elect a leader that perhaps guarantees termination but somewhat sacrifices safety. Another way to handle the livelock problem is to use random exponentially increasing delays, resulting in a client having to wait for a while before proposing again. I think these delays may well also be introduced at proposers, which will result in one proposer taking a bit of precedence over another and getting its value accepted before the acceptors could receive another prepared message with a higher proposal number. Note that there is no requirement in classical Paxos to have a single elected leader, but in practical implementations, it is commonly the case to elect a leader. Now if that single leader becomes the single point of failure, then another leader must be elected.

A key point to remember is that $2f + 1$ acceptors are required for f crash faults to be tolerated. Paxos can also tolerate omission faults. Suppose a prepare message is lost and didn't make it to acceptors, the proposer will wait and time out and retry with a higher proposal number. Also, another proposer can propose meanwhile with a higher proposal number, and the protocol can still work. Also, as only a majority of acceptor responses are required, as long as a majority of messages $(2f + 1)$ made it through to the proposer from acceptors, the protocol will progress. It is however possible that due to omission faults, the protocol takes longer to reach consensus or may never terminate under some scenarios, but it will always be safe.

Safety and Liveness

The Paxos algorithm solves the consensus problem by achieving **safety** and **liveness** properties. We have some requirements for each property. Under safety, we mainly have the agreement and validity. An **agreement** means that no two different values are chosen. **Validity** or sometimes called **nontriviality** means no value is decided unless proposed by some process participating in the protocol. Another safety requirement which stems from the validity property and may be called "**valid learning**" is that if a process **learns** a value, the value must have been decided by a process. An agreement ensures that all processes decide on the same value. Validity and valid learning requirements ensure that processes decide only on a proposed value and do not trivially choose to not decide or just choose some predefined value.

Under **liveness**, there are two requirements. First, the protocol eventually **decides**, that is, a proposed value is eventually decided. Second, if a value is decided, the learners eventually **learn** that value.

Let's now discuss how these safety and liveness requirements are met.

Intuitively, the agreement is achieved by ensuring that a majority of acceptors can vote for only one proposal. Imagine two different values v1 and v2 are somehow chosen (decided). We know that the protocol will choose a value only if a majority of the acceptors accept the same accept message from a proposer. This condition implies that a set of majority acceptors A1 must have accepted an accept message with a proposal (n1,v1). Also, another accept message with proposal (n2, v2) must have been accepted by another set of majority acceptors A2. Assuming that two majority sets A1 and A2 must intersect, meaning they will have at least one acceptor in common due to the quorum intersection rule. This acceptor must have accepted two different proposals with the same proposal number. Such a scenario is impossible because an acceptor will ignore any prepare or accept messages with the same proposal number they have already accepted.

If n1 <> n2 and n1 < n2 and n1 and n2 are consecutive proposal rounds, then this means that A1 must have accepted the accept message with proposal number n1 before A2 accepted the accept messages with n2. This is because an acceptor ignores any prepare or accept messages if they have a smaller proposal number than the previously promised proposal number. Also, the proposed value by a proposer must be from either an earlier proposal with the highest proposal number or the proposer's own proposed value if no proposed value is included in the accepted message. As we know, A1 and A2 must intersect with at least one common acceptor; this common acceptor must have accepted the accept messages for both proposals (n1,v1) and (n2,v2). This scenario is also impossible because the acceptor would have replied with (n1,v1) in response to the prepare message with proposal number n2, and the proposer must have selected the value v1 instead of v2. Even with nonconsecutive proposals, any intermediate proposals must also select v1 as the chosen value.

Validity is ensured by allowing only the input values of proposers to be proposed. In other words, the decided value is never predefined, nor is it proposed by any other entity that is not part of the cluster running Paxos.

Liveness is not guaranteed in Paxos due to asynchrony. However, if some synchrony assumption, that is, a partially synchronous environment, is assumed, then progress can be made, and termination is achievable. We assume that after GST, at least a majority of acceptors is correct and available. Messages are delivered within a known upper bound, and an elected unique nonfaulty leader proposer is correct and available.

In Practice

Paxos has been implemented in many practical systems. Even though the Paxos algorithm is quite simple at its core, it is often viewed as difficult to understand. As a result, many papers have been written to explain it. Still, it is often considered complicated and tricky to comprehend fully. Nevertheless, this slight concern does not mean that it has not been implemented anywhere. On the contrary, it has been implemented in many production systems, such as Google's Spanner and Chubby. The first deployment of Paxos was in a Petal distributed storage system. Some other randomly chosen examples include Apache ZooKeeper, NoSQL Azure Cosmos database, and Apache Cassandra. It proves to be the most efficient protocol to solve the consensus problem. It has been shown that the two-phase commit is a special case of Paxos, and PBFT is a refinement of Paxos.

Variants

There are many variants of classical Paxos, such as multi-Paxos, Fast Paxos, Byzantine Paxos, Dynamic Paxos, Vertical Paxos, Disk Paxos, Egalitarian Paxos, Stoppable Paxos, and Cheap Paxos.

Multi-Paxos

In classical Paxos, even in an all-correct environment, it takes two round trips to achieve consensus on a single value. This approach is slow, and if consensus is required on a growing sequence of values (which is practically the case), this single value consensus must repeatedly run, which is not efficient. However, an optimization can make classical Paxos efficient enough to be used in practical systems. Recall that Paxos has two phases. Once phases 1 and 2 both have completely run once, then, at that point, a majority of acceptors is now available to that proposer who ran this round of phases 1 and 2. This proposer is now a recognized leader. Instead of rerunning phase 1, the proposer (leader) can keep running phase 2 only, with the available majority of acceptors. As long as it does not crash, or some other proposer doesn't come along and propose with a higher proposal number, this process of successive accept messages can continue. The proposer can keep running the accept/accepted round (phase 2) with even the same proposal number without running the prepare/promise round (phase 1). In other words, the message delays are reduced from four to two. When another proposer comes along or the previous one fails, this new proposer can run another round of phases 1 and 2 by following classical Paxos. When this new proposer becomes the leader by receiving a majority from the acceptors, the basic classical Paxos protocol upgrades to multi-Paxos, and it can start running phase 2 only. As long as there is only a single leader in the network, no acceptor would notify the leader that it has accepted any other proposal, which will let the leader choose any value. This condition allows omitting the first phase when only one elected proposer is the leader.

This protocol is known as optimization Paxos or multi-Paxos. A normal run of multi-Paxos is shown in Figure 7-4.

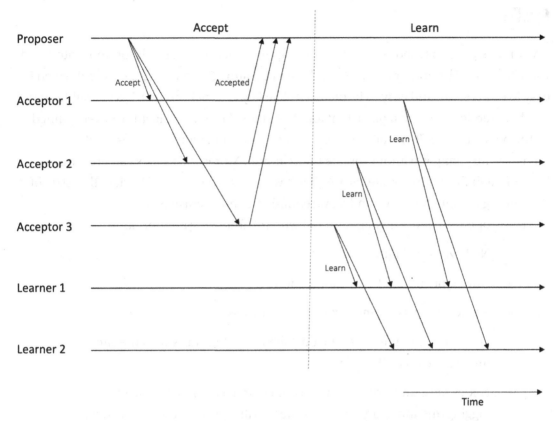

Figure 7-4. *Multi-Paxos – note the first phase, prepare phase, skipped*

Original Paxos is a leaderless (also called symmetric) protocol, whereas multi-Paxos is leader driven (also called asymmetric). It is used in practical systems instead of classical Paxos to enable state machine replication. Commonly in implementations, the role of the proposer, acceptor, and learner is contracted to so-called servers, which may all assume these three roles. Eventually, only a client-server model emerges. With roles collapsed, a steady leader and prepare phase removed, the protocol becomes efficient and simple.

Paxos is seen as a difficult protocol to understand. This is mostly due to underspecification. Also, the original protocol described by Lamport is a single decree protocol, which is not practical to implement. There have been several attempts, such as multi-Paxos, and several papers that try to explain Paxos, but, overall, the protocol is still considered a bit tricky to understand and implement. With these and several other points in mind, a protocol called RAFT was developed. We introduce RAFT next.

RAFT

RAFT is designed in response to shortcomings in Paxos. RAFT stands for Replicated And Fault Tolerant. The authors of RAFT had the main aim of developing a protocol which is easy to understand and easy to implement. The key idea behind RAFT is to enable state machine replication with a persistent log. The state of the state machine is determined by the persistent log. RAFT allows cluster reconfiguration which enables cluster membership changes without service interruption. Moreover, as logs can grow quite large on high throughput systems, RAFT allows log compaction to alleviate the issue of consuming too much storage and slow rebuild after node crashes.

RAFT operates under a system model with the following assumptions:

- No Byzantine failures.

- Unreliable network communication.

- Asynchronous communication and processors.

- Deterministic state machine on each node that starts with the same initial state on each node.

- Nodes have uncorruptible persistent storage with write-ahead logging, meaning any write to storage will complete before crashing.

- The Client must communicate strictly with only the current leader. It is the Client's responsibility as clients know all nodes and are statically configured with this information.

RAFT is a leader-based (asymmetric) protocol, where one node is elected as a leader. This leader accepts client requests and manages the log replication. There can only be one leader at a time in a RAFT cluster. If a current leader fails, then a new leader is elected. There are three roles that nodes (more precisely the consensus module within nodes) can assume in a RAFT cluster: leader, follower, and candidate.

- The **leader** receives client requests, manages replication logs, and manages communication with the followers.

- **Follower** nodes are passive in nature and only respond to Remote Procedure Call (RPCs). They never initiate any communication.

- A **candidate** is a role that is used by a node that is trying to become a leader by requesting votes.

Time in RAFT is logically divided into terms. A term (or epoch) is basically a monotonically increasing value which acts as a logical clock to achieve global partial ordering on events in the absence of a global synchronized clock. Each term starts with an election of a new leader, where one or more candidates compete to become the leader. Once a leader is elected, it serves as a leader until the end of the term. The key role of terms is to identify stale information, for example, stale leaders. Each node stores a current term number. When current terms are exchanged between nodes, it is checked if one node's current term number is lower than the other node's term number; if it is, then the node with the lower term number updates its current term to the larger value. When a candidate or a leader finds out that its current term number is stale, it transitions its state to follower mode. Any requests with a stale term number received by a node are rejected.

Terms can be visualized in Figure 7-5.

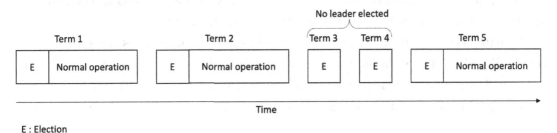

Time

E : Election

Figure 7-5. *Terms in RAFT*

A RAFT protocol works using two RPCs, AppendEntries RPC, which is invoked by a leader to replicate log entries and is also used as a heartbeat, and RequestVote RPC, which is invoked by candidates to collect votes.

RAFT consists of two phases. The first is leader election, and the second is log replication. In the first phase, the leader is elected, and the second phase is where the leader accepts the clients' requests, updates the logs, and sends a heartbeat to all followers to maintain its leadership.

First, let's see how leader election works.

Leader Election

A heartbeat mechanism is used to trigger a leader election process. All nodes start up as followers. Followers will run as followers as long as they keep receiving valid RPCs from a leader or a candidate. If a follower does not receive heartbeats from the leader for some time, then an "election timeout" occurs, which indicates that the leader has failed. The election timeout is randomly set to be between 150ms and 300ms.

Now the follower node undertakes the candidate role and attempts to become the leader by starting the election process. The candidate increments the current term number, votes for itself, resets election timer, and seeks votes from others via the RequestVote RPC. If it receives votes from the majority of the nodes, then it becomes the leader and starts sending heartbeats to other nodes, which are now followers. If another candidate has won and became a valid leader, then this candidate would start receiving heartbeats and will return to a follower role. If no one wins the elections and election timeout occurs, the election process starts again with a new term.

Note that votes will only be granted by the receiver node in response to the RequestVote RPC if a candidate's log is at least as up to date as the receiver's log. Also, a "false" will be replied if the received term number is lower than the current term.

The specific process of a leader election is shown in Figure 7-6.

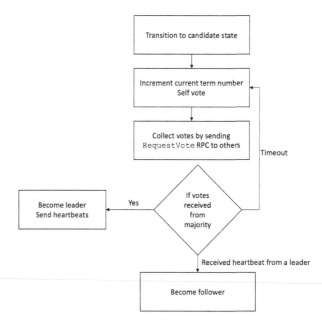

Figure 7-6. *RAFT leader election*

A node can be in three states; we can visualize server states in the state diagram shown in Figure 7-7, which also shows leader election.

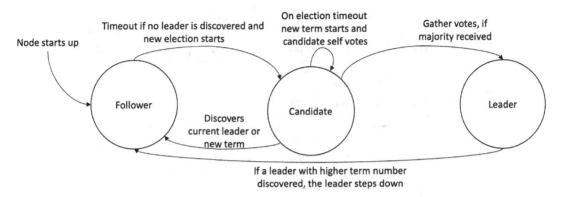

Figure 7-7. *Node states in RAFT*

Once a leader is elected, it is ready to receive requests from clients. Now the log replication can start.

Log Replication

The log replication phase of RAFT is straightforward. First, the client sends commands/ requests to the leader to be executed by the replicated state machines. The leader then assigns a term and index to the command so that the command can be uniquely identified in the logs held by nodes.

It appends this command to its log. When the leader has a new entry in its log, at the same time it sends out the requests to replicate this command via the AppendEntries RPC to the follower nodes.

When the leader is able to replicate the command to the majority of the follower nodes, that is, acknowledged, the entry is considered committed on the cluster. Now the leader executes the command in its state machine and returns the result to the client. It also notifies the followers that the entry is committed via the AppendEntries RPC, and the followers execute committed commands in their state machines. A set of logs from five nodes is shown in Figure 7-8.

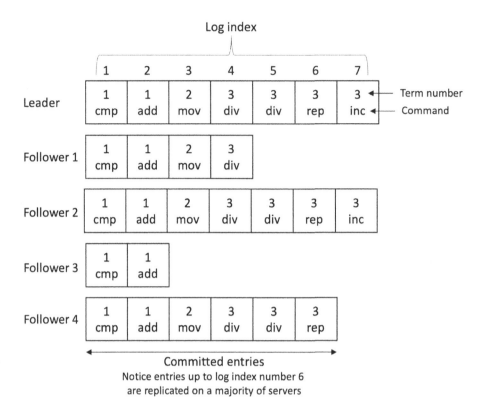

Figure 7-8. *Logs in RAFT nodes*

Notice that entries up to log index number 6 are replicated on a majority of servers as the leader, follower 3, and follower 4 all have these entries, resulting in a majority – three out of five nodes. This means that they are committed and are safe to apply to their respective state machines. The log on followers 1 and 3 is not up to date, which could be due to a fault on the node or communication link failure. If there is a crashed or slow follower, the leader will keep retrying via the AppendEntries RPC until it succeeds.

The log replication process is shown in Figure 7-9.

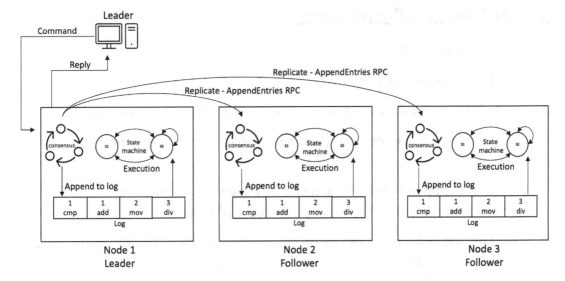

Figure 7-9. *RAFT log replication and state machine replication*

When a follower receives an AppendEntries RPC for replication of log entries, it checks if the term is less than the current term it replies false. It appends only new entries that are not already in the logs. If an existing entry has the same index as the new one, but different terms, it will delete the existing entry and all entries following it. It will also reply false if the log does not have an entry at the index of the log entry immediately preceding the new one but the term matches.

If there is a failed follower or candidate, the protocol will keep retrying via the AppendEntries RPC until it succeeds.

If a command is committed, the RAFT cluster will not lose it. This is the guarantee provided by RAFT despite any failures such as network delays, packet loss, reboots, or crash faults. However, it does not handle Byzantine failures.

Each log entry consists of a term number, an index, and a state machine command. A term number helps to discover inconsistencies between logs. It gives an indication about the time of the command. An index identifies the position of an entry in the log. A command is the request made by the client for execution.

Guarantees and Correctness

Guarantees provided by RAFT are

- **Election correctness**

  - **Election safety**: At most, one leader can be elected in each term.

  - **Election liveness**: Some candidate must eventually become a leader.

- **Leader append-only**: A leader can only append to the log. No overwrite or deletion of entries in the log is allowed.

- **Log matching**: If two logs on two different servers have an entry with the same index and term, then these logs are identical in all previous entries, and they store the same command.

- **Leader completeness**: A log entry committed in a given term will always be present in the logs of the future leaders, that is, leaders for higher-numbered terms. Also, nodes with incomplete logs must never be elected.

- **State machine safety**: If a node has applied a log entry at a given index to its state machine, no other node will ever apply a different log entry for the same index.

Election correctness requires safety and liveness. Safety means that at most one leader is allowed per term. Liveness requires that some candidate must win and become a leader eventually. To ensure safety, each node votes only once in a term which it persists on storage. The majority is required to win the election; no two different candidates will get a majority at the same time.

Split votes can occur during leader election. If two nodes get elected simultaneously, then the so-called "split vote" can occur. RAFT uses randomized election timeouts to ensure that this problem resolves quickly. This helps because random timeouts allow only one node to time out and win the election before other nodes time out. In practice, this works well if the random time chosen is greater than the network broadcast time.

Log matching achieves a high level of consistency between logs. We assume that the leader is not malicious. A leader will never add more than one entry with the same index and same term. Log consistency checks ensure that all previous entries are identical. The leader keeps track of the latest index that it has committed in its log. The leader broadcasts this information in every AppendEntries RPC. If a follower node doesn't have an entry in its log with the same index number, it will not accept the incoming entry. However, if the follower accepts the AppendEntries RPC, the leader knows that the logs are identical on both. Logs are generally consistent unless there are failures on the network. In that case, the log consistency check ensures that nodes eventually catch up and become consistent. If a log is inconsistent, the leader will retransmit missing entries to followers that may not have received the message before or crashed and now have recovered.

Reconfiguration and log compaction are two useful features of RAFT. I have not discussed those here as they are not related directly to the core consensus protocol. You can refer to the original RAFT paper mentioned in the bibliography for more details.

PBFT

Remember, we discussed the oral message protocol and the Byzantine generals problem earlier in the book. While it solved the Byzantine agreement, it was not a practical solution. The oral message protocol only works in synchronous environments, and computational complexity (runtime) is also high unless there is only one faulty processor, which is not practical. However, systems show some level of communication and processor asynchrony in practice. A very long algorithm runtime is also unacceptable in real environments.

A practical solution was developed by Castro and Liskov in 1999 called practical Byzantine fault tolerance (PBFT). As the name suggests, it is a protocol designed to provide consensus in the presence of Byzantine faults. Before PBFT, Byzantine fault tolerance was considered impractical. With PBFT, the duo demonstrated that practical Byzantine fault tolerance is possible for the first time.

PBFT constitutes three subprotocols called normal operation, view change, and checkpointing. The normal operation subprotocol refers to a mechanism executed when everything is running normally, and the system is error-free. The view change is a subprotocol that runs when a faulty leader node is detected in the system. Checkpointing is used to discard the old data from the system.

The PBFT protocol consists of three phases. These phases run one after another to complete a single protocol run. These phases are pre-prepare, prepare, and commit, which we will cover in detail shortly. In normal conditions, a single protocol run is enough to achieve consensus.

The protocol runs in rounds where, in each round, a leader node, called the primary node, handles the communication with the client. In each round, the protocol progresses through the three previously mentioned phases. The participants in the PBFT protocol are called replicas. One of the replicas becomes primary as a leader in each round, and the rest of the nodes act as backups. PBFT enables state machine replication, which we discussed earlier. Each node maintains a local log, and the logs are kept in sync with each other via the consensus protocol, PBFT.

We know by now that to tolerate Byzantine faults, the minimum number of nodes required is $n = 3f + 1$ in a partially synchronous environment, where n is the number of nodes and f is the number of faulty nodes. PBFT ensures Byzantine fault tolerance as long as the number of nodes in a system stays $n \geq 3f + 1$.

When a client sends a request to the primary (leader), a sequence of operations between replicas runs, leading to consensus and a reply to the client.

This sequence of operations is composed of three phases:

- Pre-prepare

- Prepare

- Commit

In addition, each replica maintains a local state containing three main elements:

- A service state

- A message log

- A number representing that replica's current view

Let's look at each of the phases in detail.

Pre-prepare phase – phase 1

When the primary node receives a request from the client, it assigns a sequence number to the request. It then sends the pre-prepare message with the request to all backup replicas.

When the backup replicas receive the pre-prepare message, they check several things to ensure the validity of the message:

- Whether the digital signature is valid.

- Whether the current view number is valid, that is, the replica is in the same view.

- Whether the sequence number of the operation's request message is valid, for example, if the same sequence number is used again, the replica will reject the subsequent request with the same sequence number.

- If the hash of the request message is valid.

- No previous pre-prepare message received with the same sequence number and view but a different hash.

If all these checks pass, the backup replicas accept the message, update their local state, and move to the prepare phase.

In summary, the pre-prepare phase

- Accepts a request from the client.

- Assigns to it the next sequence number. This sequence number is the order in which the request is going to be executed.

- Broadcasts this information as the pre-prepare message to all backup replicas.

This phase assigns a unique sequence number to the client request. We can think of it as an orderer that applies order to the client requests.

Prepare phase – phase 2

Each backup replica sends the prepare message to all other replicas in the system. Each backup replica waits for at least $2f + 1$ prepare messages to arrive from other replicas. They check

- Whether the prepare message has a valid digital signature.

- The replica is in the same view as in the message.

- The sequence number is valid and within the expected range.

- The message digest (hash) value is correct.

If all these checks pass, the replica updates its local state and moves to the commit phase.

In summary, the prepare phase performs the following steps:

- Accepts the pre-prepare message only if the replica has not accepted any pre-prepare messages for the same view or sequence number before

- Sends the prepare message to all replicas

This phase ensures that honest replicas in the network agree on the total order of requests within a view.

Commit phase

Each replica sends a commit message to all other replicas in the network in the commit phase. Like the prepare phase, replicas wait for $2f + 1$ commit messages to arrive from other replicas. The replicas also check the view number, sequence number, digital signature, and message digest values. If they are valid for $2f + 1$ commit messages received from other replicas, the replica executes the request, produces a result, and finally updates its state to reflect a commit. If some messages are queued up, the replica will execute those requests first before processing the latest sequence numbers. Finally, the replica sends the result to the client in a reply message.

The client accepts the result only after receiving $2f + 1$ reply messages containing the same result.

The commit subprotocol steps

- The replica waits for $2f + 1$ prepare messages with the same view, sequence, and request.

- It sends a commit message to all replicas.

- It waits until a $2f + 1$ valid commit message arrives and is accepted.

- It executes the received request.

- It sends a reply containing the execution result to the client.

This phase ensures that honest replicas in the network agree on the total order of client requests across views.

In essence, the PBFT protocol ensures that enough replicas process each request so that the same requests are processed and in the same order.

We can visualize the normal mode of operation of the protocol in Figure 7-10.

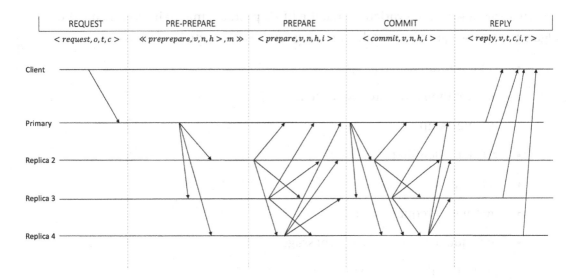

Figure 7-10. *PBFT normal mode operation*

During the execution of the protocol, the protocol must maintain the integrity of the messages and operations to deliver an adequate level of security and assurance. Digital signatures fulfill this requirement. It is assumed that digital signatures are unforgeable, and hash functions are collision resistant. In addition, certificates are used to ensure the proper majority of participants (nodes).

Certificates in PBFT

Certificates in PBFT protocols establish that at least $2f + 1$ replicas have stored the required information. In other words, the collection of $2f + 1$ messages of a particular type is considered a certificate. For example, suppose a node has collected $2f + 1$ messages of type prepare. In that case, combining it with the corresponding pre-prepare message with the same view, sequence, and request represents a certificate, called a prepared certificate. Likewise, a collection of $2f + 1$ commit messages is called a commit certificate.

There are also several variables that the PBFT protocol maintains to execute the algorithm. These variables and the meanings of these are listed as follows:

- **v**: View number

- **o**: Operation requested by a client

- **t**: Timestamp

- **c**: Client identifier

- **r**: Reply

- **m**: Client's request message

- **n**: Sequence number of the message

- **h**: Hash of the message m

- **i**: Identifier of the replica

- **s**: Stable checkpoint – last

- **C**: Certificate of the stable checkpoint ($2f + 1$ checkpoint messages)

- **P**: Set of prepared certificates for requests

- **O**: Set of pre-prepare messages to be processed

- **V**: Proof of the new view ($2f + 1$ view change messages)

Let's now look at the types of messages and their formats. These messages are easy to understand if we refer to the preceding variable list.

Types of Messages

The PBFT protocol works by exchanging several messages. A list of these messages is shown in Table 7-1 with their format and direction.

Table 7-1. *PBFT protocol messages*

Message	From	To	Format	Signed by
Request	Client	Primary	<REQUEST, o, t, c>	Client
Pre-prepare	Primary	Replicas	<<PRE-PREPARE, v, n, h>, m>>	Primary
Prepare	Replica	Replicas	<PREPARE, v, n, h, i>	Replica
Commit	Replica	Replicas	<COMMIT, v, n, h, i>	Replica
Reply	Replicas	Client	<REPLY, r, i>	Replica
View change	Replica	Replicas	<VIEWCHANGE, v+1, n, s, C, P, i>	Replica
New view	Primary	Replicas	<NEWVIEW, v + 1, V, O>	Replica
Checkpoint	Replica	Replicas	<CHECKPOINT, n, h, i>	Replica

Note that all messages are signed with digital signatures, which enable every node to identify which replica or client generated any given message.

View Change

A view change occurs when a primary replica is suspected faulty by other replicas. This phase ensures protocol progress. A new primary is selected with a view change, which starts normal mode operation again. The new primary is chosen in a round-robin fashion using the formula $p = v \bmod n$, where v is the view number and n is the total number of nodes in the system.

When a backup replica receives a request, it tries to execute it after validating the message, but for any reason, if it does not execute it for a while, the replica times out. It then initiates the view change subprotocol.

During the view change, the replica stops accepting messages related to the current view and updates its state to a view change. The only messages it can receive in this state are *checkpoint, view change*, and *new view* messages. After that, it broadcasts a view change message with the next view number to all replicas.

When this message reaches the new primary, the primary waits for at least $2f$ view change messages for the next view. If at least $2f + 1$ view change messages are acquired, it broadcasts a new view message to all replicas and runs normal operation mode once again.

When other replicas receive a new view message, they update their local state accordingly and start the normal operation mode.

The algorithm for the view change protocol is as follows:

1. Stop accepting pre-prepare, prepare, and commit messages for the current view.

2. Construct a set of all the certificates prepared so far.

3. Broadcast a view change message with the next view number and a set of all the prepared certificates to all replicas.

Figure 7-11 illustrates the view change protocol.

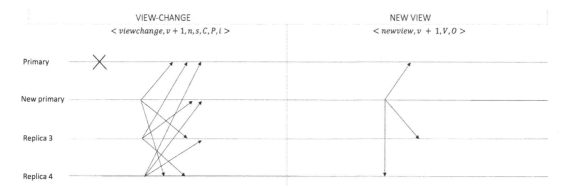

Figure 7-11. *View change protocol*

The view change subprotocol is a means to achieve liveness. Three clever techniques are used in this subprotocol to ensure that:

1. A replica that has broadcast the view change message waits for 2f+1 view change messages and then starts its timer. If the timer expires before the node receives a new view message for the next view, the node will start the view change for the next sequence but increase its timeout value. This situation will also occur if the replica times out before executing the new unique request in the new view.

2. As soon as the replica receives f+1 view change messages for a view number greater than its current view, the replica will send the view change message for the smallest view it knows of in the

set so that the next view change does not occur too late. This is also the case even if the timer has not expired; it will still send the view change for the smallest view.

3.   As the view change will only occur if at least $f + 1$ replicas have sent the view change message, this mechanism ensures that a faulty primary cannot indefinitely stop progress by successively requesting view changes.

It can happen especially in busy environments that storage becomes a bottleneck. To solve this issue, checkpointing is used in the PBFT protocol.

The Checkpoint Subprotocol

Checkpointing is a crucial subprotocol. It is used to discard old messages in the log of all replicas. With this, the replicas agree on a stable checkpoint that provides a snapshot of the global state at a certain point in time. This is a periodic process carried out by each replica after executing the request and marking that as a checkpoint in its log. A variable called "low watermark" (in PBFT terminology) is used to record the last stable checkpoint sequence number. This checkpoint is broadcast to other nodes. As soon as a replica has at least $2f + 1$ checkpoint messages, it saves these messages as proof of a stable checkpoint. It discards all previous pre-prepare, prepare, and commit messages from its logs.

PBFT Advantages and Disadvantages

PBFT is a groundbreaking protocol that has introduced a new research area of practical Byzantine fault–tolerant protocols. The original PBFT have many strengths, but it also has some weaknesses. We introduce those next.

Strengths

- PBFT provides immediate and deterministic transaction finality. In comparison, in the PoW protocol, several confirmations are required to finalize a transaction with high probability.

- PBFT is also energy efficient as compared to PoW, which consumes a tremendous amount of electricity.

Weaknesses

- PBFT is not very scalable. This limitation is why it is more suitable for consortium networks than public blockchains. It is, however, considerably faster than PoW protocols.

- Sybil attacks are possible to perform on a PBFT network, where a single entity can control many identities to influence the voting and, consequently, the decision.

- High communication complexity.

- Not suitable for public blockchains with anonymous participants.

PBFT guarantees safety and liveness. Let's see how.

Safety and Liveness

Liveness means that a client eventually gets a response to its request if the message delivery delay does not increase quicker than the time itself indefinitely. In other words, the protocol ensures progress if latency increases slower than the timeout threshold.

A Byzantine primary may induce delay on purpose. However, this delay cannot be indefinite because every honest replica has a view change timer. This timer starts whenever the replica receives a request. Suppose the replica times out before the request is executed; the replica suspects the primary replica and broadcasts a view change message to all replicas. As soon as $f + 1$ replicas suspect the primary as faulty, all honest replicas enter the view change process. This scenario will result in a view change, and the next replica will take over as the primary, and the protocol will progress.

Liveness is guaranteed, as long as no more than $\left\lfloor \dfrac{n-1}{3} \right\rfloor$ replicas are faulty, and the message delay does not grow faster than the time itself. It means that the protocol will eventually make progress with the preceding two conditions. This weak synchrony assumption is closer to realistic environments and enables the system to circumvent the FLP result. A clever trick here is that if the view change timer expires before a replica receives a valid new view message for the expected new view, the replica doubles the timeout value and restarts its view change timer. The idea is that the timeout timer doubles the wait time to wait for a longer time as the message delays might be more extensive. Ultimately, the timer values become larger than the message delays, meaning messages will eventually arrive before the timer expires. This mechanism ensures that eventually a new view will be available on all honest replicas, and the protocol will make progress.

Also, a Byzantine primary cannot do frequent view changes successively to slow down the system. This is so because an honest replica joins the view change only when it has received at least $f + 1$ view change messages. As there are at most f faulty replicas, only f replicas cannot cause a view change when all honest replicas are live, and the protocol is making progress. In other words, as at most f successive primary replicas can be faulty, the system eventually makes progress after at most $f + 1$ view changes.

Replicas wait for $2f + 1$ view change messages and start a timer to start a new view which avoids starting a view change too soon. Similarly, if a replica receives $f + 1$ view change messages for a view greater than its current view, it broadcasts a view change. This prevents starting the next view change too late.

Safety requires that each honest replica execute the received client request in the same total order, that is, execute the same request in the same order in all phases.

PBFT is assumed safe if the total number of nodes is $3f + 1$. In that case, f Byzantine nodes are tolerated.

Let's first recall what a quorum intersection is. If there are two sets, say S1 and S2, with $\geq 2f + 1$ nodes each, then there is always a correct node in $S1 \cap S2$. This is true because if there are two sets of at least $2f + 1$ nodes each, and there are $3f + 1$ nodes in total, then the pigeonhole principle implies that the intersection of S1 and S2 will have at least $f + 1$ nodes. As there are at most f faulty nodes, the intersection, $S1 \cap S2$ must contain at least 1 correct node.

Each phase in PBFT must acquire $2f + 1$ certificate/votes to be accepted. It turns out that at least one honest node must vote twice on the same sequence number to result in a safety violation, which is not possible because an honest node cannot vote maliciously. In other words, if the same sequence number is assigned to two different messages by a malicious primary to violate safety, then at least one honest replica will reject it due to a quorum intersection property. This is because a $2f + 1$ quorum means that there is at least one honest intersecting replica.

The commit phase ensures that the correct order is achieved even across views. If a view change occurs, the new primary replica acquires prepared certificates from $2f + 1$ replicas, which ensures that the new primary gets at least one prepared certificate for every client request executed by a correct replica.

Order Within a View

If a replica acquires a prepared certificate for a request within a view and a unique sequence number, then no replica can get a prepared certificate for a different request with the same view and sequence number. Replicas can only get a prepared certificate for the same request with the same view and sequence number.

Imagine two replicas have gathered prepared certificates for two different requests with the same view and sequence number. We know that a prepared certificate contains 2f+1 messages, which implies that a correct node must have sent a pre-prepare or prepare message for two different requests with the same sequence and view due to quorum intersection. However, a correct replica only ever sends a single pre-prepare for each view and sequence, that is, a sequence number is always incremented when the client request is received by the primary and assigned to the request. Also, a correct replica only sends one prepare message in each view and for a sequence. It sends out a prepare message only if it has not accepted any pre-prepare messages for the same view or sequence number before. This means that the prepare must be for the same request. This achieves order within a view.

Order Across Views

The protocol guarantees that if a correct replica has executed a client request in a view with a specific sequence number, then no correct replica will execute any other client request with the same sequence number in any future view or current view. In other words, every request executed by an honest replica must make it to the next view in the same order assigned to it previously.

We know that a request only executes at a replica if it has received $2f + 1$ commit messages. Suppose an honest replica has acquired $2f + 1$ commit messages. In that case, it means that the client request must have been prepared at, at least, $f + 1$ honest replicas, and each of these replicas has a prepare certificate for it and all the previous client requests. We also know that at least one of these $f + 1$ honest replicas will participate in the view change protocol and report these requests along with their certificates. This implies that the request will always carry the same sequence number in the new view.

This completes our discussion on PBFT. However, it's a vast subject, and you can further explore the original papers and thesis to learn more.

Blockchain and Classical Consensus

We can implement classical algorithms in the blockchain. However, the challenge is modifying these protocols to make them suitable for blockchain implementations. The core algorithm remains the same, but some aspects are changed to make the protocol suitable for the blockchain. One issue is that these traditional consensus algorithms are for permissioned environments where all participants are known and identifiable. But blockchain networks are public and anonymous, for example, Bitcoin and Ethereum. Therefore, classical algorithms are primarily suitable for permissioned blockchain networks for enterprise use cases where all participants are known. Also, blockchain network environments are Byzantine, where malicious actors may try to deviate from the protocol. And Paxos and RAFT are CFT protocols that are not suitable for Byzantine environments. As such, either these protocols need to be modified to BFT protocols to tolerate Byzantine faults, or different BFT protocols need to be used. These BFT protocols can be a modification of existing classical CFT or BFT protocols or can be developed specifically for blockchains from scratch. One attempt to modify an existing classical protocol to suit a permissioned blockchain environment is IBFT, which we will introduce in Chapter 8. We will discuss more about blockchain protocols in the next chapter.

Dynamic membership (reconfiguration) and log compaction using snapshots are two very useful features which RAFT supports. These two features are particularly useful in consortium blockchains. Over time, the blockchain can grow significantly large, and snapshotting would be a useful way to handle that storage issue. Also, membership management can be a useful feature where a new consortium member can be onboarded in an automated fashion. RAFT, however, is CFT only, which is not quite suitable for consortium chains. Nevertheless, introducing Byzantine fault tolerance in RAFT is possible, as Tangaroa shows - a BFT extension to RAFT. Some issues however are reported in Tangaroa, but it is quite possible to build a BFT version of RAFT. Alternatively, these two features can be implemented in a PBFT variant for blockchain networks. Variants of PBFT include IBFT, HotStuff, LibraBFT, and many others.

Summary

In this chapter, we covered a number of topics including viewstamped replication, practical Byzantine fault tolerance, RAFT, and Paxos. Paxos and viewstamped replication are fundamentally important because they provide very fundamental ideas in the history of the distributed consensus problem. Paxos especially provided formal description and proofs of protocol correctness. VR bears resemblance with multi-Paxos. RAFT is a refinement of Paxos. PBFT is in fact seen as a Byzantine-tolerant version of Paxos, though PBFT was developed independently.

This chapter serves as a foundation to understand classical protocols before blockchain age protocols in the next chapter. Many ideas originate from these classical protocols that lead to the development of newer protocols for the blockchain.

Bibliography

1.   A Google TechTalk, 2/2/18, presented by Luis Quesada Torres. `https://youtu.be/d7nAGI_NZPk`

2.   Lindsey Kuper's lectures on distributed systems: `https://youtu.be/fYfX9IGUiVw`

3.   Bashir, I., 2020. Mastering Blockchain: A deep dive into distributed ledgers, consensus protocols, smart contracts, DApps, cryptocurrencies, Ethereum, and more. Packt Publishing Ltd.

4.   Bully algorithm: `https://en.wikipedia.org/wiki/Bully_algorithm`

5.   Zhao, W., 2014. Building dependable distributed systems. John Wiley & Sons.

6.   Unique Leader election is equivalent to solving consensus – Gray, J. and Lamport, L., 2006. Consensus on transaction commit. ACM Transactions on Database Systems (TODS), 31(1), pp. 133–160.

7.   Leader election algorithms – Aguilera, M.K., Delporte-Gallet, C., Fauconnier, H., and Toueg, S., 2001, October. Stable leader election. In International Symposium on Distributed Computing (pp. 108–122). Springer, Berlin, Heidelberg.

8. https://en.wikipedia.org/wiki/Paxos_(computer_science)

9. Aspnes, J., 2020. Notes on theory of distributed systems. arXiv preprint arXiv:2001.04235.

10. Howard, H., 2014. ARC: analysis of Raft consensus (No. UCAM-CL-TR-857). University of Cambridge, Computer Laboratory.

11. Ongaro, D. and Ousterhout, J., 2015. The raft consensus algorithm.

12. Ongaro, D. and Ousterhout, J., 2014. In search of an understandable consensus algorithm. In 2014 USENIX Annual Technical Conference (Usenix ATC 14) (pp. 305–319).

13. Tangaroa issues: Cachin, C. and Vukolić, M., 2017. Blockchain consensus protocols in the wild. arXiv preprint arXiv:1707.01873.

14. Liskov, B., 2010. From viewstamped replication to Byzantine fault tolerance. In *Replication* (pp. 121–149). Springer, Berlin, Heidelberg.

15. Wattenhofer, R., 2016. *The science of the blockchain*. Inverted Forest Publishing.

CHAPTER 8

Blockchain Age Protocols

This chapter covers blockchain age protocols. Some novel protocols and some variants of classical blockchain consensus protocols were discussed in Chapter 7. We start with Ethereum and finish this chapter with a discussion on Solana. Along the way, we will cover in detail the characteristics, strengths, weaknesses, properties, and inner workings of major consensus protocols used in platforms such as Cosmos, Ethereum 2.0, and Polkadot.

We already covered proof of work in detail in Chapter 5. So, I will not repeat that here; however, Ethereum's PoW will be discussed in this chapter.

Introduction

Consensus protocols are at the core of any blockchain. A new class of consensus protocols emerged with Bitcoin. Therefore, we can categorize all consensus protocols for a blockchain that emerged with and after Bitcoin as "blockchain age consensus protocols."

The primary aim of a consensus protocol in a blockchain is to achieve an agreement on the state of the blockchain while preserving the safety and liveness of the system. The state generally refers to the value, history, and rules of the blockchain. An agreement on the canonical history of the blockchain is vital, and so is the agreement on the governing rules of the chain. Additionally, consensus on values (data) added to the chain is fundamentally critical.

Like traditional pre-blockchain protocols, safety and liveness are two key properties that should be fulfilled by a consensus protocol to ensure the consistency and progress of the blockchain.

Blockchain consensus protocols can be divided into two main categories: the probabilistic finality protocols and absolute finality protocols – in other words, probabilistic termination protocols and deterministic termination protocols. Probabilistic protocols are abundantly used in cryptocurrency public blockchains like Ethereum and Bitcoin. Deterministic protocols, usually from the BFT class of

© Imran Bashir 2022
I. Bashir, *Blockchain Consensus*, https://doi.org/10.1007/978-1-4842-8179-6_8

protocols, are commonly used in enterprise blockchains; however, they are also used in some public blockchains. While PBFT variants are more commonly used in enterprise blockchains, their usage in public chains is somewhat limited only to some public blockchains. For example, TowerBFT used in Solana is a deterministic finality consensus protocol. BFT-DPOS used in EOSIO is another example. Deterministic finality is also known as *forward security* where a guarantee is provided that a transaction once finalized will not be rolled back.

From the perspective of how the consensus algorithms work, blockchains or distributed ledgers are based on one or a combination of the following types of consensus algorithms:

- **PoW based**: Such as Nakamoto consensus in Bitcoin, which relies on solving a math puzzle using brute force.

- **Leader based**: Such as usual BFT protocols where a leader acts as a primary proposer of blocks/values.

- **Voting based**: Usually applicable in BFT protocols where a leader gathers votes from followers to finalize a decision. Also called "quorum based."

- **Virtual voting**: Usually, voting in BFT protocols is complex from a communication point of view, where each voter has to send and receive several messages to the leader. Virtual voting is a technique in the Hashgraph algorithm used in Hedera where votes are evaluated by looking at the local copies of the Hashgraph instead of complex communication with other nodes. This process eventually leads to achieving a Byzantine agreement.

- **Economy based**: Such as proof of stake mechanisms that rely on a stake bonded in the network.

After Bitcoin's inception, many blockchains emerged, and alternative PoW algorithms were introduced, for example, Litecoin. As PoW consumes excessive amounts of energy, the community felt very early that alternatives that are not excessively energy consuming need to be designed. In the wake of introducing less energy-consuming protocols, developers introduced proof of stake. With PoS, the sustainable public blockchain networks have become possible to build. There are, however, some challenges and caveats. After going through the mechanics of how PoS works, we will discuss these limitations.

Proof of Stake

Even though Bitcoin's PoW has proven to be a resilient and robust protocol, it has several limitations:

- Excessive energy consumption

- Slow rate of block generation

- Becoming centralized due to the requirement of specialized hardware and large mining pools

- Probabilistic finality which is not suitable for most of the applications

- Not a perfect consensus algorithm, some attacks exist, for example, Goldfinger attack, 51% attack

- Barrier to entry getting higher as a special hardware requirement to mine

- Not scalable enough to support usual high throughput applications

Significant research has been ongoing to address the abovementioned weaknesses. Especially, high energy consumption from the limitations mentioned earlier led to the development of alternatives. Proof of stake is one such alternative.

Proof of stake first appeared in Peercoin in 2012. Later, many blockchains adopted this mechanism, such as EOS, NxT, Steem, Tezos, and Cardano. In addition, Ethereum, with its Serenity release, will soon transition to a PoS-based consensus mechanism. Proof of stake is also called virtual mining. This is so because in PoS instead of requiring miners to allocate compute resources to solve a puzzle, the right to produce the next block is decided on the basis of what value the miner possesses. This valuable possession can be anything of value (usually coins) that aligns with the interest of the network. PoW's motto was one CPU = one vote, whereas we can think of PoS as one coin = one vote.

The next proposer is usually elected randomly. Proposers are incentivized either with transaction fees or block rewards. Like PoW, control over the majority of the network in the form of controlling a large portion of the stake is required to attack and control the network.

PoS protocols usually select stakeholders and grant suitable rights based on their staked assets. The stake calculation is application specific but is typically based on the total balance, deposited value, or voting between the validators. Once the stake is calculated and a stakeholder is selected as the block proposer, the block proposed by the proposer is readily accepted. The higher the stake, the better the chances of winning the right to propose the next block.

A general scheme of a PoS scheme is shown in Figure 8-1.

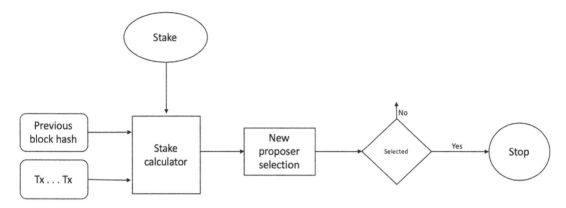

Figure 8-1. *Proof of stake scheme*

As shown in Figure 8-1, PoS uses a stake calculator function to calculate the amount of staked funds, and, based on that, it selects a new proposer.

The next proposer is usually elected randomly. Proposers are incentivized either with transaction fees or block rewards. Control over most of the network by having a large portion of the stake is needed to attack the network.

There is some element of randomness introduced in the selection process to ensure fairness and decentralization. Other factors in electing a proposer include the age of the tokens, which takes into account for how long the staked tokens have been unspent; the longer the tokens have been unspent, the better the chances to be elected.

There are several types of PoS:

- Chain-based PoS

- BFT-based PoS

- Committee-based PoS

- Delegated proof of stake

- Liquid proof of stake

Chain-Based PoS

This scheme is the first alternative proposed to PoW. It was used first in Peercoin in 2012. This mechanism is like PoW; however, the block generation method is changed, which finalizes blocks in two steps:

- Pick transactions from the memory pool and create a candidate block.

- Set up a clock with a constant tick interval. At each clock tick, check whether the hash of the block header concatenated with the clock time is less than the product of the target value and the stake value. We can show this simple formula as follows:

$$Hash\left(B_h \,\|\, clock\ time\right) < target \times stake\ value$$

The stake value depends on how the algorithm works. In some chains, it is proportional to the amount of stake. In others, it is based on the amount of time the participant has held the stake. The target is the mining difficulty per unit of the value of the stake.

This mechanism uses hashing puzzles, as in PoW. But, instead of competing to solve the hashing puzzle by consuming high energy and using specialized hardware, the hashing puzzle in PoS is solved only once at regular clock intervals. A hashing puzzle becomes proportionally easier to solve if the stake value of the miner is high. This contrasts with PoW where repeated brute-force hashing is required to solve the math puzzle.

Committee-Based PoS

In this scheme, a group of stakeholders is chosen randomly, usually using a verifiable random function (VRF). The VRF produces a random set of stakeholders based on their stake and the current state of the blockchain. The chosen group of stakeholders becomes responsible for proposing blocks in sequential order.

A general scheme is described as follows:

- A validator joins the network and deposits a stake.

- Participate in the committee election process and keep checking its turns.

- When it's the turn, collect transaction, generate block, append the new block in the chain, and finally broadcast the block.

- At the other receiver nodes, verify the block; if valid, append the block into the blockchain and gossip the block to others.

The committee election produces a pseudorandom sequence of turns for validators to produce blocks. Ouroboros Praos and BABE are common examples of committee-based PoS.

BFT-Based PoS

In this scheme, the blocks are generated using a proof of stake mechanism where a block proposer is chosen based on the proof of stake which proposes new blocks. The proposer is elected based on the stake deposited in the system. The chance of being chosen is proportional to the amount of stake deposited in the system. The proposer generates a block and appends it to a temporary pool of blocks from which the BFT protocol finalizes one block.

A general scheme works as follows:

- Elect a block proposed based on the PoS mechanism, proportional to a stake.

- Proposer: Propose a new block, add to a temporary block pool, and broadcast the new block.

- Receiver: When other nodes receive this, they validate the block and, if valid, add to the local temporary block pool.

- During the consensus epoch

  - Run BFT consensus to finalize a valid (most voted) block.

  - Add the most voted valid block to the main blockchain.

  - Remove other blocks from the temporary block pool.

Tendermint in Cosmos is one example where the validator is chosen based on a stake, and the rest of the protocol works on BFT principles. Other examples include Casper FFG.

BFT-based PoS is fault tolerant as long as two-thirds of validators remain honest. Also, blocks are finalized immediately.

Delegated PoS

DPoS works like proof of stake, but a critical difference is a voting and delegation mechanism which incentivizes users to secure the network. DPoS limits the size of the chosen consensus committee, which reduces the communication complexity in the protocol. The consensus committee is composed of so-called delegates elected by a delegation mechanism. The process works by stakeholders voting for delegates by using their stake. Delegates (also called witnesses) are identifiable, and voters know who they are, thus reducing the delegates' chance of misbehavior. Also, a reputation-based mechanism can be implemented, allowing delegates to earn a reputation based on the services they offer and their behavior on the network. Delegates can represent themselves for earning more votes. Delegates who get the most votes become members of the consensus committee or group. Usually, a BFT-style protocol runs between the members of the chosen consensus committee to produce and finalize blocks. Each member can take a round-robin fashion to propose the next block, but this activity remains within the elected consensus committee. Delegates earn incentives to produce blocks. Again, under the BFT assumptions, the protocol within the consensus committee can tolerate f faults in a 3f+1 member group. In other words, it can tolerate one-third or 33% of delegates being faulty. This protocol provides instant finality and incentives in proportion to the stake of the stakeholders. As network-wide consensus is not required and only a smaller group of delegators oversee making decisions, the efficiency increases significantly. Delegated PoS is implemented in EOS, Lisk, Tron, and quite a few other chains.

Liquid PoS

LPoS is a variant of DPoS. Token holders delegate their validation rights to validators without requiring transferring the ownership of the tokens. There exists a delegation market where delegates compete to become the chosen validator. Here, the competition is primarily on fees, services offered, reputation, payout frequency, and possibly other factors. Any misbehavior such as charging high fees by a validator is detectable quickly and will be penalized accordingly. Token holders are also free to move to any other validator. LPoS supports a dynamic number of validators as compared to DPoS's fixed validator set. Token holders are also allowed to become validators themselves by self-electing. Token holders with small amount can delegate to larger amount holders. Also, a number of small token holders can form a syndicate. Such "liquid" protocol allows much flexibility as compared to other PoS protocols and helps to thwart creation of lobbies to become a fixed validator set. LPoS is used in the Tezos blockchain.

There are some attacks against PoS, such as the nothing-at-stake attack, long-range attack, and stake grinding attack. We explain these attacks as follows.

Attacks

PoS suffers generally from a costless simulation problem where an adversary can simulate any history of the chain without incurring any additional cost, as opposed to PoW where the cost is computational power. This no-cost block generation is the basis of many attacks in PoS.

Nothing-at-Stake Problem

The nothing-at-stake or double bet problem occurs when multiple forks occur. An attacker can generate a block on top of each fork without any additional cost. To solve this problem, economic penalties are introduced in protocols that prevent attackers from launching this attack. If a significant number of nodes do this, then an attacker holding even less than 50% of tokens can launch a double-spend attack.

Long-Range Attacks

Long-range attacks exist due to weak subjectivity and costless simulation. Long-range attacks are also possible because of costless simulation where an adversary creates a new branch starting from the genesis block with the aim to take over the main good chain, once the bad chain becomes longer than the real main chain. This can create an alternate history which is detrimental to the blockchain.

A weak subjectivity problem affects new nodes and the nodes which were offline for a long time and rejoined the network. As nodes are not synchronized and there are usually multiple forks available in the network, these nodes are unable to differentiate between which node is correct and which one is malicious; they may as well accept a malicious fork as valid.

Other Attacks

Liveness denial is another attack that PoS can suffer from. In this attack, some or all validators collectively decide to stop validating the blocks, resulting in halting block production. Penalizing such activities by the protocol can prevent these types of attacks.

A **selfish mining** or block withholding attack occurs when an adversary mines their own chain offline. Once the chain is at a desired length, the adversary releases this chain to the network with the expectation that the bad chain will take over the main good chain. It can cause disruption on the network as it can result in causing honest validators to waste resources.

A **grinding attack** on PoS occurs if a slot leader election process is not random. If no randomness is introduced in this process, then a slot leader can increase the frequency of its own election again and again, which can result in censorship or disproportionate rewards. An easy way to solve this is to use some good random selection process, usually based on verifiable random functions (VRFs).

Next, we discuss Ethereum's proof of work – Ethash.

Ethereum's Proof of Work

We discussed PoW for Bitcoin in detail in Chapter 5. In this section, we'll see how ETHASH works, the PoW used in Ethereum.

Ethash is the evolved form of the Dagger-Hashimoto algorithm. The key idea behind mining is to find a nonce (an arbitrary random number), which, once concatenated with the block header and hashed, results in a lower number than the current network difficulty level. Initially, the difficulty was low when Ethereum was new, and even CPU and single GPU mining was profitable to a certain extent, but that is no longer the case. So now, only pooled mining or large GPU mining farms are used for profitable mining purposes.

Ethash is a memory-hard algorithm, making it challenging to implement on specialized hardware due to the requirement of large and fast memories on ASICS, which is generally not practical.

Note that for quite some time, this memory hardness of Ethash prevented the development of ASICs, but now various ASIC miners are available for Ethereum mining.

This algorithm requires subsets of a fixed resource called a directed acyclic graph (DAG) to be chosen, depending on the nonce and block headers.

DAG is a large, pseudorandomly generated dataset. This graph is represented as a matrix in the DAG file created during the Ethereum mining process. The Ethash algorithm has the DAG as a two-dimensional array of 32-bit unsigned integers. Mining only starts when DAG is fully created the first time a mining node starts.

This DAG is used as a seed by the Ethash algorithm. The Ethash algorithm requires a DAG file to work. A DAG file is generated every epoch, 30,000 blocks. DAG grows linearly as the chain size grows.

The protocol works as follows:

- The header from the latest block and a 32-bit random nonce are combined using the Keccak-256 hash function.

- This produces a 128-bit structure called mix which determines which data, that is, a 128-byte page, to select from the DAG.

- Once the data is fetched from the DAG, it is "mixed" with the mix to produce the next mix, which is then used to fetch data from the DAG and subsequently mixed again. This process repeats 64 times.

- Eventually, the 64th mix is run through a digest function to produce a 32-byte sequence called the mix digest.

- This sequence is compared with the difficulty target. If it is less than the difficulty target, the nonce is valid, and the PoW is solved. As a result, the block is mined. If not, then the algorithm repeats with a new nonce.

We can visualize this process in Figure 8-2.

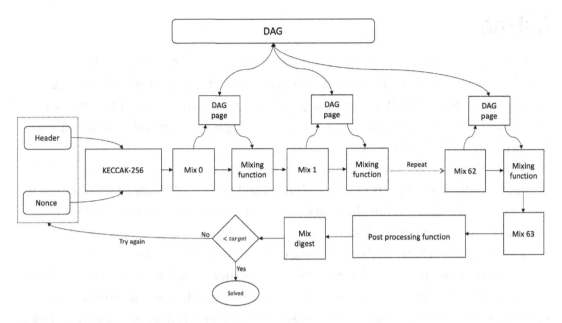

Figure 8-2. *Ethash process*

Ethash has several objectives:

- The algorithm consumes almost all available memory access bandwidth, which is an ASIC resistance measure.

- Mining with Ethash using GPUs is easier to perform.

- Light clients can verify mining rounds much efficiently and should be able to become operational quickly.

- The algorithm runs prohibitively slow on light clients as they are not expected to mine.

As the Ethereum execution layer (formerly Eth1) advances toward the consensus layer (formerly Ethereum 2), this PoW will eventually phase out. When the current EVM chain is docked into the beacon chain, that is, the so-called "the merge" happens, Casper FFG will run on top of PoW. Eventually, however, Casper CBC, the pure PoS algorithm, will finally take over.

Also, with ice age activation, the PoW will become almost impossible to mine due to the extreme difficulty level induced by the "ice age," and users will have no choice but to switch to PoS.

Solana

Solana is a layer 1 blockchain with smart contract support introduced in 2018. Developers of Solana aimed for speed, security, scalability, and decentralization. At the time of writing, it is in Beta, and it is growing in popularity quickly. Though it is an operational network with production systems running on it, there are some technical issues which are being addressed.

The ledger is a verifiable delay function where time is a data structure, that is, data is time. It potentially supports millions of nodes and utilizes GPUs for acceleration. SOL coin is the native token on the platform used for governance and incentivization. The main innovations include the following.

Proof of history (PoH) enables ordering of events using a data structure–based cryptographic clock instead of an external source of time, which then leads to consensus.

TowerBFT is a protocol for consensus derived from PBFT. Note that PoH is not a consensus protocol, it is simply a mechanism to enable ordering of events using a data structure–based clock. A consensus mechanism is still needed to enable nodes to vote on a correct branch of the ledger.

Turbine is another innovation which enables block propagation in small chunks called shreds, which helps to achieve speed and efficiency. There are no memory pools in Solana as transactions are processed so fast that memory pools do not form. This mechanism has been named the Gulf stream.

Solana supports parallel execution of smart contracts, which again results in efficiency gains.

Transactions are validated in an optimized fashion using pipelining in the so-called transaction processing unit residing within validators.

Cloud break is a name given to the database which is horizontally scalable. Finally, archivers or replicators are nodes which allow for distributed ledger storage, as in a high throughput system such as Solana data storage can become a bottleneck. For this purpose, archivers are used which are incentivized to store data.

As our main focus is consensus algorithms, I will leave the introduction to blockchains here and move on to discussing the actual consensus and relevant mechanisms in Solana.

Solana uses proof of stake and TowerBFT consensus algorithms. One of the key innovations in Solana is proof of history, which is not a consensus algorithm but allows to create a self-consistent record of events proving that some event occurred before and after some point in time. This then leads to consensus. It results in reducing the message complexity in a BFT protocol where effectively communication is replaced by local computations. This immediately results in high throughput and subsecond finality times. It has been long known in the distributed systems research community that if somehow communication can be replaced with local computation, then significant performance can be achieved, and many clock synchronization protocols emerged as a result. However, generally all of these relied on an external source of time either via atomic clocks or GPS and then use an NTP type of protocol to synchronize. PoH is a proof for cryptographically proving order and passage of time between events without relying on an external source of time.

Proof of History

As discussed in Chapter 1, time in distributed systems is crucial. If time is synchronized among processes, that is, a synchronized clock is available in a distributed network, then communication can be reduced, which results in improved performance. A node can deduce information from past events instead of asking another node repeatedly about some information. For example, with the availability of a global clock where all nodes are synchronized, the system can establish a notion of the system-wide history of events. For example, a timestamp on an event can inform a node when this event occurred in reference to the globally synchronized time across the network, instead of asking a node again who produced that event when this event occurred.

Another application of a synchronized clock is that entities in the system can deduce if something has expired, for example, a timestamped security token can immediately tell a node how much time has elapsed since its creation. The node can infer if it is valid anymore or not and not something that occurred in the distant past, making this token no longer applicable and expired.

In replication protocols, clock synchronization also plays a crucial role. If nodes don't have clocks synchronized, that can lead to inconsistency because every node will have a different view of the order of events.

If the time is not synchronized among nodes, the system cannot establish a global notion of time and history. It is usually possible in practical systems using an NTP protocol. We discussed this in Chapter 2 before in the context of time and order in distributed systems.

So far, we have established that synchronized time is indeed a valuable construct in distributed systems for performance gains. In other words, if we can somehow replace communication with local computation, then we can gain tremendous efficiency.

Also, synchrony and time together solve consensus easily. Safety and liveness, the two fundamental requirements, are easy to implement with a trusted clock and synchronous network. However, networks are empirically asynchronous. We also know that a trusted synchronized clock in distributed networks is difficult to maintain. Blockchains and distributed systems are characterized by no clocks, which make them slow due to inherent asynchrony and the need for complex message passing for ordering of events and agreement.

On the other hand, a reliable, trusted clock makes network synchronization much simpler and quicker, which leads to very fast networks. Solana's PoH is a solution where the system can keep time reliably between nontrusting computers. In short, PoH enables clocks in clockless blockchains.

Solana's PoH is a way to establish the history and provide that global notion of synchronized time among nodes in a distributed network. The key innovation here is that it does not use any external source of time and synchronize nodes using that, for example, via an NTP protocol; instead, it uses a cryptographic proof to show that some time has passed, and other nodes directly accept this history of events due to cryptographic guarantees. So instead of relying on a source of global time, this mechanism is built into validators that generate a sequence of events with a proof when an event has occurred. The following describes how it works.

In a blockchain network, the right of adding a new block is won after solving a puzzle, that is, PoW, which takes a long time. Although this mechanism is secure and thwarts Sybil attacks (as we saw in Chapter 5), it is slow. If BFT-style consensus is used, the leader validator that proposes a block only gets to commit after at least two sequential phases, which is also time-consuming even under a normal environment. In case of failures, it can ever further slow down with new leader selection (election) and view changes. What if somehow there is a deterministic leader election algorithm that can select leaders in quick successions, and each leader quickly proposes, and then the algorithm moves to the next leader and so on? All this without going through complex leader election, acknowledgment from other nodes, and running multiple phases to reach consensus. The problem here is that it's quick to create a deterministic algorithm that can select the next leader, but how do I ensure that what they propose is correct and that selected leaders are not malicious and will not censor transactions or exhibit other malicious behaviors?

This is where PoH comes in. In Solana, one leader at a time processes transactions and updates the state. Other validators read the state and send votes to the leader to confirm them. This activity is split into very short successive sessions where one leader after another performs this. It can be thought of as if the ledger is split into small intervals. These small intervals are of 400ms each. The leader rotation schedule is predetermined and deterministic based on several factors such as the stake and behavior of previous transactions. But how can we ensure that the leader rotation is done at the right time and does not skip the leader's turn?

In PoH, the passage of time is proven by creating a sequence of these hashes, as shown in Figure 8-3.

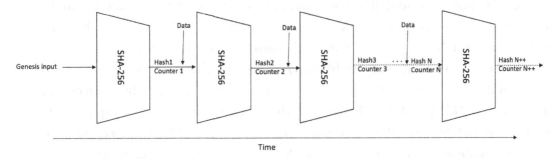

Figure 8-3. *Solana proof of history sequence*

In Figure 8-3, a sequence of hash operations is shown. The genesis input (shown at the left in the diagram) is first provided to the hash function. In the next iteration, the output of the previous hash function is used as an input to the hash function, and this process continues indefinitely. This sequence is generated using the SHA-256 function on a single core. This process cannot parallelize it because the output of the previous hash function can only be known if and only if the hash function has processed the previous input. It is assumed that the functions are cryptographic hash functions that are preimage resistant. Therefore, this is a purely sequential function. However, this sequence can be verified in parallel using multicore GPUs. As all the inputs and outputs are available, it becomes just a matter of verifying each output, which GPUs can do in parallel. This property makes this sequence a verifiable delay function (VDF) because the time taken (i.e., delay) in generating the hash sequence can be verified using quick parallel verification. However, there is some debate between cryptographic VDFs introduced by researchers at Stanford and hardware VDF introduced by Solana researchers. See the reference in the bibliography.

We can then sample this sequence at regular intervals to provide a notion of the passage of time. This is so because hash generation takes some CPU time (roughly 1.75 cycles for SHA-256 instruction on an Intel or AMD CPU), and this process is purely sequential; we can infer from looking at this sequence, that since the first hash is generated, up to a later hash in the sequence, some time has passed. If we can also add some data with the input hash to the hash function, then we can also deduce that this data must have existed before the next hash and after the previous hash. This sequence of hashes thus becomes a proof of history, proving cryptographically that some event, let's say event e, occurred before event f and after event d.

It is a sequential process that runs SHA-256 repeatedly and continuously, using its previous output as its input. It periodically records a counter for each output sample, for example, every one second, and current state (hash output), which acts like clock ticks. Looking at this structure of sampled hashes at regular intervals, we can infer that some time has passed. It is impossible to parallelize because the previous output is the input for the next iteration. For example, we can say time has passed between counter 1 and counter N (Figure 8-3), where time is the SHA-256 counter. We can approximate real time from this count. We can also associate some data, which we can append to the input of the hash function; once hashed, we can be sure that data must have existed before the hash is generated. This structure can only be generated in sequence; however, we can verify it in parallel. For example, if 4000 samples took 40 seconds to produce, it will take only 1 second to verify the entire data structure with a 4000 core GPU.

The key idea is that PoH transactional throughput is separated from consensus, which is key to scaling. Note that the order of events generated, that is, the sequence, is not globally unique. Therefore, a consensus mechanism is needed to ascertain the true chain, as anyone can generate an alternate history.

Proof of history is a cryptographically proven way of saying that time has elapsed. It can be seen as an application-specific verifiable delay function. It encodes the passage of time as data using SHA-256 hashing to hash the incoming events and transactions. It produces a unique hash and count of each event, which produces a verifiable ordering of events as a function of time. This means that time and ordering of events can be agreed without waiting to hear from other nodes – in other words, no weak subjectivity where nodes must rely on other nodes to determine the current state of the system. This results in high throughput, because the information that is usually required to be provided by other nodes is already there in the sequence generated by the PoH mechanism and is cryptographically verifiable, ensuring integrity. This means that a global order of events can be enforced without going through a communication-wise complex agreement protocol or trusting an external source of time for clock synchronization. In summary, instead of trusting the timestamp, proof of history allows to create a historical record proving that an event e occurred at a particular point in time t, before another event f and after an event d.

Using PoH, leadership can be switched without needing to communicate with other nodes, which results in increased block production frequency. PoH results in high node scalability and low communication complexity as compared to BFT-style protocols with high communication complexity and limited node capacity.

It provides global read consistency and cryptographically verifiable passage of time between two events. With PoH, nodes can trust the ordering and timing of events, even before the consensus stage is reached. In other words, it's a clock before consensus approach. Consensus then simply works by voting on different branches where nodes vote on a branch that they believe is the main chain. Over time, by keep voting on the chain they first voted on, and by voting on any other branch, they earn rewards and eventually the other branches orphan.

TowerBFT is a variant of PBFT. It is basically a fork selection and voting algorithm. It is used to vote on the chains produced by PoH to select the true canonical chain. It is less communication-wise complex because PoH has already provided an order, and now the decision is only required on the choice of canonical chain. PoH provides timing of events before consensus initiates, and TowerBFT is then used for voting on the canonical chain.

TowerBFT is BFT in the sense that once two-thirds of validators have voted on a chain (hash), then it cannot be rolled back. Validators vote on a PoH hash for two reasons: first, the ledger is valid up until that hash, that is, a point in time, and, second, to support for a fork at a given height as many forks can exist at a given height.

Furthermore, PoS in Solana is used for economics and governance to control slashing, inflation, supply, and penalties.

Tendermint

Tendermint is inspired by the DLS protocol that we covered in Chapter 6 and was originally introduced in the DLS paper. It can be seen as a variant of PBFT too with similarities in the phases.

The Tendermint protocol works in rounds. In each round, an elected leader proposes the next block. In Tendermint, the view change process is part of the normal operation. This concept is different from PBFT, where a view change only occurs in the event of a suspected faulty leader. Tendermint works similarly to PBFT, where three phases are required to achieve consensus. A key innovation in Tendermint is the design of a new termination mechanism. Unlike other PBFT-like protocols, Tendermint has developed a more straightforward mechanism like a PBFT-style normal operation. Instead of having two subprotocols for normal mode and view change mode (recovery in case of a faulty leader), Tendermint terminates without additional communication costs.

Tendermint works under some assumptions about the operating environment, which we describe next:

> **Processes:** A process is a participant on the network. Processes are expected to be honest, but they can turn faulty. Each process has a voting power that serves as a confirmation to the leader. Processes can connect loosely or with their immediate subset of processes/nodes. They are not necessarily connected directly. Processes have a local timer that they use to measure timeout.

> **Network model:** The network is a message-passing network where a gossip protocol is used for communication between processes. The standard BFT assumption of $n \geq 3f + 1$ applies here, which means that the protocol operates correctly only if the number of nodes in the network stays more than 3F, where F is the number of faulty nodes and N represents the total number of nodes in the network. In practice, this means that there must be at least four nodes in a network to tolerate Byzantine faults.

> **Timing assumptions:** Tendermint assumes a partially synchronous network. There is an unknown bound on the communication delay, but it only applies after an unknown instance of time called global stabilization time or GST.

> **Security and cryptography:** The security assumption in the system is that the public key cryptography used is secure. Also, the impersonation or spoofing of identities is not possible. All messages on the network are authenticated and verified via digital signatures. The protocol ignores any messages with an invalid digital signature.

State machine replication: SMR is used to achieve replication among the nodes. SMR ensures that all processes on the network receive and process the same sequence of requests. In addition, the agreement and order provide that the sequence in which the nodes have received requests is the same on all nodes. Both requirements ensure the total order in the system. The protocol only accepts valid transactions.

Tendermint solves consensus by fulfilling the properties listed as follows:

- **Agreement**: No two correct processes decide on different values.

- **Termination**: All correct processes eventually decide on a value.

- **Validity**: A decided-upon value is valid if it satisfies an application specific predefined predicate denoted valid( ).

State transition at processes in Tendermint depends on the messages received and timeouts. The timeout mechanism guarantees liveness and prevents indefinite waiting. Here, the assumption is that eventually, after some period of asynchrony, there will be a synchronous communication period during which all processes can communicate in a timely fashion, ensuring that processes eventually decide on a value.

A Tendermint protocol has three types of messages: proposal, pre-vote, and pre-commit. These messages can be viewed as equivalent to the PBFT protocol's PRE-PREPARE, PREPARE, and COMMIT messages:

- **Proposal:** This message is used by the leader of the current round to propose a value or block.

- **Pre-vote:** This message is used to vote on a proposed value.

- **Pre-commit:** This message is also used to vote on a proposed value.

Only the proposal message contains the original value. The other two messages, pre-vote and pre-commit, use a value identifier representing the initially proposed value.

There are three timeouts in the protocol, corresponding to each message type:

- Timeout-propose

- Timeout-prevote

- Timeout-precommit

These timeouts prevent the algorithm from waiting indefinitely for certain conditions to be met. They also ensure that processes make progress through the rounds. A mechanism to increase timeout with every new round assures that after reaching GST, the communication between correct processes eventually becomes reliable, nodes can reach a decision, and protocol terminates.

All processes maintain some necessary variables in the protocol:

- **Step:** This variable holds the current state of the Tendermint state machine in the current round.

- **lockedValue:** This variable stores the most recent value (concerning the round number) for which a pre-commit message has been sent.

- **lockedRound:** This variable holds information about the last round where the process sent a non-nil pre-commit message which implies that this is the round where a possible decision value has been locked. This means that if a proposal message and corresponding 2F + 1 messages have been received for a value in a round, then, due to the reason that 2F + 1 pre-votes have already been accepted for this value, this is a possible decision value.

- **validValue:** The role of the validValue variable is to store the most recent possible decision value.

- **validRound:** The validRound variable is the last round in which validValue was updated.

- **Height:** Stores the current consensus instance.

- Current round number

- An array of decisions

Tendermint proceeds in rounds. Each round contains three phases: propose, pre-vote, pre-commit. The algorithm works as follows:

- Every round starts with a proposal value proposed by a proposer. The proposer proposes a new value at the start of the first round for each height.

- Any subsequent rounds will only have a proposer proposing a new value if there is no valid value already present, that is, null. Otherwise, the validValue, the possible decision value, is proposed, already locked from a previous round. The proposal message also includes a value denoting the last valid round in which there was a valid value updated.

- A correct process accepts the proposal only if

  - The proposed value is valid.

  - The process has not locked on a value.

  - Or the process has a value locked.

- The correct process accepts the proposal and sends a pre-vote message if the preceding conditions meet.

- If the conditions do not meet, the process will send a pre-vote message with a nil value.

- A timeout mechanism associated with the proposal phase triggers timeout if a process has not sent a pre-vote message in the current round or the timer expires in the proposal stage.

- If a correct process receives a proposal message with a valid value and 2F + 1 pre-vote messages, it sends the pre-commit message.

- Otherwise, it sends out a nil pre-commit.

- A timeout mechanism associated with the pre-commit will initialize if the associated timer expires or if the process has not sent a pre-commit message after receiving a proposal message and 2F + 1 pre-commit messages.

- A correct process decides on a value if it has received the proposal message in some round and 2F + 1 pre-commit messages for the ID of the proposed value.

- This step also has an associated timeout mechanism, ensuring that the processor does not wait indefinitely to receive 2F + 1 messages. If the timer expires before the processor can decide, the processor starts the next round.

- When a processor eventually decides, it triggers the next consensus instance for the following block proposal, and the entire cycle of a proposal, pre-vote, and pre-commit starts again.

The protocol can be simply depicted as a recurring sequence of proposal ➤ pre-vote ➤ pre-commit, and after every commit, a new height is achieved and a new round starts, as shown in Figure 8-4.

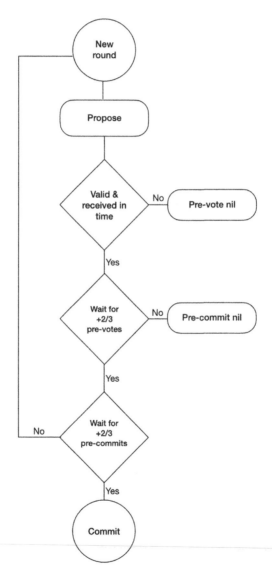

Figure 8-4. *Tendermint flow – single run*

Tendermint introduced a new termination mechanism. There are two variables, namely, validValue and validRound, used by the proposal message. Both are updated by a correct process when receiving a valid proposal message and subsequent corresponding 2f + 1 pre-vote messages.

This termination process benefits from the gossip protocol and synchrony assumptions. For example, suppose a correct process has locked a value in a round. Then all other correct processes will update their validValue and validRound variables with the locked values by the end of the very round during which they were locked. The fundamental presumption is that a gossip protocol will propagate them to other nodes within the same round once a correct processor has locked these values. Each processor will know the locked value and round, that is, the valid values. Now, when the next proposal is made, the same locked values will be picked up by the proposer, which has already been locked due to the valid proposal and corresponding 2f + 1 pre-vote messages. This way, it can be ensured that the value that processes eventually decide upon is acceptable as specified by the validity condition.

This completes our discussion on the Tendermint protocol. Next, we explore HotStuff, which improves on several limitations in previous PBFT and its variant protocols.

HotStuff

HotStuff is a BFT protocol for state machine replication. Several innovations make it a better protocol than traditional PBFT. However, like PBFT, it works under partial synchrony in a message-passing network with minimum $n = 3f + 1$ and relies on a leader-based primary backup approach. It utilizes reliable and authenticated communication links. HotStuff makes use of threshold signatures where all nodes use a single public key, but each replica uses a unique private key. The use of threshold signatures results in reduced communication complexity.

HotStuff introduced some innovations which we introduce as follows.

Linear View Change

A view change in a HotStuff protocol requires only $O(n)$ messages. It is part of the normal run instead of a separate subprotocol. In a worst-case scenario where leaders fail successively, the communication cost increases to $O(n^2)$, quadratic. Instead of a stable leader like PBFT, a leader rotation in HotStuff occurs every three rounds even if the leader doesn't fail.

In simpler words, quadratic complexity means that the algorithm's performance is proportional to the squared size of the input.

In a linear view change, after GST, any honest selected leader sends only $O(n)$ authenticators to drive a decision, including the case where a leader fails and a new one is elected. So even in the worst case where leaders fail one after another, the communication cost to reach consensus after GST is $O(n^2)$.

Optimistic Responsiveness

Optimistic responsiveness allows any correct leader after GST to only need the first $n - f$ responses to ensure progress instead of waiting for $n - f$ from every replica. This means that it operates at network speed instead of waiting unnecessarily for more messages from other nodes and move to the next phase.

Chain Quality

This property provides fairness and liveness in the system by allowing frequent leader rotation.

Hidden Lock

It also solves the hidden lock problem. A "hidden lock" problem occurs when a leader validator does not wait for the expiration time of a round. The highest lock may not get to the leader if we rely only on receiving $n - f$ messages. The highest locked value may be held in another replica from which the leader did not wait to get a response, thus resulting in a situation where the leader is unaware of the highest locked value. If a leader then proposes a lower lock value and some other nodes already have a higher value locked, this can lead to liveness issues. The nodes will wait for a higher lock or the same lock reply, but the leader is unaware of the highest lock value and will keep sending a lower lock value, resulting in a race condition and liveness violation.

HotStuff has solved this problem by adding the precursor lock round before the actual lock round. The insight here is that if $2f + 1$ nodes accept the precursor lock, the leader will get a response from them and learn the highest locked value. So now the leader doesn't have to wait for Δ (delta – an upper bound on a message delivery delay) time and can learn the highest lock with $n - f$ responses.

Pacemaker

HotStuff innovatively separates the safety and liveness mechanisms. Safety is ensured through voting and commit rules for participants in the network. On the other hand, liveness is the responsibility of a separate module, called pacemaker, which ensures a new, correct, and unique leader is elected. Furthermore, pacemaker guarantees progress after GST is reached. The first responsibility it has is to bring all honest replicas and a unique leader to a common height for a sufficiently long period. For synchronization, replicas keep increasing their timeouts gradually until progress is made. As we assume a partially synchronous model, this mechanism is likely to work. Also, the leader election process is based on a simple rotating coordinator paradigm, where a specific schedule, usually round-robin, is followed by replicas to select a new leader. Pacemaker also ensures that the leader chooses a proposal that replicas will accept.

Better Participant Organization Topology

A PBFT protocol organizes nodes in a clique (mesh topology), resulting in a quadratic message complexity, whereas HotStuff organizes nodes in a star topology. This setting enables the leader to send or collect messages directly to or from all other nodes, which results in reduced message complexity. In simpler words, it uses a "one-to-all" communication pattern.

If a leader is responsible for all this processing, the problem of high load on a single leader can arise, which can slow down the network.

Now think of a scenario where the leader gets corrupted or compromised. The standard BFT tolerance guarantees address such situations. If a leader proposes a malicious block and is suspected faulty, it will be rejected by other correct nodes, and the protocol will choose a new leader. This scenario can temporarily slow down the network until a new honest leader takes over. If majority of the network is honest, a correct leader will eventually take over and propose a valid block. Also, for added security, the leader usually is frequently rotated between validators every few rounds, which can offset any malicious attacks targeting the leader. This property ensures fairness, which helps to achieve chain quality.

PBFT consists of a normal and view change mode, where a view change triggers when a leader is suspected faulty. This approach provides a liveness guarantee but increases communication complexity. HotStuff handles this by combining the view change process with the normal mode. In PBFT, nodes wait for 2F+1 messages before the view change occurs, but in HotStuff, the view change can occur directly without invoking a separate subprotocol. Instead, checking the threshold of the messages to change the view becomes part of the normal view.

How It Works

HotStuff is composed of four phases: prepare, pre-commit, commit, and decide phases.

A quorum certificate (QC) is a data structure that represents a collection of signatures produced by $n - f$ nodes to indicate that a required threshold of messages has been achieved. In other words, a collection of votes from $n - f$ nodes is a QC.

Prepare

Once a new leader has accumulated new view messages from N – F nodes, the protocol starts with a new leader. The leader processes these messages to determine the latest branch in which the highest quorum certificate of PREPARE messages is present.

Pre-commit

As soon as a leader accumulates N – F prepare votes, it creates a quorum certificate called "prepare quorum certificate." The leader broadcasts this certificate to other nodes as a PRE-COMMIT message. When a node receives the PRE-COMMIT message, it responds with a pre-commit vote. The quorum certificate indicates that the required threshold of nodes has confirmed the request.

Commit

When the leader has accumulated N – F pre-commit votes, it creates a PRE-COMMIT quorum certificate and broadcasts it to other nodes as the COMMIT message. When nodes receive this COMMIT message, they respond with their commit vote. At this stage, nodes lock the PRE-COMMIT quorum certificate to ensure the safety of the algorithm even if a view change occurs.

Decide

When the leader receives N – F commit votes, it creates a COMMIT quorum certificate. Then, the leader broadcasts this COMMIT quorum certificate to other nodes in the DECIDE message. When nodes receive this DECIDE message, they execute the request because this message contains an already committed certificate/value. The new view starts once the state transition occurs due to the DECIDE message acceptance and execution.

We can visualize this protocol in Figure 8-5.

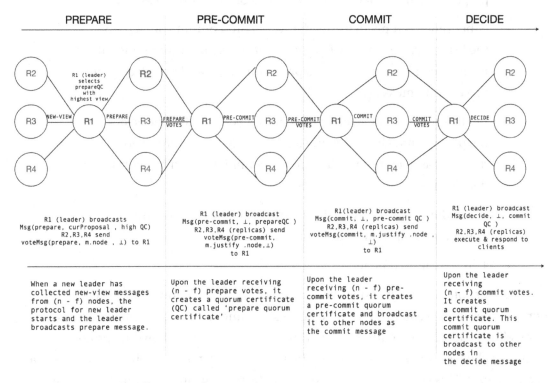

Figure 8-5. *HotStuff protocol*

More precisely, HotStuff steps are listed as follows:

- A new primary acquires new view messages from n-f nodes with the highest prepare quorum certificate that each validator receives. The primary looks at these messages and finds the prepare QC with the highest view (round number). The leader then broadcasts the proposal in a prepare message.

- When other nodes receive this prepare message from the leader, they check if the prepare proposal extends the highest prepare QC branch and has the higher view number associated than what they have currently locked.

- Other nodes reply to the leader with an acknowledgment.

- The leader collects the acknowledgments from $n - f$ prepare votes.

- When n-f votes are acquired by the leader, it combines them into a prepare QC and broadcasts this QC in a pre-commit message.

- Other replicas reply to the leader with a pre-commit vote. When the leader has received n-f pre-commit votes from other nodes, the primary combines them into a pre-commit QC and broadcasts them in a commit message.

- Replicas reply to the leader with commit votes and replicas lock on the pre-commit QC. When the leader receives n-f commit votes from the replicas, it combines them into a commit QC and broadcasts the decide message.

- When the nodes receive a decide message, they execute the operations/commands and start the next view.

- This operation repeats.

There are other optimizations such as pipelining which allows for further performance improvements. As all the phases are fundamentally identical, it's easy to pipeline HotStuff, which improves performance. Pipelining allows the protocol to commit a client's request in each phase. In a view, a leader in each phase proposes a new client request. This way, a leader can concurrently process pre-commit, commit, and decide messages for previous client requests passed on to the last leader via the commit certificate.

Safety and Liveness

HotStuff guarantees liveness by using the pacemaker, which ensures progress after GST within a bounded time interval by advancing views. This component encapsulates view synchronization logic to ensure liveness. It keeps enough honest nodes in the same view for sufficiently long periods to ensure progress. This property is achieved by progressively increasing the time until progress is made.

Whenever a node times out in a view, it broadcasts a timeout message and advances to the following when a quorum certificate of $2f + 1$ timeout messages is received. This certificate is also sent to the next leader, who takes the protocol further. Does this timeout detection sound familiar? It sounds familiar because pacemaker abstraction is basically a failure detector that we discussed before in Chapter 3. Moreover, voting and relevant commit rules ensure safety in HotStuff.

HotStuff is a simple yet powerful protocol that combines several innovations to produce a better protocol than its predecessors.

Polkadot

Polkadot is a modern blockchain protocol that connects a network of purpose-built blockchains and allows them to operate together. It is a heterogenous multichain ecosystem with shared consensus and shared state.

Polkadot has a central main chain, called a relay chain. This relay chain manages the Parachains – the heterogenous shards that are connected to the relay chain. A relay chain holds the states of all Parachains. All these Parachains can communicate with each other and share the security, which leads to a better and more robust ecosystem. As the Parachains are heterogenous, they can serve different purposes; a chain can be a specific chain for smart contracts, another for gaming, another could be for providing some public services, and so on and so forth. The relay chain is secured by a nominated proof of stake.

The validators on the relay chain produce blocks and communicate with Parachains and finalize blocks. On-chain governance decides what the ideal number of validators should be.

A depiction of the Polkadot chain with Parachains is shown in Figure 8-6.

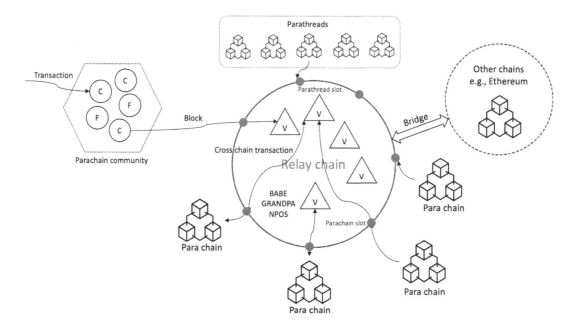

Figure 8-6. *A simple depiction of Polkadot*

Polkadot aims to be able to communicate with other blockchains as well. For its purposes, bridges are used, which connect Parachains to external blockchains, such as Bitcoin and Ethereum.

There are several components in Polkadot. The **relay chain** is the main chain responsible for managing Parachains, cross-chain interoperability, and interchain messaging, consensus, and security.

It consists of nodes and roles. Nodes can be light clients, full nodes, archive nodes, or sentry nodes. Light clients consist of only the runtime and state. Full nodes are pruned at configurable intervals. Archive nodes keep the entire history of blocks, and sentry nodes protect validators and thwart DDoS attacks to provide security to the relay chain. There are several roles that nodes can perform: validator, nominator, collator, and fisherman. **Validators** are the highest level in charge in the system. They are block producers, and to become block producers, they need to provide a sufficient bond deposit. They produce and finalize blocks and communicate with Parachains. **Nominators** are stakeholders and contribute to the validators' security bond. They place trust in a validator to "be good" and produce blocks. **Collators** are responsible for transaction execution. They create unsealed but valid blocks to validators that propose. **Fishermen** are used to detect malicious behavior. Fishermen are rewarded for providing proof of misbehavior of participants. **Parachains** are heterogenous blockchains connected to the relay chain. These are fundamentally the execution core of Polkadot. Parachains can be with their own runtime called application-specific blockchains. Another component called **Parathread** is a blockchain that works within the Polkadot host and connects to the relay chain. They can be thought of as pay-as-you-go chains. A Parathread can become a Parachain via an auction mechanism. **Bridges** are used to connect Parachains with external blockchain networks like Bitcoin and Ethereum.

Consensus in Polkadot

Consensus in Polkadot is achieved through a combination of various mechanisms. For governance and accounting, a nominated proof of stake is used. For block production, BABE is used. GRANDPA is the finality gadget. In the network, validators have their own clocks, and a partially synchronous network is assumed.

Finality is usually probabilistic as we saw in traditional Nakamoto PoW consensus. In most permissioned networks and some public networks, it tends to be deterministic, that is, provable finality, for example, PBFT and Tendermint.

In Polkadot, due to the reason that it is a multichain heterogenous architecture, there could be some situations where, due to some conflicts between chains, some rogue blocks are added. These rogue blocks will need to be removed after conflict resolution; in such situations, deterministic finality is not suitable due to its irreversible property. On the other hand, PoW is too slow, energy consuming, and probabilistic. The solution for this is to keep producing blocks as fast as possible but postpone finality for later as soon as it is suitable to finalize. This way, block production can continue and is revertible, but finality decision can be made separately and provably at a later stage.

This notion of provable finality is quite useful in a multichain heterogenous network because it allows us to prove to other parties that are not involved in consensus that a block is final. Also, provable finality makes it easier to make bridges to other blockchains.

This hybrid approach works by allowing validators to produce blocks even if only one validator is online and correct, but the finalization of the blocks is offloaded to a separate component called a finality gadget. Under normal conditions, block finalization is also quite fast, but in case of issues such as state conflicts, the finalization can be postponed until more scrutiny checks are performed on the blocks. In case of severe attacks or huge network partitions, block production will continue; however, as a fallback mechanism, Polkadot will fall back to the probabilistic finalization mechanism. This way, liveness is guaranteed even under extreme scenarios, as long as at least one validator is correct and alive. The blocks are produced by BABE, whereas they are finalized by GRANDPA. GRANDPA finalizes a chain of blocks instead of block-by-block finalization which improves efficiency. As finalization is a separate process, block production can continue at whatever speed the network allows for, but finality doesn't impact the block production speed and is done later.

There can be some forks before a "best" chain is finalized by GRANDPA. We can visualize this in Figure 8-7.

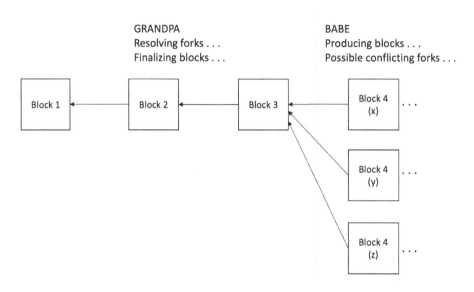

Figure 8-7. *BABE producing and GRANDPA finalizing*

The diagram shows on the right side three produced blocks by BABE in three forks; GRANDPA resolves these forks and finalizes the chain. Now let's see how blocks are produced by BABE.

BABE – Blind Assignment for Blockchain Extension

BABE is a proof of stake protocol for block production where validators are randomly selected based on their staked amount to produce blocks. It does not depend on any central clock.

Time is divided into periods spanning n seconds called slots, where a block is expected to be produced. An epoch is a sequence of slots. At each slot, validators run a VRF, which, based on randomness generated from previous epochs, decides whether to produce a block or not. We can visualize this in Figure 8-8.

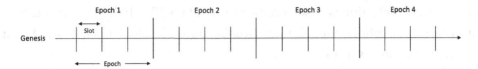

Figure 8-8. *Slots and epochs*

Validators use public key cryptography. There are two types of key pairs. A private key from the first key pair is used for block signing. The second pair is used for a verifiable random function (VRF), also called the lottery key pair. A private key from the latter pair is used as an input to the verifiable random function. Block signing provides usual nonrepudiation, integrity, and data origin authentication guarantees, verifying that the validator has indeed produced this block. In the VRF, the private key generates the randomness, but the public key proves to other nodes that the randomness generated is indeed reliable and that the validator did not cheat.

Each validator has an almost equal chance of being selected. A slot leader election is done like PoW, where, if the result of VRF is lower than a predetermined threshold, then the validator wins the right to produce the block. Also, the proof generated from the VRF enables other participants to verify that the validator is following the rules and not cheating; in other words, it proves that the randomness generated is reliable. If the value produced from the VRF is higher than or equal to the target, then the validator simply collects blocks from other validators.

Here are the phases of the BABE protocol.

Genesis Phase

In this phase, the unique genesis block is created manually. A genesis block contains a random number that is used during the first two epochs for the slot leader selection.

Normal Phase

Each validator divides its time into so-called slots after receiving the genesis block. Validators determine the current slot number according to the relative time algorithm, which we'll explain shortly. Each validator during normal operation is expected to produce a block, whereas other nonvalidator nodes simply receive the produced blocks and synchronize. It is expected that each validator has a set of chains in the current slot/epoch and has the best chain selected in the previous slot by using the best chain selection mechanism, which we'll explain shortly.

The slot leader selection is based on the output of the VRF. If the output of the VRF is below a certain threshold, then the validator becomes the slot leader. If not, then it simply collects the blocks from the leader.

The block generated by the leader is added to the best chain selected in the current slot. The produced block must at least contain the slot number, the hash of the previous block, the VRF output, VRF proof, transactions, and the digital signature. Once the chain is updated with the new block, the block is broadcast. When another non-leader validator receives the block, it checks if the signature is valid. It also verifies if a valid leader has produced the block by checking the VRF output using the VRF verification algorithm. It checks that if the output of the VRF is lower than the threshold, then the leader is valid. It further checks if there is a valid chain with the required header available in which this received block is expected to be added, and if the transactions in the block are valid.

If all is valid, then the validator adds the block to the chain. When the slot ends, the validator finally selects the best chain using the best chain selection algorithm, which eliminates all chains that do not include the finalized block by the finality gadget GRANDPA.

Epoch Update

A new epoch starts every n number of slots. A validator must obtain the new epoch randomness and active validator set for the new epoch before beginning the new epoch. The new validator set for the new epoch is included in the relay chain to enable block production. A new validator must wait for two epochs before the protocol can select it. Adding a validator two epochs later ensures that VRF keys of the new validators are added to the chain before the randomness of the future epoch in which they are going to be active is revealed. A new randomness for the epoch is calculated based on the previous two epochs by concatenating all the VRF outputs of blocks in those epochs.

The diagram in Figure 8-9 illustrates this slot leader election process.

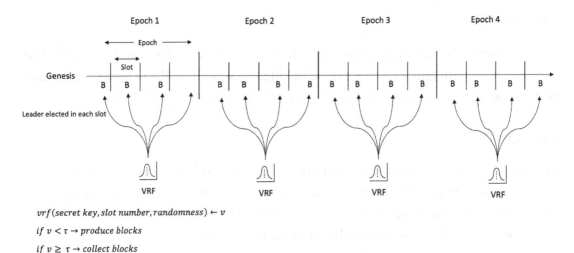

$vrf(secret\ key, slot\ number, randomness) \leftarrow v$

$if\ v < \tau \rightarrow produce\ blocks$

$if\ v \geq \tau \rightarrow collect\ blocks$

$randomness\ from\ genesis\ if\ epoch\ is\ 1\ or\ 2, otherwise\ from\ 2\ epochs\ earlier$

Figure 8-9. *Slot leader election via VRF and block production in slots and epochs*

The best chain selection algorithm simply removes all chains that do not contain a finalized block by GRANDPA. In case GRANDPA does not finalize any block, the protocol falls back to probabilistic finality, and the finalized block is chosen as the one which is several blocks (a number) before the last block. This works almost like a chain depth rule in PoW.

Time is managed in BABE using the **relative time algorithm**. It is critical for the security of the BABE that all parties are aware of the current slot number. BABE does not use a time source managed by NTP as clearly a central source of time cannot be trusted. Validators realize a notion of logical time by using block arrival times as a reference without relying on an external source of time. When a validator receives the genesis block, it records the arrival time as a reference point of the beginning of the first slot. As the beginning time of each slot is expected to be different on each node, an assumption is made that this difference is reasonably limited. Each validator updates its clock by calculating the median of the arrival times of the blocks in the epoch. Although the mechanics are different, the fundamental concept appears to be similar to the logical clocks we discussed in Chapter 1. Temporary clock adjustment until the next epoch is also possible for validators that went offline and joined the network again.

Safety and Liveness

There are four security properties that BABE satisfies: chain growth, existential chain quality, chain density, and common prefix.

Chain Growth

This property guarantees a minimum growth between slots. In other words, it's a liveness property, and chain growth is guaranteed as long as a supermajority of honest validators is available. Malicious validators cannot stop the progress of the best chain.

Chain Quality

This property ensures that at least one honest block is contributed to any best chain owned by an honest party in every x number of slots. The protocol guarantees that even in the worst case, there will be at least one honest block included in the best chain during an epoch. This ensures that the randomness is not biased.

Chain Density

This property ensures that any sufficiently long portion of blocks in the best chain contains more than half of the blocks produced by honest validators. This property is implied by chain growth and chain quality.

Common Prefix

This property ensures that any blocks before the last block in the best chain of an honest validator cannot be changed and are final. Again, this property is satisfied due to the assumption of super honest majority of honest validators. It is rare for a malicious validator to be elected in a slot, and only mostly honest validators will be elected; therefore, malicious validators are in such a minority that they cannot create another "best" chain which do not contain a finalized block.

GRANDPA – GHOST-Based Recursive Ancestor Deriving Prefix Agreement

It is a gadget that finalizes the blocks separately after they have been produced by BABE. It is essentially a Byzantine agreement protocol that agrees on a chain out of many forks. The difference here is that usually in BFT protocols, a decision is made on a single block, whereas GRANDPA decides on a chain of blocks (a fork) and decides what the final chain is. It's a finalization mechanism that resolves forks.

GRANDPA assumes a partially synchronous network. It works in rounds with each round having 3f+1 eligible voters out of which 2f+1 voters are assumed honest. In other words, it requires that two-thirds of the validator set is honest and agrees on a prefix of the canonical chain, which ultimately becomes finalized. In each round, a primary is pseudorandomly elected, which is agreed upon by the participants. Moreover, all participants agree on the voter set. Primary selection can also be based on rotation between voters.

The protocol works in two phases: pre-vote and pre-commit. The pre-vote allows validators to estimate what can be finalized, that is, validators pre-vote on a best chain. For the pre-commit, validators use the two-thirds GHOST rule to pre-votes collected and pre-commit. Finally, the pre-commits are finalized.

GRANDPA consists of two protocols. The first protocol works under partial synchrony and tolerates one-third Byzantine faults. The second protocol works in a fully asynchronous environment and can tolerate one-fifth Byzantine faults.

GRANDPA Protocol Steps

In each round, a participant is selected as a leader (primary), and other participants are also aware who the primary is:

- The new round starts.

- The primary broadcasts the highest block that it thinks might be final from the previous round.

- Validators wait for a certain network delay, then each validator broadcasts a "pre-vote" message for the highest block that it believes should be finalized. If validators receive a block from the primary with the better best chain, then the validators use that best chain. If the supermajority of the validators is correct, this block is expected to extend the chain that the primary has broadcast.

- Each validator looking at the pre-votes determines the highest block that could be finalized. If the pre-votes extend the last finalized chain, each validator will cast a pre-commit to that chain.

- Each validator waits for sufficient pre-commits to compose a commit message on the newly finalized chain.

The protocol penalizes misbehavior by slashing where a percentage of the stake is deducted for malicious behavior or even just irresponsible behavior, for example, a long-running inactive node. An increase in penalties is proportional to the number of participants.

Safety

The protocol ensures that all votes are descendants of some block that could have been finalized in the previous round. Nodes estimate the finalization possibility of a block based on pre-votes and pre-commits. Before a new round starts, nodes ensure by acquiring enough pre-commits that no block with this round's estimate can be finalized on a different chain or later on the same chain. In the next round, it also ensures that it only pre-votes and pre-commits on the blocks that are descended from the last round's estimate.

Liveness

The protocols select a validator in rotation to become the primary. The primary starts the round by broadcasting their estimate of block finalization from the last round. Validators pre-vote for the best chain, including the primary's proposed block if (1) the block is at least the validator's estimate and (2) the validator has acquired >2/3 pre-votes for the block and its descendants in the last round.

The key insight here is that if the primary's proposed block has not been finalized, it is finalized to make progress. For example, suppose the proposed block by the primary has not been finalized, and all validators have agreed on the best chain with the last finalized block. In that case, progress is made by finalizing the latest agreed final chain. If GRANDPA cannot conclude, then BABE provides its probabilistic finality as a fallback mechanism, ensuring progress.

GRANDPA and BABE are one of the latest heterogenous multichain protocols. There are other protocols in this family such as Casper FFG used in the Ethereum consensus layer (Ethereum 2, beacon chain).

Ethereum 2

Ethereum 2, also called Serenity or Eth2, is the final version of Ethereum. Currently, Ethereum is based on proof of work and is known as Eth1. It is now called the execution layer, and the previous terminology of Eth1 and Eth2 is no longer valid. Eth2 is now called the consensus layer. As per the original plan, the existing PoW chain will eventually be deprecated, and users and apps will migrate to the new PoS chain Eth2. However, this process is expected to take years, and an alternative better proposal is to continue improving the existing PoW chain and make it a shard of Ethereum 2. This change will ease the transition to proof of stake and allow scaling up using rollups instead of sharded execution. The beacon chain is already available; "the merge" phase where the Ethereum mainnet merges with the beacon chain is expected in 2022. After the merge, the beacon chain will become executable with proof of stake and EVM capabilities. Old Ethereum 1 (Eth1) will become the execution layer with execution clients, for example, "geth" from Eth1. Ethereum 2 (consensus) clients such as prysm and lighthouse will continue operating on the beacon chain. Eventually, the shard chains that expand Ethereum capacity and support execution are planned for 2023. Ethereum 2.0 "consensus" with Ethereum 1 "execution" as shard 0, along with other upgrades based on their road map, can be visualized in Figure 8-10.

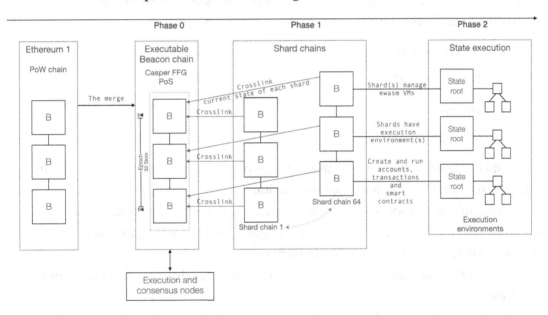

Figure 8-10. *Ethereum upgrades, showing the merge and subsequent upgrades*

In short, Eth1 is now called the execution layer, which handles transactions and executions, whereas Eth2 is now called the consensus layer, which manages proof of stake consensus. As part of the consensus layer, the "Ethereum 2" proof of stake consensus protocol is proposed, which we discuss next.

Casper

Casper is a proof of stake protocol which is built to replace the current PoW algorithm in Ethereum. There are two protocols in this family:

- Casper the Friendly Finality Gadget (FFG)

- Casper the Friendly GHOST

Casper FFG is a PoS BFT–style hybrid protocol that adds a PoS overlay to the current PoW, whereas Casper the Friendly GHOST is purely a PoS protocol. Casper FFG provides a transition phase before being replaced with Casper CBC, a pure PoS protocol. We'll discuss Casper FFG as follows.

Casper FFG

Casper can be seen as an improved PBFT with proof of stake for public blockchains. Casper the Friendly Finality Gadget introduces some novel features:

- Accountability

- Dynamic validators

- Defenses

- Modular overlay

Casper FFG is an overlay mechanism on top of a block proposing mechanism. Its sole purpose is consensus, not block production.

Accountability allows to detect rule violations and identify the validators who violated the rule. This enables the protocol to penalize the violating validator, which serves as a defense against malicious behavior.

Casper FFG also introduces a safe way to change (i.e., add/remove) participants' validator set.

The protocol also introduces a defense mechanism to protect against network partitions and long-range attacks. Even if more than one-third of validators go offline, the protocol provides a defense against such scenarios.

Casper FFG is an overlay, which makes it easier to add on top of an existing PoW chain. As it is an overlay, it is expected that the underlying chain has its own fork choice rule. In the Ethereum beacon chain, it is an overlay on top of the fork choice rule called LMD GHOST (Latest Message Driven Greedy Heaviest-Observed Sub-Tree).

The LMD GHOST fork choice rule is based on GHOST. The LMD GHOST choice rule selects the correct chain from multiple forks. The honest chain is the one that has the most attestations from the validators and stake (i.e., weight). Forks occur due to network partitions, Byzantine behavior, and other faults. We can see LMD GHOST in action in Figure 8-11.

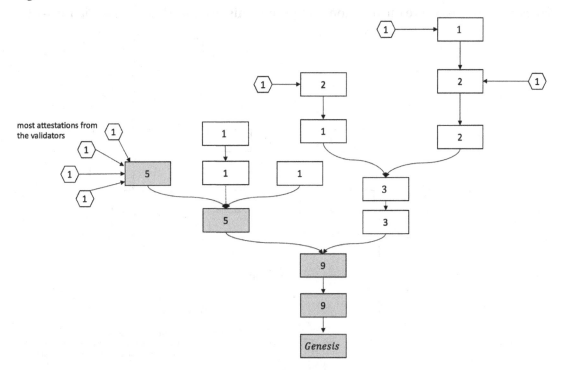

Figure 8-11. *LMD GHOST fork choice rule*

In Figure 8-11

- The number in the block represents the weight by stake in blocks.

- The hexagon represents attestations from validators carrying weight 1.

- The canonical chain is the one with shaded blocks (weight + attestations).

Usually, when proof of work or some other blockchain production mechanism produces blocks, they are produced one after another, in a sequential and linear chain of blocks, where each parent has exactly one child. But it can happen due to network latency and faulty/Byzantine nodes that the proposal mechanism produces multiple child blocks of a parent block. Casper is responsible for choosing a single child from each parent block, thus choosing a single canonical chain from the block tree.

Casper however does not deal with the entire block tree due to efficiency concerns; instead, it considers a subtree of checkpoints forming the checkpoint tree.

New blocks are appended to the block tree structure. A subtree of a tree called the checkpoint tree is where the decision is required. This structure is shown in Figure 8-12.

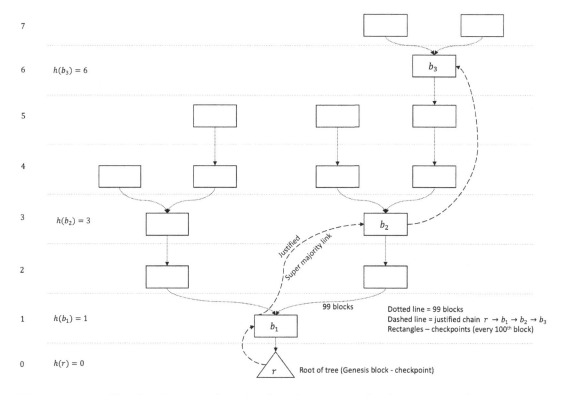

Figure 8-12. *Checkpoint tree showing heights, votes, checkpoints, and canonical chain*

The genesis block is a checkpoint, and every 100th block is a checkpoint. The distance from one checkpoint to another is called an epoch. In other words, validators finalize checkpoints every 100 blocks. Each validator that joins the network deposits their owned deposit. This deposit is subject to increase and decrease due to penalty and reward mechanism. Validators broadcast votes. A vote weight is proportional to a validator's stake. A validator can lose the entire deposit if it deviates from the protocol, that is, violates any rules. This is to achieve safety.

A vote message has some attributes, which we describe as follows:

- **s**: Hash of a justified source checkpoint

- **t**: Hash of the target checkpoint to be justified

- **h(s)**: Height of the source checkpoint

- **h(t)**: Height of the target checkpoint

- **S**: Signature on the complete vote message from the sender

Validators create the vote message, sign it, and broadcast to the network.

The hash of a checkpoint is used to identify the corresponding checkpoint. The vote is valid only if s is an ancestor of t in the checkpoint tree and the public key of the validator is in the validator set. When more than two-thirds of validators vote on a chain from a source to a target, this chain or link becomes the supermajority link. For example, cp' as a source and cp as a target, then $cp' \rightarrow cp$ is the majority link. A checkpoint is justified if it is the genesis block or if it is the checkpoint in a supermajority link where the last checkpoint is justified. Precisely, we can say a checkpoint cp is justified if there is a supermajority link $cp' \rightarrow cp$ where cp' is justified. A checkpoint cp is considered final if it is justified and there exists a supermajority link $cp \rightarrow cp'$ where cp' is a direct child of checkpoint cp.

Justified checkpoints are not considered final as there can exist conflicting justified checkpoints. To finalize a checkpoint cp, a second round of confirmation is required where a direct child cp' of cp with a supermajority link $cp \rightarrow cp'$ is justified.

Protocol steps

- Token holders deposit a stake in the network.

- During a consensus epoch

  - Identify valid checkpoints.

  - Add them to the checkpoint tree.

  - Broadcast a vote for a checkpoint pair (source, target).

  - Evaluate received votes' validity, check against slashing rules and the deposited stake of the vote signer.

- If the checkpoint pair has more than two-thirds of total deposited stakes, then the checkpoint is considered validated.

- The checkpoint pair is justified and finalized.

- Repeat the process.

Essentially, the process works in three steps. First, votes are casted for a checkpoint; if >2/3 votes are acquired, then the checkpoint is in a justified state. Finally, the chain is finalized to form the canonical chain. Justification does not mean finalized; there can be multiple justified chains in the block tree. Finality occurs when two consecutive checkpoints receive 2/3 votes.

Safety and liveness

Any validator who violates these conditions will be penalized by slashing their deposit. These are known as minimum slashing conditions:

- A validator must not publish two distinct votes for the same target checkpoint height.

- A validator must not vote again within the source to target span of its other existing vote.

There are two safety and liveness requirements:

- Accountable safety

- Plausible liveness

Accountable safety is a little different from the traditional safety requirement in consensus protocols. Safety simply means that two conflicting checkpoints can never be finalized unless more than one-third of validators deviate from the protocol. Accountability means that misbehaving validators can be identified and penalized.

Plausible liveness means that as long as there exist children that extend the finalized chain, supermajority links can always be added to produce new finalized checkpoints.

Summary

This chapter discussed the blockchain age protocols that emerged after Bitcoin. There are several types of blockchain consensus protocols; some are based on voting, some are proof of work, and another class is proof of stake protocols. All these protocols have some safety and liveness properties that ensure that the protocol is correct and works correctly in a given environment. We discussed several of these points in this chapter. A concluding comparison of these protocols is presented in the last chapter, Chapter 10.

We also discussed protocols such as ETHASH, proof of stake, its different types, and BFT variations, including HotStuff and Tendermint, in detail. Modern protocols such as Casper FFG, Solana's proof of history, and Polkadot's GRANDPA and BABE were also introduced. It is impossible to cover all protocols in this chapter, but at least adequate information is given to build a good understanding of different types of algorithms used in the blockchain. Some more protocols that we did not cover, such as PoET, HoneyBadger BFT, and Snow, will be briefly presented in the last chapter.

This area is a very active field of research, and many researchers in academia and industry are very much interested in this area. As such, only further evolution and advancement is expected in this space.

In the next chapter, we will discuss another exciting topic, quantum consensus, a subject that has emerged recently with the advent of quantum computing.

Bibliography

1. Peer coin paper: www.peercoin.net/whitepapers/peercoin-paper.pdf

2. Xiao, Y., Zhang, N., Lou, W., and Hou, Y.T., 2020. A survey of distributed consensus protocols for blockchain networks. IEEE Communications Surveys & Tutorials, 22(2), pp. 1432–1465.

3. Bashir, I., 2020. Mastering Blockchain: A deep dive into distributed ledgers, consensus protocols, smart contracts, DApps, cryptocurrencies, Ethereum, and more. Packt Publishing Ltd.

4. "Hidden lock problem": http://muratbuffalo.blogspot.com/2019/12/hotstuff-bft-consensus-in-lens-of.html

5. Web3 Foundation Consensus Tutorial – Bill Laboon: https://youtu.be/1CuTSluL7v4

6. https://polkadot.network/blog/polkadot-consensus-part-2-grandpa/

7. Buterin, V. and Griffith, V., 2017. Casper the friendly finality gadget. arXiv preprint arXiv:1710.09437.

8. "Replace communication with local computation" – Liskov, B., 1993. Practical uses of synchronized clocks in distributed systems. Distributed Computing, 6(4), pp. 211–219.

9. Buterin, V., Hernandez, D., Kamphefner, T., Pham, K., Qiao, Z., Ryan, D., Sin, J., Wang, Y., and Zhang, Y.X., 2020. Combining GHOST and casper. arXiv preprint arXiv:2003.03052.

10. Solana whitepaper: Solana: A new architecture for a high performance blockchain v0.8.13: `https://solana.com/solana-whitepaper.pdf`

11. Burdges, J., Cevallos, A., Czaban, P., Habermeier, R., Hosseini, S., Lama, F., Alper, H.K., Luo, X., Shirazi, F., Stewart, A., and Wood, G., 2020. Overview of polkadot and its design considerations. arXiv preprint arXiv:2005.13456.

12. Yin, M., Malkhi, D., Reiter, M.K., Gueta, G.G., and Abraham, I., 2018. HotStuff: BFT consensus in the lens of blockchain. arXiv preprint arXiv:1803.05069.

13. Buterin, V., Hernandez, D., Kamphefner, T., Pham, K., Qiao, Z., Ryan, D., Sin, J., Wang, Y., and Zhang, Y.X., 2020. Combining GHOST and casper. arXiv preprint arXiv:2003.03052.

14. Stewart, A. and Kokoris-Kogia, E., 2020. GRANDPA: a Byzantine finality gadget. arXiv preprint arXiv:2007.01560.

15. Buchman, E., 2016. Tendermint: Byzantine fault tolerance in the age of blockchains (Doctoral dissertation, University of Guelph).

CHAPTER 9

Quantum Consensus

This chapter covers quantum consensus. Before we explain what quantum consensus is, a basic introduction to quantum computing and its advantages is given to build an understanding about how quantum computer works. Moreover, topics like quantum networks, quantum Internet, quantum cryptography, and quantum blockchains are also covered. Then we discuss quantum consensus and explain what it is, how quantum computing impacts classical consensus in classical and quantum networks, and how quantum computing can enhance existing distributed consensus protocols. We survey what has been done so far in the research community and some open research problems.

Introduction

The roots of the idea to combine quantum mechanics and information theory can be traced back to as early as the 1970s. In 1979, Paul Benioff proposed a theoretical foundation of quantum computing. In 1982, Richard Feynman gave a lecture in which he argued that classical computers cannot possibly perform calculations that describe quantum phenomena. Classical computers are inherently limited, and to simulate quantum phenomena, the computing device must also be based on quantum principles, thus allowing quantum mechanical simulations and calculations which otherwise are not possible in the classical computing world. This was received well, and many researchers started working on this.

In 1985, David Deutsch proposed a universal quantum computer and indicated that it might perform simultaneous operations using quantum superposition. He also suggested the "Deutsch algorithm," which could determine if a quantum coin is biased with a single toss. After this, an interest sparked again but soon waned. However, quantum computing came into the limelight when Peter Shor, in 1994, described a quantum algorithm that could factorize large numbers quickly. This event sparked a

© Imran Bashir 2022
I. Bashir, *Blockchain Consensus*, https://doi.org/10.1007/978-1-4842-8179-6_9

lot of interest because primarily Internet security is based on RSA, which uses prime factorization as a hard problem for its security. More precisely, it is computationally infeasible to factor large prime numbers on classical computers, which gives RSA its security. However, this can be done efficiently with quantum computers, thus breaking RSA, hence the security on the Internet. Of course, we can imagine, this was big news. In 1996, Grover introduced his quantum search algorithm, which further renewed the researchers' interest in quantum computing. Almost 28 years later, we are at the stage where some companies have claimed quantum supremacy. Many researchers from academia and industry are working on quantum computing, and it now appears that quantum computing is at a stage where classical computing was in the 1960s. It will become mainstream in a decade or so in most large organizations, if not everywhere. Perhaps, quantum computers may not become a household reality soon. Still, one thing is clear; quantum computing is evolving rapidly and will start to impact (good or bad) quite soon on our daily lives.

Quantum computers use ideas from various fields, including computer science, engineering, quantum mechanics, physics, mathematics, and information theory. Several subjects have emerged from this, such as quantum information science and technology (QIST), a merger of quantum mechanics and information technology.

Quantum information science (QIS) is a subject at the intersection of computer science, information theory, and quantum mechanics. QIS changes how we fundamentally think about information processing and results in novel ways to solve previously unsolvable computationally complex problems. A quantum computer stores and processes data fundamentally differently from classical computing, where 0s and 1s are used to encode data. This difference in how the information is processed in quantum computers opens the door to achieving significant speedup to solve complex problems.

What Is a Quantum Computer?

A quantum computer is a device that makes use of properties of quantum mechanics to perform computations. Classical computers mimic calculations that humans can perform and are good at solving general day-to-day problems. However, many problems are still unsolvable on classical computers, called "intractable problems." These problems include modelling of natural phenomena such as atomic particle behavior and modelling climate change and many others. A simple example of a complex problem could be when you organize ten people around a table for dinner. It turns out that there are 3,628,800[1] ways to solve this. A brute-force way is to calculate factorial.

Another problem is the travelling salesman problem, which is an NP hard problem. This problem aims to find the shortest route for a round trip among multiple cities.

We can solve many complex problems on classical computers, and we have supercomputers available that can solve problems very fast, such as everyday math, algebra problems, etc. However, the intractable problems are not solvable on even modern supercomputers. This is where quantum computers come in. Especially in combinatorial optimization problems where even supercomputers fail, quantum computers provide a way to solve them.

Optimization problems are problems which try to find the best solution from all feasible solutions. Quantum computers are good at solving these types of problems where a large state space is explored.

Efficiently simulating molecules can help in new drug discovery. This problem of simulation of molecules is difficult because all variations in the way atoms behave with each other and even a small change in the way a single atom is positioned impact all other atoms. Such problems where exponentially many variations exist are expected to be solvable on quantum computers. Also, this information cannot be held on a classical computer, as we don't have such amount of space available.

For example, a caffeine molecule is composed of 24 atoms, but representing that requires 10^{48} bits, which makes this problem intractable on a classical computer; however, a quantum computer can handle this information in 160 qubits.

Route optimization of delivery companies is an exciting application where the aim is to find optimized routes in order to minimize fuel usage while still able to deliver a greater number of packages.

Quantum computing applications are vast, including but not limited to cryptography, machine learning, data analysis, computational biology, simulating chemistry, and quantum simulation.

An application in chemistry helps to discover new materials and compounds, new drugs, and improvements in fertilizer production, which leads to better agriculture. In cybersecurity, better and secure key generation and distribution mechanisms and novel

---

[1] www.ibm.com/quantum-computing/what-is-quantum-computing/

cryptology (cryptography and cryptanalysis) can be realized. Optimization problems such as efficient route discovery, risk management in financial investments, and a lot more are expected to be solvable by Quantum computers.

Quantum computing has many applications and thus the excitement and race to achieve quantum supremacy. Quantum supremacy or quantum advantage is the empirical demonstration of solving a problem that no classical computer can solve in a reasonable amount of time.

There are several building blocks which are necessary to understand the quantum computing world. We describe them as follows:

- Qubit

- Superposition

- Entanglement

- Teleportation

Qubit

A classical computer works based on two distinct states, 0 and 1. Classical computers use transistors to create the absence or presence of an electric signal which represents 0 or 1, respectively. Fundamentally, it is all transistors, even in most modern supercomputers.

With qubits in quantum computers, this fundamental paradigm shifts, which leads to extraordinary speeds at which quantum computers can operate. A qubit is the state of physical atomic particles, for example, a spin on an electron. A qubit can be in a superposition of two states 0 and 1 simultaneously. The speedup rises exponentially as more qubits are added. Eight bits together in a classical computer are called a byte. In the quantum computing world, eight qubits together are called a qubyte.

Imagine 4 bits in a classical computer. These bits can have 16 possible states and can only be input sequentially. However, in a quantum computer, 4 qubits can be in a superposition of all 16 possible states and thus be input simultaneously Instead of the classical version, where 4 bits do have 16 possible states but can only be input sequentially. This phenomenon is called quantum parallelism and is the key to speeding up certain types of problems that are intractable on classical computers.

There are many ways to build a qubit physically. These techniques include trapped ions, photons, neutral atom, NMR, and several others.

Dirac notation is used to represent qubits. Qubits are represented as $|0\rangle$ and $|1\rangle$, as compared to classical 0 and 1. The difference is that a qubit can be in a linear combination of states called superpositions. A qubit can be a superposition of, for example, an electron with spin-up or spin-down or a photon with +45-degree polarization or –45-degree polarization and many other ways.

Dirac notation is used to represent quantum states and their superpositions. Dirac notation has the form $|0\rangle + |1\rangle$ where 0 and 1 are states.

A qubit can be in a quantum state $|\psi\rangle = \alpha | 0\rangle + \beta | 1\rangle$ where $\alpha, \beta \in C$ (complex amplitudes) and $|\alpha|^2 + |\beta|^2 = 1$. This means that the state of a single qubit is represented by $|\psi\rangle = \alpha | 0\rangle + \beta | 1\rangle$, and the probability condition is $|\alpha|^2 + |\beta|^2 = 1$. This probability condition means that the values that α, β can take are limited, and in any case, both must add to one. C represents complex numbers.

Other than Dirac notation, we can also use vector representations. A single vector can represent the state containing amplitudes α and β:

$$|\psi\rangle = [\alpha\ \beta]$$

and

$$|0\rangle = [1\ 0]\ \text{and}\ |1\rangle = [0\ 1]$$

A qubit can be visualized using a Bloch sphere, as shown in Figure 9-1.

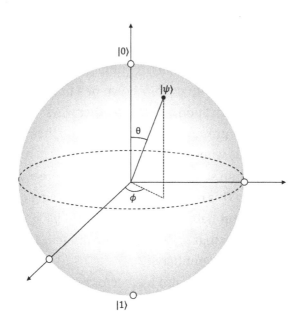

Figure 9-1. *The Bloch sphere – a convenient way to visualize qubits*

We can describe a single qubit as a point on the surface of the Bloch sphere. The North pole represents state $|0\rangle$, and the South pole represents state $|1\rangle$. Qubit angles are θ the latitude and ϕ the longitude. When a single gate operation is performed on the qubit, the state ψ (the qubit) rotates to another point on the Bloch sphere.

Superposition

Superposition is a fundamental principle of quantum mechanics. Superposition means that quantum states can be added together to get another valid quantum state. This is analogous to classical mechanics, where waves can be added together. Added quantum states are so-called "superposed." Superposition is the key to extraordinary speedup as it allows many computation paths to be explored simultaneously.

Entanglement

Entanglement is an incredibly strong correlation that exists between particles, which allows two or more particles to inseparably link with each other. It allows any two quantum particles to exist in a shared state. Any action on one particle instantly affects the other particle even at massive distances. Entanglement is usually performed by bringing two qubits close together, performing an operation to entangle them, and, once entangled, moving them apart again. They will remain entangled even if one of them is on earth and the other is moved to outer space at a vast distance.

There are two features of entanglement which makes it particularly suitable for a large range of applications: maximal coordination and monogamy.

Maximal Coordination

When two qubits at different nodes in a network entangle, that is, the quantum state of two particles become inseparably connected, they provide stronger correlation and coordination properties, which are nonexistent in classical networks. This property is called maximal coordination. For example, for any measurement on the first qubit, if the same measurement is made on the second qubit, instantaneously, the same answer is shown, even though that answer is random and was not predetermined. More precisely, they will always yield a zero or one at random, but both will produce the same output always. This feature makes entanglement suitable for tasks requiring coordination, for example, clock synchronization, leader election, and consensus. Imagine clock synchronization in a distributed network without physical transfer; it can make distributed networks extraordinarily fast. (Remember replacing communication with local computation from the last chapter.) Also, state transfer/awareness during consensus immediately makes consensus faster. The fundamental idea here is that when entangled, it is possible to change the state globally (full state) by only performing operations (changing parameters) in one qubit. This feature has far-reaching implications; imagine being able to do immediate state transfer to all nodes in the network. This can result in extraordinary speedup in consensus algorithms.

Monogamy

Quantum entanglement is not shareable. If two qubits are entangled, then a third qubit from anywhere in the universe can never entangle with either of them. This property is called monogamy of entanglement. This property can enable applications in privacy, cryptographic key generation, and identification.

Quantum Gates

Just like classical computing in the quantum world, we use gate operations for data processing. We are used to Boolean gates used in the classical world, such as NOT, AND, OR, XOR, NAND, and NOR. In the quantum world, we apply some operator to an input state which transforms into an output state. This operator is called a quantum gate. Quantum gates operate on a single qubit or multiple qubits. A rule here is that each gate must have the same number of inputs as outputs. This is what makes the gate reversible and consequently the quantum computers reversible. There are single qubit gates which make rotations on a Bloch sphere. Then there are two qubit gates which combine single gates to create more complex functions, which leads to building quantum computers.

There are many quantum gates; some common ones are introduced as follows.

Hadamard

This gate transforms a basis state into an even superposition of the two basis states. Fundamentally, it allows us to create superpositions. It operates on one qubit and is denoted by the symbol shown in Figure 9-2.

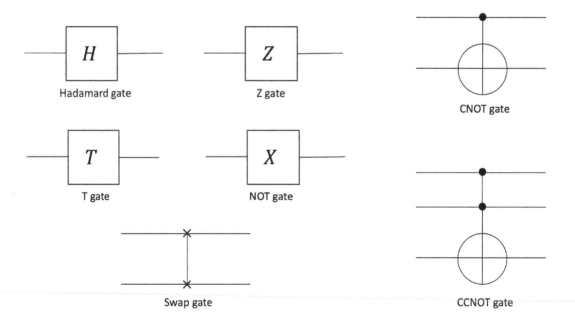

Figure 9-2. *Quantum gates*

T

The T gate induces a pi/4 phase between contributing basis states. The symbol shown in Figure 9-2 represents the T gate. Relative phase rotation is by 45 degrees in T gate.

CNOT

This gate is called the controlled NOT. It is the same as the classical XOR gate, but with the property of reversibility. It works with two qubits. The first qubit serves as the control qubit, and the second qubit acts as the target qubit. It changes the state of the target qubit only if the first qubit is in a specific state. This gate can be used to create an entangled state in a two or more qubit system.

Toffoli (CCNOT)

This is the controlled-controlled NOT gate. It operates on three qubits. It switches the third bit of a three-bit state where the first two bits are 1, that is, it switches $|110\rangle$ to $|111\rangle$ and vice versa. It is represented by the symbol shown in Figure 9-2. In other words, if the first two bits are 1, the third bit inverts.

Z

It is a phase shift gate. It maps 1 to –1 and keeps 0 as 0. In other words, the amplitude of $|1\rangle$ is negated. Fundamentally, it rotates the phase by 180 degrees. It is represented in the circuit with the symbol Z in a box, as shown in Figure 9-2.

NOT

This gate switches $|1\rangle$ to $|1\rangle$ and vice versa. It is an analogue of the classical NOT gate.

Swap Gate

The swap gate swaps two qubits. It can be visualized in Figure 9-2. Of course, there are many quantum gates, but we have introduced those which are commonly used and will help us to understand the algorithms later in this chapter.

All these gates can be visualized in Figure 9-2.

Measurement

In addition to gates, another important element is measurements. A measurement takes a quantum state and collapses it into one of the basis states. We can visualize this in Figure 9-3.

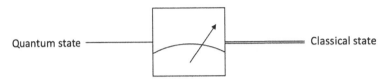

***Figure 9-3.** Measurement*

Quantum Circuits

Using quantum gates, we build quantum circuits. A quantum circuit is basically a sequence of quantum operations applied to qubits. It is composed of quantum gates (operators), quantum registers containing qubits providing input, quantum wires representing a sequence of operations over time, and measurements. Time runs from left to right in quantum circuits. Figure 9-4 shows how a quantum circuit looks like.

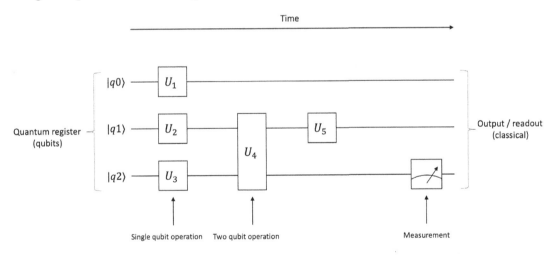

***Figure 9-4.** A quantum circuit*

Quantum gates are represented as boxes. On the left side, we have quantum registers. Quantum wires represent a qubit, that is, a photon or an electron. Each gate introduces a change in the qubit, for example, a change in the spin of an electron.

Quantum circuits implement quantum algorithms. In other words, quantum algorithms are described by quantum circuits. There are many standard quantum circuits. We describe some commonly used as follows.

Teleportation Circuit

Can we transfer a quantum state from one quantum device to another? Yes, we can; for this purpose, teleportation is used, which uses entanglement to move a quantum state from one quantum device to another.

In Figure 9-5, a teleportation circuit is shown, which can transport a quantum state from one party to another.

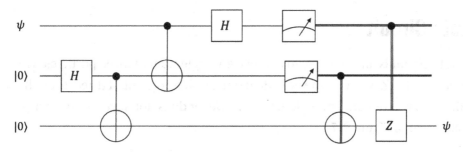

Figure 9-5. *Teleportation circuit*

Some applications of teleportation are state transportation between quantum systems. This can be valuable in quantum distributed systems where state transfer between nodes can enable applications like quantum state machine replication.

GHZ Circuit

The Greenberger-Horne-Zeilinger (GHZ) state is an entangled state of three or more qubits. If three or more particles get into an entangled state, it's called a multipartite entanglement.

Figure 9-6 visualizes this circuit.

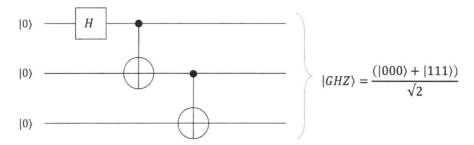

Figure 9-6. *GHZ circuit*

GHZ states have been shown to be useful in quantum cryptography and quantum Byzantine agreement (consensus) algorithms, as we'll explore later in this chapter.

W State Circuit

The W state circuit is another way to achieve entanglement of three particles. The difference with GHZ is that in the W state if one qubit is lost out of three, then the remaining two will remain entangled. GHZ however does not have this property. The circuit is shown in Figure 9-7.

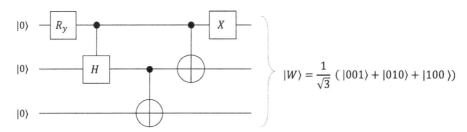

Figure 9-7. *W state circuit*

The W state circuit has application in leader election algorithms, as we'll see later in this chapter.

Quantum Algorithms

As we know, algorithms are set of instructions to solve a problem. Quantum algorithms are the same in this regard; however, they run on quantum devices and contain at least one quantum operation, for example, superpositions or entanglement operations. In other words, a quantum algorithm is the same as the classical algorithm in the sense that it is a set of instructions to solve a problem, but it has instructions for creating superpositions and entanglements.

Famous quantum algorithms include the Deutsch-Jozsa blackbox solution algorithm, Shor's discrete log problem and factorization algorithm, and Grover's search algorithm. There is a catalogue maintained at the quantum algorithm zoo – https://quantumalgorithmzoo.org.

There are primarily three classes of quantum algorithms: quantum search algorithms, quantum Fourier transform–based algorithms, and quantum simulation algorithms.

Quantum Computational Complexity

In computer science, we are used to analyze algorithms to understand the resources required to run an algorithm. The analysis looks at algorithms from two angles, the time complexity of how many steps the algorithm will take to run and how much memory or "work space" it will consume. This is usually referred to as time and space complexity, respectively.

To describe and classify the time and space complexity of algorithms, the big O notation is used. Particularly, this classification is based on the study of how the time to run or space requirements of algorithms grow as the input size grows. A chart is presented in Figure 9-8, which gives a visual indication of how the problem class behaves from a complexity point of view.

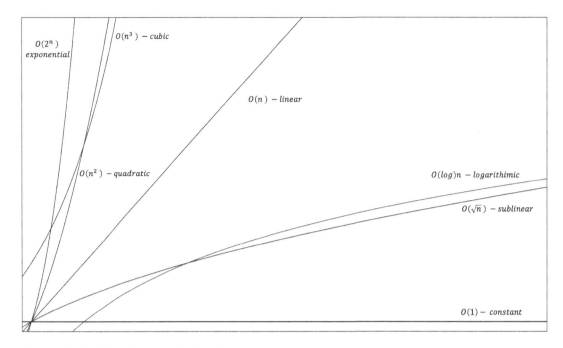

Figure 9-8. *Big-O complexity chart*

Common Big-O complexity orders are described in Table 9-1.

Table 9-1. *Big-O complexity orders*

Name	Big-O Notation	Examples
Constant time	$O(1)$	Find if a number is odd or even
Logarithmic	$O(\log n)$	Binary search
Sublinear (square root)	$O(\sqrt{n})$	
Linear	$O(n)$	Linear search
Quadratic	$O(n^2)$	Insertion sort
Cubic	$O(n^3)$	Simple multiplication of $n \times n$ matrices
Exponential	$O(2^n)$	Recursive Fibonacci

Algorithms are methods which contain a specific set of instructions to solve computational problems. Computation complexity is the study of categorization of different problems into suitable classes. Naturally, a need here arises to formally categorize the algorithms into different categories based on the computational resources required to solve a problem. For this purpose, complexity classes are considered.

With quantum computing, new complexity classes have also emerged. Quantum computers can solve NP hard problems, which classical computers cannot.

Several complexity classes exist; we describe them as follows.

P – Polynomial

A polynomial time class categorizes problems which are solvable in polynomial time, that is, a reasonable amount of time.

NP – Nondeterministic Polynomial

An NP class means that the solution to the problem can be checked quicker, that is, in polynomial time. One example of P is multiplication, whereas factorization is NP. For example, the multiplication of two numbers is in class P, whereas factoring (finding which two numbers were multiplied) is in class NP. However, if the solution is there, then it's quick to verify the solution; hence, it is in the NP class.

NP-complete problems are those if they are in NP and all NP problems are "polynomial time" reducible to the NP problem under consideration. NP hard problems are those if we know that any NP problems are reducible to the possibly NP problem under consideration, but we do not know if the problem is in NP. In other words, NP-complete are those if any NP problem can be reduced to these problems, and NP hard means they're reducible to NP but don't know if they are in NP. One famous example of an NP-complete problem is the travelling salesman problem.

BPP – Bounded Error Probabilistic Polynomial Time

This class contains P. These problems are solvable in polynomial time with probability > ½. Problems in BPP are either solvable deterministically in polynomial time or probabilistically correctly more than one-thirds of the time.

BQP – Bounded Error Quantum Polynomial Time

This new class emerged with quantum computing. A problem is in BQP if it is solvable correctly on a quantum computer in polynomial time with probability > ½, that is, high probability. In other words, this class includes problems that are thought to be hard for classical computers, but easy for quantum computers.

Figure 9-9 shows complexity classes.

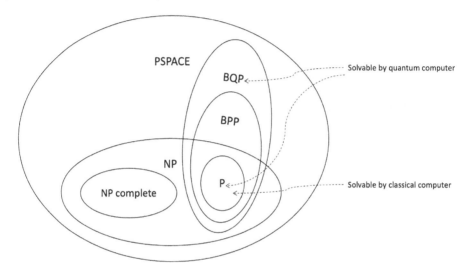

Figure 9-9. *Complexity classes*

PSPACE – Polynomial Space

This class is concerned with memory utilization, instead of time. Problems in PSPACE require a polynomial size of memory.

There is also a concept of hypercomputation that has come to limelight with quantum computing. The idea of hypercomputation is that it can even solve problems which are Turing incomplete, for example, the halting problem. It has, however, been shown that a quantum computer could be much faster than a classical one, but it cannot solve every problem that a classical computer cannot. The idea is that even on quantum computers, Turing-incomplete problems cannot be solved. However, research continues in this regard to study infinite state superposition and infinite state Turing machines which can lead to building hypercomputers.

With this we complete our discussion on complexity.

Other Quantum Systems

As quantum computing evolves, new systems utilizing quantum properties will emerge. We discuss them as follows.

Quantum Networks

Quantum networks are like classical networks with the same routing strategies and topologies. The key difference is that nodes can implement quantum computations and relevant quantum processes. Channels between quantum devices in a quantum network can be quantum or classical.

Quantum Internet

Just as the ARPANET from 1969 with just four nodes became the Internet of today with billions of entities[2] on it, it is expected that small experimental scale quantum networks will become a quantum Internet of tomorrow.

It is envisioned that a quantum network infrastructure will be developed to interconnect remote quantum devices and enable quantum communication between them. The quantum Internet is governed by laws of quantum mechanics. It transfers qubits and distributes entangled quantum states. As the number of nodes grows in the quantum Internet, so does the quantum power. This is so because, as the number of qubits scales linearly with the number of quantum devices on the network, the quantum Internet could enable an exponential quantum speedup, resulting in a "virtual quantum computer" capable of solving previously impossible problems.

Traditional operations present in classical networks such as long-term data storage, data duplication (copying), and straightforward state reading are no longer applicable in quantum networks:

- Long-term data storage is not possible because decoherence in the quantum world rapidly corrupts information, making it very difficult to rely on quantum memories/storage.

---

[2] As almost everything can connect to the Internet now, the term "entities" is used which includes users, things, devices, etc.

- Data copying is not possible in the quantum world due to the no-cloning theorem which prohibits copying an unknown qubit. This means that usual mechanisms to improve resilience on the network, such as retransmission, are no longer applicable. However, note that the no-cloning theorem is a valuable property for secure communications.

- Reading quantum states is challenging because when measured, any qubit immediately collapses to a classical single state of 0 or 1. Due to uncertainty associated with reading quantum states and the no-cloning theorem, direct transmission of qubits is only limited to very specific scenarios with short distances.

However, quantum teleportation can be used to transmit qubits. Quantum teleportation is realized using a quantum feature called entanglement, which we discussed earlier. Using entanglement, instantaneous transfer of the quantum state encoded in a qubit at a sender to a qubit stored at a receiver is possible. The surprising thing is that this transfer occurs without physical transfer of the qubit at the sender. Entanglement is the core enabler of the quantum Internet.

A quantum Internet enables several exotic applications such as blind computing, secure communications, and noiseless communications.

Quantum Distributed Systems – Distributed Quantum Computing

With the availability of the quantum Internet, it is not difficult to envisage that quantum nodes will also engage in communication with each other to cooperate and collectively solve some problem using the distributed computing approach. This development will inevitably lead to the emergence of distributed quantum systems or distributed quantum computing.

We can think of a layered approach where at the lowest layer we have a network layer composed of classical and quantum links. Then we have a layer of quantum computers running on the next layer. Next up are local and remote operations, which include local quantum operations and remote operations on qubits. By combining all operations and computing layers underneath, a virtual quantum computer can be imagined, which combines all the qubits and results in a scalable virtual quantum computer. A controller or distributed quantum compiler is then required to translate quantum algorithms into a sequence of local and remote operations. Finally, we have a layer on top which runs quantum algorithms. This layered approach can be visualized in Figure 9-10.

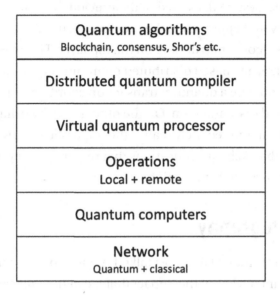

Figure 9-10. *An abstract quantum blockchain ecosystem*

Quantum Blockchain

Inevitably with the quantum Internet and quantum distributed systems, we can envisage a quantum blockchain that utilizes quantum computers as nodes and the underlying quantum Internet as the communication layer.

There are two facets of blockchains in the quantum world. The first one is the pure quantum blockchains running on top of the quantum Internet. Some work has been done in this regard, and an innovative proposal by Rajan and Visser is to encode blockchains into a temporal GHZ state.

The other aspect is the existence of classical blockchains in the post-quantum world. Quantum computers can impact the security of blockchains and consensus adversely due to the ability to break classical cryptography. More on this later in this chapter in the last section.

A quantum blockchain can comprise several elements. The quantum blockchain can have both classical and quantum channels and devices. It can exist as a quantum algorithm, among others, in the "distributed quantum algorithm" layer in the distributed quantum computing ecosystem discussed in the previous section.

We elaborated a layered approach in the previous section. We can envisage blockchains and other algorithms running on the top layer. This whole layer approach represents quantum Internet–based distributed quantum computing ecosystem.

Another element could be a quantum transaction coordinator responsible for transaction ordering and dissemination. On the other hand, by using blind computing, quantum blockchains can immediately realize the unparalleled privacy which will enable quantum scale blockchain applications that require privacy, for example, finance, health, and government-related applications.

Quantum Cryptography

Quantum cryptography is indeed the most talked-about aspect of quantum computing, especially from the point of view of the impact that it can have on existing cryptography.

There are two dimensions here; one is quantum cryptography, and the other is post-quantum cryptography. Quantum cryptography refers to cryptography primitives or techniques that are based on properties of quantum mechanics. For example, quantum key distribution, quantum coin flipping, and quantum commitment. Using quantum properties, a new type of unconditionally secure mechanisms can be developed, which have no counterpart in the classical world. Quantum key distribution (QKD) protocols, such as BB84, were proposed by Bennett and Brassard in 1984, which allow two parties to construct private keys securely using qubits. The benefit of this quantum scheme is that due to superposition any adversary trying to eavesdrop will inevitably be detected.

The other dimension of the study of quantum cryptography is the impact of quantum computers on classical cryptography. We know that using Shor's algorithm, the discrete log problem can be solved, and integer factorization can be sped up, which can result in breaking commonly used public key cryptography schemes, such as RSA and elliptic curve cryptography. Not so much impact is expected on symmetric cryptography because simply key lengths can be increased to ensure that exhaustive searches $O(n)$ in the classic world and $O\left(\sqrt{n}\right)$ using quantum techniques made possible by Grover's algorithm or similar no longer are effective.

Several approaches have been studied for post-quantum cryptography, including lattice-based cryptography, code-based cryptography, multivariate cryptography, hash-based cryptography, and isogeny-based cryptography.

As blockchain consensus mechanisms use cryptography, which is known to be impacted by quantum computing, it is essential that the blocks produced today are quantum resistant so that when quantum computers can do so, they cannot rewrite the entire history of a blockchain. For example, Bitcoin uses the digital signature scheme ECDSA, which quantum computers can break. If quantum technology becomes capable of breaking ECDSA even in ten years, they can still move funds around due to broken ECDSA. Therefore, there is a need to address this issue and apply some quantum resistance to already produced and future blocks. If quantum technology becomes capable of breaking ECDSA in future, an adversary cannot rewrite the block history. Bitcoin generally is not quantum safe, and Lamport signatures have been proposed to alleviate this issue. Note that Bitcoin is secure for the foreseeable future, and the quantum computer required to break ECC is still decades away. To break the 256-bit ECC encryption within one hour, 317×10^6 physical qubits[3] are required. However, currently the most qubits we have today are only 127 on IBM's 127-qubit Eagle processor. So breaking elliptic curve cryptography is not going to be a reality any time soon.

So far, we have discussed what quantum computing is and what effect it can have on classical computing. We also covered some applications of quantum computing and relevant technical details such as gates and circuits. One thing is clear: quantum computing is going to revolutionize the world soon, and a tremendous effort is already being put into making the technology grow and become mainstream.

With all this revolutionary advancement in quantum computing, a natural question arises whether it is possible to harness this power and apply it to solve distributed computing problems, especially the consensus problem. Can we make consensus faster, can we circumvent FLP in some novel way, or does FLP even apply in the quantum world? Is there a quantum solution for the Byzantine generals problem? How can quantum computing help in distributed systems? Can it increase its efficiency? Can quantum consensus tolerate any number of dishonest parties, and no usual lower bounds apply? Can blockchains benefit from this advancement and improve blockchain consensus and other aspects of blockchains, such as cryptography, security, efficiency, and scalability? We answer these questions in the next section.

---

[3] https://doi.org/10.1116/5.0073075

Quantum Consensus

Quantum consensus drives a quantum network with some qubits to a symmetric state. Also, with the advent of quantum computing, the problems from the classical computing world are being studied through the lens of quantum computing to see if there are any improvements that can be made to the existing algorithms from the classical world by harnessing the quantum power. One such problem is distributed consensus from the classical computing/networking world, which we have studied throughout this book. We'll study the agreement/consensus in quantum distributed systems and the impact of quantum computing on classical distributed systems, especially consensus. It has been shown that the classical distributed consensus problem when studied under a quantum framework results in enhancing the classical results and can also solve problems which are otherwise unsolvable in classical networks.

Also, in quantum networks, reaching an agreement is required in many cases; thus, pure quantum consensus for quantum networks and quantum Internet is also an area of interest.

In this section, we'll focus more on enhancement of classical results rather than pure quantum consensus where a quantum network with some qubits is brought to consensus, that is, in a symmetric state. Classical result enhancement is more relevant to our study of consensus in this book.

Quantum consensus algorithms are a very active area of research. There are four categories that have emerged in this context:

- Symmetric state consensus

- Entanglement-based consensus

- Measurement-based consensus

- Quantum key distribution (QKD)–based consensus

Symmetric state consensus refers to the convergence of arbitrary states of quantum nodes in a quantum network to a consensus symmetric state.

Entanglement-based consensus is more relevant to the classical consensus problem. This is so because classical consensus has been investigated through the lens of quantum computing. The key idea here is that quantum properties can enhance the classical consensus and can solve problems which were understood to be unsolvable in the classical consensus world.

Measurement-based consensus works on the premise that when a measurement is made on a quantum state, it collapses to a classical state, 0 or 1. Such a mechanism can be useful in quantum hybrid networks with quantum nodes but classical channels. The quantum state is kept in quantum computers, whereas the classical channels are used for communication to reach consensus. The aim is to allow convergence of quantum nodes to a common state in a hybrid quantum–classical network.

QKD-based consensus has been proposed to solve the Byzantine agreement problem between multiple nodes without entanglement. The unconditional security property of QKD is fundamental to this type of consensus.

Participants in a classical distributed system, including permissioned blockchains, are inherently slow to achieve consensus due to high time complexity incurred by the use of classical protocols like PBFT, three-phase commit, or Paxos. Usually, the time complexity of these consensus algorithms is $O(n^2)$, that is, quadratic. Is it possible to significantly reduce time complexity of classical distributed/blockchain consensus by using quantum computing? The short answer is yes. Ben-Or and Hassidim proposed a fast quantum Byzantine agreement which resolves consensus in $O(1)$ time complexity.

In the next section, we introduce some consensus and agreement algorithms that have been introduced in the literature, which due to quantum properties significantly improve classical results or provide novel algorithms for consensus and relevant problems in the quantum world.

Fast Quantum Byzantine Agreement

Michael Ben-Or and Avinatan Hassidim introduced the fast quantum Byzantine agreement protocol which reaches an agreement in $O(1)$ expected communication rounds. There are two results presented in the paper:

- A quantum protocol for synchronous consensus which tolerates t<n/3 faults and acts in an expected constant number of rounds. The adversary is fail-stop, adaptive, full information, and computationally unbounded.

- A quantum protocol for a synchronous Byzantine agreement tolerating t < n/3 faulty actors in an expected constant number of rounds. The adversary model is an adaptive, full information, and computationally unbounded adversary.

The system model comprises of n nodes, and each pair of nodes is connected through a separate two-way quantum channel. The protocol works in rounds, and each round has two phases. In the first phase, all processors send and receive messages, and the second phase is the computation phase where nodes do local computation to process received messages and decide what messages to send.

The protocol satisfies the following conditions:

- **Agreement**: All nonfaulty processors decide on the same value with probability 1.

- **Validity**: The decided value is the input value of all processors.

- **Termination**: All nonfaulty processes decide on a value with probability 1.

Remember we discussed coin flip randomized protocols earlier in Chapter 6. Especially, we discussed Ben-Or's algorithm where coin flipping was used to achieve an agreement. Fundamentally, the agreement problem is reduced to weak global coin flipping.

The idea in the quantum world is that instead of obtaining a weak global coin by classical means, we use quantum techniques to obtain a weak global coin. With this quantum technique, it is possible to tolerate Byzantine failures under synchrony if $n > 3t$ in $O(1)$ expected rounds. Consensus however is still impossible if $n < 3t$, but there's an improvement of achieving $O(1)$ rounds.

In an asynchronous model, a quantum algorithm exists if $> 3t$; however, it is impossible if $n < 3t$.

The protocol for fail-stop faults works as described in the following:

(C represents a coin, L represents a leader, and the state is GHZ.)

GHZ state is $|GHZ\rangle = \frac{1}{\sqrt{2}}|000\rangle + \frac{1}{\sqrt{2}}|111\rangle$

Each process P_i runs:

Round 1

1. Generate the state $|C_i\rangle = \frac{1}{\sqrt{2}}|0,0,\ldots0\rangle + \frac{1}{\sqrt{2}}|1,1,\ldots1\rangle$ on n qubit.

    a. Send the k th qubit to the k th player while keeping one part to yourself.

2.   Generate the state $|L_i\rangle = \dfrac{1}{n^{3/2}} \displaystyle\sum_{a=1}^{n^{3/2}} |a, a, \ldots a\rangle$ on n qubits, an equal superposition of the numbers from 1 to $n^{3/2}$.

   a. Distribute n qubits among all processes.

3.   Receive the quantum message from all processes.

Round 2

4.   Measure all L_j qubits received in round 1.

5.   Select the process which has the highest leader value as the leader of the round.

6.   Measure the leader's coin in the standard base.

7.   Obtain the measurement outcome of the leader's coin which serves as the global coin.

Using this algorithm, a weak global coin is obtained. The probability for either common outcome is at least $\dfrac{1}{3}$ if $3t < n$. The protocol works for crash faults.

Another protocol for Byzantine faults is presented in the paper, which can tolerate up to $t < \dfrac{n}{4}$ faulty nodes under an asynchronous environment.

How to Refute FLP Impossibility

An interesting claim is made in [by Louie Helm] that distributed consensus can be achieved under asynchrony even in the presence of faults, which appears to contradict FLP impossibility.

Helm proposed a protocol for solving consensus using quantum techniques. At a high level, the protocol works as follows:

- Entangled qubits are distributed to all nodes.

- Each node measures its qubit(s).

- Finally, due to measurement, the superposed quantum state will collapse, which leads to consensus.

This is so because the quantum entanglement here guarantees that entangled qubits collapse to the same state. This means that all nodes will end up with the same state, which means an agreement.

The GHZ state is used to realize this scheme. The key assumption made here is that each node receives a qubit during the setup phase and then later measures it, which results in the same collapsed state at all nodes.

The algorithm works as follows:

1. Prepare the GHZ state via entanglement of a set of n qubits.

2. Distribute a single qubit from the set of superposed qubits to each node in the network. This step distributes a shared state between all nodes.

3. Each node measures their qubit. Note there is no decision yet at this stage.

4. If qubit measurement is $|0\rangle$, choose 0. Choose 1 if qubit measurement is $|1\rangle$. This is where the quantum benefit is realized. When the measurement is made on a node, its quantum state will collapse to either $|0\rangle$ or $|1\rangle$, with equal probability. Also, with the first measurement on a node, the state of all other nodes will also collapse simultaneously and instantaneously to the exact same value as the first node that did the measurement. This is possible because of entanglement and thus strong correlation between qubits. Now as all nodes have the exact same value, this scheme achieves consensus.

An agreement is provided simply because measuring any single full entangled qubit in the GHZ state causes all other qubits in the same GHZ state to collapse to the same basis state. Validity is achieved because when the measurement is made on the first node, it's effectively proposing either a $|0\rangle$ or $|1\rangle$.

This protocol can tolerate network delays because even if a qubit arrives late on a quantum node, the other nodes will keep working without any impact. When the late qubit arrives at any time, it will already contain the agreed-upon value, again due to entanglement. The fundamental reason why FLP can be refuted using this algorithm is because it requires one-way broadcast, and no classical response is required. Even if a single process does not measure its qubit, it will not impact the overall outcome of the computation, that is, even if that single measurement is not available, the other correct nodes will continue to operate even if one qubit is missing. This algorithm will work if the distribution of the original GHZ state completes successfully. Once that's complete, missing measurements won't impact the protocol from there onward. In case of Byzantine faults, the algorithm is also resilient. Any malicious party cannot tamper with the value the algorithm will eventually choose. This is so because any measurement does not impact the correlation of other qubits in the system. This means that any adversary measuring the qubits cannot impact the final chosen value. Due to the quantum nature, the qubit will always end up as 0 or 1. This always means that the decision will eventually be made regardless of Byzantine faults. This achieves termination.

Enhanced Distributed Consensus

Seet and Griffin proposed how quantum computing can speed up an agreement on a distributed network. They proposed a novel quantum consensus mechanism. The work presented in the paper focuses on the scalability and speed of distributed consensus.

By removing the need for multicast replies, the consensus speed and scalability is accomplished. Moreover, using quantum properties, it is ensured that only a single multicast is required. The key idea for achieving consensus is to aggregate the wave function of the received qubits (from other nodes) and local qubits of a quantum node.

The scheme works as follows:

- The network is composed of quantum computers, communication channels, and classical computers. The channels can be quantum to quantum, classical-quantum, and between classical computers.

- Each quantum computer is connected with a classical computer for storage and data retrieval.

- A quantum computer creates an entangled qubit of each qubit.

- Send the duplicates to other nodes in the system.

- Consensus to be determined via the sum of each qubit wave function.

- The qubits can be measured directly from within the quantum computer to calculate the wave function of each qubit. The idea revolves around the assumption that the wave function of each qubit should be similar to each other. Here, the expectation is that the values obtained should be consistent with each other.

- Relying on the superposition, these wavelengths of qubits are a scalar multiple, that is, $n\psi$, where n is the number of nodes participating in consensus.

- The technique here is to determine the difference between an ideal and actual system state wave function.

- If all quantum nodes participating in the consensus have a consistent state, then a randomly selected result would be consistent with any other node's state. This can be compared against the actual system state wave function.

- If the same state exists on all quantum nodes, each individual node's wave function is a scalar multiple of the system's state wave function. The wave function then outputs zero.

- In case of any different state on a node, then that node's wave function will not be a scalar multiple of the entire system's state function. So, the difference between the system state wave function and the node's state wave function is not zero, indicating the discrepancy. The difference increases as the discrepancy between the node's state and system state grows. The level of fault tolerance can be determined if the difference does not fall below a certain threshold. This could be a percentage of the total system, in line with classical BFT where roughly 33% of the nodes can be faulty in a network. It is possible to apply similar thresholds here too, though not proven.

- The consensus algorithm multiplies a randomly chosen wave function with the number of nodes in the system.

- It subtracts the sum of wave functions of each qubit in the system.

- If all wave functions are the same, then the expected result is zero, indicating a coherent system. Otherwise, the system is not coherent. The larger the difference, the more incoherent the system is.

In the paper, this algorithm is expanded to a multiqubit system. Also, several improvements over the classical model are achieved such as reducing the time complexity of state verification by half. This is achieved by utilizing entanglement where the verifier only needs to receive the entangled qubit, after which verification can be done locally, by comparing the state of all qubits. This contrasts with a classical high complexity request-response style of message passing, which increases time and communication complexity. With quantum properties, this complexity is reduced, and consensus can be reached in half the time as compared to the classical consensus. Such efficiency gains can be utilized in blockchains to increase scalability. Moreover, any attempt of manipulation of the original and the sent state in isolation is immediately detectable due to entanglement, thus resulting in increased security of the system. The paper also proposes several scalability, privacy, and performance enhancements addressing the blockchain trilemma.

Quantum Leader Election and Consensus

Ellie D'Hondt and Prakash Panangaden presented a quantum solution for a totally correct leader election in quantum networks, which is considered difficult in the classical world.

For electing a leader using quantum properties, the use of the W state is proposed. In an anonymous network, if quantum nodes share the W state the leader election problem can be solved trivially.

Remember we discussed the W state earlier. For example, the entangled W state of three qubits is

$$|W\rangle = \frac{1}{\sqrt{3}}\left(|001\rangle + |010\rangle + |100\rangle\right)$$

This is used as a symmetry breaking quantum resource. The quantum leader election algorithm for each process i then simply is

1. q = ith qubit from the entangled W-state i.e., from a quantum process i

2. initialize b = 0 and result = wait

3. b = measurement of q

4. if b = 1 then result = leader, else result = follower

This protocol has time complexity of $O(1)$, that is, constant, and there is no message passing required. This is in complete contrast with the classical world where multiround protocols with higher complexity are usually common. This quantum protocol works in asynchronous networks too.

Also, a simple algorithm for consensus is presented. Leader election was based on symmetry breaking; however, this algorithm is dependent on symmetry preservation.

The idea is that to achieve totally correct anonymous quantum distributed consensus where each process has one qubit initially, the processors are required to be entangled in a GHZ state. It is shown that not only is it necessary but also a sufficient condition.

The core idea of the protocol is to share the GHZ entangled state between all nodes participating in the consensus. This allows to create symmetry in one step.

The GHZ state for three qubits is given as

$$|GHZ\rangle = \frac{(|000\rangle + |111\rangle)}{\sqrt{2}}$$

Each process i runs

```
q = ith qubit of GHZ state among n processes
result= wait
result = measure q
```

Again, this protocol has time complexity of $O(1)$, and no message passing is needed. This protocol works under different communication topologies and under asynchrony.

The result in the paper shows that GHZ for consensus is necessary and sufficient. Moreover, W is necessary and sufficient for leader election.

Other Algorithms

There is a wide range of quantum consensus algorithms and relevant proposals. It's not possible to cover them all here in detail; however, this section summarizes some of the prominent results.

Luca Mazzarella, Alain Sarlette, and Francesco Ticozzi in "Consensus for Quantum Networks: From Symmetry to Gossip Iterations" extend the classical distributed computing problem to networks of quantum systems. They proposed a general framework to study the consensus problem in the quantum world. Also, a quantum gossip–style algorithm is presented in the paper.

"Reaching Agreement in Quantum Hybrid Networks" is proposed by Guodong Shi, Bo Li, Zibo Miao, Peter M. Dower, and Matthew R. James. The problem considered in the paper is to drive a quantum hybrid network composed of quantum nodes holding qubits to a common state, thus achieving consensus. The key idea is that quantum nodes measure the qubits, and the results of the measurement are exchanged through classical communication links.

It has been shown that the classical Byzantine generals problem is unsolvable even if pairwise quantum channels are used. However, a variation of the Byzantine agreement problem called the **detectable Byzantine agreement** (DBA) can be solved by using quantum properties. The DBA protocol ensures that either all generals agree on an order or all abort, that is, the agreement property, and if all generals are loyal, they agree on an order, that is, validity.

"Multi-party Quantum Byzantine Agreement Without Entanglement" is proposed by Xin Sun, Piotr Kulicki, and Mirek Sopek. Usually, an entanglement property is used in the quantum consensus algorithm. But this algorithm is different where entanglement is not used. Instead, the protocol relies on quantum key distribution and its unconditional security. The protocol relies on sequences of correlated numbers shared between semihonest quantum key distributors.

There are other proposals where a concept of the quantum blockchain using temporal GHZ is introduced.

There are quite a few innovative results regarding quantum consensus, and researchers are presenting more and more developments. We introduced some of these results earlier. The quantum algorithms that can enhance classical distributed consensus results are of particular importance as they can impact classical distributed systems in the near future. Other pure quantum results are also fascinating but will be fully useful only in the future when quantum Internet and relevant quantum ecosystems become a reality.

Summary

As quantum computing is a vast and deep subject, we have not covered everything. Still, this chapter should give us a good understanding of quantum computing and how it can benefit distributed systems and consensus. Moore's law has almost come to an end, so with quantum computing, we can reinvigorate it. In computer science, more complexity classes are emerging due to quantum computing. For physicists, the interest is to understand more about quantum theory.

This chapter gives us an intuition to think more deeply and prepare ourselves for further research and exploration. The main point to remember is that largely quantum consensus mechanisms exploit the quantum properties of superposition and entanglement.

In the next chapter, we conclude all ideas presented in this book and some exotic ideas and future research directions.

Bibliography

1. Rohde, P.P., 2021. The Quantum Internet: The Second Quantum Revolution. Cambridge University Press.

2. Cuomo, D., Caleffi, M., and Cacciapuoti, A.S., 2020. Towards a distributed quantum computing ecosystem. *IET Quantum Communication*, *1*(1), pp. 3–8.

3. LaPierre, R., 2021. Quantum Gates. In *Introduction to Quantum Computing* (pp. 101–125). Springer, Cham.

4. National Academies of Sciences, Engineering, and Medicine, 2019. *Quantum computing: progress and prospects*. National Academies Press.

5. Marcozzi, M. and Mostarda, L., 2021. Quantum Consensus: an overview. *arXiv preprint arXiv:2101.04192*.

6. SEET, Jorden and GRIFFIN, Paul. Quantum consensus. (2019). 2019 IEEE Asia-Pacific Conference on Computer Science and Data Engineering (CSDE) 2019: December 9–11, Melbourne, Australia: Proceedings. 1-8. Research Collection School Of Computing and Information Systems.

7. Ben-Or, M. and Hassidim, A., 2005, May. Fast quantum Byzantine agreement. In *Proceedings of the thirty-seventh annual ACM symposium on Theory of computing* (pp. 481–485).

8. Quantum algorithm: `https://en.wikipedia.org/wiki/Quantum_algorithm`

9. Rajan, D. and Visser, M., 2019. Quantum blockchain using entanglement in time. *Quantum Reports*, *1*(1), pp. 3–11.

10. Stinson, D.R., & Paterson, M.B. (2018). Cryptography: Theory and Practice (4th ed.). Chapman and Hall/CRC. `https://doi.org/10.1201/9781315282497`

11. Helm, L.K., 2008, August. Quantum distributed consensus. In *PODC* (p. 445).

12. Scalability trilemma: `https://vitalik.ca/general/2021/04/07/sharding.html`

13. Lamport, L., 1979. Constructing digital signatures from a one way function. (Lamport signatures).

14. Pinski, Sebastian. (2011). Adiabatic Quantum Computing.

15. Mohr, A., 2014. Quantum computing in complexity theory and theory of computation. *Carbondale, IL*, *194*.

16. Sun, X., Kulicki, P., and Sopek, M., 2020. Multi-party quantum Byzantine agreement without entanglement. *Entropy*, *22*(10), p. 1152.

17. Fitzi, M., Gisin, N., and Maurer, U., 2001. Quantum solution to the Byzantine agreement problem. *Physical Review Letters*, *87*(21), p. 217901.

18. Webber, M., Elfving, V., Weidt, S., and Hensinger, W.K., 2022. The impact of hardware specifications on reaching quantum advantage in the fault tolerant regime. *AVS Quantum Science*, *4*(1), p. 013801.

CHAPTER 10

Conclusion

Congratulations on making this far! We've come a long way with a lot of information under our belt. In this chapter, we summarize some important topics. We will also look at some latest research and ideas and touch upon some more consensus protocols. An important aspect in consensus protocol research is formal design and verification of the algorithms. We briefly explain this important area in this chapter. Also, we compare some of the most common consensus protocols from different angles and introduce some important research directions.

Introduction

Consensus protocols are the backbone of distributed systems and especially blockchains. Throughout this book, we discussed several protocols and relevant topics. Currently, a blockchain is the most common candidate for implementing consensus protocols. In fact, they are at the core of the blockchain. With the blockchain, novel schemes are being introduced which address various problems including node scalability, transaction throughput, consensus efficiency, fault tolerance, interoperability, and various security aspects.

Distributed consensus is used almost everywhere between networked devices, not only in classical distributed systems that we are used to. This includes the Internet of Things, multiagent systems, distributed real-time systems, embedded systems, and lightweight devices. With the evolution of the blockchain, blockchain consensus adoption is expected to grow in all these systems too.

Other Protocols

In this section, we briefly introduce protocols that we did not cover before. As it is a vast area, a brief introduction only is given.

© Imran Bashir 2022
I. Bashir, *Blockchain Consensus*, https://doi.org/10.1007/978-1-4842-8179-6_10

PoET

The proof of elapsed time algorithm was introduced by Intel in 2016. Remember we discussed earlier in Chapter 5 that a key purpose that PoW fulfills is the passage of some time until the network can converge to a canonical chain. Also, the leader, the miner whose block is accepted, wins the right to do so by solving PoW. PoET is fundamentally a leader election algorithm which utilizes trusted hardware to ensure that a certain time has elapsed before the next leader is selected for block proposal. The fundamental idea in PoET is to provide a mechanism of leader election by waiting randomly to be elected as a leader for proposing new blocks.

PoET in fact emulates the passage of time that would be consumed by PoW mining. The core idea is that every node randomly waits for some time before producing a block. The random waiting process runs inside a Trusted execution environment (TEE) to ensure that true time has indeed passed. For this purpose, Intel SGX or ARM TrustZone can be used. As TEEs provide confidentiality and integrity, the network in turn trusts the block producers. PoET tolerates up to 50% faulty TEE nodes. However, there is a possibility of Sybil attacks where an actor can run many TEE nodes, which can result in shortening the random waiting time. This can result in the creation of a malicious chain if more than 50% of TEEs become malicious. Another limitation is the stale chip problem highlighted by Ittay Eyal. This limitation results in hardware wastage, which results in resource wastage. The stale chip problem stems from the idea that it is financially beneficial for malicious actors to collect many old SGX chips, which increases their odds of becoming the producer of the next block. For example, adversarial actors can collect many old SGX chips to build mining rigs. It serves only one purpose, that is, mining, instead of buying modern CPUs with SGX, which will help in PoET consensus and be useful for general computation. Instead, they can choose to collect as many old SGX-enabled chips as they can and increase their chances of winning the mining lottery. Also, old SGX-enabled CPUs are cheap and can increase the use of old, inefficient CPUs. It is like Bitcoin miners racing to get as many fast ASICs as possible to increase their chances of becoming elected miners. However, it results in hardware wastage. There is also the possibility of hacking the chip's hardware. If an SGX chip is compromised, the malicious node can win the mining round every time, resulting in complete system compromise and undeserved incentivization of miners. This problem is called the broken chip problem.

Proof of Authority

We can think of PoA as a specific kind of proof of stake where the validators stake with their identity instead of economic tokens. The identity of a validator depicts the authority associated with the validator. A usual process of earning authority involves identity verification, reputation building, and a publicly scrutinized assessment process. The resultant group becomes a highly trusted set of validators to participate in the consensus protocol and produce blocks. Any violation by a validator of the rules of the protocol or inability to justify the earned right to produce blocks results in the removal of the dishonest validator by other validators and users on the network. It's used in Rinkeby and Kovan Ethereum test nets. PoA provides good security as we have trusted validators in the network, but the network is somewhat centralized. The resilience against collusion and other security threats depends on the consensus algorithm used by the validators. If it's a BFT variant, then usual BFT guarantees of 33% fault tolerance apply.

HoneyBadger BFT

HoneyBadger BFT (HBBFT) is a leaderless and randomized consensus protocol that works under asynchrony. It is the first practical asynchronous Byzantine consensus protocol. Generally, in distributed system theory, randomized algorithms are thought to be impractical. The HoneyBadger protocol authors claim to refute this belief. The approach taken to build this protocol is to improve efficiency by fine-tuning existing primitives and introducing new encryption techniques. These techniques result in removing bottlenecks in the protocol.

The first limitation to address is the leader bottleneck, for example, in PBFT and other variants there's a standard reliable broadcast mechanism used to disseminate information from the leader to other nodes. This results in significant bandwidth consumption, for example, on the order of $O(n^B)$ where b is the blocks. To address this limitation, erasure coding can be used which allows the leader to send only erasure codes to the nodes. Then each node sends the erasure code stripe received to other nodes. This way, there is less load on the leader. Then all nodes simply reconstruct the message. This reduces the leader bandwidth to $O(n)$. Transactions are processed in batches in HBBFT, which increases the throughput.

It is fundamentally an atomic broadcast protocol based on the multivalue Byzantine agreement and agreement on common subset. HoneyBadger uses several techniques developed previously, including erasure-coded reliable broadcast and common coin–based asynchronous Byzantine agreement. It also uses a threshold public key encryption (signatures) to provide common coins for the randomized ABA protocol.

HBBFT implements the total order using the asynchronous common subset (ACS). ACS is implemented using two other protocols, reliable broadcast (RBC) and asynchronous binary Byzantine agreement (ABA).

Reliable broadcast was introduced in 1987 by Bracha, commonly known as Bracha's broadcast. This protocol tolerates f Byzantine faulty nodes where $n = 3f + 1$. It provides two guarantees, when a designated node (leader, broadcaster) broadcasts a message to all nodes. If any honest node delivers a message m broadcast by the broadcaster, then all correct nodes deliver m. Secondly, if the broadcasting node is correct, then every honest node delivers the message broadcast by the broadcaster node. Due to the message being echoed from all nodes to all, the communication complexity of this protocol becomes $O(n^2m)$, which is ok for smaller size networks, but in the blockchain world with 1000s of nodes, it is impractical.

The agreement on a common subset protocol for multiparty computation (ACS for MPC) was proposed by Ben-Or. ACS was used as a consensus primitive for multiparty computation under an asynchronous network. Multiparty computation (MPC) aims to create a mechanism to compute a function jointly over their inputs, while the inputs are kept private. ACS achieves an agreement on a common subset of at least $n - f$ correct inputs. ACS uses RBC and ABA which enables a single bit agreement between parties.

Due to the communication complexity of RBC, HBBFT implements a different bandwidth-efficient broadcast mechanism called AVID by Cachin et.al., which uses erasure coding and cross checksums to reduce the communication complexity to $O(nm)$. Here, the message m is erasure coded into different slices, and then each slice is hashed to produce a cross checksum. The broadcaster sends a slice and cross checksum to a node, and that node then echoes these to all other nodes. Once all slices reach all nodes, each node reconstructs the original message from these slices. This way, less bandwidth is consumed.

In summary, HBBFT solves consensus under asynchrony by using the asynchronous common subset protocol (ACS) and reliable broadcast (RBC), where each node proposes its value, and finally an asynchronous binary agreement protocol (ABA) runs, which decides on each proposal.

414

Avalanche

This new paradigm of consensus protocols achieves an agreement through random network sampling. The Avalanche family of protocols allow for a more relaxed form of agreement as compared to a deterministic agreement. However, it provides stronger safety than PoW and enjoys the node scalability of the Nakamoto consensus. We can think of it as a probabilistic version of the traditional quorum-based protocol but without explicit intersections in voting. The key idea is to combine the best of Nakamoto family with the best of classical family.

The safety of these protocols is probabilistic but with negligible failure possibility. In terms of liveness, these protocols terminate with high probability. For liveness, these protocols rely on synchrony. The protocol achieves safety through metastability. Safety provided by the protocol is probabilistic where an adjustable system chosen security parameter makes the possibility of consensus failure negligibly small. The protocol guarantees safety and liveness properties, with high probability:

- **Safety:** No two correct nodes accept conflicting transactions.

- **Liveness:** Every correct node will eventually accept any transaction by an honest client.

This family has several protocols that build up the complete Avalanche protocol. The protocol is built gradually, starting from the so-called slush protocol, which provides metastability, snowflake, the BFT protocol, Snowball, which affirms the state by adding confidence to the decision; and, finally, Avalanche, which adds the DAG structure to improve efficiency.

With these innovations, the protocol provides quick finality, low latency, high throughput, and scalability.

DAG-Based Consensus Protocols

Usually, a blockchain is a linear structure; however, another class of algorithms has been proposed with nonlinear blockchain structures. The primary aim is efficiency, and these protocols are based on the premise that instead of relying on a limited and slow, linearly growing chain, the ledger should be able to expand in all directions, like a DAG, which can result in improved performance, high scalability, and fast transaction confirmation. DAGs require less communication, computation, and storage, thus increasing the performance. There are two types of DAG-based ledgers: block-based DAG and transaction-based DAG.

Block-Based DAG

Every vertex of a blockDAG contains a block. Each block can be a child of multiple blocks, instead of only one parent in linear designs, SPECTRE, PHANTOM, and Meshcash.

Transaction-Based DAG

Each vertex of a transaction-based DAG contains a transaction. IOTA Tangle, Byteball, Graphchain, and Avalanche are some examples of a transaction-based DAG.

Hashgraph is a permissioned graph–based blockchain with a BFT-type consensus protocol.

Ebb-and-Flow Protocols

This work is a response to a liveness issue found in Gasper. Gasper is a PoS-based consensus mechanism proposed for Ethereum's beacon chain. It is a combination of Casper FFG, the finality gadget, and LMD GHOST, the fork choice rule. In this work, "snap-and-chat" protocols are proposed that are provably secure.

Nakamoto-style protocols provide liveness under network partitions and dynamic network participation, but they sacrifice safety over liveness. BFT protocols, on the other hand, provide safety (finality) under network partitions and low participation (participants less than $<3f+1$) but sacrifice liveness. It has been shown that it is impossible for a protocol to be both live under dynamic participation and safe under network partitions. This work answers the question of whether there exists a consensus mechanism that guarantees both availability and safety. The key idea is exquisite and proposes to create two ledgers instead of one. Remember, no protocol can ensure safety and liveness under network partitions and dynamic partitions with a single ledger. In other words, longest chain–style mechanisms favor liveness over safety and provide dynamic availability under different participation levels; however, BFT protocols favor safety over liveness and provide finality. This problem is called the availability-finality dilemma, as a single ledger cannot provide both properties. Therefore, the proposal is to create two ledgers. The first is an "available full ledger" that is always live but safe only without network partitions, similar to "longest chain–type PoW protocol." The other ledger, called the "finalized prefix ledger," is always safe but not live in low participation scenarios. This concept is the same as traditional BFT–style protocols, for example,

PBFT, which stalls unless a threshold of participants is available. As the finalized prefix ledger is the prefix of the available full ledger, both ledgers eventually converge as a single authentic chain of history. In other words, the finalized prefix ledger is safe under network partitions and if less than one-third of participants are faulty.

Moreover, the available full ledger is live under dynamic (low) participation and if <50% of active players are Byzantine. This technique of combining BFT-style with Nakamoto-style protocols and creating so-called nested ledgers has been named the "Ebb-and-Flow" property. The so-called "snap-and-chat" protocols are developed to achieve the "Ebb-and-Flow" property. The finalized ledger is always the prefix of the available ledger, thus creating a combined proper single chain. At a high level, this mechanism works by ordering transactions into a chain of blocks by using some longest chain–type protocol, for example, PoW. Next, snapshots of prefixes from this blockchain feed into a partially synchronous BFT-style protocol for example, PBFT, which produces a chain containing multiple chains of blocks. Next, any duplicates or invalid transactions are removed, which creates a finalized prefix ledger. This finalized prefix ledger is added before the output of the PoW-style protocol, and any duplicates or invalid transactions are removed. This process finally creates an available single ledger.

There is a myriad of consensus protocols that exist, but we cannot cover all of them. However, we did explore quite a few covering different types and classes including randomized, deterministic, CFT, BFT, and Nakamoto-style protocols.

Let's now turn our attention to formal verification which allows us to ensure the correctness of all these different consensus protocols.

Formal Verification

With all the activity in blockchain consensus research, we can now appreciate that it is such an active area of research. Many new protocols have been proposed to solve consensus problems in innovative ways. For example, some address efficiency, some look at scalability problems, some try to reduce message complexity, some modify the existing classical protocols to make them suitable for the blockchain, some try to speed up the consensus mechanism, and many other improvements and novelties are claimed. Here, a question arises: How do we ensure that these consensus protocols are correct and perform as we intend them to? For this purpose, usually researchers write research papers with proofs and arguments about the correctness of the protocols. Moreover, formal methods are used to ensure protocol correctness.

Formal methods are techniques used to model systems as mathematical objects. In other words, these are mathematically rigorous methods used to specify, design, and verify software or hardware systems. Such techniques include writing specifications in a formal logic and verifying them using model checking and formal proofs. Formal methods are divided into two broad domains called formal specification and formal verification. The first domain deals with writing precise and concrete specifications, and the latter concerns the development of proofs to prove the correctness of a specification.

A formal specification is a well-defined mathematical logic statement, whereas verification is the process of checking the specification by logic deductions, which is done mechanically. In other words, the specification is formally defined and then verified using a model checker or a theorem prover.

The reason why formal methods provide value is that they can symbolically check the entire state space of a design and ascertain the correctness of the design.

Generally, formal verification comprises three steps:

- Create a formal model of the system to be checked.

- Write a formal specification of the properties desired to be satisfied by our model.

- Mechanically check the model to ensure that the model satisfies the specification.

Two categories of techniques are commonly used for verification: state exploration–based approaches and proof-based approaches. State exploration–based methods are automatic but are inefficient and difficult to scale. For example, a usual problem is state explosion, where the number of states to check grows so exponentially large that the model does not fit in a computer's memory. This is the reason the model must be finite, so that it can be efficiently verified. On the other hand, proof-based approaches (i.e., theorem proving) are more precise and less memory consuming but require human interaction and more in-depth knowledge of the proofs and relevant techniques. Proof-based techniques are the most elegant way of reasoning about properties of a system without any limit on the size of the spec. This is in contrast with model checking where there must be a limit on the size of the model. With proof-based techniques, you can reason about the system states and prove that with any input the system will always work as intended. Proof assistants such as Isabelle are used to help with reasoning about systems by allowing automated theorem proving.

A model checking mechanism consists of a formal specification language and a model checker. Model checking verifies systems formally using automated tools. This approach is gaining popularity among blockchain researchers to check formal specifications of a consensus protocol and ensure its correctness. The automated checker checks for the conditions to be satisfied and then confirms if the conditions are satisfied; otherwise, it produces counter examples (i.e., exceptions).

Figure 10-1 illustrates the model checking mechanism.

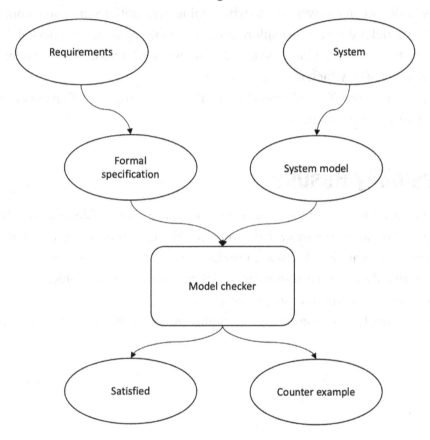

Figure 10-1. *Model checking*

TLA+ (temporal logic for actions) is a specification language designed by Leslie Lamport for describing and reasoning about concurrent systems. TLC is a model checker for design specifications written in TLA+. Another model checker is SPIN which checks specifications written in the Promela specification language.

A distributed blockchain consensus algorithm is usually evaluated against two classes of correctness properties: safety and liveness. Safety generally means "nothing bad will happen," whereas liveness suggests "something good will eventually occur." Both these properties have some subproperties, depending on the requirements. Usually, for consensus mechanisms, we have agreement, integrity, and validity conditions under the safety property, and termination is required for liveness. Consensus algorithms are mostly model checked under a system model by specifying how many nodes are in the system and what timing assumptions are made about the system. The model is then run to explore each state of the system and check if there is an execution that doesn't terminate. Usually, this is done under a four-node model, based on the formula of 3f+1, which we've seen before.

A program is correct if, in all possible executions, the program behaves correctly according to the specification.

Impossibility Results

Unsolvability results in distributed systems show that certain problems cannot be solved. Lower bound results show that certain problems cannot be solved if resources are insufficient; in other words, these lower bound results show that certain problems are only solvable if a certain threshold of sufficient resources is available, that is, minimum resources required to solve a problem.

Table 10-1 summarizes the core impossibility results related to the consensus problem.

Table 10-1. *Consensus problem impossibility results*

	Crash Faults	Byzantine Faults
Synchronous	Consensus possible if $f < n$ At least $f + 1$ rounds required where $f < n$ $> f$ network connectivity	$f \geq n/3$ impossible $> 2f$ network connectivity minimum $f < n/2$ possible $f + 1$ rounds
Asynchronous	Deterministic consensus impossible	Deterministic consensus impossible
Partially synchronous	Impossible if $n \leq 2f$	Impossible if $n \leq 3f$ $> 2f$ network connectivity $f + 1$ rounds

The results in Table 10-1 are standard impossibility results. However, there are many others.

With the innovative research on blockchains, some new results have emerged. Andrew Lewis-Pye and Tim Roughgarden announced a fascinating new impossibility result similar to the CAP theorem where we can simultaneously choose only two of three properties. It states that no blockchain protocol can operate in the unconstrained environment (e.g., PoW), is live under a synchronous environment with significant and sharp dynamic changes in network resources (e.g., participant numbers), and satisfies probabilistic finality (consistency) in the partially synchronous environment. We can only choose two properties simultaneously out of the three properties stated earlier.

For example, in an unsized environment such as Bitcoin, imagine a node stops receiving any new blocks. Now the node cannot differentiate between whether the other nodes have lost their resources and cannot produce blocks anymore and if the block messages are delayed. Now if the node stops producing blocks and other nodes are low on resources and not producing blocks, it violates the liveness property, because this node must keep producing blocks even if others don't. However, if it keeps producing blocks but the block messages are just delayed, then it is violating the consistency property, because there could be other conflicting blocks which are just delayed.

Complexity and Performance

A consensus algorithm can be evaluated from a communication complexity point of view. This involves calculations such as if the protocol is running in normal mode (no failures), then how many messages are required to be exchanged to reach consensus. Also, in case of leader failure when a view change occurs, how many messages are exchanged? Such metrics can help to understand how the algorithm behaves practically, which helps to estimate the efficiency of the algorithm.

Message delays can be defined as the number of messages required by an algorithm that cannot be sent before the previous message is received. In other words, it's a message which is sent only after the previous one has been received. An algorithm requires n message delay; if some execution contains a chain of n messages, each of which cannot be sent before receiving the previous one.

To evaluate the cost associated with an algorithm, we can think of different complexity traits. There are three costs associated with a consensus algorithm: message complexity, communication complexity, and time complexity.

Message Complexity

Message complexity denotes the total number of messages that are required to be exchanged by the algorithm to reach consensus. For example, imagine an algorithm where all processes broadcast to all other nodes. This means that $n(n-1)$ messages will be received. This means this algorithm has $O(n^2)$ message complexity.

Communication Complexity (Bit Complexity)

Communication complexity is concerned with the total number of bits required to be exchanged by the algorithm. Think of the same algorithm we imagined about in the context of message complexity. If each message contains t bits, the algorithm exchanges $tn(n-1)$ bits, which means that the communication complexity is $o(tn^2)$ bits, that is, all to all.

Time Complexity

Time complexity is concerned with the amount of time needed to complete the execution of the algorithm. The time taken to execute the algorithm also depends on the time it takes to deliver the messages in the protocol. The time to deliver messages is quite large as compared to the local computation on the message. Time can be then thought of as the number of consecutive message delays. The same algorithm from the previous example running on a faultless network has $O(1)$ time complexity.

Space Complexity

Space complexity deals with the total amount of space required for the algorithm to run. Space complexity is mostly relevant in a shared memory framework.

In message-passing distributed systems, such as blockchains, mostly message complexity is considered. Bit complexity is not so much relevant; however, if the size of the messages is big, then this can become another complexity measure to take into consideration.

Table 10-2 summarizes the complexity results of some common BFT protocols.

Table 10-2. *Message complexity orders*

Protocol	Normal Mode	View Change	Message Delays
Paxos	$O(n)$	$O(n^2)$	4
PBFT	$O(n^2)$	$O(n^3)$	5
Tendermint	$O(n^2)$	$O(n^2)$	5
HotStuff	$O(n)$	$O(n)$	10
DLS	$O(n^2)$	$O(n^4)$	$O(n)$ rounds
HoneyBadger	$O(n)$	–	–
PoW	$O(n)$	–	–

With these costs in mind, we can think of several bottlenecks in blockchain consensus protocols that result in poor performance. For example, the choice of all-to-all messages will inevitably result in more complexity.

Several techniques such as erasure coding can be used to reduce message complexity. Another technique called star topology (one to all – all to one), instead of mesh topology (all-to-all communication), can also reduce message complexity. Both these techniques are used in HoneyBadger and HotStuff, respectively.

Another class of algorithms that aims to improve performance and scalability of the consensus algorithms is to allow multiple nodes to act as leaders in parallel, that is, parallel leaders. Under this paradigm, multiple leaders can propose concurrently, which results in alleviating the CPU and bandwidth costs by distributing load evenly across all leaders. There are several algorithms in this category like HoneyBadger, Hashgraph, and RedBelly. However, it is possible that request duplication might occur with parallel leaders, which has been addressed in the Mir-BFT protocol.

Sharding is another technique that improves consensus performance. It allows breaking up the system state and validators into smaller sections. Each shard is responsible for a small subset of the entire state, and only a smaller subset of the global validator set is required to achieve consensus on that part of the state. This way, in parallel many shards exist, and by allowing consensus to run on smaller parts, great efficiency is achieved. To achieve a final state, some cross-shard communication and consolidation mechanism is also required.

Another technique to improve throughput is to offload data from the main chain to layer 2. Some techniques are developed in this regard, such as payment channels, lightning network for Bitcoin, commit chains, and Plasma. Techniques such as zero knowledge are used to provide evidence of off-chain execution. Prism and Bitcoin-NG are some of the techniques to improve consensus performance.

DAG-based consensus discussed earlier aims to improve performance by introducing graph-based structures that allow for non-interdependent commands to be committed in parallel.

Parallel execution of commands/smart contracts are also a technique that is proposed to improve performance. Parallel smart contracts (called Sealevel) are supported in the Solana blockchain.

Comparison of Protocols

We can compare consensus algorithms from different perspectives. Table 10-3 summarizes the results.

Table 10-3. *Comparison of the main consensus algorithms*

Property	POW	POS	POA	RAFT	PBFT
Safety	Probabilistic	Probabilistic	Deterministic	Deterministic	Deterministic
Adversary	Computational power control	Stake amount	Collusion/ Byzantine	Collusion/ crash	Collusion/ Byzantine
Method	Math puzzle solving	Value deposit	Authority	Leader-follower	Primary backup
Network model	Synchronous	Synchronous	Synchronous	Partially synchronous	Partially synchronous
Incentive	Yes	Yes	No	No	No
Access control	Public	Public	Permissioned	Permissioned	Permissioned
Block validation	Block header check/PoW valid	Staking rules	Identify check	Seal check	Seal check
Finality	Probabilistic	Economic	Deterministic >50% validator agreement	Immediate	Immediate
Misbehavior control	CPU/memory resources	Stake penalty	BFT	CFT	BFT
Election type	Lottery	Lottery	Voting	Voting	Voting
Liveness	Probabilistic	Probabilistic	Deterministic	Deterministic	Deterministic
CAP	A over C	A over C	A over C	P over C	P over C
Transaction capacity	10s	100s	10s	1000s	1000s
Fault tolerance	BFT	BFT	BFT	CFT	BFT
Forking	Yes	Yes	No	No	No
Special hardware	Yes	No	No	No	No

(continued)

Table 10-3. (*continued*)

Property	POW	POS	POA	RAFT	PBFT
Example	Bitcoin	Tezos	Rinkeby	GoQuorum	Sawtooth
Dynamic membership	Yes	Yes	No	Yes	No

Notes:

- PoA is assumed to be BFT based.

- While only a single example is given, there are many, for example, Ethereum uses PoW too.

- PBFT and RAFT both are state machine replication protocols with a leader-follower architecture, also called a primary backup. Usually, for PBFT a primary backup is used in the literature; however, for RAFT leader-follower terms are used. Fundamentally, they serve the same purpose.

Network Model

We can model a blockchain network in several ways, as shown in the following. Fundamentally, the networks are either synchronous, asynchronous, or partially synchronous. However, in literature several terms are used and as such explained as follows.

Synchronous

All messages are delivered within delta Δ time.

Eventual Synchrony

After an unknown global stabilization time (GST), all messages are delivered within delta Δ time.

Partial Synchrony

A protocol does not know what delta Δ is.

Weak Synchrony

Δ varies with time. In practice, the Δ increases systematically until liveness is achieved. However, the delays are not expected to grow exponentially.

Asynchronous

All messages are eventually delivered but have no fixed upper bound on message delivery time. The message delivery delay is finite, but no time bound is assumed on it.

Adversaries are primarily of two types, a static adversary and an adaptive adversary. A static adversary performs corruption before the protocol executes, whereas an adaptive adversary can cause corruption anytime during the execution of the protocol. There are two crash models, a crash failure model and a Byzantine failure model. Round-based algorithms have a send step, receive step, and compute step, which make one round.

We can think of several aspects of consensus protocols that we can use to study, evaluate, or classify them:

- **Fault tolerance/resilience level**: BFT or CFT.

- **Time complexity**: How long the protocol takes to run and how many message delays.

- **Message complexity**: What is the message complexity of the protocol in terms of the number of messages exchanged?

- **Trusted setup**: Does the protocol need any setup like PKI or no dealer is required?

- What is the adversary strength assumed in the model? Is it bounded or unbounded? What is the adversary corruption model? Is it static or adaptive?

- What is the network model? Synchronous, asynchronous, or partially synchronous and its variations.

- Is the protocol probabilistic or deterministic?

- Does it use any cryptography?

- **Computational assumptions**: Information-theoretic security or computational security.

- **Membership**: Dynamic or fixed, permissioned, or public.

Such questions are useful to ask when analyzing a consensus protocol. Just two more points to remember about consensus algorithms are as follows:

1. Consensus algorithms aim to reach consensus on a single value, whereas SMR uses a consensus algorithm to decide on a sequence of operations for replication.

2. Remember that PoW is not a consensus algorithm. It is a Sybil resistance mechanism; the consensus is reached via the choice of longest chain. Similarly, PoS is not a consensus algorithm. It is also a Sybil resistance mechanism, but decision on the canonical truth (choice of fork) is made by a BFT-style algorithm. We can think of it as a coupled mechanism where PoS is a Sybil control mechanism, whereas fork selection and finalization are done via a BFT-style algorithm. Similarly, PoH in Solana is a sequencing of events mechanism (an event orderer) which also allows for leader selection in a trustless manner; however, the decision on the final chain is made by voting on forks by a BFT-style algorithm called TowerBFT.

Research Directions

Blockchain consensus is a very ripe area for research. Even though tremendous progress has been made, still there are a few open research problems which should be addressed. Some of these problems are listed as follows, with possible direction of research:

- Most blockchain protocols, especially permissioned blockchain protocols, are based on PBFT. However, the world is evolving, and since 1999, when PBFT was introduced, a lot has changed. There have been attempts to use PBFT in blockchains by modifying it to blockchain needs, and it does work, but efficiency and scalability are still issues that need to be addressed. The future of the blockchain is multichain and heterogeneous. Also, there will be all sorts of different devices ranging from computers to lightweight resource-constrained IoT systems or mobile devices. Such a heterogeneous network requires another consensus mechanism that can withstand millions of heterogeneous devices with an asynchronous network. Cross-chain transactions and consensus are another aspect that needs further research. Some research on asynchronous BFT protocols has resulted in HoneyBadger BFT and BEAT, and, of course, we can do more. Similarly, Casper FFG, Casper CBC, GRANDPA, and BABE are the steps in the right direction for a multichain heterogeneous future. However, significant work still needs to be done.

- As the blockchain technology evolves, so do the adversaries. There is a possibility of novel attack techniques, which, due to possible economic incentives on blockchains, can manifest sooner rather than later. This is so because concerned parties are willing to invest with the hope that new novel techniques for hacking blockchain networks will result in immediate revenue.

- The use of quantum computing to enhance the classical results is an interesting topic. For example, a quantum computer can run in parallel with a classical distributed network or a blockchain. The quantum computer can elect a leader using the W state–based quantum leader election algorithm (discussed in Chapter 9) and pass the result on to the classical blockchain/distributed network. Such techniques can improve the security and efficiency of existing classical networks.

- Classical permissioned network–related results cannot be directly applied to the permissionless settings; therefore, a need to modify those protocols to suit the blockchain world is needed. Some work is already done, for example, Casper FFG is inspired by PBFT.

- Scalability and privacy of consensus protocols is an area of extreme importance. Privacy has two facets in the blockchain world: transaction value confidentiality and hiding users' identities participating on the network. Scalability is concerned with node scalability as well as transaction throughput.

- Mechanism design is a branch of microeconomics and built on the concept of game theory that studies how to design protocols that use incentivization to encourage rational actors to behave correctly. It is also called reverse game theory. It starts with an outcome and studies how entities in the system can work collaboratively to achieve a desired goal. As blockchains are cryptoeconomic incentive systems, much can be learned from the field of mechanism design. We can apply techniques and methods from the field of mechanism design to develop novel blockchain protocols that are robust.

Summary

In this last chapter, we summarized what we learned throughout this book. We also covered the algorithms that we did not before, especially new consensus protocols such as Avalanche and Ebb-and-Flow protocols. We also touched upon some research directions which require further work. We have come a long way from the Byzantine generals problem to Nakamoto consensus and now multichain consensus protocols. This is such a ripe area for research that we'll only see more progress in it with more innovative ideas in the future.

In this book, we have explored the foundations of a blockchain and distributed consensus. We learned what impact quantum computing can have on distributed consensus and how an agreement could be achieved in quantum networks. Blockchain consensus is possibly the strongest area for research in the blockchain.

Thank you for staying with me in this wonderful journey. You are now capable of applying the knowledge from this book as a blockchain researcher and continuing your learning and research in the field of blockchain consensus.

Bibliography

1. Decentralized thoughts: `https://decentralizedthoughts.github.io`

2. Xiao, Y., Zhang, N., Lou, W., and Hou, Y.T., 2020. A survey of distributed consensus protocols for blockchain networks. *IEEE Communications Surveys & Tutorials*, 22(2), pp. 1432–1465.

3. Miller, A., Xia, Y., Croman, K., Shi, E., and Song, D., 2016, October. The honeybadger of BFT protocols. In *Proceedings of the 2016 ACM SIGSAC conference on computer and communications security* (pp. 31–42).

4. Lewis-Pye, A. and Roughgarden, T., 2020. Resource pools and the cap theorem. *arXiv preprint arXiv:2006.10698.*

5. Neu, J., Tas, E.N., and Tse, D., 2021, May. Ebb-and-flow protocols: A resolution of the availability-finality dilemma. In *2021 IEEE Symposium on Security and Privacy (SP)* (pp. 446–465). IEEE.

6. Tim Roughgarden Lectures on foundations of blockchains: https://youtu.be/EfsSV7ni2ZM

7. Fokkink, W., 2018. *Distributed algorithms: an intuitive approach.* MIT Press.

8. More on mechanism design and blockchains here: https://medium.com/blockchannel/a-crash-course-in-mechanism-design-for-cryptoeconomic-applications-a9f06ab6a976

Index

A

B

Q

Printed in the United States
by Baker & Taylor Publisher Services